The Ferocious Engine of Democracy

A History of the American Presidency

Volume One
From the Origins through William McKinley

Foreword by Herbert Mitgang

Michael P. Riccards

MADISON BOOKS
Lanham • New York • Oxford

Originally printed in hardcover in 1995 by Madison Books.

Published by Madison Books
4720 Boston Way
Lanham, Maryland 20706

12 Hid's Copse Road
Cummor Hill, Oxford OX2 9JJ, England

Distributed by National Book Network

The Library of Congress has cataloged the hardcover edition as follows:

The ferocious engine of democarcy : a history of the American presidency /
  by Michael P. Riccards.
  Includes index.
  Contents: From the origins through William McKinley.
1. Presidents—United States—History. 2. United States—Politics and government. I.
Title.
E176.1.R48   1994
973'.099   94-15019
                                                      CIP

ISBN 1-56883-041-3 (cloth: alk. paper)
ISBN 1-56833-102-9 (pbk. : alk. paper)

To Margaret Riccards and
in memory of Patrick P. Riccards
(1916–1989)

Contents

Foreword

THE CRUCIBLE OF THE PRESIDENCY

The framers of the Constitution created a document for their time, but they also designed it to preserve the institutions of government for a new century. The nineteenth century was on the horizon; the twentieth century was too far in the future to contemplate. After long years of colonial domination and occupation upheld by British bayonets, the new United States at last seemed stable, with boundless promise for human progress. Unlike the fiery language in the Declaration of Independence, the Constitution was written as a legal document that could be amended, if necessary, but not fundamentally changed. Arising out of the long and divisive American Revolution—many people in the thirteen colonies chose to remain loyal to the Crown or simply sat out the war without making personal sacrifices to support the rebellion—the bold revolutionaries had a right to envision an undisturbed peace within the existing boundaries.

The possibility of becoming entangled in Europe's long history of armed conflict seemed extremely remote. The words of the first president in his Farewell Address in 1796—"'Tis our true policy to steer clear of permanent alliances, with any portion of the foreign world"—set the tone for the nation at the end of the eighteenth century and remained almost undisputed as American foreign policy for another hundred years.

What is remarkable about our anti-royalist Constitution is the great power it bestows upon the president. After winning a war against the dictatorial rule of a remote British king, it is little wonder that the framers wrote a clause in the Constitution (Article I, Section 9) that reads:

> No title of Nobility shall be granted by the United States: And no Person holding any Office of Profit or Trust under them, shall, without the Consent of the Congress, accept of any present, Emolument, Office, or Title, of any kind whatever, from any King, Prince or foreign State.

In creating the balance of powers among the three branches, the Constitution gave Congress and the Supreme Court specific tasks of governance, yet the framers placed their greatest faith in a single chief executive. Could the reason be that the same men who made a Revolution and knew and trusted each other also made the Constitution? From President George Washington to the present occupant of the White House, he (or, surely, a she at some not-too-distant time in the twenty-first century) was granted extraordinary powers to lead the nation in war and peace. Around the world, scores of kings and queens and emperors have come and gone since the founding of the United States; and those that remain after World War II are figureheads with limited powers. Today, not one foreign monarch can match an American president in written or assumed authority, even with all the quadrennial turmoil of gaining the Democratic or Republican party nomination and then winning the election.

I use the phrase "assumed authority" because it derives from one of the most important ideas expressed in *The Ferocious Engine of Democracy*. The phrase helps to explain the differences in conduct of the first forty presidents of the United States. Some of the presidents considered the job simply as an administrative office to execute the laws; others saw it as more or less a ceremonial office where the president could give party cronies coveted appointments; still others viewed it as a bully pulpit to exhort the public and convince the Congress of the need for new laws or constitutional amendments. In more recent times, we have witnessed the growth of the "imperial presidency." The strongest presidents have expanded the functions of the office—partly on their own initiative and partially through the veto power. These presidents sometimes have been branded dictators by their political opponents, often with an assist from a vituperative party press.

In *The Ferocious Engine of Democracy*, Michael Riccards uses the word "paraconstitutional" to describe the transition from what the Constitution specifically spelled out and the additional authority that presidents have assumed. In the early days of the Republic, the Jeffersonian approach was to remain in the background, working closely with the legislature. Even during Lincoln's wartime presidency, the White House staff was comparatively small in number—dozens, not thousands. One of the major developments in the twentieth century is the growth of a second staff of advisers— some down the hall from the Oval Office itself and others scattered nearby in Executive buildings. Their assignments almost exactly parallel the tasks of cabinet officers and departments.

The framers of the Constitution did not authorize these paraconstitutional offices, such as the National Security Council, the Council of Economic Advisers, and various presidential assistants and counsel—not to mention pollsters and spear carriers testing the wind of popular appeal for another election. The advisory subcabinets are not vague shadow cabinets but actual working cabinets. These intimate advisers often have the president's ear by proximity, but they frequently carry the seeds of paraconstitutional conflict with the real cabinet and the Congress. It is now generally accepted that the president does indeed require such subcabinets to provide him with advice quickly—without having to go through official channels publicly.

In delineating the role of the president, the Constitution first of all describes him as an "executive" and also includes the phrase "execution of office." In the young nation, a president was permitted to enter office at the young age of thirty-five. It has never happened; candidates have run for and held office at twice that age. The greatest qualification for office concerns not personal maturity but the ability to be the absolute leader of the nation's armed forces in peace and war: "The President shall be Commander in Chief of the Army and Navy of the United States, and of the Militia of the several States, when called into actual service of the United States." For the several states to give up their control of their militia was unusual in the early days of the Republic, yet it showed a recognition of federal dominance in times of crisis.

The United States was established only after an insurrection against a foreign occupying power. This same acceptance of a Commander in Chief with unrestricted, written constitutional authority enabled the sixteenth president of the United States to put down an insurrection by the Confederate States, including states that had ratified the Constitution. This was at the heart of President Abraham Lincoln's steadfast arguments and actions to preserve the Union. He made the "oath or affirmation" in the Constitution the escutcheon of his presidency—to "preserve, protect and defend the Constitution of the United States."

The constitutional oath requires a president not to defend the United States, as such, or any of its states, but to defend the Constitution. In their wisdom, the framers foresaw the Constitution as the ferocious engine of democracy that drives all else in order to form a more perfect Union for ourselves and our posterity.

From the beginning of the Republic, the role of the president as Commander in Chief has, for good or ill, marked the presidency. Our wars have produced military heroes who became peacetime presidents: George Washington, Andrew Jackson, Zachary Taylor, Ulysses S. Grant, Theodore Roosevelt and Dwight D. Eisenhower. But we have also had wartime presidents whose military experience was nil or very limited: James Madison, James K. Polk, Abraham Lincoln, William McKinley, Woodrow Wilson, Franklin D. Roosevelt. And yet of all these presidents, the two who stand out in the White House are Abraham Lincoln during the Civil War and Franklin D. Roosevelt during World War II.

Lincoln proved to have the instincts of a brilliant Commander in Chief. He dismissed or demoted general after general—McClellan, Burnside, Banks, Pope, Fremont, Scott, McDowell, Hooker—until he promoted General Grant to lead the Union armies. He studied the war maps, plotted strategy, examined and encouraged new weapons, and was in constant touch with front line commanders through the War Department telegraph office. Yet, though he had been elected captain of the New Salem militia in 1832, he never fired a shot in anger. After a few months of service, he was mustered out as a private. In 1861, when the lanyard of war was pulled at Fort Sumter, former private A. Lincoln found himself cast as the Commander in Chief until the end of the war in 1865.

Despite the terrible casualties and duration of the Civil War, Lincoln was against war itself. While serving as a one-term congressman during the Mexican War, which he strongly opposed, he made a speech in 1848 that described war as "fixing the public gaze upon the exceeding brightness of military glory—that attractive rainbow, that rises in showers of blood—that serpent's eye, that charms to destroy."

But the most startling section of his little-known antiwar speech preached a doctrine of people's revolution that was in the Jeffersonian spirit of the Declaration of Independence:

> Any people anywhere, being inclined and having the power, have the right to rise up, and shake off the existing government, and form a new one that suits them better. This is a most valuable—a most sacred right—a right, which we hope and believe, is to liberate the world. Nor is this right confined to cases in which the whole people of an existing government may choose to exercise it. Any portion of such people that can, may revolutionize, and make their own, of so much of the territory as they may inhabit. More than this, a majority of any portion of such people may revolutionize, putting down a minority, intermingled with, or near about them, who may oppose their movement. Such minority was precisely the case of the Tories of our own Revolution. It is a quality of revolutions not to go by old lines, or old laws; but to break up both, and make new ones.

President Lincoln—like President Franklin D. Roosevelt—was on the side of the angels and the working classes. Both were deeply involved with domestic affairs at the same time that they were Commander in Chief. F.D.R. created the New Deal to pull the country out of the Depression and raise the spirits of the people. Lincoln had less opportunity to concentrate on peacetime issues, but he also favored laws to improve the lot of the workers in the nation. Again and again, Lincoln spoke up for labor. In his first annual message to Congress in 1861, he said:

> Labor is prior to and independent of capital. Capital is only the fruit of labor; and could not have existed if labor had not first existed. Labor is the superior of capital and deserves much the higher consideration. Capital has its rights, which are as worthy of protection as any other rights.

Lincoln was prescient about equality in the workplace. On the subject of women's wages when the government was trying to economize, he told Secretary of War Edwin Stanton in 1864:

> I know not how much is within the legal power of the government in this case; but it is certainly true in equality that the laboring women in our government's employment should be paid at least as much as they were at the beginning of the war.

Like a handful of great presidents in American history, Lincoln was willing to go against the grain of popular opinion. He did not rely on pollsters or speech writers to do his thinking or writing. He was not a compromising centrist; the key to his presidency is that he was a constitutionalist. He could find roots for his radical ideas in the language of the Constitution. In the crucible of war, he was willing to be independent and, if necessary, transform the office into what the author aptly calls "the ferocious engine of democracy." These volumes provide a broadly sweeping history of the Republic through the actions of its presidents, from Washington to Bush. It is an important, even controversial, view of how some presidents exercised leadership, or failed to, and how the country survived its glories and failures in the White House.

Herbert Mitgang
University of Georgia

Preface
Models of the Presidency

This volume is a history of the office and the first forty men who served in it over two centuries. It is not a social or economic history of the United States, except where those factors influenced the macropolicies of the nation and were in turn affected by the behavior of the chief executives. Still, men and women came of age, fell in and out of love, and died, often without feeling or acknowledging the impact of this office especially before Franklin D. Roosevelt's time.

The sheer sweep of these two hundred years, which are partially seen in the development of this office, is enough to keep a reader from picking up a skimpy-sized single volume. But with all these details, with all these character sketches and political controversies, one can still lay out some overriding themes that emerge without forcing the particulars into the service of generalizations.

Two such themes are expounded in the introduction: the presidency has been a prism through which the concerns and ambitions of Americans have been refracted. And with the growth and development of the American republic and its commanding influence, the presidency has been to a remarkable extent the cutting edge for such aggrandizement.

It is also becoming clearer as we examine the presidency in its two-hundred-year history that the central, but not solitary importance of the office is in its public and communal functions—the ability of its incumbents to express ideas, ideologies, hopes, and fears for the people of their particular generations. Although the successes of presidents are surely linked to concrete realities, such as economic stability or depression, the outcomes of military battles, and fair tax and tariff schedules, the office is more importantly linked to the realm of popular impressions and symbols in which facts and administrative feats are only building blocks that can support or undermine in partial ways these overall leadership impressions. And the ability of presidents to identify with very powerful motifs, such as federalism, the perpetual Union, internationalism, Manifest Destiny, and equalitarianism did dictate to a large extent how successful they were in moving from being generational leaders to historical figures. In this volume and its successor, one can examine how Washington went from being a modestly successful commander to the father of his country, how Lincoln was transformed from a Whig Unionist into the Great Emancipator, how Wilson emerged from a schoolmasterish prime minister to the apostle of selfless internationalism, and how Franklin Roosevelt cast off the trappings of the crafty domestic politician and became the international soldier of freedom fighting against some of the terrible tyrannies of this century.

But there are also other common themes that serve to show some general unity of purpose and interests during particular times or eras. I have characterized them as models along the following lines:

1. *The Federalist Model.* Established by Washington, the Federalist model was epitomized by the first two presidents and then fell into disrepute and disuse during much of the nineteenth and most of the twentieth century, although it seems to have been somewhat rediscovered by Eisenhower, Reagan, and Bush. The main elements are broad, popular appeal of the incumbent often regardless of public policy positions, strong assertions of executive authority especially in foreign affairs, general disregard of political parties, a preoccupation with official pomp and protocol as a way of protecting and buttressing the incumbent, a conservative economic and social orientation, and an aloofness toward legislative controversies, except where they infringe on the direct prerogatives of the executive. Adams continued these orientations, although he had a more difficult time than his popular predecessor. To some extent, his son tried to return to this model of presidential leadership.

2. *The Jeffersonian Model.* Jefferson and his immediate successors provided a very different approach: strong party government, subtle fusion of the executive with the legislative branch, coherent leadership, democratic mores, and a partially hidden executive. Such

a model influenced Woodrow Wilson's very successful first term although he was not, in many ways, an admirer of Jefferson. Of course, the impact of Jefferson's philosophy and that of his associates has had an even more far-reaching influence than his model of the presidency. His appreciation of limited government, state rights, and broad limitations on political power led to the Jacksonians and to what became the mainstream conservative tradition of the Democratic party. The missionary zeal of the Jeffersonians in spreading the American faith by exporting it down the East Coast and into the hinterlands was only the first step in a clear imperial vision in which the presidency became one of the major sources of direction in those two centuries.

3. *The Jacksonian Model.* Nominally a Jeffersonian Democrat, Jackson went on to transform the party and the presidency by adhering to a very different model of the office. He, and to a lesser extent his disciples, employed a populist view of a presidency in direct communication with the people and asserted the executive's dominance over party and Congress based on specific programmatic initiatives. The foreign policy of expansion—including expansion through armed force—was more pronounced than in the Jeffersonian period and yielded enormous territorial rewards especially under James "Young Hickory" Polk and, to a lesser extent, John Tyler. In many ways, the 1850s were characterized by a struggle of weak presidents trying to be Jackson and the absence of a strong Democratic party, which would undergird their leadership.

4. *The Whig Model.* Although no Whig president ever served long enough to attach much significance to his particular election, the party did propose a fairly articulate notion of what the office and the federal government should be. Harrison and Taylor were not great theorists, but the party's position was formed initially as a reaction to Jackson's plebiscite views of direct democracy. The Whig model reemphasized a broad nationalism replete with an agenda of patriotism and internal improvements, a public respect for Congress, a general view of the executive as a chief magistrate who would be zealous against encroachments of his power, but would not engage in great demonstrations of executive leadership. The Whig model emerges occasionally in the period from William Henry Harrison through Buchanan; oddly enough, the most important Whig politician elected to the presidency, Abraham Lincoln, abandoned its central tenets under the pressure of circumstance.

But this Whig model is in many ways the major paradigm that one can use in evaluating the presidency after the Civil War between Grant and Theodore Roosevelt and, to a lesser extent, it is characteristic of parts of the period of Republican party ascendancy in 1921–33. Those men emphasized a broad national sentiment, respected Congress in a general sense, tried to protect their powers especially in appointments and foreign relations, and rarely appealed to the people in that direct Jacksonian manner. In a sense, the Whig model became partially, but not totally, absorbed into the Republican party, which is not surprising since that is where most of the northern and western wings of the Whig party went before the Civil War came. The only major exception was Grover Cleveland who served two nonconsecutive terms and whose conservative views were Jeffersonian in economics and stubbornly individualistic in his almost Whig leadership style.

5. *The Lincoln Model.* There was really nothing like it in the nineteenth century in any Western constitutional government—an executive exercising incredible discretionary powers unparalleled in American history and even in the history of parliamentary states in Europe. The Lincoln presidency clearly operated at times outside of law and outside of normal constitutional practice, a model justified by expediency and grave emergency, and divorced at least in the beginning of the war and in the early stages of Reconstruction from the approval of the legislative branch. This executive state with its vast "war powers" became increasingly important for war presidents in the twentieth century—Wilson, FDR, Truman, Lyndon Johnson, and Nixon.

6. *The Rooseveltian Model.* Starting with Theodore Roosevelt and fully expanded by his cousin Franklin, the presidency became the very focal point of the political system and the most activist branch of the federal government. The Roosevelt model is one with strong dominance over the legislative agenda, direct personal appeals to the populace for support, an expanded social welfare state, and an assertive internationalist foreign policy. With the emergence of the executive at the center of the national government and the United States at the center of the world stage, the presidency became increasingly surrounded, as has been noted, by large and often paraconstitutional bureaus of its own—the National Security Council, the Central Intelligence Agency, the Council of Economic Advisors, the White House staff, and assorted offices and officers.

Critics have characterized it as the "imperial presidency"; it may be, but it is also the Rooseveltian presidency writ large. In either case, it represents the highest tide of both executive power and national aggrandizement that the republic has seen and tolerated.

Of course, there is a mixture of elements from different models—necessary adaptions especially in the administrations of more contemporary presidents. The models presented here are meant as guides to help one understand these complexities, not as conceptual straitjackets. The presidency has grown in many ways over the past two centuries. There are similarities and differences, continuities and abrupt departures as executives matched their talents to the challenges before them, and as they interpreted the world to their fellow citizens and as that world impinged on their terms and years in office.

Acknowledgments

I am grateful to a variety of people and institutions that have supported this book and its author for over twenty years. The librarians at SUNY College at Buffalo, Hunter College, the University of Massachusetts at Boston, the Henry L. Huntington Library, St. John's College, and Shepherd College have been generous in their attention. The National Endowment for the Humanities and the SUNY Research Foundation provided financial encouragement as well. James Brennan of the University of Massachusetts has gone beyond the bounds of even friendship in reviewing the entire manuscript and providing his usual erudite comments from which I and the reader have benefited. Douglas Smith of West Virginia University and Burchenal Ault were constantly solicitous about the manuscript and encouraged publishers to review it. I am also grateful for the moral support of Jacques Barzun, one of the great humanist scholars of our time, and to Gordon Hoxie of the Center for the Study of the Presidency, James Wilson of Princeton University, Graydon Tunstall of the Phi Alpha Theta Association, Mark Snell of Shepherd College, and Julie Kirsch of Rowman and Littlefield for their assistance. A special note of thanks to my assistant, Cheryl Flagg, who is responsible more than anyone else for aiding in the preparation of this and the following volume.

Above all I am indebted to my wife, Barbara, and my children, Patrick, Catherine, and Abigail, who put up with me and with "his book." Twenty years is a long time to wait for a finished product.

Introduction

Of all the empires and great states that have made up the fabric of the human chronicle, few have been more remarkable than the United States of America. In less than three hundred years, dots of transplanted European colonies transformed themselves into a string of seaboard territories, waged a common revolution, embraced a loose national government, advanced on a steady and often rapacious march into the hinterlands, and emerged as a unique global power. Nations have risen and fallen before, but it is rare that a new nation has entered the ranks of the great and accelerated its might and prestige so quickly. In that sense, the United States of America is a marvelous success story.

But the shadows of that march loom large: a frequently brutal Indian policy, a neglectful social welfare state, a callous immigration history, a long record of slavery and social apartheid, and a foreign policy often devoid of the most basic decencies of the American spirit.

The American Founding Fathers, operating at the beginning of a new century of great colonization, sought to create an indigenous republic heavily laden with English law, custom, and culture. In the period from the 1600s to the early 1700s, the American continent was peopled by small, meager units of humanity that sprinkled the landscape. In the settlements of New England, in the early communities in Florida and the West Indies, and in the lower tiers of what is now southern California and the Southwest, English, French, and Spanish life, language, and custom prevailed alongside the tribes and pueblos of the American Indians.

In the eastern coastal area, the 1700s marked the formation of a colonial consciousness with English-style institutions of government and self-expression. The endless legalistic battles, the tiresome legislative utterances, and the long Revolution created a confederation

1

of diverse peoples that ended up accepting a national government. In this republican experiment, the Founding Fathers borrowed much from England and created one of the most fascinating institutions ever to enter human history. Except for the papacy, the American presidency is the longest running elective office. The republican executive was an old concept that had proven a failure over and over again; it had led to either breakup or to tyranny—to the Gracchi brothers or to the Caesars.

Today we see a far different office, especially since the first term of Franklin D. Roosevelt. The presidency is an institution of incredible, frightening powers and of simple elementary weaknesses. In the two hundred years of our national existence, the presidency has become the mirror in which the citizenry has often seen itself. The president was the chief magistrate in a republic of free yeomen, an expansionist in the early age of nationalism, a dedicated general in chief during a terrible civil war, a spokesman for the ethos of business and commercial interests during industrialization, and the world prophet and international powerbroker during the period of alliance and empire.

In moving the United States from its simple past to its great far-flung realm, the presidency has been more than a mirror image of our ambitions. It has become the very cutting edge of that process of national aggrandizement, national assertiveness, and national commitment. The republic has been overtaken by a government of extended sway, an empire, if you will, but an empire not modeled on the British, or the French, or the Dutch. It is not an imperialist dream that so fascinates us. It is the subtle extension of influence, of power, of might through commerce, ideas, and popular culture. With that tone and spirit, the American realm has been the major agent of modernity in our times, and its civilization has been a strange mixture of technocratic dynamics, traditional and noble human rights, and unbridled commercialism of all aspects of living. Love or hate it, nearly all the world has imitated these manifestations of the American way. Not since the Romans learned classical Greek and adopted so much Hellenistic culture has one state spread its paradigms of thought so rapidly. Not since the British unfurled their flag over the far corners of the world has one system of government so demanded and so received its way as has the United States in the post-World War II world. Surely one cannot argue that the presidency since George Washington accomplished all this alone. The influence of the United States runs deeper and wider than its executive. Yet the presidency has been both a mirror of our dreams and wishes and an agent of change especially since 1933.

While the Egyptian empire lasted 900 years, the Roman empire 400 years, and British rule about 250, there are cries that the American realm is in disrepair and the American Century, as Henry Luce called it, has supposedly shrunk down to twenty-five years ending in 1968 or so. The historian of the presidency should be interested in a narrative of the office and officeholders and an analysis of the effects of that institution on government and society. What the office will become and how the American state will fare is beyond the scope of this work. Some chroniclers of the past prefer to believe that the future is contained in what went before like seeds embedded in fully grown plants. Others like to believe that leaders and followers learn from the study of history and hopefully become wiser in the process. Yet the repetitions of error seem to undercut that very philosophy of history. Still others accept Tolstoy's conclusion in *War and Peace* that fate and its fickle sister, chance, explain why great men and great nations rise and fall despite their intentions. Presidents in that perspective would be more creatures of circumstance than makers of events. Some critics of history believe that historians are simple bards who do not seek truth as much as provide fallacious contexts in which disjointed events are forced into an order to make sense to the writer and reader.

This study charts the complex dynamics of a two-hundred-year-old institution and in that story one can see how our ideal of America has changed as well. We are, for better or worse, the self-made nation, the resting place—if we can rest—of people who remade themselves, freed from old nations and old family roots—an endlessly migrating people where 10 percent of the population changes residence each and every year. We are held together by a vague national patriotism, a nebulous creed espousing liberty and opportunity, a set of eighteenth-century political institutions, and a popular culture that is thin but pervasive especially among the young.

The presidency is one of those national institutions, an office that permeates our civic consciousness and occupies a central, but not solitary role in our national policy-making. As this century comes to a close, we must recognize that profound changes are occurring in our lives—public and private. The world that many of us were born into is as far removed from our children as ours is from that of George Washington. The America of stable, closed neighborhoods, contained and unsophisticated media, stubborn men and domestically oriented women, mild religion and nonideological politics is gone forever, and with it all the virtues and the vices of small town living and manageable urban areas.

To be a great empire, or an expanded realm, we have had to raise taxes, build armies, support militarily oriented laboratories and university centers, create paraconstitutional agencies such as the CIA, the National Security Council, the augmented Federal Reserve System, and the Council of Economic Advisors, and set up alliances and military bases all over the world. Athens has become Rome. The chief magistrate has become the first consul. The presidency is one of the linchpins of this change in American political ambitions. These developments have mainly come about because we, or those we let lead us, wish to exert American influence in the world, and because we are fearful of the vacuum some foreign powers would exploit if we were idle or negligent. The growth of the presidency and the reconstruction of foreign policy have coincided with the ascendancy of the Stalinist state in Russia. Of all the major tyrannical regimes in Western history, few can rival in scope the bureaucratic and often terroristic police state that Stalin created and that his successors finally dismantled in 1991.

Great nations need great enemies. The Macedonians had Persia, the Athenians Sparta, the Romans Carthage. In the postwar period, the presidents have been the champions and articulators of that Manichean, black and white struggle between the forces of light and darkness. It is easy to satirize that struggle, but its elements are real, powerful, dangerous, and often true. No one born into this terrible and exciting century can dare say that ideas are not important—ideas that led to Nazism, Fascism, Communism, democracy, nationalism, tribalism, and religious fervor. In the twentieth century, men and women died in battle and built strange societies believing that they served a greater cause than themselves. Looking back on our time, historians will probably remember two achievements most starkly—we were the people who urged explorers on into outer space and we were the madmen who carried genocide and war to an intense art.

The presidents, then, are witnesses of that past, manifestations of our wisdom and our follies, advocates of our expanded role in the world. Some of them were thoughtful men, some mundane and deficient. Taken together, the presidents and their presidencies can give us also a glimpse of a changing government, a restless people, and an uncertain future for one of the few republican forms of government ever struck by the mind of humankind.

Few institutions have been so examined over the years as the American presidency, and I have benefited from the works of others and their scholarly effort. I hope that a future historian of the office may say the same of this study. And I would wish that aspirants to the office would benefit in some ways by not just knowing the presidency, but by coming to keep the faith that only a free people can seem to love and truly deserve.

This first volume will cover the development of the presidency in the late eighteenth and the nineteenth centuries, the enormous geographical expansion of the nation, the democratization of the United States, and the critical role of the executive in the carnage and the nobility of the Civil War. It is especially within the last context that I have characterized the presidency as the ferocious engine of democracy. For despite its moderate lapses, the major chief executives were assertive presidents in enlarging the American realm and in articulating for many in forceful and compelling ways this new form of government and its special mission in the world and in history.

1

The Origins of the American Presidency: The British and American Backgrounds

They were the sons and daughters of Englishmen and women, born in another land and cast upon the virgin shores of a strange continent. Praying to a God of vengeance and not of love, confronted daily by the fierce quickness of death, and living in close communities for sheer survival, the new inhabitants tried to adjust their traditions to the seacoast frontiers they embraced. With their compacts, their charters, and their constitutions, they struggled to regulate the conflicts within themselves and work out a system of rational common action against the chaos that lived by their doorsteps.

In their adventure, these settlers stretched a fragile cord of memory and a broken line of sailboats across the sea from their mother country. They sought to impose on their experiments a standard far more exacting than ever existed before, and called upon the Almighty to bless their righteousness and their sacrifice. Those settlers who came to this land had set sail for a variety of reasons. Many desired to acquire land and wealth, fearing that England was becoming overcrowded and prone to produce paupers. Others came to advance the causes of the English flag and to contain the reach of the Catholic Spanish king. Still others braved the heartaches and the dangers to bring Christianity to the natives and thus to further the spread of the Holy Gospel. And, of course, some of these noble ancestors were common criminals, social misfits, and political undesirables who were shipped to the New World away from the decent peoples of the British Isles.[1]

Although an ocean separated the colonists from their ancestral homeland, they shared many of the ideas and habits of their previ-

7

ous compatriots. Their views of politics and government drew heavily on their experiences in Britain, often in opposition to the king's ministers and the king's church. Indeed, anyone seeking to understand the origins of executive power in America must be aware of the general contours of the late seventeenth- and early eighteenth-century debates over the powers and the prerogatives of the British monarch.

Those political controversies involved an ancient and uncertain tension between the monarch and the Parliament, a tension that was still unresolved at the time of the American Revolution. Supporters of a strong monarchy reached back into medieval history, arguing that Parliament existed by the grace of the Crown, and they relied on deference, divine right, and later patriarchal theory to support their view of the political world. The king was to the nation what the father was to the family, and by the nature of things, both ruled their realm, one hoped, wisely and well. The advocates of an independent Parliament, on the other hand, recalled Anglo-Saxon myth and argued that when their British forebears originally came out of the Germanic forests, they had already established traditions of self-government based on consent and mutually agreed upon customs.[2]

One of the major outcomes of this long Crown-Parliament rivalry was the creation of the nebulous but very powerful tradition called "the rights of Englishmen," a vaguely defined collection of personal and political liberties. Many British subjects, including some of the colonists, saw themselves as Englishmen who had not forfeited their heritage because of the distance that separated them from the isles. Both the Crown and the Parliament reinforced these colonial views by instituting local assemblies in the New World and allowing rudimentary representative governments to be established. The role of these local assemblies quickly became a source of controversy in the eighteenth century, and as in England, the representative body began to assume ascendancy over executive authority, in this case, the royal governors.

THAT AWFUL RESPECT

For the colonists in the New World, experiences with executive authority often revolved around two major institutions: the king in England, and the provincial governor at home. The exact powers of the monarch in eighteenth-century Britain, on the eve of the American Revolution, are difficult to define with any precision. While the more literate Founding Fathers were influenced by a variety of European philosophers and public figures, two major authorities on that question were especially well known to the Americans in that period: the philosopher John Locke and the jurist William Blackstone.

Although identified with the notions of consent and parliamentary supremacy, Locke had defended the tradition of royal prerogative. The executive, he argued, had by "the common law of Nature, a right to make use of it [the prerogative], for the good of the Society." In addition, "the Laws themselves should in some cases give way to the Executive Power, or rather to this Fundamental Law of Nature and Government, viz., that much as may be, all Members of the Society are to be *preserved*." Thus, the executive could act counter to law if guided by the public interest. Locke insisted that the prerogative was to be used only to promote desirable ends, and that by definition, the prerogative "is nothing but the Power of doing publick good without a Rule." Yet Locke was wise enough in the ways of the world to concede that the reigns of strong princes are always "the most dangerous to the Liberties of their People," for soon lesser leaders will recall the extraordinary use of power in the past and try to establish it as a new standard for their future conduct.[3]

Locke's influence on the American colonial mind is well known, and his work and words reached the common folk through the efforts and rhetoric of several of the Founding Fathers, including Jefferson, Adams, and Madison. But these men, all trained in the law or quite familiar with its background, had also studied the works of William Blackstone, the great English jurist and author of the *Commentaries on the Laws of England* (1765-1769). Central to his discussion of law and tradition was the question of the powers of the monarch and his manifold prerogatives, some of which Blackstone defined with much more precision than Locke had attempted. Although Blackstone always referred to the monarch as "the king," he undoubtedly recognized the same prerogatives could be claimed by a queen, such as the vigorous daughter of Henry VIII, Elizabeth I. In general, the monarch was to rule, in the words of the great coronation oath, "according to the statutes in parliament agreed on, and the laws and customs of the same." But Blackstone argued that, in addition, the monarch possessed two types of prerogatives: direct and incidental, and he went on to enumerate them in detail.

The first type of prerogative was rooted in the king's political person and included such important powers as the right to send ambassadors, to create peers, and to make war and peace. Another category, incidental prerogatives, was distinct from the king's person and was usually an exception to the general rules of the community, such as the dictum that no costs can be recovered against the king. Under English tradition, no one could sue the sovereign without royal permission, a stipulation that was carried over in America to the early prohibition of lawsuits against the various levels of government from local to federal.

In keeping with the sovereign majesty of the king, the monarch could do no wrong and if acts of oppression occurred within the realm, it was the fault of others around him. The law, Blackstone argued, ascribes to the king not only extensive powers and emoluments, but also "certain attributes of a great and transcendent nature; by which, the people are led to consider him in the light of a superior being, and to pay him that awful respect, which may enable him with greater ease to carry on the business of government." Since the monarch could do no wrong, "in him is no folly or weakness." The monarch is never negligent, and on taking the throne is purged of any stain of corruption, including treason. While he can not be found to have violated his trust, his ministers are not so fortunate; and the history of Britain is replete with Parliament impeaching ministers of the Crown as a way of controlling the monarch.

For Blackstone, the king is vested with a host of powers, many of them granted not by law, but by tradition and the very nature of the royal position. The monarch, for example, can reject bills passed by Parliament, make treaties, coin money, create peers, pardon offenders, wage war, declare peace, issue letters of marque and reprisal, and grant safe conduct to foreigners in the realm. The monarch is the generalissimo, has the sole power to raise and regulate fleets and armies, erect and maintain forts, prohibit the exportation of arms and ammunition out of the kingdom and, within some limits, both curtail travel abroad and demand a particular person's return.

In terms of judicial administration, the ruler is the "fountain of justice," can issue proclamations that have the force of law, confer honors and titles, control commerce by establishing markets, regulating weights and measures, and setting the standards for the coining of money. He is the head of the Church of England, has authority over all ecclesiastical synods and convocations, can fill bishoprics, and is the last appeal in cases coming from ecclesiastical courts.

Of central concern to any monarch is control over revenues, and Blackstone's discussion here ranges far and wide. The king is entitled to money from the custody of some church property, tithes and ecclesiastical taxes, rents and profits of royal lands and arbitrary tenures, fees for wine licenses, and judicial court revenues. The monarch's sway even includes the rights to "royal fish" (whale or sturgeon), which are caught or come ashore, remains of shipwrecked merchandise, treasures found buried in the earth, recovered stolen goods that are unclaimed, stray animals, forfeited lands or goods, and copyrights for many items.

These prerogatives, and many more, were seen as conferring dignity and power on the monarch, and under Blackstone's aegis they came to form an overarching theory of royal power. Although, the political world of Blackstone and Locke had changed extensively by the time the Founding Fathers read their work, nonetheless these two scholars, among others, provided the colonists with what many viewed as the major English tradition on the topic of executive authority. By the time the House of Hanover and the three Georges took over the throne in the eighteenth century, however, the English political system had become one in which royal patronage and parliamentary cliques ensured the ascendancy of the Crown-in-Parliament, that is, the monarch acting in league mainly with royal supporters in the House of Commons.[4]

THE FIRST EXECUTIVES

In the New World, however, the Americans had their real exposure to executive authority in the person of the royal governors who were appointees of the Crown and the Privy Council, and who became the object of much colonial distrust and opposition. The royal governors were assisted by local councils of notables who were appointed to their position by the British government. In addition, the original documents creating these provincial institutions usually included provisions for a local assembly. In the eyes of the royal authorities, these assemblies were not legislative bodies, but simply consultative groups established by the grace and good favor of the Crown. To the colonists, who were anxious about their security and their status, these assemblies of suspicious and often pompous local leaders, became great bodies to protect their rights as Englishmen. The Crown and its partisans had tried by mighty design to contain and control the Parliament in Britain, yet by their grace and favor, the monarchs had created a host of little parliaments across the ocean, fertile plots in which the seeds of resistance and rebellion were inadvertently planted generations before the battles at Lexington and Concord.

At the center of this developing controversy was the royal governor. Sitting with his provincial council, usually twelve people, the governor could create and regulate the lower courts, appoint judges, commissioners, ministers, and other officers, issue money, establish martial law in time of war, and be the highest court of appeals in the province. The governor was usually the commander in chief and captain general of the armed forces, and he could require inhabitants to serve in those forces, could create ports and harbors, set up customs and warehouses, and examine rates and shipping duties. By the 1750s, however, most of the patronage positions in the New World colonies were filled by the authorities in London, and the power of the governors over the military and their ability and opportunity to deal directly with the British secretaries of state were weakened.

Surely though, the real undoing of the provincial governors was the local assemblies. While the Crown and Parliament across the sea did not recognize these bodies as representative forms of government with the power to tax and make laws, the assemblies took a different view. As the assemblies matured, they began to develop an opinion of themselves that in a remarkable way paralleled the parliamentary assertion of power against the Stuart monarchs. The local bodies insisted on having the sole right to raise revenues, to dispense funds, and to pay the salaries of the governors and other royal officials. In New York, New Jersey, New Hampshire, and the Massachusetts Bay colonies, assemblies frequently withheld or delayed governors' salaries as a way of expressing disapproval with their actions or those of the Crown's ministers in England.

The royal governors became an easy target of opportunity for the patriot leaders with their sense of quick organization and their propensity for immediate and direct action. Isolated from the people, far from the protection of the British court, the governors became symbols of an increasingly objectionable set of policies—policies they often had little impact upon, and which they had to carry out, as the British administration insisted on more and varied taxes on the colonies. As for the Americans, these royal governors were the first real executives they encountered, and discussions of tyranny often became linked up with the notion of executive authority. It fell to the new war governors in the states to recast somewhat the link between popular sovereignty and executive responsibility in ways both familiar and acceptable to the fiercely independent American provincials.

When the Revolution came, the states were advised by patriot leaders to write new constitutions, republican documents purged of references to the Crown and its once recognized favors and graces. To guide such discussions, George Wythe of Virginia wrote John Adams in early 1776 for advice on how to proceed. Adams put forth a constitutional blueprint, which he later published in a pamphlet titled "Thoughts on Government." He warned against concentrating all powers in a congress or legislative branch, yet he still retreated from supporting a strong governor or executive. His contemporary, James Wilson of Pennsylvania, explained that before the war, the executive and judicial powers were "placed neither in the people, nor in those who professed to receive them under the authority of the people. They were derived from a different and a foreign source: they were regulated by foreign maxims: they were directed by a foreign purpose." As Thomas Jefferson noted, "Before the Revolution we were all good English Whigs, cordial in their free principles and in their jealousies of their executive Magistrates. These jealousies are very apparent in all our state constitutions."[5]

REPUBLICAN EXECUTIVES

Yet despite the apparent movement away from executive authority, most of the state constitutions provided for some recognition of the role of the governors—even if many of the important powers had to be shared with a council or the legislature itself. Significantly though, two major states, Massachusetts and New York, departed from the general temper of the times and provided for comparatively strong executives. Their constitutions were to influence greatly the Founding Fathers as they gathered in Philadelphia to write the new federal document with its strong executive article.

Article II, which contains most of the language in the Constitution on the presidency, enumerates the powers of the office and provides for the election process. The president is given "the executive power," is commander in chief, can grant reprieves and pardons (except for impeachments), has the authority to make treaties, which have to be ratified by two-thirds of the Senate, makes major appointments with the advice and consent of a majority of the Senate, and is allowed to fill vacancies during Senate recesses. The executive can also require written opinions from the heads of departments, address Congress on the state of the Union, recommend measures for its consideration, convene Congress, and adjourn it if the two houses disagree on the date. The executive can veto bills subject to two-thirds override by both houses, receive foreign ministers, commission all officers of the United States, and is instructed to "take care that the laws be faithfully executed." The president is guaranteed a fixed salary while in office, can be reelected indefinitely for four-year terms, and can be removed only for high crimes and misdemeanors after indictment by the House and conviction by the Senate. Brief in length and succinct in style, this is Article II, the basic constitutional foundation upon which is built the most powerful elective office in the world.

The phrasing of Article II is very similar, but not identical to some of the major state constitutions. The New York Constitution of 1777, for example, provided for a popularly elected governor with a three-year term, who was general and commander in chief of the state militia and admiral of the navy. He was empowered to convene the legislature, prorogue or discontinue it for up to sixty days on extraordinary occasions, grant reprieves and pardons except in cases of treason or murder, recommend measures he deemed important, and inform the legislature about the condition of the state. In words similar to Article II, the governor was required to "take care that the laws are faithfully executed to the best of his ability." Unlike the president though, the governor shared the veto power with a council made up of the chancellor and judges of the state supreme court. In terms of the appointment power, the constitution provided that the assembly would nominate a group of senators who in turn would give its advice and consent concerning the governor's nominees. The assembly also had the power to begin impeachment charges against officials for "real and corrupt conduct," with a court of select senators and state judges pronouncing the final verdict.

The second major constitution that was well known to the Founding Fathers was the 1780 Massachusetts charter. In *The Federalist*, Hamilton recorded that on several occasions this document was the model from which the federal constitution was adapted. The Massachusetts Constitution provided for a "supreme executive magistrate" who was chosen yearly by popular vote. He retained the veto power which could be overridden only by a vote of two-thirds of both houses, could in some cases, with the advice of the council, adjourn or prorogue the legislature, and, with the advice and consent of the council, pardon offenders, except in impeachment cases.

Over the years, especially since Franklin D. Roosevelt's terms in office, there has been considerable discussion over what exactly are "the war powers" of the presidency. The Massachusetts Constitution gives an interesting list of those powers in the case of the governor:

> The governor of this commonwealth, for the time being, shall be the commander-in-chief of the army and navy, and of all the military forces of the state, by sea and land; and shall have full power, by himself, or by any commander, or other officer or officers, from time to time, to train, instruct, exercise and govern the militia and navy; and for the special defense and safety of the commonwealth, to assemble in martial array, and put in warlike posture, the inhabitants thereof, and to lead and conduct them, and with them to encounter, repel, resist, expel, and pursue, by force of arms, as well as by sea as by land, within or without the limits of this commonwealth, and also to kill, slay, and destroy, if necessary, and conquer, by all fitting ways, enterprises, and means whatsoever, all and every such person and persons as shall, at any time hereafter, in a hostile manner, attempt or enterprise the destruction, invasion, detriment, or annoyance of this commonwealth.

Thus, despite all the bitter criticisms of royal government, of its prerogatives, and of the abuses of power perpetrated by energetic ministers and sycophant agents, the American political leadership showed somewhat of a consensus about what properly constituted executive authority in a rather narrow sense at least. What the Revolutionary War years provided was the experience of some successful republican executives at the state level who could be admired and held up favorably to public scrutiny. Energy and dispatch were once again prized attributes in government, and as many influential individuals began to look more critically at a weak national government run by congressional committees, they came to rethink the value of executive authority.

Article II of the federal Constitution was not a brilliant innovation but rather, like most of the American system of government, an adaptation of the familiar to the novel, a blending of tradition and experience to the uncertain world that demanded both authority and restraint. Of course, paper constitutions are not the same as political history, and a collection of clauses does not an office make. The true tale of executive power in that period can be best related by looking at the actual wartime governors in order to comprehend how they dealt with the problems of leading their states during the confusing and demanding War of Independence.

Overall, the men who served in these positions during the Revolution had both experience in local politics and a special understanding of the national war effort. They were not provincial lawyers and merchants who knew only success in the neighborhood and the friendships of the local folk. In fact, about half of the governors had at one time or another served in the early Congress, and were familiar with the representatives from other states in the new Union. Delegates elected to Congress corresponded regularly with the governors, and that body actively sought the views of the governors and usually supported them in disputes with Continental army officers. Some of the governors could draw warrants on the national treasury to pay for supplies and bounties and for expenses incurred in defending the frontiers. The governors also could remove recruiting officers and appoint Continental agents and Indian affairs commissioners.

As a group, the governors were strong supporters of General Washington and, unlike some congressional leaders, they were mainly unimpressed with his rivals in the military ranks. Washington, in turn, kept in close contact with the state executives, especially those in the war zones and, after 1779, he communicated more frequently with them than with Congress to which he nominally reported. The governors then became important leaders in the struggle for independence, and set the style for republican executive authority. In the real seats of government—the state capitals— many of them recast the balance of political power, and made it fit into the new order of things. America had strong governors and weak ones during this revolutionary period, but when it came time to reframe the national government, the Founding Fathers looked more toward the New York and Massachusetts models for guidance.[6]

CREATING THE PRESIDENCY

After the Revolution was successful and the peace treaty with Britain signed, some of the patriot leaders became more convinced that a new constitution was essential. To individuals engaged in commerce, the separate states posed major obstacles to free trade; to men and women of affairs the American nation lacked a firm presence and financial stability; and to ambitious leaders, their confederation had no vigor or national authority. Shay's Rebellion in 1786 proved for many people that the state governments were weak, and that the spirit of anarchy among the lower classes had grown stronger and represented a threat to those of power and wealth. In that same year, the Commonwealth of Virginia organized a general trade convention, which was attended by five states. From that session, a report was circulated that urged the state legislatures to call a national convention for the sole purpose of putting forth a plan to rectify the alleged serious defects in the Confederation. Twelve state legislatures, led again by Virginia, responded positively, and Congress concurred on February 21, 1787. Only Rhode Island was unwilling to join in the proposed convention.

When the delegates arrived in Philadelphia, it soon became obvious that some of them wished not to modify the Articles of Confederation, but to write a totally new charter. After George Washington was chosen presiding officer and some procedural rules were laid down, Edmund Randolph on May 29 presented the Virginia delegation's sweeping proposals. In a long speech, he enumerated the defects of the government of the Articles of Confederation: it provided no security against foreign invasion, offered little direction in the way of regulating commerce, could not defend itself from encroachments by the more aggressive states, and overall, lacked authority. In place of the current system of government, Randolph proposed a bicameral legislature, with one branch to be elected by the "free inhabitants" of the states, and the second branch to be chosen by the first from a list of people nominated by the state legislatures. The National Legislature was to have broad powers to pass laws, void state acts contravening the constitution, and use force against recalcitrant states. The executive—whether it was a single or plural one was not specified in the proposal—would be elected by the legislative branch for only one term, guaranteed a fixed salary, and given "the executive rights vested in the Congress by the Confederation." A council of revision, made up of the executive and some judges was to exercise a qualified veto.[7]

At first, the Virginia Plan seemed to command quick assent, and a majority of state delegations went on record supporting the bold nationalistic position. But some of the delegates from the smaller states felt that they could not get approval back home for such a radical departure from the past. And so the convention continued with extensive debates, focusing in the first week of June on the executive article. Charles Pinckney of South Carolina argued that while he personally favored a vigorous executive, to give that position the power to declare war and peace would lead to "a monarchy, of the worst kind, to wit, an elective one." Randolph now argued that he himself feared having only one person assume all the executive powers, for that was "the foetus of monarchy."[8]

James Wilson, the distinguished Pennsylvanian jurist and constitutional scholar, emerged as one of the strongest defenders of a powerful executive as he argued that the "best safeguard against tyranny" was being able to hold one person responsible for the execution of the office. He argued for the popular election of the executive and cited the experiences of New York and Massachusetts. The delegations agreed by a vote of six to three to have a single executive, and then took up the question of whether to give him a veto, or "negative" as they called it.

Wilson again stressed the need for a strong president who would be granted either an absolute veto, or one jointly shared with the judiciary as a way to protect those two branches of government from legislative intrusion. But opposition mounted as Benjamin Franklin reported that one governor in his home state of Pennsylvania had used the veto in order to extort money from the legislature. George Mason added to the criticism by warning that a "hereditary monarchy" might grow up in America. At the end of the discussion, the convention approved, by a vote of eight delegations to two, a veto power with a two-thirds override by both houses. Madison and Wilson later tried to have the question reopened by introducing again the provision that the veto be shared with a sort of council of revision made up of federal judges sitting with the executive, but the convention delegates felt that this was an improper use of the judiciary, which would upset the separation of powers.

Then delegates from New York and several smaller states joined with William Paterson of New Jersey in introducing a proposal to reform modestly the Articles of Confederation. Paterson's plan would grant Congress some new powers to raise revenue and regulate commerce and would create an executive (the number of people was undesignated) to enforce the laws and treaties. The executive(s) would also chose a supreme court to hear cases of impeachment and appeals in particular controversies involving foreigners, criminals on the high seas, and ambassadors. The Paterson plan had no chance of being adopted, but it was clear that the nationalists were going to have a very difficult time pushing for a major revision of the Articles without making significant concessions.

The convention was further split on the issues of representation of the states in the new government, and to a lesser extent on the question of slavery. The moderate delegates and those from some of the smaller states were unwilling to accept the distribution of seats in both houses based on population alone. After considerable debate, the convention created a Congress based on population in one house and on equal representation in the other. In terms of slavery, the convention counted the slave population as three-fifths of its total for the purposes of both taxation and representation, and put some restrictions on the slave trade after 1808. The Constitution, however, never mentions the specific word "slave" even in passing.

With these two divisive issues settled, the convention still had to grapple with the executive power article, especially with the question of how to elect the president. Although Madison kept meticulous notes, and several others have given us their remembrances, it is obvious that at several critical junctures in the discussions, the delegates were unable to accommodate their differences and turned the issues over to select committees to work on. There over ale, in the backrooms of taverns and rooming houses, much of the difficult work of rewriting and recasting Article II, as it came to be called, was done.

From July 17 to July 26, in the steamy Philadelphia summer, the delegates wrestled with the method of electing the executive.

Gouverneur Morris repeated that to have Congress involved would violate the separation of powers and make the executive "the mere creature" of the legislative branch. Citing the New York and Connecticut experiences, he noted that popular elections worked because the "people would never fail to prefer some man of distinguished character or services." Wilson agreed, and advocated once again the popular election of the executive. But Charles Pinckney argued that such an election would favor the larger states, and George Mason warned that popular election was as unnatural as referring "a trial of colors to a blind man." The convention then refused to support either popular election or election by state-chosen electors. Instead, the delegations voted unanimously for election by Congress despite the serious reservations of several of its most influential leaders.[9]

As the debates continued, the convention reaffirmed its sense that the executive should have the veto power, but refused to give him the right to name judges, allocating that responsibility to the Senate. Morris then raised again the separation of powers issue when discussing the election process. In his view, the legislature would seek to aggrandize itself, and the "Executive Magistrate should be the guardian of the people, even of the lower classes, against legislative tyranny, against the great and the wealthy who in the course of things will necessarily compose the legislative body. Wealth tends to corrupt the mind and to nourish its love of power, and to stimulate it to oppression. History proves this to be the spirit of the opulent." He went on to support the idea of eligibility for reelection because, "the love of power is the great spring to noble and illustrious actions. Shut the Civil Road to glory and he may be compelled to seek it by the sword." Rather than arguing that power corrupts, Morris insisted that in a republican society leaders hope to gain fame and glory, and to accomplish these objections "they had to be re-elected and thus accountable to the people."[10]

The convention agreed that the executive should be eligible for reelection, and voted for a six-year term and for election by electors chosen by the state legislatures. Then the delegates dealt with the subject of impeachment. Although Morris and Pinckney argued that impeachment was not a wise process, George Mason asked, "Shall any man be above justice? Above all shall that man be above it, who can commit the most extensive injustice?" Madison agreed, for how else could citizens defend "the community against the incapacity, negligence or perfidy of the Chief Magistrate." Morris in the end also concurred, and the convention by a vote of eight states to two added an impeachment provision. The delegates then voted against a council of revision and continued to give the judicial appointment power to the Senate.[11]

The next week, though, the delegates reopened the whole election process and the length of the term, and finally the executive article was referred to a special Committee on Detail. That committee presented a draft on August 6 that vested the executive power in a single person, to be called "The President of the United States" and addressed as "His Excellency." He was elected by the legislature for only one seven-year term and could be removed for treason, bribery, or corruption. The president was to see that the laws were faithfully executed, would commission officers, receive ambassadors, grant pardons and reprieves, appoint most officers, veto legislation, and be commander in chief. When debate on the draft began, Charles Pinckney tried to add a stipulation that a prospective president must have at least $100,000 in property, but Franklin sharply attacked the idea, noting that he had a personal dislike "of everything that tended to debase the spirit of the common people."

The delegates, as they went over the draft, rejected a clause giving to Congress the power to make war; instead they substituted "declare war," with the understanding that the executive would have the power to repel sudden attacks. The convention accepted the alteration, and then rejected Pierce Butler's proposal to give the legislative branch "the power of peace." The debates on the war powers, so important to posterity, are unfortunately disjointed and confusing. Overall though, while the executive did retain the power to repel invasions, no prolonged military action would be undertaken without congressional approval and oversight. The delegates must have realized that undeclared war was the norm in eighteenth-century Europe, a reality brought close to home by the Seven Years War between Britain and France. The delegates, though, allocated to Congress important parts of what could be termed the war powers. They gave to the legislative branch the power to provide for the common defense; to define and punish piracies and felonies committed on the high seas, and offenses against the law of nations; to declare war, grant letters of marque and reprisal, and make rules concerning captures on the land or water; to raise and support armies and navies; to make rules for the government of those forces; to call forth the militia; to suppress insurrections and repel invasions, and related matters. No state could keep troops or ships of war in peacetime or enter into an agreement with another state or foreign power or engage in war without Congress's approval. Last, the power to suspend the writ of habeas corpus was specified in Article I, which deals with Congress, rather than in Article II on the presidency.

Several years after the convention, Madison wrote to Jefferson, who was in Paris during the period when the Constitution was drafted, that the power to let loose the "Dog of War" was transferred from the executive to the legislative branch, from those "who are to spend to those who are to pay." At the time, Madison wanted to require that peace treaties would need only the approval of a majority of those members present in the Senate, rather than the two-thirds proposed. The convention ended up agreeing at first to Madison's proposal, but the next day it voted his condition down.

On a matter of lesser importance, the convention discussed the proper length of time an immigrant should have to wait before becoming a citizen. In a new nation with fairly flexible requirements about residence and nationality, the issue was of concern, especially to some of the Founding Fathers who were not native-born. Morris was particularly insistent in wanting to extend the probationary period before allowing full citizenship. When a proposal that required four years' citizenship before election to the Senate was suggested, he insisted on fourteen instead. Morris sarcastically noted the "some tribes of Indians carried their hospitality so far as to offer strangers their wives and daughters. Was this a proper model for us?" In the end, the convention required that a person wishing to be a senator would have to be a citizen for nine years, a representative for seven years, and the president was to be both a resident for fourteen years and a natural-born citizen at the time of the adoption of the new constitution. Except for the founding generation, which included such prominent immigrants as Wilson and Hamilton, all future presidents had to be born Americans, a requirement that presumably assumed that they were therefore free of foreign attachments.

As the delegates pondered once again the method of election, they decided to send the matter to a new Committee on Postponed Matters. That committee's draft added a minimum age requirement (thirty-five years), residence and citizenship requirements, and mandated a four-year term with unlimited eligibility for reelection. In terms of election procedures, the committee had the president chosen by electors, who were in turn selected by the states in a manner each state legislature directed. Thus, the delegates neatly sidestepped a point of endless contention and allowed each state to choose how much popular control would be permitted.

The committee gave the president the right to make appointments subject to a majority vote in the Senate, and the authority to finalize treaties with the concurrence of two-thirds of that body. Up to two weeks before the end of the convention, the Senate had been designated as the body to appoint ambassadors and judges and to make treaties, only to have those critical powers delegated to the executive. A third committee on style eliminated the right of Congress to appoint the treasurer, and readied the Constitution for a full vote by the state delegations.

At that point, Pinckney argued that the final draft was deficient and showed "contemptible weakness and dependence of the executive." Another delegate, Pierce Butler, wrote, however, that the powers of the president were great after all, and that the executive article would not have been so broad "had not many of the members cast their eyes toward George Washington as President, and shaped their ideas of the powers to be given a president by their opinions of his virtue." As they concluded their work, Madison observed, "Dr. Franklin, looking toward the President's chair, at the back of which a rising sun happened to be painted, observed to a few members near him, that painters had found it difficult to distinguish in their art a rising from a setting sun. I have, said he, often and often in the course of the session, and the vicissitudes of my hopes and fears as to its issue, looked at that behind the President without being able to tell whether it was rising or setting: But now at length I have the happiness to know that it is a rising and not a setting Sun."[12]

So it was that the American presidency was created, a product of intense debate, committee compromises, historical precedents— all influenced by a long-held suspicion of political power, and yet infused with the confidence that only the first generation of nation builders can bring. Perhaps, once again, it was Benjamin Franklin who best summed up the Founders' deep ambiguity, though. Legend has it that as the aged statesman shuffled down the streets of Philadelphia, an inquisitive woman stopped him and asked, "What have you given us?" And Franklin is supposed to have responded, "A Republic, Madam, if you can keep it."

THE RATIFICATION CONTROVERSY

The new Constitution was forwarded to the states where special conventions were selected to consider the document. The period between 1787 and 1788 was a time of extraordinary political debate, unique even in the brief annals of free republics. The newspapers were filled with commentaries, aimed at influencing the state conventions and molding the opinions of merchants and yeomen alike. The most effective defense of the new Constitution came from "Publius," the joint pen name of Hamilton, Madison, and John Jay. Some eighty-five essays were printed in various newspapers between October 27, 1787, and August 16, 1788, and several of these pieces dealt with the presidency. John Jay reminded his readers that secrecy and dispatch are essential in negotiating treaties and that the executive should embody such attributes. Jay observed that while the proposed Constitution required that "the President . . . act by the advice and consent of the Senate, yet, he will be able to manage the business of intelligence in such a manner as prudence may suggest."

Madison, who had played a major role in the drafting of the document, reassured his readers that the method of election by state electors showed that the proposed government was a federal and not a national structure. While "the executive department is very justly regarded as the source of danger and watched with all the jealousy which a zeal for liberty ought to inspire," nonetheless, the Constitution contained careful limits on the executive. Although it was Madison himself who was the leader of the nationalists, now he was quite willing to point out the virtues of a much more limited document than the one he had proposed.

A similar conversion took place with Hamilton who defended the new Constitution and argued that the presidency was unlikely to become a monarchy; in fact he found that "the executive's powers were in few instances greater, in some less than those of the governor of New York." He rejected the view that the new executive office was patterned after the British monarchy; instead it was the state governors who provided the model for the Founding Fathers. In terms of the veto power, for example, Hamilton cited the

Massachusetts Constitution, "the original from which this Convention have copied." He went on to insist that the method of election had been accepted by nearly all, and that even some of the critics of the Constitution found that provision praiseworthy. Hamilton predicted that "the office of President will never fall to the lot of any man who is not in an eminent degree endowed with the requisite qualifications." He then cited the advantages of having a vigorous executive, an argument more to his temperament and liking. "Energy in the executive is a leading characteristic in the definition of good government," he asserted. Such energy is derived from a unity of authority, duration in office, an adequate provision for its support, and competent powers.

The proposed Constitution then had its strong defenders, but it also had many able critics as well. Elbridge Gerry, who was a delegate in Philadelphia, warned that the executive and legislative branches were "so dangerously blended as to give just cause of alarm." George Mason of Virginia, also a delegate, pressed again for a six-man council of state, made up of two representatives from each section. In this way, a region could be protected from executive abuse, and could also guard its navigation interests. Still another critic, Jonathan Jackson, argued the very opposite: the president should be totally independent of the Senate, so that he could be held personally responsible for actions done in his administration.

Another area of controversy was the method of election and the length of term—two topics that had so divided the delegates themselves. While Hamilton had remarked that this section of the Constitution drew little criticism, he seems to have overlooked some rather influential dissenters, including Jefferson, and more importantly, the governor of New York. Still in Europe, Jefferson expressed to his friends his objection to the reeligibility provision. Governor George Clinton proved to be a more important foe of the new document. Taking up his pen and using the name "Cato," Clinton argued that a term longer than one year was dangerous. He foresaw the development of a despot surrounded by a court of flatterers and sycophants. In charged language, he recited the familiar litany of horrors that such power might incur:

> The deposit of vast trusts in the hands of a single magistrate enables him in their exercise to create a numerous train of dependents. This tempts his *ambition*, which in a republican magistrate is also

remarked, *to be pernicious*, and the duration of his office for any considerable time favors his views, gives the means and time to perfect and execute his designs; he *therefore fancies that he may be great and glorious by oppressing his fellow citizens, and raising himself to permanent grandeur on the ruins of his country.*

Instead of lamenting the lack of a council of state, Clinton derided the cabinet as being the most dangerous type of council in a free country. "The language and the manners of this court will be what disguises them from the rest of the community, not what assimilates them to it; and in being remarked for a behavior that shows they are not *meanly* born, and in adulation to people of fortune and power." He concluded that the presidency and the governorship of New York are quite different, "this government is no more like a true picture of your own than an Angel of Darkness resembles an Angel of Light."

Still others agreed with Clinton and attacked various provisions of the new Constitution. They pointed out how the pardoning power might be used to hide a president's political associates from receiving proper punishment if they were guilty of crimes; how the veto was a violation of the separation of powers; how the commander in chief provision could lead to an elected kingship supported by a standing army, sycophantic officers, and the starvelings of the Cincinnati. One critic noted that the lack of a religious test for the office meant that a Jew, Roman Catholic, or worse still, a Universalist might become president of the United States.

As intense as these newspaper and pamphleteer debates were, the really important theaters of action were the state conventions. In New York, many of the delegates had expressed reservations, but the supporters of the Constitution convinced the convention to approve unconditionally the document, and then to propose a series of amendments. Regarding the presidency, those amendments included provisions that the executive be limited to one seven-year term, that he not command the armed forces without the consent of Congress, that there be a congressionally selected council to advise the executive on appointments, that Congress had to approve the pardoning of traitors, and that the executive with the consent of Congress be able to establish commissions to review Supreme Court decisions. In Pennsylvania, many of the same issues were raised. There, James Wilson, who had argued for a strong presidency in the Philadelphia Convention, was elected to the state ratifying convention. He quickly dismissed the charge that the presidency was a weak office, "a tool of the Senate," as one dissenting voice characterized it. He informed the state convention that he had favored the direct election of the president, but that most of his fellow delegates thought that the very size of the new nation made that design impractical. Wilson maintained that the president had considerable powers: he was commander in chief, controlled the departments of government, possessed the right to grant pardons, and was entrusted with the faithful execution of the laws. In the end, Pennsylvania ratified the new Constitution.

The major battle that the friends of the new document had was in Virginia where the opposition was being led by the frontier Demosthenes, Patrick Henry, whose rhetoric quickened the hearts of patriots and whose very words were already legendary. Looking over the state convention delegates, Henry began, "This Constitution is said to have beautiful features: but when I come to examine these features, sir, they appear to me horribly frightful. Among other deformities, it has an awful squinting, it squints toward monarchy." Then Henry, the one individual who had done more than almost anyone else before the Revolution to challenge the abuses of the king, denounced the proposed presidency in telling terms, "I would rather infinitely—and I am sure that most of this convention are of the same opinion—have a king, lords and commons, than a government so replete with such insupportable evils." Swept up in the raw emotions of old, he went on, "Away with your president! We shall have a king: the army will salute him monarch: your militia will leave you, and assist in making him king, and fight against you; and what have you to oppose this force? What then will become of you and your rights? Will not absolute despotism ensue?" At this point the record we have breaks off, and the stenographer simply summarizes, "Here Mr. Henry strongly and pathetically expiated on the probability of the President's enslaving America, and the horrid consequences that must result." One observer who left his impressions wrote that he found Henry's description so frightening that he "involuntarily felt his wrists to assure himself that the fetters were not already pressing his flesh and that the gallery in which he sat seemed to become as dark as a dungeon."

The Constitution's advocates countered with rhetoric and reasoning of their own. But no one in the Virginia convention was Henry's

equal; as he went on, he praised Washington: "We gave a dictatorial power to hands that used it gloriously; and which were rendered more glorious by surrendering it up. Where is there a breed
of such dictators? Shall we find a set of American presidents of
such a breed? Will the American president come and lay prostrate
at the feet of Congress his laurels. I fear that there are few men
who can be trusted on that hand." And he concluded with a single
sentence that became the credo of much of the anti-Constitution and
later Antifederalist sentiment: "Cannot people be happy under a mild
as under an energetic government?"

But when Henry finished, when the great passions had run their
course, and people ceased to admire the sheer virtuosity of his performance, the vote was taken. The Constitution received the support of the majority of the delegates, and the powerful endorsement
of Virginia was lined up in favor of the new experiment. Only North
Carolina and the normally recalcitrant Rhode Island still lagged
behind as much of the opposition to the Constitution ended. So it
was that in the context of revolutionary memories and legalistic
exercises the early presidency was born. Patriots who had fought
the abuses of a foreign king and his local ministers now came to
accept the necessity for a new national executive and a new national constitution.

From one end of the seaboard to the other, the partisan pam-
phleteers and the political elites carried on a public debate unparalleled in the history of their era. Fresh from the unifying experiences
of war, they were now divided on the future of the very republic
they had created. What was at stake were not only matters of self-
interest, power, and privilege; the Federalists and the Antifederalists,
as they came to be called, subscribed to different dreams of the
future. The opposition would repeatedly rephrase Patrick Henry's
simple question, "Cannot people be as happy under a mild as under
an energetic government?" And the answer of the more ambitious
nation-builders was clear: they wanted not just liberty, but grandeur,
not just republican virtue, but also a place in the sun. For those
purposes, they created a set of strong institutions, and later buttressed them with an alliance of finance and privilege. Yet during
this long and tortuous debate, the Federalists acknowledged, and,
perhaps, even shared in some of the Antifederalists' misgivings.
Their first order of business in the new Congress would be a Bill
of Rights, and in looking for a national executive, they chose es-

sentially a figure of the past—a man who symbolized the revolutionary struggle to his three million fellow countrymen. Washington's selection was obvious. Throughout the rancor of the ratification debates, both factions agreed on one point: they knew that their Cincinnatus could never become a Caesar.[13]

2

The Federalists and the National Agenda (Washington and John Adams)

Of all the leaders who emerged from the crucible of the Revolution, no one combined better the attributes of experience, sagacity, and "gravitas," which so captivated the imaginations of his fellow countrymen, than George Washington. Many educated Americans regarded Washington as their Cincinnatus, the noble Roman who had left his plowing, saved his country, and then returned to his farm, personally uncorrupted by the lure of power. With a hint of jealousy and some admiration, John Adams once said that Washington's main assets were that he was tall and a Virginian. Indeed he was both, but he was also a man of considerable means who had risked his life and his future in a seemingly hopeless gamble. While not one of the signers of the Declaration of Independence served in the Continental army, Washington shared in the soldiers' misery and despair, and went on to reap quite rightfully the powerful glory that only military victory can bring. Like so many of the Founding Fathers, he sought fame and desired to have posterity remember him for his patriotic services. To many Americans of his time, however, Washington was already the living embodiment of republican virtue, a testament that men raised by proper breeding might very well be able to handle honestly the lure and trappings of power.

Washington was born on February 22, 1732 (February 11, Old Style Calendar), in Pope's Creek, Virginia, the first child of his father's second marriage. Although the family could trace its roots deep in English history and was closely aligned with the Stuarts, in America, Washington's forebears were unable to move into the innermost circle of colonial society. George was raised in a family

31

where his father was often absent, his mother overprotective, and his brothers off on their own. George grew up withdrawn, restrained, and often self-reliant. Frequently in his early career, he had difficulties relating to his elders, often appearing impetuous and headstrong. He spent a considerable amount of his time teaching himself personal control and creating in the process a public persona of aloofness and reserve under which flowed the strong torrents of pride, ambition, and temper.

He was on occasion a surveyor and a lieutenant colonel in the British army. Treated unfairly by British senior officers, Washington finally resigned from the army, married a wealthy widow, and at the age of twenty-seven retired to his estate. Later he was elected to the Virginia House of Burgesses and became associated with George Mason in creating a network of opposition to British colonial policies. He was chosen in 1775 to lead the American Continental army; in part his selection was due to the fact that he was a Virginian in a conflict that was identified mainly with New England. Washington became a standard around which the new unformed America was to rally, and he persevered in what was to become a legendary struggle of a ragtag army under an inexperienced commander against the greatest empire on earth.

After a series of lucky engagements against the British and exploiting invaluable French assistance, the Americans prevailed. Washington, like Cincinnatus, returned to Mount Vernon wearing well his newly found glory and dedicated to the republican ideals of tolerance and civilian control of the military.

Although a few other names were occasionally mentioned for the presidency, there was near universal agreement that the office was Washington's if he wanted it. Washington, however, having established his reputation was reluctant to risk it anew. He wondered if he was too old at fifty-six to take on another arduous public position, and he was sure his views were not acceptable to the Antifederalist elements. On the other hand, he was uncertain if his fellow citizens would criticize him for refusing to discharge his duty and answer the call to service. While he was debating with himself, his associates were already deciding whom to support for the vice presidency. Most of the Federalist leadership wanted John Adams, but Adams during the war had sought to curtail the general's power, citing the ever-present danger of standing armies. Recognizing the problem, an old friend of the general, Benjamin Lincoln, wrote to Washington and warned that those who opposed Adams really wanted to elect an opponent of the Constitution as vice president. Washington responded tactfully that he would support any true friend of the Constitution, and later added that it might be wise for the independent electors to chose a vice president from Massachusetts. Privately, the general let it be known to his closest associates that he favored Adams over Governor George Clinton of New York, who had expressed reservations about the new Constitution. By the end of February, Washington was unanimously elected president and Adams garnered enough votes for the second slot.[1]

By April 14, 1789, Washington was officially notified of his election by Charles Thomson, the secretary of the Congress, who had traveled to Mount Vernon to make the formal announcement. Prepared already, Washington left two days later and began his week-long journey from his country estate to New York City. His trip prompted the most remarkable outpouring of public goodwill and affection ever shown in the new nation. As he passed through Virginia, he was honored at a farewell dinner at Alexandria, was greeted by large crowds in Maryland, and was presented in Delaware with an address thanking him for his willingness to give up retirement and once again come to the aid of his country. In Pennsylvania, he was greeted again by large crowds and a huge flower-covered arch bearing banners and slogans draped across laurel roses and green boughs. A chorus of young maidens sang his praises as a flowered crown descended onto his head from the overhanging structure.

Moving across New Jersey, Washington was greeted by more crowds and saw the faces of some of the old veterans of the last great war. By the time he reached Elizabethtown, he was surrounded by a vast throng of people who led him to a special barge, which was to take him across the river onto the shores of New York City, the first capital of the new nation. Washington was saluted by bands, gunfire from ships, church bells, singers, and a school of porpoises that followed his barge part of the way. At the base of Manhattan, near what is Wall Street, Washington was greeted by more celebrities and a military guard. He declined to ride in the elegant carriage held for him, and instead walked toward his new Cherry Street residence past a cheering and shouting crowd. The first administration was about to begin amid pageantry and pomp in a republic dedicated nominally to the simple virtues of thrift and moderation.

The New York City that Washington entered in 1789 was the second largest city in the new nation and, despite the migrations of

German, French, English, and African inhabitants, it was still heavily influenced by the Dutch. Few of the streets were paved, and Benjamin Franklin once sarcastically observed that one could always spot a New Yorker by the way he shuffled. Livestock roamed the avenues and lanes, and thousands of pigs feasted on the garbage that people threw into the streets.

Many of the government leaders lived near Wall and Queen streets, and Abigail Adams described her house on Richmond Hill as "the most delicious spot I ever saw." Near the fields, today's City Hall Park, were an almshouse, bridewell, debtors' jail, and gallows. In 1789, ten persons were executed on the Chinese pagoda-style gallows, none for a crime more serious than burglary. Close to the gallows were the whipping posts and the stockades. In New York City, prices then as now seemed to travelers generally high. Washington paid eighty dollars a month to livery his horses; a skilled worker earned fifty cents a day and an unskilled one about half that amount. A loaf of bread sold for three cents, and it cost a working person a week's wages to buy a ticket to Philadelphia and two days wages to see a theater production. There were numerous brothels and 330 licensed drinking places or more than one for every hundred inhabitants, including women and children.

The new republic that witnessed the inaugural of General George Washington was in many ways still a confederation. Although the Articles of Confederation was discarded, the underlying assumptions of American life were really more decentralized and generally looser than the ardent Federalists could abide. Washington knew the sentiments of his people, and he was by temperament a conservative in many ways.

Nearly all Americans worked the land, and land was plentiful indeed in the United States. Many distrusted paper money, and at the time of the first inaugural there were only three commercial banks in business. In the Deep South states of South Carolina and Georgia, rice-producing plantations in the lowlands were worked by black slaves. World markets were generally open and 40 percent of those two states' rice crops were sold to England. In the tobacco areas, especially in Virginia and Maryland, the problem of overproduction was apparent. By 1788, prices for that commodity had dropped sharply, and some planters sought to renege on debts owed to the British, while others began to diversify their crops.

In the Northwest Territory, the British still had not honored the provisions of the Treaty of Paris, and they retained a dozen trading posts near the Indian tribes. South of the Ohio, the flood of Americans met the constraints of the Spanish empire, which restricted travel down the Mississippi and its tributaries leading toward the great port of New Orleans. In the East, among the yeoman farmers there grew up three moderate-sized cities: Philadelphia (population 42,444), New York (33,131), and Baltimore (13,503) with the beginnings of a cosmopolitan culture in each. In New England, the seafaring business was the central source of wealth with Boston, Providence, and to a lesser extent, Newport conducting a lively trade with Europe and the West Indies.

This complex and diverse society fascinated European visitors as they noted the Americans' love of freedom, the lack of extremes of wealth and poverty, the emphasis on industry and hard work, and the absence of religious and hereditary distinctions. Americans were generally materialistic, at times crude, and usually enterprising. There were notable character differences between the practical and stingy Yankees, the uncouth frontiersmen, and the cultured tidewater aristocracy of the South, which were to produce tensions in the new nation.[2]

THE FIRST MONTHS

After Washington's inaugural, the new president waited patiently while Congress debated what would be the outline of the new bureaucracy and executive agencies. The Confederation, both during the war and after, had a series of such offices, which oversaw the functions of the state, war, treasury, and post office departments, and those agents continued their work during the first administration. As Washington watched the weeks pass by, Congress began its deliberations with an extremely difficult decision to make: who had the power to remove subordinates. The new Constitution said little about removing administrative officers, and it mentioned dismissal only by means of the cumbersome impeachment process.

The House of Representatives, with some nineteen members of the original Philadelphia Convention of 1787, should have known all too well what the Constitution said and what the delegates originally meant. Yet, they were in disagreement as to whether the president had the power to remove such officials and if he needed the consent of Congress, or at least the Senate, which initially would approve many of these individuals. In fact, as the debate progressed, no fewer than four separate views emerged. Some congressmen, such as James Madison, argued that the power to remove the heads of the departments must rest with the executive alone. Others argued that the only method of removal was through the cumbersome impeachment process. A third group argued that the Constitution delegated to Congress the authority to create new offices and to make laws, and that therefore it was the legislative branch that could determine tenure, duties, and compensation of officers. However, some of the representatives who held this view still believed that Congress should delegate its removal power to the president. And last, some members felt that the president and the Senate shared the removal power. In the end, the president was "given" the power to remove subordinates, but whether the power was inherently his in the Constitution or whether it was delegated to him by the Congress never became clear. By the time of Reconstruction, the Radical Republicans would resurrect the controversy by charging that President Andrew Johnson had acted improperly in dismissing major cabinet officials against the express will of the legislative branch.[3]

While that issue was being decided, Washington was spending a considerable amount of time worrying about questions of etiquette. Although he was a republican by nature and by inclination, Washington was no democrat. He had worked long and hard to separate himself from the mass of his fellow citizens, and he was sure that a solid base for the presidency had to include a decent respect for ceremony and decorum. Privately, he admitted that without Martha beside him in that first month, he found much of the socializing burdensome. He spent nearly every day receiving visitors, and many nights returning calls and going to civic events. Overwhelmed, he brooded that there was no time left for public business. As he was aware, the presiding officers of the Confederation Congress had entertained lavishly and their tables were often open to the public. Washington reviewed the situation and bluntly observed that the presiding officer was a "maître d'hôtel," and he was determined to avoid that fate.

In addition to being very time-consuming, such entertainment was costly. In the first nine months in office, Washington spent nearly $2,000 on liquor alone—an astronomical figure in 1789. As some of the more vocal republican representatives watched the new president, they found him to be a bit pompous and rather pretentious. But Washington was anxious to present a good impression in office, and he personally exhibited an old soldier's awkwardness rather than entertaining any illusions about his own position. To one confidant, he wrote that he would rather be at Mount Vernon with a friend or two than to be "attended at the seat of government by the officers and representatives of every power in Europe." When Martha finally arrived, Washington began to relax somewhat, and at informal tea parties he was seen to pass by the men and spent more time with the ladies whose gracious company he always enjoyed.[4]

THE FIRST ADMINISTRATION

The most pressing issue facing the new republic though was not etiquette or appointments, but the state of the economy. Much of the pressure for passing the new Constitution and creating a new form of government was based on the widely held view, especially in the commercial classes, that the Confederation was too weak to promote economic development and guarantee financial stability. For those groups it was fortuitous that the most brilliant and energetic cabinet member in the administration was Alexander Hamilton.

Hamilton took office as secretary of treasury on September 11, 1789, and ten days later he received a request from the House of Representatives that he send to it a plan for the "adequate support of the public credit." That simple inquiry was the immediate cause of Hamilton's far-reaching design to expand the federal government's power and tie it to the merchants and bankers. Blessed with a remarkable mastery of detail and a gift for tactical leadership, Hamilton unfolded a monumental economic policy. In his own mind, he was the prime minister of this new administration and the mainstay of what was to become the Federalist faction.

The Revolutionary War had been financed by a crazy-quilt array of measures, and the states and national government had been unable to settle the problem of who owed what to whom. The largest part of the debt was intergovernmental credits and obligations. The total amount the state governments spent for the war was somewhat over $100 million, and under the Articles of Confederation and various ordinances passed by Congress, those expenditures were to be credited and the costs reapportioned. Those states that had given more than their share would be reimbursed from the general treasury, and those who had paid less than their share would have to pay into it. Since the New Englanders kept more meticulous records than the Southerners, the reimbursement proposals were bound to create problems. Also, the United States owed $8 million to the government of France and $2 million to banks in Holland, and Congress had issued unsecured paper money that had depreciated enormously. Speculators had bought up a good number of governmental securities at a discount rate. Should they end up with a currency that was worth full value? Many of these speculators had purchased vast tracts of land from the federal government or the states, and paid for them with securities at face value. In addition, some states had already repaid their debts, while others had not.

Facing those vexatious questions, Hamilton put forth a brilliant mosaic. He would have the federal government assume the war debt, refinance the old securities under a variety of options, make no distinctions between the original and current holders of governmental securities, allow purchasers of Western lands to pay for them with the full value of inflated currencies, continue the tariff, and create a national bank.

Major opposition immediately came over the method of calculating the debts of the states. Facing intense opposition in Congress, Hamilton appealed in desperation to the new secretary of state, Thomas Jefferson, to secure important support. Hamilton, Jefferson, and Madison ended up approving a deal whereby the national capital would be moved to the Potomac River area, and the Commonwealth of Virginia received confirmation that the allowable debt assumption total in Hamilton's plan would jump to nearly $19 million. Thus, to Jefferson's later consternation, the first piece of the Hamiltonian system—the debt assumption scheme—passed with his help.[5]

Jefferson and his republican colleagues were less amenable to the next keystone, the establishment of a national bank. Jefferson and Madison openly challenged the constitutionality of the measure, insisting that the Constitution provided no specific grant of power to create such a bank. But Hamilton brilliantly demolished those criticisms and ended up making a case in the process for a broad interpretation of federal powers. In those major economic battles, the president retained his position of being above the fray, although he publicly supported the debt plan and had personal reservations, which he overcame, about a federal banking system.

While most accounts of the first term of the Washington administration concentrate on the economic program, another major issue that occupied the president's attention was the situation on the frontier. Some of the tribes constituted a clear danger, while others were still aligned with the British and Spanish. Western politicians demanded increased federal protection and when they did not get it, some talked of setting up a new nation divorced from the weak American republic.

Congress was at that time engaged in a protracted debate over reorganizing the modest military establishment. Strong opposition to a standing army and its costs was expressed by New England representatives while petitions of concern over the Indian threat came in from the Ohio Valley, Kentucky, and elsewhere. The administration resorted to the same strategies used by the Confederation government—peace treaties, bribes, and an occasional show of force. But not all the Indian tribes were willing to be pushed or cheated into the deep hinterlands. In the Northwest Territory, the army suffered serious setbacks at the hands of the tribes, and Congress ordered an investigation.

The House of Representatives, after the demise of General Arthur St. Clair's forces, insisted on getting relevant War Department documents, and the president and his cabinet secretaries discussed the question of invoking what later was called executive privilege or the right to withhold information. Washington finally forwarded the papers to the House and sent his secretaries of war and treasury to testify in person before Congress. As a consequence of these developments, the president through Secretary of War Henry Knox exercised increasing responsibilities both in terms of frontier diplomacy and in the activities of the army in those regions. Dealing with General "Mad" Anthony Wayne, the president ordered reevaluations of court martial proceedings, instructed Wayne where to lay camp and how to discipline and train troops, identified where the destinations of the troops should be, approved all promotions to higher ranks, stopped a proposed expedition to the rapids of the Miami River, and laid out the terms of a peace treaty to be presented to the Indians. Wayne desperately wrote to Knox, "Would to God that my hands were untied."

The president also continued to meet with less-bellicose tribal leaders, and in summit conferences with the Seneca chief Cornplanter in December 1790 and with the leaders of the Six Nations in late 1791 and early 1792, he urged moderation and friendship. At times, the administration's Indian policy seemed a confusing mixture of diplomacy and brute force. Faced with tribal suspicion

of the white man's push for more and more land and the restless-
ness of Western politicians, the president and Knox tried to curtail
the excesses of land speculators and lawless elements. They resisted
the brutality that so characterized other later administrations' policies toward the tribes, thwarted as best they could the mischief making of the British and the Spanish, and tried to contain the strong
pressures to enact measures for the wholesale removal of the Indians. Faced with a loose republic, a weak army, and limited options,
the president walked a fine line between restraint and bellicose
action.[6]

In another development, the impetus for political parties had been
muted for a while by Washington's election. He was indeed a symbol of unity and continuity with the Revolution. But in his own
cabinet and in Congress, two factions were emerging that threatened to polarize the administration. The sources of that division lay
embedded in many controversies: the Hamilton economic plan, the
powerful sectional differences that were evident before the Constitution was ratified, the relative importance of a strong frontier defense and a standing army, and, most especially, the intense wars
in Europe. By making the executive branch a center of initiative
and the federal government a visible establishment, Washington inadvertently facilitated that division. At first, the partisan hostility
swirled around him like currents around the calm. But by the middle
of his second term, with Hamilton and Jefferson gone and Europe
aflame, Washington provided the strong leadership that caused both
opposition leaders and the opposition press to attack him openly.
Steadfastly, Washington reached beyond the narrow confines of the
capital and elites in those controversies and prevailed again and
again.

By December 1793, the two factions (which later became known
as the Federalists and the Democratic-Republicans) were locked in
a bitter controversy over the establishment of a national bank then
being discussed in the Senate. In the House, during the next session, the two factions became increasingly cohesive in voting on
issues involving the Whiskey Rebellion, Democratic-Republican
societies, frontier security, and Indian affairs.

The growth of these factions and later full-fledged parties was
facilitated by the increase in communications and the general rise
in what one might call political consciousness. In the decade from
1790 to 1800, the number of newspapers doubled to two hundred,
and by 1810 there were more journals of public opinion per capita

in the United States than anywhere else in the world. There was also a dramatic upsurge in the number of post offices from 28 in 1776 to 75 by 1790 and 453 in 1795. America was becoming a literate and participatory political culture, the likes of which was unknown in the world at that time.

Politics became more popularly covered, as news, even delayed news, was widely disseminated. There also began to grow up partisan clubs, the most visible being the "Democratic-Republican societies," first appearing in 1793 among the Germans in Philadelphia. Jefferson exuberantly called these clubs a rekindling of "the spirit of 1776." But the real focus of the partisan strife revolved around Hamilton and Jefferson, with the latter being supported by the energetic efforts of his fellow Virginian James Madison. Hamilton had laid out the Federalist agenda, an alliance of wealth and privilege harnessed to the new experiment. Jefferson, at first diffident, later surreptitiously involved in partisan intrigue, became the lightning rod for Federalist animosity and Republican acclaim. Actually, the real engine of the opposition was Madison who was once both a close Hamilton ally and a confidant to the president. But by the 1790s, Southern and Western ranks began to coalesce around regional leaders who in turn opposed the Hamiltonian agenda. Joined with the unscrupulous and ambitious Aaron Burr in New York, the Democratic-Republicans of Virginia were creating the first real political party.

Through the early 1790s, Washington tried to ignore the controversies and attempted to mediate the differences, especially in his own cabinet. He pleaded with his secretaries for an end to "tearing our vitals out." Hamilton insisted he was the main victim in these partisan controversies as attacks on his character and policies continued in the opposition newspapers. Jefferson's response was even more bitter; Hamilton was "a man whose history . . . is a tissue of machinations against the liberty of the country which had not only received and given him bread, but heaped honors on his head." The president tried reason, flattery—even a cabinet picnic! But nothing worked. Washington privately expressed a desire to retire from all this acrimony, but the leaders of both factions insisted on his continuing.

He was unanimously reelected in the election of 1792 but partisanship flared up in the choice for the second office. Adams won reelection over Governor Clinton of New York, although the governor carried not only New York, but did very well in the South also.

Even with the national vote of confidence he received, Washington was not immune to the increasing controversies taking place. The major whirlwind he endured was the American division of opinion about the French Revolution and the wars in Europe.[7]

France had been the one true ally whose support made the U.S. Revolution a success against incredible odds and turned Washington from a beleaguered guerrilla fighter into a national hero. The two nations—the new republic and the ancien régime—were bound together by treaty, self-interest, and affection. As a reminder of British presence after the peace, His Majesty's government still refused to abandon some of its forts in the West and helped to stir up the tribes against the fragile American Union, leaving the United States still with strong positive sentiments toward its old ally France.

Washington at first joined with nearly all Americans in welcoming the French Revolution—seeing it as a child of his own nation's upheaval. He was deeply moved when the legendary Marquis de Lafayette sent him the main key of the Bastille prison, that "fortress of despotism." Linking up the two great revolutions he had been part of, Lafayette gave the key "as a tribute which I owe as a son to my adoptive father, as an aide-de-camp to my general, as a missionary of liberty to its patriarch."

But as the French Revolution became more extreme and violent, as the cycle of events began to eat its own fathers, Washington wondered if the French were not being overwhelmed by their "too great eagerness in swallowing something so delightful as liberty." Even Jefferson, who spoke of the need for a revolution every twenty years or so to water the tree of liberty, began to have misgivings about what was happening.

In politics, imitation is often more important than rational public discourse. The radical spirit of the French Revolution began to develop in the United States, and the Federalists regrouped to battle the influx of an ideology of atheism, anarchy, and excess. The new regime in France turned its energies to Europe, proclaiming the liberation of those enslaved by old monarchies and despots and using patriotism as a unifying cry for the French people. And so the wars of ideology began.

Faced with a meager military establishment and a clear sense of the folly of European wars, Washington insisted on announcing American neutrality. Hamilton pushed for a total repudiation of the treaties of friendship and armistice between France and the United States. Jefferson vigorously rejected any such step and opposed even using the word neutrality. But Washington was clearly unwilling to be drawn into conflicts not of his own making. The United States would stay out of those wars of ideology in Europe. Some Republicans denounced him in the capital and in the newspapers, but public sentiment was with the president. While Madison and Hamilton—each using pen names—debated in partisan newspapers whether the president had the authority in foreign affairs to issue a neutrality proclamation, Washington moved to implement his policy. He was soon attacked by the French minister to the United States, Edmond Genet, for abandoning treaty commitments to his country, and Genet eventually appealed to Republican leaders and to the nation as a whole.

At one cabinet meeting, the president lost his temper and denounced the criticisms of the pro-French Republican editor, that "rascal [Philip] Freneau." Years later, Adams remembered the opposition to Washington, as he recalled probably in exaggerated terms:

> Ten thousand people in the streets of Philadelphia, day after day, threatened to drag Washington out of his house, and effect a revolution in the government, or compel it to declare war in favor of the French Revolution and against England. The coolest and firmest minds, even among the Quakers in Philadelphia, have given their opinions to me, that nothing but the yellow fever . . . could have saved the United States from a fatal revolution of government.

But when Genet threatened publicly to appeal over the president's head to the people, the patriotic response was swift and predictable. Genet was bitterly denounced in all quarters for his foreign presumption, and public opinion quickly swung to the Washington of old. The Republicans quietly walked away from their French friend.

In the beginning of 1794, the Republicans in the Senate tried again and demanded from the president copies of correspondence from Gouverneur Morris, the American minister to France. Once again the cabinet discussed the question of invoking executive privilege, but Washington sent the correspondence, except for one sensitive dispatch. Meanwhile in France, the radical Jacobins had seized control of the faltering French republic, and they wanted Genet sent home for arrest and probably the guillotine. Genet pleaded for asylum, relief that the president graciously granted.[8]

Besides opposition to his foreign policy, the president was also faced with some nasty rumblings from western Pennsylvania. In several counties, excise taxes on whiskey enacted by Congress at Hamilton's request were the focal point for an insurrection. Hamilton saw that uprising as a fine opportunity to assert the power of the new federal government; Washington was more cautious and started with several warnings admonishing all to obey the law and respect the authority of revenue agents.

For the frontiersmen of western Pennsylvania whiskey was more than a beverage at mealtimes or an elixir in extending hospitality. The farmers had little cash and were unable to transport lumber, grain, and meat at reasonable costs across the mountains to market. Instead, they often turned rye to whiskey, which could be easily transported in bulk and sold at a profit. The excise on whiskey, then, was a direct burden on their livelihoods and a restriction on one of the few sources of cash they could generate. From their point of view, the federal government provided little protection on the frontier against the Indians, and yet it demanded taxes to run its administration way back east.

While Hamilton continued to push for strict prosecution, Washington temporized and in 1792 the violence seemed to have been curtailed. But gradually though 1793 and into the next year, the controversy mounted and an excise agent in western Pennsylvania was attacked. Finally, the president called up several state militias and rode with them to the areas supposedly in rebellion.

But as the president and the armed forces moved into the western counties, no real resistance was encountered. Several of the ringleaders of the rebellion were tried and two were convicted and sentenced to death. Washington issued a proclamation pardoning all those who were not then under indictment or sentenced, and he pardoned the two found guilty, remarking that one was a simpleton and the other insane.

Hamilton regarded the whole episode as a sterling demonstration of the new assertiveness and power of the nascent national administration. Yet the rebels in their crude way were also correct in their assessment that this was an administration more sensitive to the problems of the bondholders, speculators, merchants, and bankers than those of laborers, farmers, and frontier democrats in the hinterlands. Meanwhile, the Federalists in the 1794 elections adroitly used the rebellion against the Republicans. Even Washington went out of his way to criticize the so-called Democratic-Republican clubs that he felt had instigated the rebellion. He called them "self-created societies," and the Federalist-controlled Senate approved a resolution censuring the groups, while the more Republican-oriented House refused to concur. The controversy was mild, however, compared to the intense controversies that swirled around the president's support for the Jay Treaty.[9]

The upheavals in Europe profoundly changed the Old World and the New. The wars of interest and ideology begun by revolutionary France and the wars of empire heralded by Napoleon resulted in the demise of parts of the Spanish colonial system and eventually in the curbing of the power of the French nation. The United States during Jefferson's presidency was to double its size as Napoleon gladly gave up the Louisiana Territory, and American leaders were soon after to proclaim confidently that European influence would no longer be expanded in the Western Hemisphere.

But in 1794, there was no way that Washington could have known what would be the benevolent outcomes of the brutal European war that was destroying the old regime and inflaming the hearts of many Americans. At first, the president had to contend also with the increasing number of British violations of American rights. Jefferson, leaving the position of secretary of state, and Madison in the House pushed Republicans to demand retaliatory steps against the British. But then the French increased their seizing of American ships bound for England. Federalist leaders fearful of hostilities with both countries pressed Washington to reach some accommodation with the British; finally the president sent Chief Justice John Jay to England. Jay was an experienced diplomat and a former secretary of foreign affairs during the Confederation period. He negotiated a treaty that moderated many of the major points of contention between the two nations, fostered British-American amity, and led the Spanish to reevaluate their policies in the American Southwest, which finally culminated in the Pinckney Treaty approved by the Senate on March 3, 1796.

The Jay Treaty however was barely presented to the Senate when the Republican politicians and their newspapers began criticizing its provisions. In the midst of all this controversy, Washington received some evidence that his trusted secretary of state, Edmund Randolph, had been compromised in dealing with the French and had supposedly asked for bribes from the French ambassador. The charges were unsubstantiated, but Randolph resigned and the last major Republican figure in the administration was gone.

Washington ended up signing the controversial Jay Treaty and then faced an intensified campaign in the House of Representatives against providing funds to implement the agreement. By 1796, the president was under varied attacks from Republican newspapers and leaders. One editor, Benjamin Bache of the Philadelphia *Aurora*, said Washington's behavior was more characteristic of an "omnipotent director of a seraglio instead of the first magistrate of a free people." Even Madison informed Jefferson who had retired to Monticello that Washington's popularity was ebbing and that he was marked "in indelible character as the head of a British faction."

When the Republicans in the House pushed for information on Jay's instructions and all relevant correspondence, the president dug in his heels and refused to bow to the request. He argued that the House had no role in the treaty-making process and pointedly remarked that the only relevant purpose for such a request would be to provide information for impeachment proceedings.

Federalist leaders appealed to the Constitution, the integrity of the president, and the economic interests most likely to be affected by continued stresses in U.S.-British relationships. Banks and insurance companies began to sound alarms about what the consequences would be if the treaty were rejected. The Federalist establishment demonstrated all too well how Hamilton's alliance of political power and economic influence could be quickly and effectively mobilized just as the Republicans had feared. But the major factor in settling this controversy was once again the immense popularity of the president. Observing the unexpected setback to the Republican cause in the House, Jefferson simply concluded, "One man outweighs them all in influence over the people."

With the major figures of his administration gone—especially Hamilton and Jefferson—Washington took over more of the day-to-day responsibilities of his administration, especially in foreign affairs. He insisted on staying with his neutrality proclamation, and as the French ambassadors, Edmond Genet and later Pierre Adet, tried to rally popular sentiment against the president, public support for Washington mounted instead. The administration squarely faced not just French discontent, but concerns over British attacks on U.S. ships and the impressment of American seamen.

Criticisms of the president came even from Thomas Paine, Randolph, Jefferson, and other notable Republican figures, and Washington at times wondered if he had in any way hurt his reputation by continuing on in public service. Weary with the burdens of office, Washington refused to consider a third term and issued on September 17, 1796, his farewell address to the American people. The Federalist mantle passed on to John Adams who was able to squeak out a victory over Thomas Jefferson who in turn became vice president. Washington returned home to Mount Vernon, soon to be deified by the contentious people he had headed in war and peace.[10]

THE FEDERALIST LEGACY

Washington's successor, John Adams, was a well-known figure in American public life even before the Revolution. Adams was born in Braintree (now Quincy), Massachusetts, on October 30, 1735, and following the example of his father, a farmer and part-time shoe-maker, attended Harvard College. After graduation, he taught school for a year in Worchester and decided to become a lawyer. At the age of 29, while a struggling lawyer in Braintree, he married a gifted and witty daughter of a local clergyman, Abigail Smith—one of the most extraordinary women in American history.

In 1765, John and his older cousin, Samuel Adams, took the lead in opposing the Stamp Act. In 1770, John Adams helped to solidify his reputation for courage and audacity when he defended a British captain and eight soldiers who fired into a mob during the Boston Massacre, and won acquittal for the captain and six of the soldiers. During the early 1770s, Adams became a major force in the new politics, and he worked tirelessly in Congress and in New England earning himself the name, "Atlas of Independence." In 1778, he was sent to Paris to be one of the commissioners to negotiate military and economic assistance. He returned home in 1779, and later went back to Europe serving in other posts including minister to Great Britain. Short, plump, and at times overly serious, Adams was, like Washington and more than Jefferson and Hamilton, a true national figure for over a generation.

Adams entered office in 1797 with a honeymoon period, having even some Republicans compare his integrity and judgment favor-ably to the alleged shortcomings of his predecessor. Adams agreed with Washington's controversial neutrality proclamation, but he also made a major overture to the French regime and sent a special commission to Paris to try to end the split. At first the French gov-ernment rebuked the plan, and Adams ended up asking a reluctant Congress to approve an increase in military preparedness.

Riding high because of Napoleon's recent victories in Europe, French Foreign Minister Charles Maurice de Talleyrand-Perigord bluntly warned of the "power and violence of France," and demanded bribes as a precondition for peace talks. Like most nations of the time, the United States had paid bribes in the past, but this time the price was too high, especially from a supposed ally. One of the American delegates on the commission, Charles Pinckney, bluntedly responded, "It is no, no; not a six pence." The exclamation became a slogan, and Federalists back home were to add the famous refrain, "Millions for defense; not one penny for tribute."

The peace process did not go well in Paris, and in the United States intense partisanship increased as Republicans insisted on reasserting American friendship with the French, while the Federalists moved to push restrictive legislation to hamstring the Republican press and abridge the liberties of foreigners. When the Republicans in the House demanded copies of Adams's instructions to the American commissioners in Paris, the president gladly complied by making public the full record. The so-called XYZ correspondence underscored the arrogance of the French regime, and predictably the public rallied around Adams as they had behind Washington during the Genet affair. Henry Knox, Washington's secretary of war, observed of Adams, "The President shines like a God."

The Federalist-controlled Congress, caught up in the patriotic fever, now approved an increase in the size of the armed forces and the naming of a reluctant George Washington as commander in chief in the field. Congress also passed a Federalist-sponsored series of laws aimed at curtailing dissent and controlling foreigners by prolonging the waiting period for citizenship. These acts, known collectively as the Alien and Sedition Acts, were clearly aimed at the Republicans and at immigrants who were seen as too closely aligned to that party.

But despite the fire of arch-Federalists, Congress in general was reluctant to approve going to war, especially if it meant having to raise taxes. The president also began to see the scheming hand of Hamilton working his way into the so-called New Army. In addition, Adams, a sincere civil libertarian, was wary of enforcing some of the provisions of the Alien Acts. He did have fewer problems in implementing the Sedition Act though, as opposition editors who had attacked him or his administration were tried and convicted. Even Vice President Jefferson was under informal surveillance by zealous Federalists. He and Madison, in turn, secretly tried to induce friendly state legislators to interpose their governments between the federal government and their local citizens, thus offering a states-right check on the national government—a proposal that added support to the fires of secession a generation later. But only Virginia and Kentucky would follow along, and the scheme failed. The real relief came as Jefferson had predicted, "the doctor is now on his way to cure it, in the guise of the tax collector."

Suppressing newspapers and deporting aliens were inexpensive exercises. But the raising up of an army was not, and Congress had to impose more taxes, duties, and customs on the people. Historically, Americans love liberty and hate taxes, and sometimes it is difficult to find out which holds the main allegiance in their hearts—indeed, the Revolution showed that the two could really be the same. The Federalist assault began to come undone because the populace did not want war and did not wish to pay for preparedness, and also because Adams was concerned about the role of Hamilton in the grand design.

By early 1799, the president began to receive general reports from Europe and from one of his envoys back from France that the attitudes of Napoleon and Talleyrand were changing toward America. Adams embarked on an abrupt peace initiative and appointed another special commission to go to France to resolve the problems. When his cabinet opposed his decision, Adams decided to return from his home in Massachusetts and take command of his own administration. Finally, in the summer of 1800, the president demanded the resignations of his secretaries of state, war, and treasury. The peace mission eventually was successful, but its results arrived too late to influence the presidential election. Adams was left in retirement with the consolation that the peace missions were, in his words, "the most disinterested and meritorious actions of my life." He was correct in that flattering judgment.[11]

The defeat of Adams and the confusingly tense, but pacific passing of power to the opposition party were extraordinary sights. Free people had created republics before, only to see them flounder during crisis and be consumed in domestic struggle. The election of 1800 completed the development of the early presidency—executive authority had been redefined, reasserted, and institutionalized, and executive power had passed without the clash of arms to a new faction, although rumblings were heard when it appeared that Jefferson might be cheated out of his due.

The Federalist party was to die off quickly as a national political force, but its model of the presidency endures. The major tenets of that model emphasize the paramount importance of the executive—an office that at times seems to be above party, above section, above interests, reaching out for the common good.

3

The Jeffersonians: Democracy and Expansion (Jefferson, Madison, Monroe, and John Quincy Adams)

As the republic enlarged and the franchise expanded, the forces of democratic sentiment and popular reform became more apparent. In the South and in the West, Republican strength increased, and in the spring of 1800, the party even captured control of the New York legislature. The stage then was set for a changing of the guard.

As they approached the election, the Republicans nominated Thomas Jefferson for president and Aaron Burr for vice president, but in the process, the party leaders forgot to make sure that Burr would receive one vote less in the electoral college than Jefferson so there would be no tie. The result was that the lame-duck House of Representatives was forced to decide the contest, and the Federalists threw their support to Burr, resulting in a deadlock for thirty-five ballots. Burr, a veteran intriguer, instead of disavowing that tactic said nothing publicly and infuriated his own party's leaders. Finally, it was Hamilton who persuaded his fellow Federalists to support his old enemy, Thomas Jefferson, arguing quite rightly that while Jefferson was a dreamy ideologue, Burr was a dangerous man. Thus, the Founding Fathers, for all their differences, knew each other well enough to appreciate the differences between rhetoric and reality.

The election of 1800 and the long controversies after the electoral college deadlock produced some understandable bitterness among Jefferson and his followers. But when the dust settled and the House of Representatives did its constitutional duty, the new nation witnessed a peaceful transition of power into the hands of the loyal opposition. Jefferson's response was typical of him: a generous sentiment captured in a felicitous phrase covering over real malice. In his first inaugural address, probably the finest ever given by a president, he pronounced, "We have called by different names brethren of the same principle. We are all republicans; we are all federalists."

Then in a vein of public confidence and political tolerance, he fell back on the familiar sentiments of the Enlightenment, "If there be any among us who would wish to dissolve this Union or to change its republican form, let them stand undisturbed as monuments of safety with which error of opinion may be tolerated where reason is left free to combat it."[1]

As Jefferson took office in 1801, the population had grown by 25 percent since 1790 and would grow at the same rate between 1800 and 1810. A sixth of Americans were slaves and only one out of twenty-five people lived in a city. The capital was a swampy village with clusters of houses and the beginnings of a row of government buildings. There were about two hundred newspapers in the United States in 1801, and every political faction seemed to have its own organ of opinion. The country was an agricultural nation with substantial trading and commerce; the Land Act of 1800 provided for the sale of tracts of 320 acres for a minimum price of $2.00 per acre. From 1790 to 1810, the amount of cotton produced in the South jumped from 3,000 bales to 178,000 bales. There were very few free laborers in a nation where free land was so abundant and the indentured servant system was dying. Workers in towns and cities made up 2 to 3 percent of the population, and by 1815, personal income was ranging from 80 cents a day in rural areas to $1.50 in the cities. Roads were poor, although some privately run toll roads and canals were in place. The United States, in the language of the late twentieth century, had a third world economy with a fairly literate and politically aware population for that period.

The Jeffersonians, or Democratic-Republicans as they were sometimes termed, were the party of the yeoman farmers, the small businessmen, the South, and the West. However, by the end of the Jeffersonian era, the Federalist party would be thoroughly routed even in its stronghold of New England.

At the center of this first political party was the thought and the enigmatic personality of Thomas Jefferson. At six feet, two inches tall, Jefferson conveyed an impression of a dreamy, loose-limbed planter dressed casually with an easy way about him. His detractors saw him as a dangerous partisan and a subtle manipulator of people and events. But he was in the words of one woman, "so meek and mild, yet dignified in his manners, with a voice so soft and low, with a countenance so benignant and intelligent." He avoided public controversies, but privately he could be a political operator not above recrimination and petty retaliation. Like many Southerners he was imbued with a sense of formal manners and was unwilling to confront people directly. And like so many individuals from that region, because of that studied politeness, he gave people at times a sense of reassurance when he was simply avoiding disagreement, and this reticence often led to charges of hypocrisy. To Jefferson, the election of 1800 was a reaffirmation of the principles of the American Revolution, the "Spirit of '76," as he liked to characterize it. But at fifty-seven, he had spent nearly all his adult life thinking about politics and becoming aware that people are shaped by prejudices, moved by self-interest, and often swayed by the basest of sentiments.[2]

His stated intention was to split off the Federalist voters from their leaders, and to do that he insisted that his own followers and friends see the need for some public moderation, especially during his first term. Jefferson refused to begin his term with a radical agenda, arguing in part that slender majorities such as his do not lend themselves to political upheavals. He seemed to be satisfied with some patronage changes, a cut in military spending, and a balanced budget. To those moderate prescriptions, he attached the label "Revolution of 1800."

But under pressure from more radical Republican leaders and followers, Jefferson decided to make major changes in government offices, especially in the lucrative customs agent positions and in the law enforcement areas. During the period of the Alien and Sedition Acts, the Jeffersonians had learned all too well that the administration of justice was discretionary, and that politicians were not above using the law as a weapon to indict, try, and sentence opponents. Jefferson had not forgotten the "reign of the witches" and which individuals were the instruments of oppressive Federalist policies. Actually, though, in the Adams administration there were only fifteen indictments and ten convictions under the Sedition Act of 1798. Still, Jefferson swept the enforcement stables clean and replaced them with Republicans. And retaining the bitterness of memory, he publicly approved the end of the Alien and Sedition

Acts, citing them as inimical to a free people, while privately urging some of his closest and most discrete followers to undertake
similar indictments on the state level against Federalists.

The Jeffersonians had to come to grips with the most difficult
vestige of Federalist dominance—the federal judiciary. Critics
charged that Adams had nominated judges and a chief justice up to
the last days of his lame-duck term, and Congress had expanded
the number of positions and court layers even while litigation declined. The people could cast the Federalists out of the presidency,
trim down the number of elected Federalist congressmen and senators, but still one branch of government was beyond their reach.
The Jeffersonians attacked the federal judiciary in two ways: impeachment and contraction. The new Congress in 1801 began with
the repeal of the Judiciary Act in order to slice away at the new
judgeships and the Federalists embedded in them. Congress then
demanded that the Supreme Court go into recess so as to avoid
reviewing its actions. The Republican-controlled House of Representatives and Senate also began to look at the impeachment option, focusing on Federalist judges who were obviously unfit or
obnoxiously partisan. But the failed attempt to impeach Supreme
Court Justice Samuel Chase ended the enthusiasm for that labori-
ous process.[3]

The Jeffersonians accepted the basic economic structure put in
place by Hamilton, and Jefferson and Madison—both critics of
Washington's neutrality policy—proved to be less belligerent toward
Britain than the Federalists expected. The president's chief economic
advisor, the Swiss-born Albert Gallatin, accepted Hamilton's nationalism although he advocated a more frugal and less-ambitious government. But the basic pillars of the Hamiltonian system remained:
refinancing of the debt, the bank, and a strong treasury department.
In setting its foreign policy, the Jefferson administration was filled
with individuals who had served in past positions of responsibility.
Jefferson and Madison, Monroe and Robert Livingston may have
engaged in pro-French rhetoric, but in the quiet parlors of diplomacy, when they were among friends, they detested the airs of
Europe and struggled to promote American interests as firmly as
Washington, Adams, and Jay. As Jefferson commented, it would have
been better if the Atlantic were an ocean of fire to prevent the
contamination of court politics and the decadence of European life
from permeating pristine American shores.

To the Republicans, the presidency was the chief instrument of the very policies they were elected to end. Jefferson, as a symbolic concession and also because of his own predilections, refused to make the State of the Union address personally. It smacked of the speech from the throne—instead, he had his speech hand-delivered to be read by the clerk of the House, a custom continued until Woodrow Wilson. To further differentiate himself from the Federalist presidents, he deliberately avoided balls, disregarded traditional court etiquette, wore slippers in his meetings with some foreign diplomats, and conducted bright cheery dinners where fine light wines and Renaissance-style conversation dominated the tone. He was the planter squire, the Enlightenment intellectual, the reserved but friendly man of letters. Gone was the Washington preoccupation with etiquette and the Adams obsession with mannered dignity. Jefferson walked to his own inaugural, rode to Congress on his own horse, and wrote his own speeches.

Although he did not publicly ask Congress to follow his prescriptions, Jefferson had spent too much time in legislative politics not to know that things just do not happen by chance. While he avoided outward displays of leadership, in fact he and his cabinet officials and friends in Congress served as conduits for his words, sentiments, and proposals. With respectable majorities in both houses of Congress, Jefferson's first term and the beginning of his second showed remarkable results. Because of the president's stature in the nation, his long record as a leader in republican causes, and the lack of a structured leadership in Congress, Jefferson was able to provide strong guidance in a subtle but effective way. But as in all presidencies, the last several years are usually the undoing, and his undoing came over his foreign policy.[4]

THE FIRST REPUBLICAN AGENDA

Jefferson's attitude toward federal appointments drew some criticism from the ardent supporters of the Republican party for being too lenient and from the Federalists for being too extreme. He did try to stop some last minute Adams appointees from taking office, and later the new president enlarged that group to those appointed in the last three months of Adams's term. Many of the Republicans regarded the whole host of them as "midnight" appointments. One of them was William Marbury who never received his formal notice as justice of the peace for the District of Columbia from the

Jefferson administration after his appointment by Adams. Consequently he sued. The Supreme Court under Chief Justice John
Marshall granted Marbury no relief, but proclaimed in a landmark
decision the doctrine of judicial review instead.

Jefferson insisted that his appointments had to tilt toward the
Republicans until they received a just proportion of the offices to
make up for Federalist neglect over the years and to reflect better
the true popular majority they commanded. The president also took
a dim view of Federalist officeholders using their positions "to overthrow the cause," as he put it. However, he drew from the gentleman class in making his appointments, picking men who were more
often similar in background to the Federalist civil servants than those
chosen later by the more democratic Andrew Jackson.

Faced with his narrow election margin, Jefferson was pragmatic
and limited in placing his public agenda before Congress. As he
wrote to his friend Pierre Samuel du Pont de Nemours, "What is
practicable must often control what is pure theory: and the habits
of the governed determine in a great degree what is practicable."[5]

In the area of foreign policy, the president at first saw only peace
on the horizons except along the Barbary coast of North Africa
where Tripoli had committed acts of war against the United States.
Jefferson's reaction to the pirate state was at first rather indecisive.
He argued that he needed congressional sanction to act, a position
that Hamilton writing under one of his many pen names attacked
as another sign of weakness. "What will the world think of the fold
which has such a shepherd?," the New Yorker speculated. Jefferson
did send the U.S. Navy to do battle, and after four years of conflict, the United States finally defeated the Tripoli pirate regime.[6]

Overall, Jefferson minimized America's presence in other ways.
He retained missions only to Great Britain, France, and Spain, and
began an active campaign to cut the U.S. Navy, except the frigate
fleet. Aided by Secretary of the Treasury Gallatin, the president
pushed for retiring the national debt, then about $83 million.
Jefferson as a matter of philosophy opposed a public debt that was
passed on to future generations. As he once observed, "The earth
belongs always to the living generation."[7]

Jefferson exercised considerable control over Congress even
though the ideology of his party tended to depreciate presidential
leadership. He accomplished his objectives through close informal
relationships with his party's legislative leaders and because of the
high regard in which he was held among the rank and file as a

symbol of the very march of democracy. Not until Woodrow Wilson with his very different prime ministerial style of leadership was Congress to be so dominated by the executive. As Jefferson once observed, if he just limited himself to formal recommendations, his administration would be "a government of chance and not of design."[8]

At the top on the president's and the party's agenda was the repeal of the Judiciary Act of 1801. That act had become effective three weeks before the end of the last Federalist Congress, and it was clearly meant to enlarge the judiciary branch in order to stack it with Federalist party faithful. Not one Republican was seated on the federal bench at any level when Jefferson took office. The judiciary in general was a friend to creditors over debtors, and Republicans were worried about its attitude toward disputed land titles in the South and the West. The arrogance of the Federalist judiciary in the Alien and Sedition cases was legendary among the Jeffersonians, and the president shared in expressing those standard Republican criticisms. As has been noted, Congress repealed the Judiciary Act and then in a highly controversial step mandated that the Supreme Court would not meet for another fourteen months—a demand seen as a move to stop judicial review of its action.[9] During the dispute, Vice President Burr, already distrusted for his ambiguous role in the deadlocked election of 1800, let it be known that he opposed his party's policy on the repeal.

Although Jefferson's popularity grew enormously in his first years in office, he was subject to a continuing barrage of criticism. Some of it was harmless such as Thomas Pinckney's characterization of the president as "the moonshine philosopher of Monticello."[10] But others were more vitriolic such as James Thomson Callender, a former ally of Jefferson, who turned on him and carried on a personal attack for months. Among other stories, Callender spread the rumor that Jefferson had a slave mistress named Sally, had tried to seduce a friend's wife years before (which was probably true), and had tried to pay off a debt to a friend in depreciated currency. The "Dusty Sally" story remains in currency down to the present being revived in biographies and in fiction. And once again the opposition press resurrected charges of corruption and incompetence during his lackluster term as wartime governor of Virginia.

One can see why the Jefferson who so often praised a free press, and once commented that if he had to he would prefer it to the government itself, began to change his mind. Midway in his first term, he concluded that "our newspapers, for the most part, present only the caricatures of disaffected minds. Indeed the abuses of the freedom of the press here have been carried to a length never before known or borne by any civilized nation."[11] As noted, he had early in his term recommended to Republicans on a state level a few selected prosecutions of opposition journalists—a position similar to the Federalist objectives in passing the Sedition Act. Still he returned almost as a reflex action to his faith in the people, concluding, "The firmness with which the people have withstood the late abuses of the press, the discernment they have manifested between truth and falsehood, show that they may safely be trusted to hear everything true and false, and form a correct judgment between them."[12]

THE LOUISIANA PURCHASE

One persistent issue that concerned Americans of all parties and many areas of the nation was the fate of the Mississippi Valley region then held by Spain. The matter was complicated by the European wars begun as a consequence of revolutionary and later Napoleonic France's dreams of republican ideology and imperial conquest. Jefferson had hoped that a weakened Spain would continue to hold on to the Mississippi lands until the United States was able to assert itself and take them over. As Arthur Whitaker has written, in the Western region "neither unionism nor disunionism was deeply rooted in the West at the end of the century."[13] Still, as with his Federalist predecessors, Jefferson understood that he had to show that the national government cared about the West, and his party's strength in that region was based heavily on his successes.

As for Spain, the royal court's ministers saw Louisiana and the Floridas as a buffer between the United States and its more valued empire around the Gulf of Mexico. To facilitate growth in population in those colonies, Spain had adopted a generous immigration policy including religious toleration and commercial advantages. Administratively, Louisiana and West Florida were placed under a single governor with New Orleans as the capital; East Florida had a separate governor at Saint Augustine. Both governors were under the authority of the captain general who resided in Havana. About 80 percent of the colonists were concentrated in the lower areas of Louisiana and in the lands west of Mobile Bay in West Florida.

However, in 1795, Spanish Minister Manuel de Godoy signed the Treaty of San Lorenzo, which granted the Americans free navigation of the Mississippi River and the right of deposit at New Orleans port. He recognized the thirty-first parallel as the southern boundary of the United States and promised to withdraw Spanish garrisons from the areas his country was giving up. Godoy also had changed his views toward Louisiana, which he came to believe was unmanageable and a drain on the Spanish treasury. Consequently, he decided to offer France the Louisiana Territory in return for the Italian kingdom of Parma. Overall, the costs of being in Louisiana exceeded the modest revenues that came in from custom duties and other levies. Louisiana had to be supported by a Mexican subsidy for its administrative costs, and Godoy wearily examined the defense problems and concluded, "You can't lock up an open field."[14] The Spanish minister feared that conflict over Louisiana would involve his nation in controversies with both Great Britain and the United States, which he and the royal court did not want, and which they feared would jeopardize the more important southwestern empire of Mexico and New Spain. When Spain finally gave Louisiana to Napoleon, he typically insisted on possessing the Floridas as well, a demand they rejected. Napoleon then promised that he would not part with Louisiana without giving Spain the opportunity to reclaim it. In the end, he never turned over the Italian territory to the Spanish king, and he sold Louisiana to the Americans without Spanish approval.

Between the American Revolution and the Louisiana Purchase, commerce in the Mississippi Valley changed the very nature of that area. The major items exported from Louisiana were tobacco, indigo, furs and skins, and lumber; the Treaty of San Lorenzo increased the export trade for the Americans west to New Orleans and down to the West Indies. By the end of 1798, American goods were allowed to enter and leave New Orleans, but they could not be sold there.

Meanwhile on the frontier, there were increasing problems linked with the troubles in Natchez in 1797, with the Blount conspiracy, and with the Yazoo land scandal. William Blount had been a territorial governor and was later a United States senator who was nearly impeached before he left that body. He was charged by his enemies with seeking to split off the West and push the Spanish out of the hinterlands. Blount's path also crossed that of the roving Aaron Burr who had his own visions of empire. In addition, there were also some ties between Blount and other Yazoo land companies, one of which was involved in rampant land speculation and illicit contacts with the Georgia legislature.

The West was a bubbling cauldron of intrigue and reckless adventurism. At that time, Alexander Hamilton was planning a similar campaign to attack Louisiana and the Floridas with troops from the South and West and to connect up with the British fleet. But Hamilton's plans were, as has been seen, threatening to Adams, and the president pressed for peace rather than war with France. A war with France would have probably led to war with its surrogate, Spain, and Hamilton may have even envisioned a path of conquest down through New Spain with himself cast as the new Cortez. His primary concern was to dominate Louisiana and the Floridas; as he put it, "All on this side of the Mississippi must be ours including both Floridas." Characteristically, Hamilton was to conclude in 1802, "I have always held that the *unity of our Empire*, and the best interests of our nation, require that we should annex to the United States all the territory east of the Mississippi, New Orleans included." Thus, the Louisiana Territory, the Southwest, and the hinterlands fired the lustful ambitions of many individuals, some of them old-fashioned adventurers and some frustrated and out of power establishment figures.

Ironically, what provided the Louisiana Territory to the United States was not force but commerce, not the weakness of Spain but the shifting priorities of Napoleon. With the treaty in place, the port of New Orleans saw a steady and impressive flow of sugar, flour, and cotton from the Illinois region, the Ohio Valley and the Natchez district, which moved down the Mississippi and into the West Indies and even to Europe. Then on October 18, 1802, the acting indendant of Louisiana, Juan Ventura Morales, closed American access to New Orleans, and the United States reacted with a sense of outrage and deep vulnerability. Americans responded that the declaration was a violation of the treaty, and national pressure was generated to consider even war in order to reassert U.S. rights. Jefferson carefully balanced his Western strength and European "real politik" and bought time while he himself talked and wrote tough statements linking honor and war.

Federalists led by Hamilton now attacked Jefferson for being too weak in his defense of the rights of the West. Using these public pronouncements, Jefferson shrewdly convinced the French and Spanish ministers to the United States that war was near, and that he was holding it back as best he could. To pacify the West, he sent James Monroe—an avowed friend of that region—to Europe as a special envoy. The Republican-controlled Congress opposed extreme resolutions and instead gave the president the right to call up eighty thousand militia if he saw the need. Drawing on goodwill in the West, Jefferson kept that region in the fold while he practiced the uncertain arts of diplomacy.[15]

Added to the intrigue and problems in the West was the Yazoo land scandals. The word "Yazoo" quickly entered into the early American vocabulary as a shorthand for land fraud and greedy speculation. The state of Georgia laid claim to a huge tract that was west from the Chattahoochee River to the Mississippi and south from present-day Tennessee to western Spanish Florida. In the 1780s and 1790s, that state had pushed for a liberal policy granting land tracts to new prospective settlers, and Georgia officials decided to grant "perpetual" title for twenty-nine million acres in an area that contained less than nine million acres.

The Georgia legislature agreed to sell three land companies nearly sixteen million acres for $200,000 in cash to be paid over two years. That deal fell through, but in the mid-1790s four new land companies with more capital pushed for a better proposal and were aided by powerful political friends and armed with extensive bribery money. They were successful in getting a bill passed in late 1794, and for a mere $500,000, the four companies received a grant of thirty-five million acres of land.

A wave of public indignation and charges of widespread corruption led to a political upheaval, and a new governor and legislature demanded that the state reverse the deal, which it did. But on the national level, the Federalists insisted on upholding the arrangement, citing the sanctity of contracts and knowing that important supporters of their causes in New England were involved with the land companies. Jefferson appointed three of his cabinet secretaries as a committee to negotiate and settle the issue with Georgia. Their recommendations were that Georgia should transfer her western lands to the federal government for $1,250,000 and hold back one-tenth of the Yazoo lands to satisfy land claims. But some Republicans in the House, led by John Randolph, refused to accept the administration's agreement, and for years it languished in the legislative branch. Finally in *Fletcher v. Peck*, Chief Justice Marshall wrote an opinion for the Supreme Court that upheld the original Georgia legislature's corrupt bargain as an appropriate exercise of the contract power.[16]

By 1802, it was apparent that Louisiana had been given by Spain to France. In addition, Napoleon's brother-in-law, General Charles V. E. Leclerc, was sent to overthrow the black leader of Santo Domingo, General Pierre Toussaint L'Ouverture. In the end, Leclerc's disastrous defeats convinced Napoleon to forget for a while about reviving any dreams of a New World empire. Thus, ironically, it was a black liberator who helped the United States acquire the Louisiana Purchase and consequently open up that region to slavery.

Shrewdly, the president warned the French that their occupation of the Louisiana province would change the relationships between France and the United States and that the only way of avoiding problems was to cede the island of New Orleans to the United States. Through other diplomatic channels, he and Madison began to talk about an alliance with Great Britain and eventually, war with France. Jefferson's goal was to control New Orleans and the Floridas, but he insisted he had no designs on Mexico.

As has been noted, when the Spanish government demanded the end of the right of deposit in New Orleans, Congress and the American public were outraged, and Jefferson tried to embark on diplomatic overtures to calm what he called the fever and ferment that had seized the public mind. In executive session, Congress approved his request for an appropriation of $2 million for the purpose of negotiating with the French and Spanish governments to purchase the island of New Orleans and the provinces of East and West Florida.

Jefferson's critics charged that he had so cut the defense budget that there was no military option left if diplomacy failed. Actually, the president and his aides had augmented troop strength in the Mississippi Territory near Natchez, and the administration had decided to push the Indians back even farther. Jefferson sought to acquire Indian lands along the Mississippi River area so that the river would become a natural barrier. The Indians would then be forced into agriculture and made more dependent on trading posts. The president cynically hoped that in this way the tribes would accumulate debts and be made to give up even more of their lands. He concluded, "In this way our settlements will gradually circumscribe & approach the Indians, & they will in time either incorporate with us as citizens of the United States or remove beyond the Mississippi." The president had also already decided to send Meriwether Lewis and William Clark out on what was really a reconnaissance mission as well as an exploratory nature walk across the Louisiana area, which the United States had acquired by the time they departed.

The Federalists watching the New Orleans problem continued to criticize the allegedly feeble response of the administration. When Jefferson sent Monroe to join Robert Livingston in the negotiations, the *New York Evening Post* characterized it "the weakest measure that ever disgraced the administration of any country." Hamilton, writing under the pen name of "Pericles," called for more strength and advocated naval and military preparations. Only such determined measures "might yet retrieve his [Jefferson's] disaster." Federalists in the Senate, led by James Ross of Pennsylvania, took up the attack and asked that the president be authorized to take "immediate possession" of places necessary to secure the rights of Americans on the Mississippi and in New Orleans.[17]

The Republicans, though, saw the resolution as a transparent attempt to embarrass Jefferson and substituted a motion to allow the president to organize and call up eighty thousand militia. Ironically the warlike talk in Congress strengthened Jefferson's position in dealing with the Spanish minister to the United States, Don Carlos Martinez de Yrujo, who, watching the public outrage, pushed his government for a repeal of the indendant's restrictive orders in New Orleans.

On July 3, 1803, two months after Livingston's successful negotiations in France, Jefferson received formal notice of the outcome Napoleon had become disgusted with the New World and focused his attentions instead on the monumental war he was waging for hegemony over Europe. When he learned of the death of his brother-in-law in Santo Domingo, he is supposed to have cursed, "Damn sugar, damn coffee, damn colonies." He also probably was aware of Jefferson's deliberate tilting toward Great Britain and realized that he did not need to add to the strength of his great enemy.

At home, a few Federalists grumbled about the purchase—the United States had given money, which was scarce, for land, which was already so plentiful in the new nation. Others saw the new territory as destroying the old Union as they knew it and adding land that would be divided into a large number of new states. Jefferson himself wondered whether the nation needed a constitutional amendment to acquire these lands, but more sensible Republicans prevailed and urged him to simply accept the windfall and abandon his usual constitutional scruples. The total price was $11,250,000 to go to France in stock and the assumption by the United States of its own citizens' claims against France, which totaled about $3,750,000. Thus, for $15 million or so, the United States had more than doubled the size of its domain. Jefferson's empire of liberty was to become a reality not just for his generation and its children, but for generations far beyond his dreams.

The administration was unsure where the boundaries were, and Jefferson and his associates insisted that the grant included parts of western Florida—a claim about which Napoleon was ambiguous. Jefferson was also troubled about the proper administration of a vast area that contained unexplored regions in the north and west and a large concentration of people in the south. The president was concerned about emigration into the first area, seeking probably to postpone the establishment of territorial governments and the massive expansion of the Union. In addition, he and others were preoccupied with administering the New Orleans region with its very different legal code. In the past, Jefferson had foreseen not annexation, but a series of sister republics, and he was generally indifferent to the Federalist fear of an independent regime growing up in the Mississippi Valley.

Jefferson wisely abandoned his constitutional reservations especially with the news that Napoleon was having second thoughts concerning the sale. Jefferson was later to remark, "A strict observance of the written laws is doubtless *one* of the high duties of a good citizen, but it is not the highest. The laws of necessity, of self-preservation, of saving our country when in danger, are of higher obligation. To lose our country by a scrupulous adherence to written law, would be to lose the law itself, with life, liberty, property and all those who are enjoying them with us; thus absurdly sacrificing the end to the means."[18] Even the most determined literalist can depart from prophecy if the price is right. Finally, Jefferson delivered the treaty to the Senate where it was passed 24 to 7, and all ignored the question of whether France really had true title to the Louisiana area after all.

When control of Louisiana passed from Spain to France to the United States on December 20, 1803, the provisional governor, William C. C. Claiborne, was faced with having no judicial system for the region. He promptly declared all past laws in effect, and on March 26, 1804, Congress divided Louisiana into two districts. The governor in the more populous New Orleans region was appointed by the president and was to be aided by a council of thirteen. A court system was set up and common law practices such as the writ of habeas corpus, the right to reasonable bail, and other guarantees were instituted. Still the mixture of Spanish and French law and custom and the Anglo-American system of jurisprudence was confusing as these various codes were based on very different views of landownership, family relationships, and personal liberties.

Jefferson was committed to guaranteeing the predominance of Anglo-American law and encouraged immigration into that region by American citizens. Claiborne urged a slower pace, opposing for example jury trials in civil suits arguing that people wanted review not by their peers but by "great Personages."[19] Also in the past, military commanders of Spanish garrisons had exercised considerable civil and quasi-judicial powers—a practice at variance with Anglo-American separation of powers. In 1804, objections to the new system were presented in the Louisiana Remonstrance. The petitioners complained about the use of English in the courts, the novel reliance on oral argument in cases, the uncertain mix of legal principles between civil and common law, and the general thrust of changes that had already taken place.

By March 2, 1805, Congress sought to apply the major provisions of the Northwest Ordinance to the territory, and established in principle a government that was to be similar in all respects to those in the Mississippi Territory. That guarantee would have meant that the common law would have prevailed. But Congress then circumscribed that guarantee in certain ways in the Louisiana area in order to deal with the increasing controversy. The territorial legislature and Governor Claiborne were at loggerheads for a while over the issue, with the executive's position not being the popular one. Jefferson pushed for settling thirty thousand volunteers on the west side of the Mississippi River in order to change the political and ethnic balance in the region. His attitude toward the Louisiana natives was that they were "as yet as incapable of self-government as children."[20]

There is no question that Jefferson aided by Madison, Monroe, and Livingston had turned a difficult and politically explosive situation in the port of New Orleans into a brilliant diplomatic and political coup. In one fell swoop, the president silenced the Federalists, solidified the West to the Republican party (and the seaboard Union), doubled the size of the United States, cleared the frontier of many of America's European opponents, and changed the very nature of the vague republican empire of land and liberty.

DOMESTIC CONTROVERSIES

In the capital, the Republican caucus refused to renominate Burr as vice president on its ticket and celebrated Jefferson's willingness to run for a second term. In the election of 1804, the president lost only the states of Connecticut and Delaware and two electors in Maryland as he and George Clinton, his new running mate from New York, swept the nation with 162 electoral votes to 14 for Charles Cotesworth Pinckney of South Carolina and Rufus King of New York. Jefferson had become the very symbol of democracy and the greatest practitioner of its politics of liberty and expansion. John Quincy Adams said Jefferson had an "itch of popularity"—and indeed it was contagious across the country as the Republicans were to prove. Observing the Federalists, the president calculatingly wrote, "To me will have fallen the drudgery of putting them out of condition to do mischief."[21]

Yet, oddly, following this incredible triumph, Jefferson, by temperament a reserved person, became in the next congressional session rather passive and aloof in office. The major issues being discussed in Congress were the settlement of the Yazoo land claims and the impeachment and trial of Associate Justice Samuel Chase, a Federalist partisan of long standing. Jefferson had been used to dealing with a supportive leadership in Congress, but in the 1801 to 1802 term, the party's major leader in the House, William Branch Giles from Virginia, was succeeded by John Randolph who provided Jefferson with less support and considerably less skill. Randolph at the age of twenty-eight represented the area of Bizarre, Virginia, which his critics insisted was a good description of his behavior— bizarre. He was tall, slight, with a rather high-pitched voice that led to rumors about his lack of virility. Randolph at first supported the administration, but was especially vocal in attacking the administration's settlement of the Yazoo question, insisting that for Jefferson it would be "a libel on his whole political life."[22]

As noted, the Republicans had good reasons to despise Federalist judges and their hold on the bench over the years. After his election in 1800, Thomas Jefferson concluded that his political enemies had "retired into the judiciary as a stronghold. There the remains of federalism are to be preserved and fed from the treasury, and from that battery all the works of republicanism are to be beaten and erased." The Republicans in Pennsylvania had led the way and gone after the state Federalist judiciary as the president gave those efforts his quiet support. On a national level, Republicans moved to impeach and convict Judge John Pickering who was both insane and an ardent Federalist.

The president again called to the attention of his congressional supporters the conduct of Justice Chase, and the Republicans in the House formally brought charges against him. The major accusation was that he had acted improperly and in an outrageously partisan manner in instructing a grand jury in Baltimore in May 1803. Publicly staying quiet, the president privately encouraged his supporters to push on, for as he noted, "Ought the seditious and official attack on the principles of our Constitution, and or the proceedings of a State, to go unpunished?" Chase was impeached but not convicted, in part because some Republican senators from the North did not agree that he had committed "high crimes and misdemeanors." In the midst of all these activities, the president was working on a life of Jesus Christ, stripping the Gospels of the miracle stories and concentrating on what Jefferson took to be Christ's true philosophy.[23]

THE RESPONSE TO THE EUROPEAN WARS

In June 1805, a treaty was finally signed ending the war with Tripoli, and in September, the president received news that Tobias Lear had successfully negotiated a treaty in Algiers, which included returning U.S. prisoners for a ransom of $60,000. Difficulties continued with the Barbary states, however, especially Tunis and Algiers until the War of 1812. But in the more important European theater, the Monroe mission to Spain in 1805 was unsuccessful. The administration wanted the Royal government to accept the Perdido River as the eastern boundary of the Louisiana Purchase and to give up the Floridas to the United States. Once again Jefferson and Madison expressed in a guarded way how Spain's recalcitrance would hazard peace in the area. A frustrated Jefferson wrote to his secretary of state, "I do not view peace as within our choice." And once again as with Louisiana, the leaders of the administration rattled sabers among themselves if their imperialist vision were dimmed.[24]

The president at that time even indicated he would support a provisional alliance with England if and when the United States should go to war against France, Spain, or both. But the policies of the British government under William Pitt the Younger accentuated U.S. concerns about increasing interference with neutral shipping and the imprisonment of seamen. Then, in 1805, the British in the *Essex* case insisted that trade forbidden in times of peace could not be carried out in wartime. The policy was an important change from the so-called British Rule of 1756, which had allowed that if a ship had stopped and paid a nominal duty in a neutral port, that trip would be seen as a broken voyage, which would not fall under the tighter restrictions.

The greatest failure of the Jefferson administration's foreign policy, however, came out of the turmoil of the Napoleonic wars that the president and his advisors had so skillfully exploited initially in acquiring the Louisiana Territory. While Great Britain stood alone against the French emperor, the United States, committed to decentralization, demobilization, and economy, insisted on both its neutrality and on profiting from the carrying trade. But America's historic demand for freedom of the seas ran directly counter to the British war strategy. Central to Britain's defense was control of the oceans and coastlines, and that nation vigorously and often arbitrarily impressed seamen from American merchant ships to man the Royal Navy, charging them with being, in the first place, deserters or British subjects.

By October 1805, Horatio Nelson had clearly established British supremacy on the seas, while Napoleon swept from one great land victory to another across the European continent. He easily defeated the Austrians and the Russians at Austerlitz and signed a peace with the decimated Hapsburg Empire. He then moved on to crush the Prussians at Jena and Auerstadt, and later in the spring, he humiliated the Russians at Friedland. July 1807 saw Napoleon and Czar Alexander reaching a personal peace at Tilsit, and consequently the Third Coalition against Napoleon was ended. As in 1940–41, Britain and her leaders felt that she alone stood between liberty and the triumph of barbarism.

Because British power was due predominantly to the Royal Navy, its policy toward neutrals, most especially the United States, was often harsh and arbitrary on the seas. Also, much of the English leadership class retained a deep disdain toward the former colonists in America and their peculiar form of government, an attitude galling to Republican politicians such as Jefferson and Madison. When the president rejected the Monroe-Pinckney Treaty with England because it did not deal with the impressment of seamen, the British government insisted that the Jeffersonians were pro-French after all. Later, though, the Crown went on to appoint the so-called Ministry of All the Talents, and Americans hoped that it would mean a salutory change in policy, especially with Charles James Fox's presence in the cabinet. Fox had been sympathetic to the United States in the past, but he died too soon to have any impact, and by 1807 the controlling faction in the government of George III was determined to pursue the European war vigorously and American concerns were secondary.

To some Englishmen, the Americans were also commercial rivals that used the war as a chance to supersede British mercantile interests. Indeed, America hurt British colonies in the Caribbean area by growing competing crops on their Southern plantations and also by carrying to Europe the non-British produce in that region. As Bradford Perkins has summarized: from 1801 to 1805, the British West Indies imported each year about $6.5 million in U.S. goods. But soon American cotton trade increased dramatically, and U.S. shipping was intensely involved in the reshipping trade. By 1806 and 1807, U.S. reexports totaled $60 million. Still, both nations remained linked together by trade. Americans purchased about one-third of all British exports and, in 1806, more than $20 million worth of goods produced in the United States were shipped to Britain or over 40 percent of all domestic produce, much more than to France or Spain. As the British empire continued its war, U.S. trade with other nations increased; one result of that increase of trade was that the British blockade against Napoleon's empire was being weakened.

Napoleon, in turn, sought to crush Great Britain and called for a "remorseless war against English merchandise." In November 1806, he issued in Berlin a decree blockading the British Isles and prohibiting all trade with the British or in British merchandise. Napoleon lacked the navy to enforce the decree and a year later, while in Milan, he expanded the scope of his decree by declaring that all ships that submitted to British regulations or allowed themselves to be searched at sea by the British navy would no longer

be considered as neutral and would therefore be subject to confiscation. By the end of 1807, both Britain and France were violating
U.S. rights at sea.

One of the most explosive issues for Americans was the impressment of seamen. Added to that insult was the legal controversy over
the vessel *Essex* and the decision of the British courts to curtail the
reexport trade. Many former Englishmen served on U.S. ships, and
of the 11,000 naturalized seamen who were registered with American papers in 1805, most had been British. Gallatin concluded that
a total of 9,000 men fell into that category. Estimates of impressment reached 6,500 although about 3,800 is probably a closer count.
To exploit U.S.-British tensions, Talleyrand informed the Americans
that the emperor had decided to use his good offices to get the
Spanish to give up the Floridas and acknowledge the Colorado River
in mid-Texas as the western boundary of the Louisiana Purchase.
Spain would in turn get $7 million as payment.[25]

Confidentially, Jefferson informed Congress of the failure of
Monroe's mission and also asked for authority to use $2 million of
public money for negotiations with Spain. Several times in these
frontier intrigues, the administration would come close to the edge
of indiscretion. One such incident that attracted attention was
Jefferson's and Madison's contacts with General Francisco de
Miranda who wanted to liberate his native Venezuela from Spain.
Miranda set sail with 180 to 200 men on an American-owned ship
to accomplish his mission. Jefferson, hearing of those plans, decided
to order an investigation to see if any federal laws had been violated, hoping in the process to head off French and Spanish authorities who took a dim view of alleged U.S. involvement in Miranda's
cause. Two individuals were arrested in New York after Jefferson's
order, and at the trial it was asserted by the accused that the U.S.
government had told Miranda that it would not thwart his plans.
The acknowledgment that Miranda had spoken with Madison and
had dined with Jefferson added to the credibility of the claim. In
an extraordinary move, the defendants appealed to Congress against
the executive branch for assistance and had the court subpoena
cabinet officers. The Federalists lovingly exploited the controversy
and the defendants were acquitted. As for the president, he was never
able to reach a settlement with Spain and his major biographer,
Dumas Malone, has concluded that West Florida became an "obsession" to him.[26]

Meanwhile Congress began to react to British intrusions on U.S.

shipping and the impressment of seamen. Congressman Andrew Grigg of Pennsylvania introduced a resolution calling for the exclusion of all British imports until those issues were settled. The Senate, in turn, passed several strongly anti-British resolutions and asked the president to demand restoration of confiscated property and the indemnification of American citizens for loss. John Randolph deserted Jefferson and the party in the House on the issue and attacked the administration in general for its lack of leadership, but Republican congressmen as a group supported more moderate expressions drawn up by Joseph H. Nicholson of Maryland. Reports flew about that only Madison in the cabinet supported the president's policies of economic retaliation. Finally, Congress passed the Non-Importation Act, based on Nicholson's resolutions, which banned a list of specific articles and commodities, but which would not go into effect until November 15, 1806. Randolph was somewhat correct when he observed, "What is it? A milk and water bill, a dose of chicken broth to be taken nine months hence. . . . It is too contemptible to be the object of consideration or to excite the feelings of the pettiest state in Europe." To add to Jefferson's problems, the British ship *Leander* off the New Jersey coast shot at a merchant vessel in American waters and killed one person. Jefferson issued a proclamation charging the captain of the vessel with murder, stipulating that he was to be tried if he landed on American territory, and ordering the three British vessels in that area out of American waters.

Jefferson was able to contain much of the American discontent on this and other issues because of his towering presence both as a symbol of the democratic faith and as a successful party leader, playing an important and decisive role behind the scenes. He was, Randolph bitterly concluded, a "political idol" whose "colossal popularity . . . seemed to mock at all opposition."[27] He skillfully used his natural hospitality and good manners to reassure people who frequented his table. The president was a master both at conversation and at conviviality, and he rarely dined alone when in the capital. Although he was the great Apostle of Freedom in the eyes of many, he in fact rarely appeared in public and made no presidential trips as did his successors. Nonetheless, in the period of 1806–1807, he received a barrage of messages from individuals and public resolutions that supported his policies and urged him to consider a third term.

BURR AND THE CONSPIRACIES OF THE WEST

Jefferson's delight was increased in 1806 when he received the news that Lewis and Clark had successfully reached their destination at St. Louis. Surely the president's own vision now moved toward seeing the United States expand into the Oregon Territory and even to the Pacific coast. In 1803, he had written, "The object of your mission is single, the direct water communication from sea to sea formed by the bed of the Missouri and perhaps the Oregon." Later, he wrote to a friend, "The work we are now doing is, I trust, done for posterity, in such a way that they need not repeat it. . . . We shall delineate with correctness the great arteries of this great country. Those who come after us will extend the ramifications as they become acquainted with them, and fill up the canvas we begin." He also approved a second expedition by Captain Zebulon Pike who sent the president two grizzly bear cubs captured on his trip, which Jefferson in turn gave to Charles Willson Peale's museum.[28]

But there was more than exploration going on in the hinterlands, and the president at times was remarkably naive in his dealings with some of the unsavory characters there, most notably General James Wilkinson, an associate of Burr and a man on and off in the pay of the Spanish, who had been involved in so many intrigues that his biography is a string of plots and counterplots. Burr, apparently in 1805 after having left the vice presidency and after having the year before killed Hamilton in a duel in New Jersey, was hatching a vague plan to separate the Western states from the United States with British assistance and was contemplating leading armed forces to seize Spain's possessions and create perhaps a new western empire of his own. In the scheme, Burr and Wilkinson quietly joined forces, while Jefferson, too often more loyal than wise, continued to heap honors on Wilkinson, including naming him governor of the Louisiana Territory.[29]

On December 1, 1805, the president received an anonymous letter concerning the intrigues of Burr, which alleged that Wilkinson was a Spanish agent, an accusation that Jefferson seems to have discounted. Whether Jefferson knew it or not, the files of the Adams administration contained charges that Wilkinson was indeed a pensioner of the Spanish government. The president surely must have heard of Burr's western tour in the late spring and summer of 1805, which led to speculation about the latter's plans for the West. For some reason, though, Jefferson had Burr to dinner as these rumors swirled around and explored possibilities of a future role in politics for the discredited vice president. Burr apparently also talked with the British minister to the United States, Anthony Merry, and his Spanish counterpart, the Marqués de Casa Yrujo, about splitting the West off from the United States. Burr also added to his web Senator Jonathan Dayton of New Jersey, with whom he explored the possibilities of a coup d'état in Washington.

Jefferson had faith in the loyalty of the West, so important to the Republican party, but finally he confidentially ordered governors and district attorneys in those regions to have Burr watched, and the president concluded that Wilkinson was under "very general suspicion of infidelity." On November 6, 1806, Jefferson wrote his son-in-law that Burr was "unquestionably very actively engaged" in taking steps to sever the West from the United States. Wilkinson had caught the drift, began to abandon Burr, and suddenly emerged as a pillar of support for the administration, sending the president dispatches about conspiracies extending from New York to the West. The purpose of these conspiracies was allegedly to transport eight to ten thousand men to New Orleans and then join with naval forces going to Vera Cruz around February 1. There was also supposed to be support for a revolt against the Mexican government with some assistance from the British navy. Wilkinson claimed he was overwhelmed by "the magnitude of the enterprise, the desperation of the plan, and the stupendous consequences."

Jefferson decided to issue a presidential proclamation warning against any military adventures directed at Spain, a nation with which the United States was at peace. In addition, the president also asked an ally in Congress to introduce a bill to give him the authority to use land and naval forces to suppress domestic insurrections, shades of the federal government's response to the Whiskey Rebellion.

Burr's intentions and movements were confusing. He apparently indicated that the administration had given its approval to his ventures. He waxed eloquent, "The gods invite to glory and fortune; it remains to be seen whether we deserve the boon." In Congress, sentiment began to increase that the president should lay before the legislative branch information that he might have about such conspiracies. When the president responded and prejudged some of the developments, Burr had already surrendered to authorities in the Mississippi Territory. The Senate in secret session passed quickly a bill to suspend the writ of habeas corpus for three months, but the

House, more imbued with Republican ideology, overwhelmingly
rejected it.[30]

Burr was called before the grand jury which found that he was
not involved in any illegal action, and he had not given any cause
for alarm, but the court refused to allow him to be discharged. The
prisoner vanished, but surrendered after learning of Wilkinson's
treachery and was incarcerated at Fort Stoddert on February 19,
1807. Finally, Burr was tried in the Fifth Circuit Court in Richmond,
before Chief Justice Marshall with Judge Cyrus Griffin at Marshall's
side. Burr was received as a celebrity there rather than an accused
traitor. His attorneys were astute in their strategy: they insisted on
getting a subpoena to be issued to the president for correspondence
essential to Burr's case. Jefferson through the district attorney trying the case informed the court that the government would turn over
any evidence that was proper.

Marshall concluded that the president like any citizen could be
subpoenaed, but recognized that he obviously had other demands
on his time as chief executive. Jefferson wrote to the district attorney that he was ready to cooperate, but reminded him of "the necessary right of the President of the U.S. to decide, independently
of all other authority, what papers, coming to him as president, the
public interests permit to be communicated, & to whom." The president, in Edward Corwin's words, "neither obeyed the writ nor swore
anything on its return, though he forwarded the papers required."[31]
Richard Nixon was later to cite the Burr case as a precedent supporting the withholding of information under the claim of executive privilege. Nixon was criticized for having misquoted the case,
but it appears from the confused record that Jefferson did recognize a claim of executive privilege as a principle, but probably did
not press it in this instance. However, neither Jefferson nor Marshall
wanted to convert the Burr trial into a major confrontation between
the executive and judiciary branches of government.

The grand jury reported two indictments against Burr, one for
treason and the other a misdemeanor. The Constitution defines treason specifically as levying war against the United States or adhering to their enemies, giving them aid and comfort. A person can
only be convicted on the testimony of two witnesses "to the same
overt act, or on confession in open court." Burr's attorneys argued
that since he was two hundred miles from where the alleged con-
spiratorial activity took place, he could have advised war, but could
not have been involved in the overt act of levying war. Despite

Marshall's previous opinion in a similar case in whch he took a broader view of conspiracy, the chief justice accepted this limited interpretation, and the jury subsequently found Burr not guilty by the evidence submitted. An annoyed Jefferson pushed the district attorney to seek an indictment for the misdemeanor, which was attempting a military expedition against Spain, in order to get evidence for a possible impeachment of Marshall.

In addition, there was an attempt by Republicans to investigate the conduct of General Wilkinson and his ties to Spain, and the secretary of war set up a military tribunal to review the general's behavior. There was also some talk about removing federal judges on address of two-thirds of both houses of Congress, a Republican proposal that gathered some initial support. Others talked of redefining treason to overturn Marshall's precedent, but these changes all died on the vine.

The Burr trial does not represent one of the high points of Marshall's great legal career and illustrates some of the most partisan and shadowy aspects of Jefferson's leadership. The president influenced the district attorney beyond fair limits, encouraged the assault of the judiciary he never trusted, and was genuinely foolish in his dealings and loyalty to Wilkinson.

The gap between Jefferson's libertarian rhetoric and his encouragement of his followers to prosecute editors on a state level for their activities has already been noted. Despite their hatred of the Federalist Sedition Act, the Jeffersonians gave as good as they got. In intensely Federalist Connecticut, a Republican judge appointed by Jefferson charged a grand jury to look at the problem of a vitriolic press there. Six persons were indicted for libel in one such case. Jefferson had been subject to an incredible barrage of attacks on his philosophy, alleged atheism, sexual life, personal courage, and a variety of other areas. His policy was to refuse to answer them. Such attacks were delivered not just at political rallies and in the press, but in the church pulpit as well. While Jefferson did not encourage Connecticut officials, he probably took some quiet comfort that his enemies were getting some just retribution. As he put it, a spirit of indignation and retaliation should have been expected. Much later in his life, Jefferson observed that a newspaper should be divided into truths, probabilities, possibilities, and lies—a remark unusual for a man so canonized today as a proponent of a totally free press.[32]

Jefferson's main problems in his second term were not due to

the New England remnants of Federalist orthodoxy or Burr's ambiguous intrigues in the West. His second term was seriously dam-
aged by the increasing difficulties of trying to balance American
interests and national esteem with the imperatives of the British to
use their naval power to strangle Napoleon, and the French
emperor's lack of sympathy for American sensitivities and commerce.

The president had instructed Monroe and Pinckney to negotiate
a treaty with the British and to pay particular attention to the issue
of impressment. As noted, the Americans had counted on making
some progress after Charles James Fox, a figure friendly toward the
United States, was named foreign secretary, but Fox died on September 13, 1806. The American commissioners finally signed a treaty
that ignored Jefferson and Madison's admonitions on impressment
of seamen, and the president refused to submit the document to the
Senate, fearing a domestic outcry and also a weakening of the
American position toward Napoleon.

The impressment issue came to the forefront again in the *Chesapeake* affair. Some seamen had run away from British vessels and
enlisted on U.S. vessels, one of them being the frigate *Chesapeake*,
which was docked at Norfolk, Virginia. The British authorities demanded that these men be returned to British service, and Secretary of State Madison refused. After a war of nerves, the British
vessel *Leopard* fired on the U.S. frigate and British officers took
several deserters off that vessel. The people of Norfolk were furious and refused to sell provisions and supplies to the British warships and their agents off their coast. The administration
acknowledged that outrage and encouraged "honorable reparation"
to get past the crisis. Jefferson ordered all British armed vessels
out of U.S. waters, but instead of recognizing the president's steps
as a moderate response, one British commodore responded by blockading Norfolk.

The British foreign secretary, George Canning, responded cautiously at first, and insisted on knowing the nationality of the alleged deserters. Jefferson, meanwhile, presented the whole matter
to Congress, although Gallatin insisted that the president tone down
the message. Jefferson had already added to military and naval supplies beyond what had been previously authorized by Congress, and
the president and the nation were clearly running out of options to
the extremes of humiliation or war. In late 1807, the president concluded that Congress would have to chose "war, embargo or noth-

ing," but one of the president's most astute critics, and a frequent ally, John Quincy Adams, saw him as engaged in simple procrastination toward Britain. Indeed, Jefferson was hoping to avoid war believing that diplomacy might still work as it had in the New Orleans crisis.[33]

In late 1807 and early 1808, Jefferson watched as Napoleon tightened his grip on Europe and through his Berlin decree sought to close the Continent to all British products, including those carried by neutral nations. King George reasserted in even stronger terms the British right of impressment. As the president sought some encouragement from somewhere, he received Gallatin's warning, "In every point of view, privations, sufferings, revenue, effect on the enemy, politics at home, & c, I prefer war to a permanent embargo." But Jefferson was probably more realistic, and Congress with its strong Republican majorities approved an embargo, which severely limited American imports and exports with belligerents. The vote was more of a motion of confidence in the executive than a clear understanding of the consequences of cutting off trade to and from European countries.

Jefferson's embargo has been, in his time and down to the present, much criticized as a naive pacifist response to a complex problem. There is still some dispute about whether the embargo affected Britain as seriously as the administration had hoped, and historians still disagree as to whether the embargo crippled U.S. commerce as much as New England merchants and Federalist politicians claimed at the time. But there is no question that politically the anti-embargo pressure became too powerful to resist, and it was repealed just before Jefferson left office. The criticisms of the policy, however, have to be weighed against the judgment of what the alternatives were for a weak nation with no real navy, a small army, and only the loosest ties of nationalism. And if the United States went to war, on whose side would it enter? Both Britain and France were hurtful of American interests: should the Americans go to war against both great empires?[34]

Jefferson and his Republicans had been partially responsible for cutting the military and for the ideology of economy and loose union. Even while war loomed on the horizon, Gallatin presented an ambitious internal improvement plan of $20 million for roads, canals and assorted projects. But in fairness, in 1805–1806 the president was personally more assertive in his defense buildup as he recognized what was happening in Europe where minor navies, such

as the Danish fleet, had been destroyed rather easily. The administration favored gunboats and the president asked Congress later for
188 more such vessels. His secretary of navy, Henry Dearborn, requested that Congress also increase the army by six thousand regulars and twenty-four thousand volunteers, but even then Congress
had no real enthusiasm for the full plan, deciding instead to raise
the strength of the regular army to a total of ten thousand men.

In late 1807, Jefferson noted that opposition to the embargo had
quieted down when Americans learned of the British Order in Council of November 11, which declared that any vessels trading to or
from the ports of France or her allies or colonies were liable to
confiscation. Napoleon's response on December 17 was a decree
that all vessels submitting to British regulations or sailing to or from
any port under British control were subject to confiscation as British property.

Congress followed up those moves with supplemental acts to the
original embargo, which gave the executive branch more enforcement powers. Added to the president's problems was the fact that
talks on reparations over the *Chesapeake* incident were not going
well. After criticism for his secrecy, the president sent Congress a
mass of papers and reasserted the wisdom of the embargo. Defensively, Jefferson observed that the embargo was not imposed by him
or his ministers, but was a true expression of the will of the legislative branch.

Americans have historically talked tough and advocated strict
enforcement of the laws except when those actions affect them
personally. With regard to the embargo, this same backsliding occurred, and Jefferson faced a morass of legalisms and public petitions on his hands. In May of 1808, the president indicated to
Gallatin, "I am clear we ought to use it freely that we may, by a
fair experiment, know the power of this great weapon, the embargo." While the administration was concerned about the coastal trade,
troubles multiplied in the northern borders. Soon the Republican
administration, so associated with laissez faire government and protestations of individual liberty during the Federalist era, was involved
in a vigorous enforcement of what was becoming a rapidly unpopular act. Enforcement was more difficult where politicians were in
the opposition party or not particularly enamored with Jefferson's
rule. Candidly the president in August 1808 concluded, "This embargo law is certainly the most embarrassing one we have ever had

to execute. I did not expect a crop of so sudden & rank growth of fraud & open opposition by force could have grown up in the U.S." One authority on the embargo, Walter Wilson Jennings, has found,

> If, in conclusion, the effects of the embargo on industry can be epito-mized in one final sentence, that sentence will read: "The embargo stimulated manufactures, injured agriculture, and prostrated com-merce." In the years 1805, 1806, and 1807, the value of the exports of domestic produce and manufacture was $134,590,552 or an aver-age of $44,863,517 per year; during the same years the exports of foreign produce and manufacture amounted to $173,105,813 or an average of $57,701,937 per year. Re-exports thus exceeded domes-tic exports by $38,515,261 for the three years or $12,838,420 per year.[35]

The Federalists saw the embargo as giving them a new lease on life, a short-term calculation that proved correct but that did not hold for the long haul. Resolutions poured in especially from New England town meetings for an end to the embargo. Jefferson's atti-tude was that the embargo was a national policy and that critics should be pointing to the cause of the problem—the British and the French. Later Jefferson was to admit, "I felt the foundations of the government shaken under my feet by the New England townships." Having in 1808 refused to consider a third term, Jefferson watched as Madison carried the nation by 122 to 49 electoral votes, running well except in New England and Delaware.

With months to go, Jefferson became a spectator overlooking the debacle of his own policies. He left deliberations on the embargo to Congress and called himself "an unmeddling listener." Gallatin and Madison asked for some leadership with the legislature and Secretary of Navy Robert Smith called for preparations for war. Meanwhile, New England Federalists introduced resolutions to re-peal the embargo. Congress wavered, first passing in January 1809 a rather tough enforcement act and then leaning toward eviscerat-ing the embargo act altogether. The president received resolutions of support now from the legislatures of New York, Virginia, South Carolina, and Georgia, and from Philadelphia, and various groups and committees in Massachusetts, Connecticut, Maryland, and Dela-ware.

But it was apparent that the Republicans in Congress were ready for repeal, and an old Jefferson friend, Wilson Cary Nichols, introduced such a resolution and urged that the effective date be June 1. But other Republicans wanted the controversy over and done with in March as sentiment in the New England and New York delegations proved too strong to stop quick repeal. Jefferson called it "a panic" and indeed it was a quick lurch. The bill's provisions embodied a limited control over commerce with non-intercourse toward Great Britain's and France's imports. President Jefferson signed the bill and prepared to return to Monticello. He was to write on March 2, 1809, "Nature intended me for the tranquil pursuits of science, by rendering them my supreme delight. But the enormities of the times in which I have lived have forced me to take a part in resisting them, and to commit myself on the boisterous ocean of political passions."[36]

MR. MADISON'S DIPLOMACY

Unlike most presidential heirs apparent, Madison received a foreign policy legacy that he himself had created by his predecessor's side. But by 1809, the administration was left with few options to express its outrage on British impressment, and Republican solidarity was becoming frayed as public pressures increased. In the end, Madison would abandon diplomacy and the embargo and move the nation into war, presiding over a disjointed, unpopular, and confused effort. The War of 1812, as it was called, showed all the weaknesses inherent in the Republican ideology—its parsimonious vision of government, its antimilitary ethos, its faith in a barely enlightened common people, its insistence on decentralization of public institutions, and its disregard of a national bank and national financial structures.[37]

In the election of 1808, Madison easily beat Federalist Charles Cotesworth Pinckney and two Republicans, Governor Clinton of New York and James Monroe of Virginia. The final electoral vote was 122 for Madison, 47 for Pinckney, and 6 for Clinton. As has been seen, as Jefferson diffidently ended his term, Madison and Gallatin were pushing the party to enact a substitute for the embargo—a law that prohibited trade with Britain and France and gave the executive the power to issue letters of marque and reprisal. Such letters were commissions that governments of belligerent powers granted to private shipowners authorizing them to seize the vessels and property of enemy subjects on the high seas. Congress approved non-intercourse but opposed the delegation of its constitutional power to issue such letters.

Madison immediately faced problems in trying to name his own cabinet, with special opposition coming from a small group of Republican senators led by William Giles of Virginia and Samuel Smith of Maryland, who often voted with the Federalists in the upper house. Giles, posing early on as a friend of Madison, remarked that it was most unfortunate that Jefferson had "differed so materially respecting the characters of individuals from his friends in the Senate and elsewhere."[38] Giles's special target was Gallatin, Madison's original choice for secretary of state. Madison kept Gallatin as secretary of treasury and nominated Robert Smith to be secretary of state in part to appease his brother, Senator Samuel Smith. Secretary Smith turned out not to be a valuable appointment, especially as Anglo-American relations deteriorated, and Madison paid dearly for his early capitulation.

In the closing days of the Jefferson administration, Secretary of State Madison met privately with the British minister, David M. Erskine, and he laid out the options—either war between the two nations or a common alliance against France if Napoleon continued to implement his decrees. But in another vein, Madison concluded privately that if the embargo were repealed and the British orders remained in force, then war with that nation was inevitable. As noted, by March 1809, Congress had passed a Non-Intercourse Act that forbade British and French ships from entering U.S. waters. In practice, that law would obviously impact more on the former nation than on the latter, since Napoleon was virtually restricted in any major naval adventures by the imposing Royal Navy. Madison kept his maneuvering quiet, thus giving the impression of being a pacifist at heart. In fact, he seemed to have decided early that an alliance with one of those nations at war was preferable to violations of U.S. rights on the high seas by both belligerent nations.

To his delight and surprise, Madison was informed that the British government had authorized Minister Erskine to settle all outstanding differences with the United States. On April 19, Madison issued a proclamation announcing that the British Orders in Council would be withdrawn, and that by June 11 trade with Great Britain would be resumed. The president's persistence and skill seemed to have prevailed, and he was compared favorably—even by some Federalists—to his predecessor, Thomas Jefferson.

Soon, the French minister, Louis Marie Turreau, began to be concerned about this new expression of friendship and about U.S. intentions toward the Floridas and Cuba. Jefferson previously had told Turreau that the United States "must have the Floridas and Cuba," and other informants warned him that Madison was equally committed to the annexation of those territories. The new president believed that with Spain conquered, Spanish America would become the "great object of Napoleon's pride and ambition," a prophecy that came true.[39]

Madison tried, however, to allay Turreau's fears and sent Gallatin to disassociate the new president from Jefferson's more candid remarks. Gallatin insisted that the preoccupation with the Floridas was "the hobby of Mr. Jefferson" and was not supported by the cabinet. Madison would only take the Floridas if they proved to be indispensable to preventing any dispute with Spain and were able to serve as an outlet for Southern produce. As for Cuba, the United States could not accept it. In between the lines, however, the Spanish and others could see what were true American intentions toward the Floridas, which became the keystone of Madison's foreign policy interests.

Meanwhile, in May, British Foreign Minister Canning declared that Erskine's agreement was not consistent with his instructions. Why the British government repudiated its own minister is unclear. It may have been that the king was insulted by some of Madison's published remarks about the controversies, that the military situation in Europe was moving more in favor of the British, or that the Crown's ministers had become aware of American disunity and dissent especially in New England. A disappointed Madison restored the provisions of non-intercourse on August 9, 1809, and anti-British sentiment built up in the United States. Erskine was replaced by Francis James Jackson who privately wrote that the president was "a plain and rather mean-looking little man" and Dolley was "fat and forty but not fair."[40]

The new British minister, Secretary of State Smith, and Madison discussed endlessly what Erskine had agreed to, what the British had really meant, and what the two governments would not compromise on. The repudiation of the agreement with Britain would obviously limit the administration's ability to force Napoleon to make concessions. And the loss of French and especially British trade had led to a sharp drop in customs revenue from $16 million in 1807 to $6.5 million in 1809. To add to Madison's problems,

Gallatin, a stubborn Republican, insisted that the army and navy appropriations be cut in half just as war seemed even more imminent. Meanwhile, Congress received a message from the president asking for authorization to allow him to require the states to arm and equip one hundred thousand militiamen.[41]

Congress convened and considered more commercial retaliations, debating what became known as the "Macon Bills" named after Nathaniel Macon, former speaker of the House. Macon Bill 1 would prohibit all public and private ships from Great Britain and France from entering the United States. British and French goods could only be imported in American vessels. That bill was eventually killed, as Congress was unable to reach an agreement on it or on the president's request for a military buildup. As this was occurring, Gallatin expressed concern about the financial situation of the nation, and pushed for a renewal of the Bank of the United States due to expire in 1811. The "Old" Republicans, as they were called, reminded the administration of Madison's and Jefferson's earlier opposition to Hamilton's original bank proposal, and insisted on consistency regardless of circumstance.

Macon then introduced a second bill intended to break the deadlock between the House and the Senate. With the Non-Intercourse Act about to expire, Macon's bill provided that if either Great Britain or France ended its edicts and orders before March 5, 1811, or modified them so they respected U.S. commercial rights, then the Non-Intercourse Act of 1809 would be reinstated against the other belligerent who failed to respect such rights.

While the president awaited some news on the European situation, he focused his attention on the Floridas, a territory that the Republicans had looked on enviously for a long time. There was some concern that Napoleon or the British would move into the region, and throughout the Spanish empire in the New World revolutions sprung up as that old realm began to crumble. When Gallatin urged a parsimonious approach to consular expenses, Madison warned, "everything relating to Spanish America is too important to be subjected to a minute economy, or even to unnecessary delays."[42]

In expanding the Republican "empire of liberty," as the party leaders liked to call it, the president once again received advice from that shadowy master of intrigue, General Wilkinson. The general advised Madison that Governor Vizente Folch was waiting for an order from Spain to allow him to deliver West Florida to the United

States in order to thwart Napoleon's designs. Meanwhile, the president made it clear to Congress that the United States still claimed the Mobile region and demanded the right of free navigation there.

To add to the intrigue, the administration quietly through its agents encouraged the inhabitants in West Florida to request that the United States take possession of their region. While the administration denied any intention to incorporate the area, its policies were quite dramatically opposed to that guarantee. Indeed, the president asked his secretary of war what steps were within his executive powers if he decided to place the territory under U.S. authority, which many people there seemed to desire. However, Secretary William Eustis warned that acceptance of a West Florida overture would lead to formal protection and eventually the use of force to protect it; the administration finally tried to control the pro-U.S. West Florida leaders who had begun to move toward self-government and pressed them to moderate their demands.

Still a constitutional republican at heart, Madison questioned whether he had the authority to deal with the incorporation of territory, just as Jefferson had pondered in the Louisiana Purchase. He wrote his predecessor, "The crisis in West Florida, as you will see, has come home to our feelings and our interests. It presents at the same time serious questions as to the authority of the Executive, and the adequacy of the existing laws of the United States for territorial administration." And he added, "From present appearances, our occupancy of West Florida would be resented by Spain, by England, by France, and bring on not a triangular, but quadrangular contest."[43]

When the inhabitants of that region declared at a convention in Baton Rouge that the territory of West Florida was a free and independent state, Madison finally acted. The president ordered territorial officials to take possession of the region, citing U.S. claims to the area under the Louisiana Purchase—a rather shaky historical assertion—and insisting that he had moved because of the collapse of Spanish authority. Writing to Minister Pinckney, the president also stressed the importance of East Florida, and concluded that the U.S. had an interest in seeing that Cuba did not fall under the control of a hostile European power. The imperial agenda was expanding.

On January 3, 1811, the president sent a secret message to Capitol Hill concerning legislation covering all of the Floridas. Congress, after some partisan squabbling, supported the president's plan to take possession of Florida from the Perdido River to the Atlantic Ocean and to use armed force if necessary, and the executive was given the power to establish a government there. Madison concluded, "Although the government does not wantonly seek an extension of territory, it frankly avows the pursuit of an object essential to its future peace and safety upon honorable and reasonable terms. The United States cannot see with indifference a foreign power, under any pretext whatever, possess itself of the Floridas."[44] If the Spanish authorities in the east were willing to turn over the region contingent on repossessing the country at a future date, then the United States could agree to that if such territory was not part of the West Florida region.

While some Federalists took the opportunity to attack the president more for timidity than for overreaching his authority, Josiah Quincy bade farewell to the old United States concluding that Madison had welcomed in the "wild men on the Missouri" to the Union. The Federalists also continued their criticisms in late 1810 on another topic, as the president reinstated the Non-Intercourse Act against Great Britain. The administration, seeking to court the French, emphasized this change in policy, and Madison even went out of his way to congratulate Napoleon on his recent marriage to Archduchess Marie Louise of Austria. In Congress, an aggressive group of Republicans, called the "War Hawks," led the more belligerent responses toward British recalcitrance. But as France was late in responding positively to Madison's overtures, the congressional mood became more confused.

The president's ability to handle these secretive and often inconclusive foreign relations was also impeded by his weak secretary of state, Robert Smith. The personal tension between Gallatin and the Smith family had been accentuated by the philosophical controversy over the national bank, which was up for renewal. Would the Madison administration, which touted republican principles, accept this Hamilton innovation that the president had himself so attacked when he served in Congress? In the Senate, Vice President Clinton broke a 17 to 17 tie by opposing its renewal. Opposition was expressed in the House as well, while Madison remained quiet and stayed consistent.[45]

Madison learned that one of his major challengers in the Republican ranks, Governor Monroe of Virginia, would be willing to forget past slights and join the administration. The president, wary of Smith's ineptitude and fearing his disloyalty, decided to replace him with Monroe and to offer Smith the U.S. ministership to Russia. Meanwhile, Gallatin resigned as secretary of treasury arguing that his continuance served no "public utility." Smith at first accepted the Russian post but then decided otherwise. Finally, he was left with writing a pamphlet denouncing the president and his policies.

The messages the administration was getting in early 1811 from France were less than reassuring. The emperor would only say that he would respect U.S. commerce as far as he could unless such leeway led to his nation's disadvantage in his war against Britain. The French encouraged the Americans to reiterate to the British U.S. rights, and Napoleon waited to see if that tough stand bore any changes in policy. Napoleon, though, did indicate that the United States should proceed in the Floridas as it so desired.

When the new British minister to the United States, Augustus Foster, arrived in America, he seemed willing to deal with the question of reparations in the *Chesapeake* dispute if the matter of the alleged American attack on the English ship *Little Belt* was also cleared up. Foster, however, understood that the Orders in Council would be continued until the French repealed the Berlin and Milan decrees without condition and ended various regulations that prohibited British ships and national goods from coming into certain continental ports. British policy once again stiffened the administration's resolve as did Foster's protests against American occupation of West Florida. Madison's discontent with the British was becoming matched by more evidence of French intransigence in several areas: delay in returning U.S. vessels they had captured, adding restrictions for ships sailing directly for the United States, and insisting on establishing licenses to be issued by French consuls. The administration, which had hoped to use concessions on one side to force concessions from the other, now faced two determined rivals whose main concern was the war in Europe, and not the sensitivities of the proud but weak Americans.

Madison in his public address criticized both the British and the French and pushed for more harbor fortifications, replenishment of the army, an auxiliary military force, greater emphasis on volunteers, more supplies, and a larger navy. Madison sounded an ominous note with his remark, "the period is arrived." John Quincy Adams concluded to Monroe that even the "Tories in our city" praised the president. Jefferson called Madison's address to Congress on the foreign controversies "the most excellent, rational and dignified message of the president." But to a troubled Gallatin, the president was moving from non-importation to preparedness and to a more belligerent and dangerous tone toward British war policies.[46]

Minister Foster, however, interpreted Madison's message as a request to enlarge the military in order to take East Florida. Then, in response to American pressures, Foster presented a plan of his own for settlement of these lasting disputes. That proposal was formally announced to Congress on November 13 and was nearly identical to the one Erskine agreed to in 1809, which was subsequently rejected by the British cabinet. But negotiations with Britain proved fruitless again, and Madison and Monroe decided to respond positively to Napoleon's reported intention to cooperate in "liberating" Spanish-American colonies.

Madison was increasingly sensitive to the criticisms that his policies were vacillating and weak; approaching the election of 1812, he was also aware of a possible challenge from George Clinton. In Congress, the Senate on December 20 had passed the Giles Army bill, which the British minister saw as a "means to overthrow Mr. Madison and his administration."[47] But the congressional Republicans were not themselves united. There were concerns over raising taxes for prosecuting a war, the size of a standing army if war did indeed come, and the proper means to achieve Madison's original objective, which was to end British curtailment of U.S. commerce. Madison dejectedly wrote to Jefferson that while Congress wanted to enable the executive to be more assertive, it delayed raising up an army and providing for it.

MR. MADISON'S WAR

By early March 1812, the Republicans of Virginia and Pennsylvania pledged their electors to Madison, and his prospects then for reelection looked good. At that time, Henry Clay, speaker of the House and one of the leaders of the so-called War Hawks, was quoted as saying war was inevitable, and Clay went on to tell Madison that a majority in Congress would support a declaration of war if the president recommended it. On June 1, the president asked for such a declaration against Britain citing the grounds of impressment, illegal blockades, the Orders in Council, and an allegation that British agents had been responsible for the renewal of Indian attacks on the northwest frontiers in the winter of 1811–12. He called on Congress to make a decision "worthy of the enlightened and patriotic councils of a virtuous, a free, and a powerful nation."[48]

Later studies of the congressional debate indicate that voting behavior was more determined by partisan and political factors than by individual or sectional attitudes toward the issues in question. On June 3, the Republican majority carried a vote for war in the House by 79 to 49, but the Senate nearly defeated the declaration, passing it only 19 to 13. The president's decision to ask for such a declaration came as a response to long-term diplomatic efforts that had not yielded any solution. In his own party, pressures were building for such a bold action.

But the president would find that a consensus for action dissolved when the demands for new taxes and the need for more military force and social discipline came. Now the nation would pay for its Republican party leadership's emphasis on decentralization and demobilization. From 1801 to 1812, it was Gallatin with his concern for balanced budget, repayment of the debt, and shrinking military who had commanded the support of the party and two administrations. Trying to strike a balance, Jefferson agreed to both a reduction of costs and an upgrading of the navy, especially including the introduction of gunboats. Like Hamilton, Gallatin's plans to balance the budget depended on customs duties especially from British goods. During the European war, the receipts from those sources dropped from $16 million in 1807 to $6.5 million at the end of 1809. Consequently, Gallatin tried to limit the size of the army and characterized the navy as "a substantial evil."[49] The Republican legacy and the Republican stewardship were confusing indeed.

Inevitably, the United States faced the problems associated with having no real military staff department, no effective supply management, and an uncertain organizational structure for the armed forces. The president had to deal with the politically vexatious problem of appointing a steady stream of officers, while about a quarter of them refused to serve or resigned after a few months. Madison even toyed with naming Clay as the head of the army to derail some of the political difficulties he was facing with Congress, but finally decided against it. In the field, recruiters used liquor freely to persuade men to sign up, and the adjutant general refused to ban the practice, concluding candidly that a prohibition would cut enlistments by one-half. Even after these men were assigned to regiments, many companies were still manned at only one-third to two-thirds strength as it was.

As the administration prepared for war, it paid little attention to the growing belligerent tone of the Indian tribes in the Northwest. Increased white encroachment, British encouragement of resistance, and the rise of some gifted leaders led to Indian opposition toward U.S. policies. Most important in setting that tone was "the Prophet," the Shawnee Tenskwatawa, and his brother, the brilliant Tecumseh. The Prophet called for an end to trading with the whites and a return to traditional tribal practices, while his more bellicose brother criticized Indians making land cessions to the American government. By the end of 1812, the campaign in the Northwest to deal with the Indian tribes was unsuccessful because the generals and the governor in the that area could not agree on defense priorities.[50]

The real center of strategic interest for the administration was to seize and control parts of Canada, for it was thought the British would then be forced to give in to American demands for an end to maritime restrictions. Supporters of the administration in the House wanted a large force ready by mid-May 1812 in order to invade as soon as the St. Lawrence River was free of ice. Montreal and Quebec were the prizes, especially the former, which was more accessible to invasion.

Almost from the beginning, the administration faced problems in prosecuting the war because of the reluctance of the eastern states to support the effort to take Canada. At times, the criticisms of the war effort from certain politicians in that region seemed to border on treason. To many Americans living on the frontier near Canada, the problem was not that they were unsympathic toward their fellow citizens who resisted Great Britain; they were just more concerned with how the hostilities would impact on their livelihoods, especially the border trade. Since Great Britain and not the United States held naval supremacy on Lake Ontario, one could understand their fear of retaliation and disruption of trade if the Madison administration carried the war into Canada.

Overall, the leadership of the United States Army was weak and its forces were unorganized. The major historian of the war, J. C. A. Stagg, has concluded that "the American army began to disintegrate, even as it was still being formed."[51] To add to Madison's troubles, the Federalists and Clinton Republicans carried New York state in the election, and thus rendered it of little assistance to the war effort. In Massachusetts, the Republicans lost the governorship and a majority of seats in the lower house, and the Federalist party ended up controlling three of the five state executive offices in New England—the most important region of action in the war, outside of New York. Congregational clergy spoke against the war, pamphlets were circulated denouncing it, and communities designated days of fasting to protest. Army recruiters were even presented with writs of habeas corpus to stop them from enlisting minors and apprentices.

In the first year of the war, the administration suffered a series of embarrassments in its campaigns and plans. In addition, the British made some major diplomatic concessions, except on impressment. News was reaching the states that Napoleon had driven deeply into the heartland of Russia and then had withdrawn ignominiously, thus emboldening the British. On the American front, the U.S. War Department on the most basic level was still unable to put together an American fighting army. It is little wonder that the administration finally accepted an offer by the Russian czar to mediate the conflict.

Incredibly, Gallatin insisted on pressing for more cost cutting and an abandonment of the navy's building plan, his position being that the money needed to run the war was in short supply. When Monroe optimistically speculated that Great Britain would agree to cede to the United States at least upper Canada and accept U.S. control over East Florida, Gallatin bluntly responded that to prolong the war for the sake of possibly gaining East Florida would "disgust every man north of Washington."[52]

Rejuvenated in late 1812, the Federalists began a series of attacks in the House of Representatives on the administration by demanding all diplomatic correspondence with France since August 1810. Monroe's response on behalf of the administration was a convoluted report that addressed in a general way relations with Great Britain and France. Meanwhile, even the Republican-controlled Senate was criticizing the administration's agreeing to Russian mediation, and there was considerable opposition to Gallatin being named as one of the commissioners to Russia while he was to keep the treasury post. In response to these criticisms, the Senate rejected Gallatin's nomination after it approved the other two nominees on the commission.

The war did have some American successes, most graphically Captain Oliver Perry's victories at Lake Erie and the Battle of the Thames. But in terms of capturing and holding parts of Canada, the

United States was rather unsuccessful overall. In early March 1813, General Wilkinson situated in New Orleans was ordered north to enter the war efforts—an additional chapter in his strange career. The War Department and the northern command were in constant disagreement over strategy, logistics, and support efforts. Food supplies for the United States Army at the Canadian frontier were often poor or contaminated. Wilkinson proved to be a cautious commander who resisted cries of "on to Montreal." There was at the end of 1813 a host of recriminations among military leaders as the objectives of the administration were still unresolved.

In the winter of 1813–14, the Creeks began to grow increasingly restive. In the fall of 1811, Tecumseh was preaching to his tribe his gospel of resistance, and his stature was enhanced when his prediction of a comet came true in late 1811 and when earthquakes shook the South and the Midwest in early 1812. Other Indian revivalists passed through the area also exploiting the manifold discontents of an already exploited people. The administration tried to intervene in the disputes, in part because of the desire of Southern states to extend U.S. boundaries to the Gulf of Mexico—a position that Madison and Monroe approved. The United States, however, had few troops to spare and the state militia was the first line of defense. One military leader, Andrew Jackson, the commander of the west Tennessee militia, was ready to go to war with the Creeks and did wage several major battles against them. But overall, there was little systematic cooperation between and among the states and their governors in defending the increasingly precarious frontiers.[53]

American plans for progress in the Canadian campaign required more U.S. troop strength and a better militia system. A proposal to reform the militia brought forth cries of "slavery" and "conscription"—a term associated with Napoleon's armies. Meanwhile, Secretary of State Monroe was undercutting Secretary of War John Armstrong, partially to thwart the latter's desire to succeed Madison as president. As for Congress, it not only refused to recognize the military's needs, but it also ignored its responsibilities to provide a proper tax structure to finance the war. One of the consequences of the Indian wars in the South and Northwest was the decline of federal income from the sales of public lands; this loss was compounded by the absence of customs duties due to the embargo and non-importation laws. The administration could borrow money if it would charter another bank of the United States, and some Republicans were moving in that distasteful direction. But still it proved to be a divisive issue, especially in an administration led by Madison who had so criticized Hamilton. One Republican, Madison's kinsman James G. Jackson of Virginia, introduced a constitutional amendment to authorize the establishment of a bank, but the House postponed discussion. The war was not only going poorly militarily, but financially the cupboards were bare.

In New England, fierce opposition was developing to the war, especially in Massachusetts. The state legislature there debated calling for a state convention to discuss alleged violation of its citizens' rights, to raise up a state army to protect those rights, and even to explore secession and a separate peace with Great Britain. In New York, the Federalist-controlled lower house refused to help raise funds to retaliate against the British raids of December 1813. The British position in Europe and North America was helped by Napoleon's serious troubles as his foes crossed over the Rhine and the Pyrenees, moved on to capture Paris, and finally deposed him.

Across the ocean, Madison decided to end commercial restrictictions. To the Federalists his actions showed just how incorrect his assumptions were in the first place.[54] In May, the British announced that the entire American coastline was under a blockade of the Royal Navy. It was the beginning of a serious British offensive and a string of catastrophes for the administration. In mid-1814, the total strength of the army was only thirty-one thousand with twenty-seven thousand effective troops. The United States had a slight superiority in the number of vessels on the Great Lakes and on Lake Champlain but lacked trained seamen. On the Atlantic coast, the superiority of the Royal Navy was obvious. And at home, American money to wage the war had simply dried up.

Madison's cabinet had not worked harmoniously in the past, but by 1814, the president and Secretary of War Armstrong were at loggerheads. The president circumvented Armstrong and intervened in the daily activities of the department, so much so that he required that Armstrong consult him on all matters of policy. In addition, the president seemed to be the only one present in cabinet discussions who was worried about a possible British attack on the capital. Because of the administration's commitment to an offensive in Canada, there were few regular troops available to defend local communities and coastlines. While the president expressed concern for the safety of the capital, he did not check on defense preparations in July and August.[55]

The British then decided to invade the capital and, despite some earlier planning efforts, American forces retreated in a disorganized way after three hours of fighting. The enemy entered the capital with no impediment and burned public buildings on August 25 and 26, and then left quickly. On August 27, the president reentered the city. Madison asked the citizens to take up arms and resist, and ordered Monroe, in Armstrong's absence, to take command of the defense of the region. Armstrong resigned and Monroe assumed his heavy responsibilities as well. Almost immediately he had to face the collapse of the financial structure as well, and a beleaguered Monroe borrowed money from local banks to help fund coastal defenses.

The president was uncomfortable with his onetime rival Monroe holding two major cabinet positions and looked for a new secretary of war. In addition, he had to replace the departing Gallatin, and fill the spot of secretary of navy as William Jones also wanted to resign. For a time after the fall of Washington, D.C., Madison was singularly responsible for restoring the government and in holding together an inexperienced cabinet. He publicly recalled the exploits and heroism of the Revolution and pushed for changes in the organization and functioning of the armed forces. He asked for "large sums" to fight the war, as his new secretary of treasury, Alexander James Dallas, attempted to take control quickly of the deteriorating situation and push through a Hamiltonian-type bank. But in the midst of these failures and fiascos, Congress could not pass an effective bill. To many Republicans, a new national bank would be a betrayal of basic principles, and a disgusted Dallas soon resigned as well. Once again, the Republican ideology had triumphed over reality.[56]

Congress was equally recalcitrant in approving policies to reorganize the army and increase recruitments. In October 1814, the administration again considered conquering Canada, while Monroe pushed for more changes in the armed forces, but to no avail. During the war, the president and his colleagues faced a real secession movement in New England, and the commencing of the Hartford Convention raised their anxieties. When the British occupied Maine and threatened New England, the reaction of the Federalist leadership in that region was not resistance, but a push for peace and a call for a regional convention. On October 18, 1814, the Massachusetts General Court (the state legislature) endorsed such a call for a convention to be held in Hartford, Connecticut, to began "a radical reform in the national compact." Federalist leaders hoped that the delegates would deal with the issues of the war, and then move on to the long-standing grievances of New England: embargoes, representation of slaves based on the three-fourths formula, and the easy admission of new Western states.[57]

The Republicans feared that such a convention would lead to a separate peace with the enemy and ultimately encourage states to secede from the Union. Those concerns were not unfounded. Governor Caleb Strong of Massachusetts sent an agent to the British commander at Halifax, Sir John Sherbrooke, to explore possibilities for a separate peace. In the city of Hartford, the state and city governments in Connecticut had prevented the U.S. Army from recruiting there and even from playing martial music within the city limits. Monroe finally had to send two infantry regiments into Connecticut to assert federal authority.

From December 15 to January 5, the convention met in secret and discussed issues of mutual concern. But the temper of the convention cooled and two states in the region—Vermont and New Hampshire—were not represented. The report of the convention condemned the administration for failing to defend the region, but did support local defenses. There was a restatement of New England's positions on familiar issues, but no real call for secession. The Hartford convention showed the general disapproval of many New Englanders toward the war, and also the overall weakness of the Republicans in that region.

Elsewhere, the American forces defeated the British at Baltimore and at Plattsburg in September 1814, and U.S. concerns focused on the Royal Navy along the coast of the Southern states. There was a fear that the British would attack the Gulf coast and threaten New Orleans, and the British provided a vice admiral with a fleet and ten thousand men for just such an expedition. Far away from that city and facing problems after the fall of the capital, the Madison administration gave its approval to Andrew Jackson's aggressive campaigns against the British.

After his celebrated victories over the Creek Indians in March 1814, Jackson had become a recognized military figure. The administration initially supported a limited defensive effort to protect New Orleans, but Jackson insisted that the British desired to control the whole Indian territory of the Southwest. The governor of his home state, William Blount, and some of the political leaders in Tennessee agreed with his appraisal of the situation. Finally, Jackson advanced to capture Pensacola on November 7 and he was successful. The administration was uncomfortable with Jackson's movements, but it was far away from the scene of action. Jackson even encouraged the establishment of a troop of free "colored" volunteers and made an alliance with the pirates of Barataria headed by the legendary Jean Laffite. Finally, in the Battle of New Orleans, Jackson used artillery skillfully and defeated the British. A great hero was born in the heat of real battle.

The war was over by the time of his victory, but Jackson had not received the news. His use of martial law even after peace was announced was criticized by the Louisiana state legislature and Governor Claiborne who attacked "the violence of his character," a comment to be made frequently against the impulsive Jackson. Indeed, Old Hickory had enthusiastically expelled the French consul and ordered 130 uncooperative French nationals sent to Baton Rouge. After the war, he had to appear in court and was fined $1,000 for his refusal to obey a writ of habeas corpus, but by then he was a household name in a war that had produced few American victories or victors.[58]

On February 14, Monroe gave Madison the proposed treaty with Great Britain completed at Ghent. The *National Intelligencer* presented the administration's view that the treaty "is a restitution and recognition of the rights and possessions of each party, as they stood before the war." Disputed boundaries were to be brought to a neutral sovereign for third-party review. The prince regent had already ratified the treaty, and on February 17, Madison proclaimed the war over.

Madison who had the dubious honor of having the war named after him, later concluded that the first struggle in 1776 was "a war of infancy, this last was that of our youth; and the issue of both, wisely improved, may long postpone if not forever prevent a necessity for exerting the strength of our manhood."[59]

With the war over, the president opposed attempts to cut back quickly on defenses. But the Republican-controlled House took the opposite tack—it ended military conscription, killed the revised national bank, and left the nation with a $16 million budget deficit. The president wanted to keep twenty thousand troops under arms as there were still thirty-five thousand British troops in North

America. But again the House cut the troop strength to six thousand with the Senate pressing for ten thousand. Officers descended
on the capital to avoid discharge and to press personal cases. The
news also arrived in Washington that Napoleon had fled Elba and
moved toward Paris, entering on March 20. Would Europe enter into
another war that would affect the liberties of Americans? But
Napoleon's triumph was short-lived and he was returned to permanent exile.

The president on February 23 turned his attention to a different
front and focused on the hostilities of the dey of Algiers against
U.S. citizens in 1812, and he pressed for a declaration of war. The
president had sent Commodore Stephen Decatur to head up a squad-
ron to move into the Mediterranean as Jefferson had done with
Tripoli.[60]

Decatur proved to be successful, and a peace treaty was
presented to the president, ending the episode. Indian conflicts in
the Detroit and St. Louis regions quieted down, and the president
was informed by Secretary of Treasury Dallas that state banks were
agreeing to a proposal for depositing treasury notes for governmental
business, which was seen as offering some fiscal stability. In April
1816, the president signed a bill creating the Second Bank of the
United States. The Hamiltonian vision had triumphed on that issue
at last. In the same month, the president focused his attention on a
reduction of forces on the Great Lakes and on increasing West
Indian trade. Resurrecting an old Republican reservation, Madison
did veto a bill for federal development of roads and waterways,
arguing from a strict constructionist view of the Constitution that
such efforts were outside the legitimate scope of the national
government.

Madison's two terms in office were almost totally concerned with
tense diplomacy, uncoordinated war and military disasters, and international problems. The War of 1812 is often seen as "Mr.
Madison's War," the implication being that he was the instigator and
manager of that conflict. His policies were initially patient and, at
times, diplomatically skillful, but in the end the United States had
no business taking on the greatest military power in the world especially when the nation was so divided. Surely New England's
response at times bordered on treason, but the Republican ideology
of localism, disarmament, and decentralized authority was a prescription for national disaster as well.[61]

AN ERA OF GOOD FEELINGS
AND PETTY INTRIGUES

Secretary of State Monroe's election continued Virginia's control of the presidential nomination process despite a challenge from William H. Crawford of Georgia and Governor Daniel D. Tompkins of New York. He had garnered significant support among state party leaders and early endorsements from the Pennsylvania legislature and party conventions in Rhode Island and Massachusetts. Republican congressmen fell in line to support Monroe, while the remnants of the Federalist party decided to nominate Rufus King. Monroe swept the election with 183 electoral votes to 34, with Tompkins getting the vice president spot on his ticket.

Monroe stressed his role as a nonpartisan chief of state, but he refused Jackson's suggestion and those of others that he extend offers of public office to Federalists. He named John Quincy Adams as secretary of state and Crawford as secretary of treasury; he offered the secretary of war position to Clay who rejected it, giving John C. Calhoun the opportunity to accept. Adams, a former Federalist, had since moved into the moderate orbit of the Republican party, abandoning the party of his father. He called himself "a man of reserve, cold, austere and forbidding manners; my political adversaries say a gloomy misanthropist, and my personal enemies an unsocial savage." But he and Monroe worked rather well together for two terms, although at first Adams was put off by the president's slowness in making decisions.[62]

The new president reflected the sentiments of many Americans in seeking to avoid the excesses of partisanship and aggressive parties. As Nicholas Biddle was to conclude after Monroe's election, "The nation has become tired of the follies of faction and the ruling party has outgrown many of the childish customs with which they began their career 20 years since."[63]

Monroe dressed in the simple garb of the older generation, and on ceremonial occasions, he wore a blue coat, black knee breeches and black silk hose—a throwback to the military uniform of the Revolutionary era. Watching the president over the years, Calhoun concluded in 1831, "Tho' not brilliant, few men were his equals in wisdom, firmness and devotion to the country. He had a wonderful intellectual patience; and could above all men, that I ever knew, when called on to decide an important point, hold the subject immovably fixed under his attention, until he had mastered it in all of its relations. It was mainly to this admirable quality that he owed his highly accurate judgment."[64]

Monroe pledged to end the influence of parties, but he also insisted that the Republican party alone was committed to the new nation. To broaden his political base and to foster feelings of national amity, he decided to visit the northern and eastern states, and, later in 1819, the southern and western states. Many citizens came to see this president who had been one of the Founding Fathers, and who exhibited the simple hospitality and quiet confidence of that first generation of nation builders. Even in New England, the president was generally greeted warmly. Abigail Adams called it an "expiation" on the part of the region, and indeed Monroe must have recognized the changing winds. He wrote Madison that in New England, there was "a desire in the body of the people to show their attachment to our union."[65] This "era of good feelings," as a Boston Federalist newspaper in 1817 called it, led to the predominance of the Republican party nearly everywhere. Indeed, by 1819, every New England state except Massachusetts was controlled by Monroe's party, and in Congress the remaining Federalists generally supported the president.

The nearly total triumph of the Republican party led to factionalism within that party. Rufus King was to note that after the first year of Monroe's administration underneath the harmony were "strong passions." Monroe found that congressional leaders often opposed his proposals for personal reasons, rather than because of what is often loosely called in politics "principles." Also, aspirants to succeed him were already setting up rival factions to exploit advantages, and later sectional divisions helped shatter the alleged good feelings. As for Monroe, he accepted the general Republican principles of his two predecessors with their rhetoric on limiting the executive, although those experienced men recognized the need for more direction in foreign affairs. Standing committees in Congress were growing more powerful, and Monroe tried to use his cabinet to influence the legislature's actions. Sometimes as with Crawford, such assistance in dealing with partisans and factional loyalties was not forthcoming. Still, even with the astute Clay in opposition, Monroe never lost on a single major administration proposal.[66]

Monroe inherited quickly the controversies over internal improvements. The president asked Madison what was the discussion in the cabinet when Jefferson signed the Cumberland Road bill, an important deviation from strict Republican principles. Madison was uncertain as to Jefferson's views and why that bill and related subsequent ones passed at the end of his term were signed, but Madison's own position was clear since he had vetoed the improvements bill that Congress had sent him. Monroe, adhering then to the literal Republican tradition, expressed early his reservations on the constitutional questions and went on to hope for a constitutional amendment to expressly permit such expenditures. After 1819, the rage for public internal improvements declined somewhat, in part due to the poor economic conditions nationally, and the pressure on Republicans subsided for a while. Still, in 1822, Congress passed a bill providing for the collection of tolls to maintain the Cumberland Road and Monroe vetoed it. Yet he approved a bill the next year to appropriate $25,000 for repairing the same road.[67] At times, the Republican legacy appeared confusing even to its patriarchs.

In foreign affairs, the collapse of the Spanish empire presented problems and opportunities for the United States and led to the doctrine that bears Monroe's name. The administration concentrated on three major objectives: to secure possession of Florida without war, to stop European states from restoring Spanish authority, and to establish friendly relations with the new South American nations without incurring European hostility. Jefferson and Madison had oriented American foreign policy in each of these directions, and Monroe was continuing those overtures.

The French urged the administration to help foster a rapprochement with Spain and her colonies and agreed to a joint effort to curtail British commercial expansion. Monroe refused to strike such a deal believing that independence was inevitable in the Southern Hemisphere. Continuing Madison's policies, Monroe expressed concern for the fate of Amelia Island, which was within the boundaries of Spanish Florida and which was becoming a haven for pirates, slave traders, and smugglers. The president then decided to send forces onto the island and in the process pressure Spain to cede Florida. Jackson was ordered into the area, and he advised Monroe to seize East Florida also in order to compensate for alleged past outrages by the Spanish. The president refused to allow Jackson to attack any Spanish-occupied posts, but to his dismay, Monroe received notice that Jackson had summarily executed two

British subjects who had supposedly incited the Indians against the United States. The general had also attacked Pensacola on May 24, driving the Spanish out of the area and back to Havana.

Except for Adams, the cabinet secretaries denounced Jackson. Monroe's own position remained unclear. The president subsequently did not endorse the general's actions, and reasserted diplomatically the administration's more moderate policy. The posts were returned to Spain, while Monroe tried to soothe Jackson's feelings with the assurance that at times a general should exceed his authority when it was to "essential advantage to his country."[68]

As so often happens in politics, the bold are in the service of the deliberate, and it is clear that even if Monroe did not direct Jackson's various actions, the administration and the nation benefited from the general's determination. In May 1818, the cabinet had previously held a lengthy meeting in which all agreed that American forces should be kept in Florida until Spain provided adequate guarantees about that territory, and that the United States also would oppose any European interference in Latin American while the Spanish empire was crumbling. Fortunately it was the naval supremacy of Great Britain that underlined that commitment, for the British were increasing their trade with these new regimes and were unwilling to support Spanish designs to reassert their authority.

For all of the criticism of Jackson, his impetuous actions helped the administration convince Spain to cede Florida and negotiate a favorable western boundary for the Louisiana Territory. Adams wanted the cession of Florida and the establishment of the Louisiana border at the Sabine River, north to the Red River and along the forty-first parallel west to the Pacific Ocean. As for General Jackson, his opponents in the capital tried to exploit his difficulties in order to bolster the fortunes of Clay and Calhoun, likely candidates for the presidency later. The House Committee on Military Affairs condemned Jackson's executions, but when news arrived in the capital of Spain's ceding of Florida, anti-Jackson sentiment disappeared, and the general became even more of a hero. The administration eventually signed an advantageous treaty covering Florida, the Louisiana border, and Spanish claims.

In December 1818, the president continued to ponder the question of Latin America and the new regimes that were being established there. A primary concern was what the position of Great Britain would be in these matters; Monroe and Adams instructed the American minister Richard Rush to sound out His Majesty's government's views as the United States moved toward recognizing Buenos Aires and perhaps Chile and Venezuela. British Foreign Secretary Castlereagh proved to be unsupportive, not wishing to antagonize other European nations, and Monroe postponed any action. In the summer of 1819, the president toured the South and West, which applauded his successes in dealing with Spain, and by late 1819, Monroe was working on a message that asked Congress for authority to occupy Florida while he considered recognizing Buenos Aires.

Monroe's problems were complicated by the beginnings of intense sectionalism and the slavery debate arising from the question of admitting Missouri to the Union as a slave state. Success in gaining land from the Spanish only opened up more deeply the divisions in Congress and in the nation. When Jefferson pushed Monroe to suspend negotiation of the treaty with Spain until Texas was included, the president refused. Monroe was concerned that U.S. claims to that region were weak, and that controversy would arouse the same forces that went to the forefront in the Missouri crisis. When the Transcontinental Treaty was ratified in February 1819, the United States and Spain agreed on the Louisiana boundaries and also on the cession of Florida.

This glut of land produced a more profound impact on American politics than most had expected. The Missouri crisis began in early 1819 when Representative James Tallmadge, Jr. of New York introduced a bill to organize a state government there and included a proposal to require emancipation of all slaves over twenty-one years old and to forbid the introduction of new slaves. The issue caught the concerns and conscience of a rising antislavery sentiment in the North and led to Southern defensiveness. Chroniclers of the crisis have generally ignored Monroe's role and focused on the dramatic debates in the Senate led by Clay. Quietly behind the scenes, the president worked for a compromise. Monroe consistently opposed any restrictions on Missouri's entrance into the Union, arguing that the Constitution provided for equality with other states. Monroe worked closely with Senator James Barbour of Virginia who was an important figure in putting together an agreement. Barbour tried to link Missouri and Maine in order to push a bill through Congress admitting both to the Union as states. Meanwhile, Senator J. B. Thomas of Illinois introduced another bill excluding slavery from the Louisiana Purchase in the areas north of the 36°30' line. Monroe supported Barbour and met on February 9 with a group of congressmen to push for the compromise; later, the president focused on getting the important Virginian delegation to support that accommodation.[69]

The president was concerned that behind the intense sectionalism was a base desire of some to introduce a new partisanship. There were some strong criticisms when Monroe accepted the restrictions of 36°30′, and Virginia Republicans in the caucus balked at the deal and had second thoughts about supporting Monroe for reelection. The Senate, however, finally voted to admit Missouri and Maine and approved the Thomas Amendment, aimed at prohibiting slavery north of the 36°30′ line. As for the president, he had no real opposition in reelection, with only one vote being cast for another candidate. Thus the facade of unity stood side by side with the mounting forces of sectionalism and slavery.[70]

Opposition leaders were also aided by the severe economic and social dislocations of the panic of 1819. Historian Harry Ammon has cited numerous causes of the depression: overexpansion of credit, the collapse of export markets after a bumper crop in 1817 in Europe, the low prices of imports from Europe which impeded domestic industries, instability from the excessive expansion of state banking after 1811, high unemployment, and the unsound banking practices of the Second Bank of the United States in authorizing a drastic curtailment of loans in 1818 and 1819. The depression also encouraged the rise of a dissident group of conservative Republicans and broadly based factions pledged to different candidates for succession to the presidency. In addition, the economic downturn cut seriously into government income, derived mainly from customs duties, and led to cries for more republican economy. Bills were introduced in Congress for a protective tariff, which would also raise income, and it became another issue that would add to the fires of sectionalism.

Despite early Republican orthodoxy, Monroe supported a national bank, but his attempts to gather adequate information about the economy were hindered by Secretary of Treasury Crawford's reluctance to provide the data. Crawford had his allies in Congress who were pushing for cuts rather than unpopular taxes, and the secretary hoped to use the outcry to gain the White House. A very involved Clay concluded, "Mr. Monroe has just been re-elected with apparent unanimity, but he has not the slightest influence on Congress. His career is closed. There was nothing further to be expected by him or from him."[71]

As the year passed, the administration decided to develop some statement of hemispheric principles as Monroe originally advocated. On October 28, the president and Secretary of State Adams were considering a proposal from British Foreign Minister George Canning that the two nations issue a public manifesto opposing any attempt by European powers to restore Spain's place in Latin America. The British were concerned about stopping French influence after that nation, with the concurrence of Russia, Prussia, and Austria, placed Ferdinand VII back on the Spanish throne in 1823. Madison and Jefferson gave Monroe support in cooperating with Great Britain, but Monroe decided to turn down the idea of a joint accord. Instead, the United States would issue its own statement of principles, one that also would be in line with British interests and intentions.

Monroe's final declaration (called only after 1850 the "Monroe Doctrine") stated that the American continents should thereafter not be subject to future European colonization, and it reaffirmed the United States' policy of noninterference in European affairs as well. Any such new European movement into the hemisphere would be seen as an unfriendly act toward the United States. John J. Crittenden of Kentucky called it a dignified and heroic policy that made the United States "the protector of free governments of South America and arrayed as boldly against any attempts on the part of the Holy Alliance to extend to this hemisphere that despotism and slavery which it has fastened on Europe."[72]

The Monroe Doctrine has been seen by later and more critical generations as a blueprint for U.S. imperialism. But, in fact, it was originally a statement of principles by a president who genuinely cared about revolutionary governments and opposed their suppression. Monroe was a cautious and skeptical man, but he also drew intensely from his own experience as the last of the Revolutionary Founding Fathers presidents. The doctrine that bears his name probably owes more to that profound influence than to any nascent imperialist vision of a South America run by the United States.

During the president's second term, great interest focused on who would be his successor with the names of Crawford, Clay, Calhoun, Adams, and Jackson being mentioned. Calhoun was the first to drop out in 1824, indicating his desire for the vice presidency instead. Adams and Monroe were linked closely in the public mind, and Clay, Jackson, and even Secretary Crawford attacked the president's policies to eliminate Adams as a prime contender.

While the partisan lines were drawn, Monroe probably without any knowledge of what he was doing signed the Tenure of Office Act of 1820, which would open up large numbers of offices especially in the Treasury Department and which, consequently, strengthened Crawford's position. The act also established a precedent for congressional control over removals, a point to be made against Andrew Johnson years later. But Monroe and John Quincy Adams automatically reappointed mostly all officeholders unless charged with misconduct. Patronage disputes had led Monroe into some conflicts with the New York machine and with Martin Van Buren who supported at first Crawford and later Jackson for president. Monroe concluded that sniping at his policies increased in Congress as factional lines grew sharper, and he was accused of secretly desiring a third term by those who publicly coveted his position.

As his term ended, the president continued his work on modest diplomatic matters. A treaty of commerce with France was negotiated and as a result of the Convention of 1818, the United States and Great Britain moved toward a settlement of their fisheries dispute and other long-standing problems. The administration even considered a draft inspired by the British to suppress the slave trade. Adams pushed as well for a settlement of the Maine boundary controversy, and congressional critics demanded a tougher line on the Oregon question. But many of the administration's efforts to deal with Great Britain hit the shoals of partisanship and factional rivalry, and agreements and proposals often died in the Senate.

Crawford's bid for the presidency was suddenly stopped when he suffered a stroke that left him for a while almost totally incapacitated. Weary of the increased vituperation, Monroe complained to a friend, "Every kind of malignant effort is made to annoy me, by men of violent passions, some of whom are very ignorant, and others little restrained by principle." Monroe found himself under pressure, for example, from the Georgia delegation because of his moderate Indian policy, a policy that Adams continued and Jackson abandoned. Monroe refused to accept the desire of Georgia to push the Indians out, arguing, "Any attempt to remove them by force would, in my opinion, be unjust."[73]

Monroe had kept the Republican faith alive, by standing by its basic principles, but in a more moderate and less manipulative way than Jefferson's and in easier times than Madison's. He endeavored to make cabinet government work within that tradition, but he also suffered as the rivalries in his cabinet reflected in part the factions arising in the nation.[74] The Era of Good Feelings was the artificial backdrop for the Era of Sectional Disputes, and the Missouri controversy was, as Jefferson astutely prophesied, "the firebell in the night." Monroe as the last of the Founding Fathers presidents ended the Virginia dynasty. He died nearly penniless never having been reimbursed fully even for the expenses he incurred in a lifetime of public service.

JOHN QUINCY ADAMS AND
THE NATIONALIST AGENDA

It may seem odd to group John Quincy Adams in with Thomas Jefferson and his Virginia circle, but, in fact, the son of John Adams became increasingly identified with his father's rival and his associates as his own political aspirations blossomed. Early in his distinguished career, John Quincy had accompanied his father on a diplomatic mission to France and later to Great Britain. He went on to serve his government in Czarist Russia, the Hague in the Netherlands, and in Berlin. He was elected in 1803 to the U.S. Senate with the support of the Federalists. But gradually he became a critic of their views especially with regard to Britain, and Adams found the Federalist position a "glaring absurdity and hypocrisy of their professed veneration for the policy of Washington." Above all and in all things, he was his own man; as the historian Alan Nevins observed, "Few of our great statesmen have had an individuality so marked; perhaps no other has combined so many aufractoxities, humors, and prejudices with so much ability, liberality, and high rectitude of character."[75]

Adams's election was, in some ways, rather remarkable, for he had no real popular following, no strong partisan machine, no articulate platform. The congressional caucus had fallen into disrepair, and in February 1824, only 68 of 261 members of Congress participated in the caucus, and the majority backed Crawford's candidacy. Adams was an honest and irascible individual of great talents who was elected in a deadlocked electoral procedure, a man respected for his great family's service and his own talents as secretary of state in Monroe's administration. He sought to put together a cabinet that would combine the leaders of the major factions, and he offered posts to Jackson, Clay, and Gallatin. Like Washington, he would then be the president of the whole nation, above intrigues, partisanship and section. But that was not to be. Although General Jackson had a plurality of the electoral votes for president in 1824, he did not garner a majority, and so the election was thrown into the House of Representatives where each state delegation had only one vote. After some machinations, the Clay delegations supported Adams and he was elected. Adams, in turn, named Clay secretary of state—the position usually given to one's prospective successor. Jackson became bitter toward Adams and Clay for the "corrupt bargain," and he joined with Calhoun in putting together a Southern-Western opposition to curtail the future influence of Clay—"Harry of the West" as his followers called him.[76]

Clay did not really engage in such a blatant swap, but there were conversations between him and Adams and their agents to smooth over the informal understandings that gave each of them national office. As for the new president, Adams entered the White House with a strong commitment to American nationalism, a respect for liberty guaranteed by the Constitution, and a propensity to stress commercial negotiations to further U.S. aims abroad. Adams was above all a nationalist, one dedicated to the Union. He wanted a stronger central government to exploit the resources of a rapidly expanding American presence in North America, and he pushed for internal improvements in a manner very different from the other Jeffersonian presidents.

On other matters, the new president was concerned for some reason that private property was not as securely protected as liberty, and that a national bankruptcy statute was needed as well. In addition, Adams supported an Indian removal policy to transfer the tribes to west of the Mississippi and encouraged education and some assimilation for the natives. These newly opened up lands in the public domain, connected by national roads and canals knitting the republic together, would provide a vast domestic market. Thus, in many ways, he accepted Clay's "American System"—a program of internal improvements and economic expansion. The president, years later, summarized his view at the time: "The federalism of Washington, Union, and Internal Improvement have been the three hinges upon which my political life and fortunes, good and bad, have turned."[77] It was more Washington and Hamilton than early Jefferson or even his own petulant father. It also became clear that Adams would continue to stress foreign policy in his administration and accentuate the goal of world trade. The problem was that regional economic differences politicized U.S. commercial policy which limited, in turn, American assertiveness abroad.

The new president immediately found a Congress controlled by hostile factions. Adams, who refused to use patronage as a way of building his political base, quickly lost his initial advantages. His messages to Congress were filled with allusions to this nationalist vision, and yet were not well received. He pushed for a new Department of Interior, a national naval academy, a new university in Washington, D.C., an astronomical observatory that would be one of the "light houses of the skies," a national militia law, a national system of weights and measures, a more effective national patent law, and a system of internal improvements. "Liberty is power," the president concluded. "The nation blessed with the largest portion of liberty must in proportion to its members be the most powerful nation upon earth, and the tenure of power by man is, in the moral purposes of his Creator, upon conditions that it shall be exercised to ends of beneficence, to improve the condition of himself and his fellow-men." It was a brilliant vision, which would be overshadowed by the intrigues of sectional politicians and the maneuvers of powerful political operatives.[78]

The opposition of Calhoun, Crawford, and Jackson laid the groundwork for the new Democratic party. Clay was a great political figure in his own right, but the alliance against him and Adams was becoming too powerful, and although he respected the president, Adams's nonpartisan profile was less than helpful to his own supporters. Added to congressional fears of a national agenda was the South's increasing sensitivity over its "peculiar institution"—an economy and social system based on slavery and racism.[79]

In foreign affairs, the administration had initially supported a treaty with Great Britain and with the Republic of Colombia to suppress the African slave trade. The opposition in the Senate to the treaty at first focused on British abuses in searching ships and in impressment, but also there was a rising concern about interfering with slavery. Early in his term, Adams's modest proposal to send a representative to attend the Latin American Congress ran into the same sort of mixture of isolationism and fear that the international conference would touch on the slave trade question, the possibilities of diplomatic relations with the black state of Haiti, or the status of the island of Cuba. The United States Congress finally approved Adams's initiative, but the conference was not successful and the American minister got there too late to participate. The opposition though was one of the first signs of the new alliance of Southern planters and Northern Republicans that the wily Martin Van Buren of New York was midwifing.

Adams also tried to steer a compromise course on the difficult issue of public lands. Representatives from the West, led by Senator Thomas Benton of Missouri, wanted to place the rights of squatters before other buyers in those new lands. Initially, the president viewed the public lands as a source to pay off the nation's debt and to generate income to fund his ambitious internal improvements. But he was reluctant to alienate Southerners and voters from the Western states by getting in the middle of the dispute.[80]

The president did have to deal with the question of the Indian tribes and the substantial public clamor, especially in Georgia, to push them west. When he took office, Adams found that the Senate had already approved the Treaty of Indian Springs, which was completed with a group of Creeks and which swapped lands in Georgia for lands west of the Mississippi plus a cash bonus. Soon knowledgeable people attacked the treaty as unfair and the Indian delegation as unrepresentative of the full Creek nation, but Adams signed it.

Adams did encourage some renegotiation of the objectionable document, and his secretary of war, James Barbour, advocated that the Indians should be incorporated within the states and be placed under the same laws that governed whites. The administration advocated a new treaty in which the Creeks would cede all their lands in Georgia except for the area west of the Chattahoochee River by January 1, 1827. Georgia's governor, George M. Troup, ignored the new treaty and insisted on having surveys done of the Indian lands. The cabinet supported Adams's threat to send in troops to uphold U.S. policy, but finally the Creeks ceded all their lands and Georgia took over control.

It was left to Andrew Jackson to show how mild and moderate Adams had been in comparison in his handling of the Indian problem. Years later, John Quincy Adams concluded, "We have done more harm to the Indians since our Revolution than had ever been done to them by the French and English nations before. . . . These are crying sins for which we are answerable before a higher jurisdiction." But other leaders were less sympathetic: Calhoun insisted, "By a proper combination of force and persuasion, of punishments and rewards, they ought to be brought within the pales of law and civilization."[81] His sometime ally, Clay, thought it was impossible to civilize the Indians and concluded that they were destined for extinction; while he did not support inhuman actions toward them, he did not think their race worth preserving. At times, Adams seemed to agree with Clay's pessimism, but not his policies.

Adams also had to face another issue with states' rights implications: the protective tariff. The tariff of 1824, which increased the schedules of 1816, had drawn the ire of Southern politicians, and the president tried to stay away from the issue as best he could, being content to let his secretary of treasury, Richard Rush, support the tariff on his own. On March 1, 1827, Vice President Calhoun cast the deciding vote against a new revision, but Southern discontent was accentuated by a drop in cotton prices and the inability or unwillingness of local branches of the Bank of the United States to supply credit. The price of cotton dropped from 30.8 cents a pound in 1818 to 8.9 cents in 1831, wreaking havoc on the plantation economy.[82]

The president supported some protection to advance internal improvements and protect domestic industries, but he refused to be fixed on a particular formula—leaving that issue to Congress, which was supposed to be the one body chosen to represent all sections of the nation. Jackson's supporters, now led by Van Buren, tried to outflank the president by pushing for a tariff so unreasonable that it would be defeated. To their surprise, this "tariff of abominations," as it was called, passed both houses of Congress and Adams complacently signed it, alienating for good the vociferous South, as the issue became a major concern in the electoral campaign of 1828.

In the area of foreign policy, where Adams was so experienced, the United States was seeking to press its various claims against France, Naples, Denmark, and Russia. The administration also wanted to develop trade with the Latin American republics, especially Brazil, Colombia, Haiti, and Mexico. Overall, the administration pushed for reciprocity to open up world markets to U.S. commerce. On December 5, 1825, Secretary of State Clay signed a treaty with the Federation of Central America that was a model of the Adams administration's efforts to establish commercial ties with an emphasis on reciprocity and most favored nation treatment. The agreement was to run for twelve years, but in 1826, the Central American Federation began to disintegrate, and the treaty was null and void. Earlier in 1824, the United States also suspended discriminating duties on direct trade with the Netherlands; Prussia; the

Hanseatic cities of Hamburg, Lubeck, and Bremer; Oldenburg; Norway; Scandinavia; and Russia. The administration moved in 1827 to extend the commercial convention originally signed with Great Britain in 1815, negotiated agreements with the bountiful islands of Tahiti and Hawaii, and even made overtures to the Ottoman Empire, which were unsuccessful.

Unfortunately, the administration was unable to break into the mercantilistic European system, and between 1825 and 1829, commodity prices dropped, thus alienating farmers from Adams's policies. The British continued their restrictions on U.S. trade with the West Indies and with Canada, stating it was "the intention of the British Government to consider . . . any relaxation from the colonial system as an indulgence, to be granted on such terms as might suit the policy of Great Britain at the time, when it might be granted." In response, Congress voted to close U.S. ports to retaliate against British restrictions on American trade.

The administration also attempted to extend the nation's claims in continuing boundary disputes in the Texas area, Maine, the Great Lakes, and Oregon, although little progress was made. Clay had been a strong advocate of a more aggressive posture, especially with regards to Texas, arguing that the Sabine boundary line was too close to "our great western mart." In other areas, the administration supported the Greek independence movement, which in turn foreclosed overtures to the Ottoman Empire. Also in 1825, the administration was approached by influential Central Americans about the possibility of a Nicaraguan canal. Clay, however, stressed caution, and the idea was abandoned since money could not be raised for such a venture.

The administration reaffirmed its commitment to the Monroe Doctrine, but in several instances, Latin American nations seeking some assurance of support against possible foreign intervention received only vague replies or evasions. Instead, the United States pushed for a diplomatic offensive to get the Spanish to recognize the independence of its former colonies. American administrations—before and after John Quincy Adams—focused on one special Spanish possession, Cuba. Jefferson and Madison had both quietly supported annexation at one time or another, and Monroe's cabinet discussed the possibility at some length. On that island, local nationalists with support from Mexico and Colombia were in revolt against the Spanish New World empire, while the U.S. publicly counseled moderation. Meanwhile, the more adventurous liberator Simon Bolivar was calling for a confederation of states to further hemispheric emancipation and deter European interference and imperialism.

Many of Adams's initiatives reflected a continuity with his Republican predecessors in the area of foreign policy. Indeed, in his earlier years, Adams had been one of the most articulate spokesmen for an aggressive continental vision, which would have the United States stretch across from one ocean to another as a single and powerful republic. Jackson and especially James K. Polk were to some extent heirs of that early vision.[83]

Despite his successes in foreign policy, Adams received little public credit for his efforts. By the time of his bid for reelection, he had declining popular support against a very powerful and appealing opponent. Jackson, the winner of the Battle of New Orleans, became a vivid democratic hero in a period with a rapidly expanding electorate. Actually, the stern, imperious Jackson had compiled a record as a brave, but headstrong military man, a rich cotton planter who was a supporter of slavery, states' rights, and sound money, and an opponent of relief laws for debtors.

Ironically, Adams had been a strong supporter of Jackson especially in the controversies during the Monroe years arising from his 1818 movement into Florida. And Jackson had a high regard for Adams, even welcoming his disputed election at first. But it was Clay's support for Adams and the president-elect's naming of the Kentuckian as secretary of state that thoroughly soured Jackson. After his friends and aides used the cries of a corrupt bargain between Adams and Clay to focus public indignity, Jackson came to believe those charges himself.

Throughout Adams's term, Van Buren and his associates used every occasion to embarrass and ridicule his actions. In 1826, they called Adams a spoilsman and sought to investigate in the Senate his use of executive patronage. Actually, despite the law governing tenure of federal officials, Adams only made twelve removals, all for substantial cause. The congressional elections in 1826 resulted in both houses being controlled by majorities hostile to the administration, further frustrating Adams. In the House of Representatives, the brilliant and erratic John Randolph of Roanoke focused the opposition efforts on alleged examples of waste of public funds. Randolph's animosity extended back to John Quincy's father, and he bragged that he brought down "John the First" and he would do the same for the "dynasty of John the Second."[84]

Adams was attacked for corruption, the bargain with Clay, abuse of patronage, making West Point into a rich man's club, allegedly opposing the Louisiana Purchase, ceding Texas to the Spanish, even buying an expensive table out of White House funds. The partisan newspapers attacked each other mercilessly. One editor, Thomas L. Arnold of the *Daily National Journal*, charged Jackson was a man who spent "the prime of his life in gambling, in cock-fighting, in horseracing and has all his life been a most bloody duelist; and to cap all his frailties he tore from a husband the wife of his bosom, to whom he had been for years united in the holy state of matrimony." Jackson had married his wife Rachel after both thought her divorce was final, but it turned out the divorce was not granted properly. Of all the vitriolic attacks launched on Jackson, there was none he so resented as those on his wife, and when she died of natural causes after the election, he never forgave those who attempted to assassinate her character. Still other opponents spread the rumor that the general's mother, whose memory he loved dearly, was a prostitute who had married a black man. The Jacksonians had an editor equal to the tone of the times, Duff Green of the *United States Telegraph*, who was tagged by Adams as "the prince of slanderers." And another editor in New Hampshire charged that John Quincy Adams, while minister to Russia, had provided a pretty Boston girl to satisfy the sexual appetites of Czar Alexander I.[85]

The one divisive issue that was to prove most significant later—slavery—was avoided by both candidates. Jackson, who was a slaveowner, shared in the profits of that way of life, but he did not want to alienate the Republicans in the North by coming out boldly in favor of its aggrandizement. Adams, who was to be later a bitter critic of slavery, did not at this time choose to denounce the evil either.

Meanwhile in New York, another controversy arose unexpectedly. The Anti-Mason movement brought strong public censure on the Masonic Order after the abduction and murder of William Morgan, a brick and stone mason who had exposed the secrets of the group. Adams was not a Mason, but Jackson was, and the national notoriety of the order spilled over into the campaign.[86]

The election of 1828 was decided in the large states of New York and Pennsylvania where Jacksonians chanted their powerful slogan, "Jackson and Reform." In the end, the general carried Pennsylvania and the western and southern regions. Adams won New England, New Jersey, Delaware, six of eleven electoral votes in Maryland, and sixteen of New York's votes, helped in part by the Anti-Masonic vote. Jackson, however, swept the electoral college 178 to 83 with a margin of 647,276 to 508,064 in the popular vote. Adams attributed the victory to sectional disagreements, and he observed later that people generally supported internal improvements until the South fell under the spell of states' rights and nullification. To the surprise of some, Jackson was to prove that he, too, shared in John Quincy Adams's intense commitments to the Union when Southern secessionist sentiment moved toward the brink.

John Quincy Adams, like his father, had been a dedicated public servant, but also like his father he lacked the ability to weld national policies to popular discontents and aspirations. The Hero of New Orleans did to the son what the Sage of Monticello did to his father. They created myths larger than themselves and sold them to the changing populace as their birthright. John Quincy Adams had hoped to create a personal political base that rested on a pronounced sense of nonpartisanship and nationalistic vision. He took his weaknesses—the lack of a party label and strong partisan appeal—and hoped to turn those into assets. But the days of presidents being above parties were over. The Age of Jackson was not the Age of Washington.

The Jeffersonians thus took the earlier model of the presidency and changed it by making it both less remote and more consequential. Jefferson and his ideological allies laid aside much of the pomp of office that Washington and Adams believed was so necessary to add stature to the unformed position. Their constituents were the "new men" of the republic— the rugged Westerner, the yeoman, the artisan, but not the patrician class from which the Republic's earliest leaders, including the Jeffersonian elite, so often came. But in day-to-day activities, the Jeffersonian presidents often intruded themselves in indirect ways into the legislative branch using their like-minded colleagues in the cabinet and in Congress to create and enact a Republican agenda. And having considerable experience in foreign policy, they were under no illusions that diplomacy and open deliberations go hand in hand. They were more at home in the world of European court diplomacy than they would dare admit. There was not a Wilsonian among them. Much of their foreign policy was conducted by special emissaries making secret agreements arrived at behind closed doors. Congress, controlled by Republican majorities, generally accepted broad delegations of authority to the executive and received little information at least until John Quincy Adams's term. Jackson would strip away many of the old subtleties, communicating directly and boldly with the people and openly challenging friend and foe alike.

4

The Jacksonians: The Common Man and Manifest Destiny (Jackson, Van Buren, William Henry Harrison, Tyler, and Polk)

Sometimes it seems that the Federalists and the Republicans would have their partisans believe that the very directions of the earth depended on how completely their opinions prevailed. There surely were differences in policies, philosophies, and views of the ideal republic and the dangers of the outside world. But in many ways, there was a continuity that reflected the general homogeneity of the Founding Fathers. Jackson, however, was a very different sort of man, one who terrified Federalist descendants and elicited leery reviews from older Jeffersonian Democrats.

Jefferson had heard Jackson's name in connection with Burr's schemes. The Sage of Monticello concluded that Jackson was, at the very least, not dependable, and while his colleagues Madison and Monroe acknowledged the exploits of the man who became the Hero of New Orleans, one of the few American generals who ever won a definitive victory in the War of 1812, they too had reservations. As noted, Monroe actually had presided over cabinet discussions as to whether to discipline Jackson for his actions in Florida, and it was his secretary of state, John Quincy Adams, who defended the headstrong military leader. As for Jackson, he had strong views about some of his predecessors. He had criticized Washington and Adams for what he felt was their abuse of office. He thought that Washington had grasped after power and often exercised authority that he was not constitutionally invested with; in fact, Jackson had proposed that Washington be impeached for his attempts to influence the passage of the Jay Treaty. As for Adams, Jackson suggested that he was guilty of violating constitutional liberties. Jackson said of Jefferson that he was "the best Republican in theory and the worst in practice."[1]

But even beyond all that, Andrew Jackson by the sheer drama of his personality came to be considered a national figure, and from 1824 to 1828, a systematic campaign was waged to gain him the White House and to discredit Adams and Clay in the process. But Jackson was a strange choice considering the state of the presidency at the time. The chief executive position had gone into a period of nonpartisanship and general decline. Jefferson had been somewhat successful in creating a presidency that was deeply enmeshed for over six years in the daily operations of Congress and in promoting the Republican party on both the national and state levels. As has been seen, Jefferson was a superb behind the scenes operator, but his talents were sorely tried by the embargo, and his successor, Madison, was never able to exercise the level of leadership that one would have expected considering his previous successes in legislative bodies. Monroe substituted a patina of good feelings publicly while his own cabinet members attacked each other, and the second Adams tried to make his absence of a party base into a public virtue.

The Jacksonian model of the presidency was so very different. Jackson was a product and a promoter of a plebiscite democracy. No president before and probably no president until Franklin D. Roosevelt so directly appealed to the people over and over again. The general did not use surrogates as the Jeffersonians did to deal with controversies or to prod Congress into action. He confronted the great disputes of his time, personalized them, and drew the restive farmers, frontiersmen, and artisans into his orbit. He regarded his elections and congressional elections in off years as personal votes of confidence, and he drew his inspiration and power from the approval of the people—in a way that would seem alien if not undignified to his predecessors and most of his successors in the nineteenth century.

Obviously then, the Jacksonian model was unique from what had gone before. In its strongest expression under General Jackson, it was characterized by a plebiscite view of democracy, a strong affirmation of limited national government, an activist presidency, and an aggressive, expansionist foreign policy. Unlike the Federalists who maintained a judicious separation from Congress, and the Jeffersonians who provided leadership of the legislature in an informal, guileful way through associates, the Jacksonians were not apologetic about direct intrusions into the legislative branch when they regarded them as warranted.

Van Buren and Polk were surely less aggressive than the general, but they lived off his refracted glory, and off his political capital and great popular appeal. Jackson imagined he had a special and personal relationship with the common people, and all exaggeration aside, he did indeed. He was the first president to urge abolition of the electoral college because it was undemocratic, the first to use the veto not just because of constitutional scruples but on matters of public policy, the first to exploit unashamedly patronage to reward the faithful, and the first to engage in public campaigns to rally directly the people. Not until Theodore Roosevelt would a president so robustly use the office, not until Franklin D. Roosevelt would the chief executive become so identified with popular hopes and democratic resentments.

The explosive style of Andrew Jackson was like gasoline poured on the fires of that period of democratic expansion. The 1830s was an epoch of major economic changes, social upheavals and reform movements, a passionate reaffirmation of tariff protectionism, and a strident form of American nationalism. Jackson was a product and also a promoter of those sentiments. He embodied them, he advocated them, he furthered their impetus. And his closest associate Martin Van Buren, the new type of political man, saw that the old parties based on deference and republican tradition were no longer viable vehicles for the movement that he followed and eventually led.

THE JACKSONIAN PERSONALITY

To Jackson's foes, he was an illiterate, ignorant, harsh, and vindicative man. One senator, Elijah Hunt Mills, judged that the general was only "a little advanced in civilization over the Indians with whom he made war."[2]

At times, he seemed to be a man possessed of only one genuine emotion—undifferentiated anger. But to his allies and friends, Jackson was a mythic man who exemplified the true strengths of democratic America. Andrew Jackson was born in Waxhaw, South Carolina, in 1767, and at the age of fourteen he fought alongside adults against the British during the Revolutionary War. He and his brother were captured, and when they refused to clean the boots of a redcoat officer, they were both slashed by his sword. They were later imprisoned and caught smallpox, from which Jackson's brother died. In 1781, his mother who had been nursing prisoners at Charleston caught a fever and died as well. For forty years he unsuccessfully searched for her grave. All he had left were the memories of her last words, "Andy . . . never tell a lie, nor take what is not your own, nor sue . . . for slander. *Settle them cases yourself.*"[3]

Like many individuals plagued by insecurity, Jackson came to exude a public sense of incredible self-confidence and firmness. He grew in wealth and influence, becoming a military hero and slaveowner on the American frontier. As late as 1821, he dismissed the idea of being president by observing, "Do they think that I am such a demented fool as to think myself fit for the president of the United States? No, sir; I know what I am fit for. I can command a body of men in a rough way; but I am not fit to be president." But because of the controversy of 1824–25, Jackson felt he was cheated out of the office, and so did a good number of Americans. His behavior began to change; by his mid-fifties, he had curtailed his famous temper. Jackson was either mellowing or had realized that his political ambitions required a more moderate public posture. When he arrived in Washington in 1824, he observed to a friend, "Many do indeed believe me unfit for civil life; and many here, strangers to me, had expected, I believe, to see a most uncivilized, unchristian man when they beheld me." Instead, observers saw a lean, tall, almost ascetic-looking gentleman, slightly stooped over, and personally courteous to a fault. He even patched up old rivalries, most importantly with Thomas Hart Benton of Missouri whose bullet from an early duel was embedded for years in Jackson's body.

Throughout his career, he personalized differences and saw conspiracies all around him. Once when informed he violated international law in Florida, he cursed the scholarly authorities, "Damn Grotius! Damn Pufendorf! Damn Vattel! This is a mere matter between Jim Monroe and myself." One obvious reason for his irritability was probably bad health, which would fray anyone's nerves. He suffered from chronic diarrhea and indigestion, had tuberculosis, rheumatism, and bouts of migraines. Until 1832, he carried Benton's bullet in his left arm and a ball in his chest, which rested close to his heart. This harsh warrior, though, was a true and kind companion and a devoted family man.

He had an incredible hold over the masses, being seen as a glorious military hero and a romantic spirit of the age. He fought duels of honor, killed Indians, beat the British and Spanish, and stood strong and straight. His nickname, "Old Hickory," summed it up best. As no other president, he was identified as a man of courage and audacity. At the age of sixty-eight, he was attacked by a would-be assassin carrying two pistols. The president charged forward with only a cane to fight off the miscreant. No one ever accused Jackson of being a superb and subtle democratic thinker, but he was not the ignorant savage he was portrayed to be by his enemies. His state paper against South Carolina's nullification is equal to Lincoln's logic and Webster's eloquence on the same topic.

Jackson's political philosophy might be summarized as entailing a simple faith in the people, majority rule, limited government, a Jeffersonian respect for states' rights, opposition to "class legislation," a distrust of banks and middlemen, and a profound commitment to the preservation of the Union. One scholar, Albert Somit, has noted that Jackson was different from most Jeffersonians in three ways. He emphasized the direct relationships between economic interests and political action, and brought that issue into the campaigns. He emphasized a social conception of government's obligations to the people, and he expanded the Democratic party's appeal to the masses, especially the nascent urban dwellers. This in the 1830s was remarkable.[4]

Jackson's major biographer, Robert V. Remini, has concluded that the candidate rode to victory on a wave of public indignation about alleged political corruption. There were numerous instances of fraud involving banks, especially the branches of the Bank of the United States, and many congressmen took money from corporations that wanted favorable legislation passed. In the Senate, Thomas Hart Benton started an investigation of the Office of Indian Trade within the War Department amid charges of improprieties; the conclusions exposed a swindle against both the Indians and the federal government. Other departments, it was also charged, were riddled with graft, bribery, and kickbacks. To add to the administration's problem was James Monroe's decision to borrow personally $5,000 from businessman John Jacob Astor and his rescinding of a previous order prohibiting foreigners from engaging in the fur trade—seen by some as a quid pro quo.

The allies of Crawford especially went after the enlarged War Department, headed by rival John C. Calhoun, and sought to cut the army from twelve thousand to six thousand men.[5] Calhoun was also hurt by the so-called Yellowstone Expedition, when the secretary and Monroe threw good money after bad to support an expedition going up the Missouri River. The contracts had gone to the brother of a Calhoun's ally in Kentucky, Colonel Richard M. Johnson. Still another contract of $300,000 was given by Calhoun's chief clerk to his brother-in-law for supply stores in the construction of Fortress Monroe. In addition, there was criticism of Calhoun's chief enemy in the cabinet, Secretary of Treasury William Crawford, for the handling of money received from the sale of public lands. Even Secretary of State John Quincy Adams was accused of being influenced by New England insurance interests in his negotiations of the Florida treaty. Thus, the whole cabinet seemed to be under scrutiny for misconduct.

Part of the talk about corruption was directly due to the intense cabinet jockeying for the right to succeed Monroe. His era of good feelings provided the veil behind which men of inordinate ambition promoted vicious attacks on each other and conveyed the overall impression of widespread corruption, malfeasance and general disarray. From Jackson's point of view, they had already robbed him of the presidency once in 1824, and he was not surprised at any charges levied at them.

THE FORCE OF DEMOCRACY

Swept up in the tidal wave of "Jackson and Reform" and aided by the machinations of a new generation of professional politicians such as Van Buren, the aging general came into the White House as the people's choice. Deprived of the love of his wife who died after the bitter election, Jackson emerged in the public eye as even more of a solitary and courageous man, dressed in the very color of mourning. For that period, he was to form an extraordinary and at times personal attachment to the people and they to him.

Early on, Jackson let it be known that he wanted strict economy in government, a liquidation of the national debt, a "judicious" tariff, and a distribution of the budget surplus on the basis of representation to promote education and internal improvements. The key word in the Jackson lexicon was "reform." The administration saw itself as a period of cleansing after an era of corruption. Daniel Webster caustically remarked, "Persons have come five hundred miles to see General Jackson, *and they really seem to think that the country is rescued from some dreadful danger!*"[6]

The inaugural itself reflected those initial feelings as Jackson opened up the "president's palace," and people of all classes pressed into the house. Justice Joseph Story concluded, "The reign of KING MOB seemed triumphant." Barrels of orange punch were laid out, but as the mob rushed forward and pails of liquor fell to the floor, fixtures were broken, and china and glassware were smashed. Men with muddy boots stood on the fine furniture in order to see the famed general better. For his safety, Jackson was ushered out of the house, and he spent the night at Gadsby's Tavern. In a different tone, the *Argus of Western America* wrote on March 18, 1829, "General Jackson is *their own* president. Plain in his dress, venerable in his appearance, unaffected and familiar in his manners, he was greeted by them with an enthusiasm which bespoke him the Hero of a popular triumph."[7]

Jackson started his administration with a call for some changes in the distribution of patronage. He was confident that "rotation in office will perpetuate our liberty." In that way he would weed out corruption and prevent the growth of an "official aristocracy." Or as one of Van Buren's allies in New York, William L. Marcy, in the Senate summarized it all shorn of any philosophical pretense, "To the victor belong the spoils of the enemy." An anti-Jacksonian critic however portrayed a different picture, "The government formerly served by the *elite* of the nation, is now served, to a considerable extent, by its refuse."[8]

The president's focus was a little different. He told one associate early in his first term, "Assure my friends we are getting on here *well*, we labour night and day, and will continue to do so, until we destroy all the rats, who have been plundering the Treasury." Within a year of taking office, the administration discovered that some $280,000 had been stolen from the Treasury Department alone—a further proof of the corruption of the previous government. This was another indictment of the educated, trained elite that Jackson so hated, people "who are on the scent of Treasury pap. And if I had a *tit* for every one of these pigs to suck at they would still be my friends." While the president did insist that in a democracy "no one man has any more intrinsic right to official station than another," there were very few dismissals of incumbent officials—about 10 percent of the total over eight years.

Jackson's biographer Remini has concluded that with the combined episodes of misconduct involving Indian affairs, army and navy contracts, and the operations of the Bank of the United States, the previous period is more aptly called the "Era of Corruption" rather than the "Era of Good Feelings." Surely, if one compares the Monroe-Adams era to the corruptions of the Grant, Harding, Truman, or Reagan years, there is little fault. But coming as it did after the comparatively pristine Federalist and early Jeffersonian presidencies, there was surely some moral slippage during the Monroe-Adams period. However, what made Jackson also susceptible later to criticism on his choices was his overall poor record for judging candidates for major offices and his selection to his cabinet of men of very limited ability. His crusade against corruption, for example, was hurt by a very bad appointment of his own, the collector of the Port of New York, Samuel Swartwout, who vanished to Europe with over $1.2 million.[9]

His bad judgment was especially apparent in his choice of John Eaton as secretary of war, and the president's persistent defense in almost total defiance of Washington society of Eaton's wife's honor. The circle of petticoat gossip had branded Peggy Eaton a woman of loose morals and had turned a collective cold shoulder to her. Jackson, perhaps remembering the nasty mess that preceded his own wife's death, defended Mrs. Eaton with a blind vigor and demanded that his cabinet officers and their wives show their loyalty to him by opening up their hearts and homes to the secretary's wife. Only Van Buren was shrewd enough to comply, and his flexibility moved him closer to the general's affections. Calhoun did not follow suit, and soon in Jackson's eyes he was even more suspect for his disloyalty to the president. Later, after the nullification crisis precipitated by South Carolina, the vice president was displaced in the Jackson official family.

JACKSON AND UNION

In his first term, Jackson's slogan became in his own eyes a mandate—"retrenchment and economy." In foreign policy, he was like his Republican predecessors, a strong nationalist bent on expansion. However, Jackson was at times more aggressive, at least in tone, and he was especially committed to Indian removal and driving the Spanish out of North America—two causes he had been identified with in his earlier public career. In addition, Jackson initially desired to annex Texas, an area excluded from U.S. possession because of the boundaries Jefferson accepted when he took over the Louisiana Territory. Only later in office, did Jackson seem to have second thoughts about the timing. For the next several decades, most of the Democratic party would be committed to bringing the Texas republic into the Union. Jackson told Van Buren he would push for $5 million from Congress to buy the territory in order to keep any foreign power from gaining control of the Mississippi and New Orleans. He concluded that the "god of the universe had intended this great valley to belong to one nation."[10]

Jackson also wanted to move the frontier border in order to acquire more land to relocate Indians living east of the Mississippi. His argument was that a natural and accepted boundary would promote amity between the two groups. But his minister to Mexico, Joel Poinsett of South Carolina, was inept and heavy-handed in the way he proposed the purchase, and the Mexican government demanded his recall. In addition, the Creeks and Cherokees did not accept Jackson's logic that relocation was a humane alternative to the inevitable annihilation that would result if they stayed where they were. The policy of the government, he blandly announced, was to introduce to Indians the ways of civilization and lead them away from nomadic wanderings to a happy and comfortable life.

Jackson also respected limited government, individual initiative, and states' rights. But his definition of the last excluded any acknowledgment of the right to nullify federal laws or to advocate secession. The president swore that he would rather die in the last ditch than have the Union dismantled. In the Senate the godlike Daniel Webster, as he was called, challenged Robert Y. Hayne in a monumental debate that started with a discussion of public lands and concluded with questions about the very nature of the Union. Webster's words could have been Jackson's, and they were to be Lincoln's sentiments, "I go for the Constitution as it is, and for the Union as it is. It is, Sir, the people's Constitution, the people's government, and answerable to the people."

Then, at a Jefferson Day dinner, the president and Vice President Calhoun headed up the Democratic delegation. The president added to the tension with his toast, "Our Union. *It must be* preserved." Calhoun's response was quick, "The Union. Next to our liberty, the most dear." Neither sentiment was radical, but soon the dinner became the occasion of drawing a line in the dust between Jackson and Calhoun adherents. A delighted Van Buren noted prophetically, "The veil was rent."[11]

Previously, Calhoun and his friends in South Carolina had staked out their position against the "tariff of abominations," which had not been repealed after Jackson's election. They asserted the right of states to nullify federal laws if need be, to interpose their state government between the federal government and the citizens of the state. One could trace that tradition to the Kentucky and Virginia resolutions and to the Hartford convention and the opposition in New England to the War of 1812, and now it became the political theory of the slaveholders' most accomplished theorists.[12]

Jackson's position was clear—there could be no secession from the Union, and he warned his friends in South Carolina that if a single drop of blood were shed by those opposing federal laws, he would find out who was responsible and have them hanged. Seeking to succeed Calhoun as vice president and to show support for the president, Van Buren had the New York Democratic party pass a resolution advocating a second term for Jackson. John Quincy Adams, however, claimed that Van Buren had generally misunderstood the Jefferson dinner confrontation. But Amos Kendall, closer to Jackson than Adams, concluded, "Van Buren glides along as smoothly as oil and as silently as a cat." Additionally, Jackson learned that in the Monroe administration, Calhoun as secretary of war had not supported him in the Florida invasion, and had pushed for his arrest and punishment. Consequently, Jackson pronounced Calhoun "the most profound hypocrite he had ever known."[13]

When Congress returned in December 1829, the president was able to make another statement of his political philosophy by vetoing a bill to extend the National Road from Maysville to Lexington, Kentucky. Jackson opposed spending federal funds for obviously local public works projects, even though he was warned that a veto would hurt his party in the West and gain adherents for Clay. But Jackson concluded that the "great body of the people hail the act [his veto], as a preservative of the constitution & the union." Fearful that internal improvement bills would lead to hasty appropriations, corrupt elections, and a general decline of civic virtue, Jackson vetoed the Washington Turnpike bill, measures for building lighthouses and beacons, and a proposal for dredging harbors. He also stopped a bill to purchase stock in the Louisville and Portland Canal Company. His use of the veto restored presidential power and reaffirmed the office as a separate branch of government. In addition, Jackson became the first president to use the "pocket" veto, whereby the executive can kill a bill by simply not signing it when Congress has already adjourned.

Jackson was a soldier and a patriot, but one of his greatest claims to fame was his history as an Indian fighter. He was bold, ferocious, and brutal, and no president including Grant with his terrible campaigns has been so cavalier in meting out death to his opponents. His philosophy of human liberty and laissez faire was meant for white men only; as for the Indians, he was insistent that they be driven to remote areas west of the Mississippi River. Jefferson had originally proposed removal of Indians unwilling to assimilate. But Jackson did not flinch from the consequences of a policy of confrontation.

In Congress, considerable opposition arose to Jackson's proposal to eject the Indians in the South. But on May 28, 1830, the Indian Removal Act passed the legislative branch, and Jackson assumed he had approval to press on. The president had publicly vowed that no Indian would be forced to leave, but he soon abandoned that guarantee. The apostle of economy and retrenchment proceeded to advocate a removal policy that cost the government an astronomical $68 million and 32 million U.S.-controlled acres west of the Mississippi River in order to gain 100 million acres of coveted Indian lands.

Friends of the Indians, however, went to court to protect their interests, and they hired William Wirt, a constitutional lawyer of national renown. Jackson seemed to be taken aback at the lack of confidence the Indians had in his leadership and protection. He warned that the Indians could refuse to leave, but then they would be subject to the laws and harsh devices of the states. Jackson played the role of solicitous great white father to the hilt, and initially the Indians tried to appeal to his paternalistic instincts, but they soon learned that they would have to resort to other strategies to guard their lands. Jackson stood firm and concluded, "I have exonerated the national character and now leave the poor deluded Creeks and Cherokees to their fate, and then annihilation, which their wicked advisors has induced."[14]

The Choctaws finally ceded to the United States 10.5 million acres of land east of the Mississippi River. Their removal was a chronicle of corruption, theft, and mismanagement, which led to the near destruction of that tribe. Even Jackson was shocked when he learned of their extensive sufferings, and he sought to establish new policies to govern future removals. In fact, the brutal treatment of the tribes was a logical outcome of Jackson's support for a wholesale removal policy devoid of humanitarian treaty commitments. In

1832, treaties were signed with the Creeks, Seminoles, and Chickasaws. Only the Cherokees refused to join the exodus.

But that tribe finally exhausted all levels of appeal as well. In 1831, Chief Justice Marshall, writing for the Supreme Court, found the Indians to be "domestic dependent nations" subject to the authority of the United States but not that of the states. The Court in a second case found the Georgia laws regulating the tribes unconstitutional. Georgia refused to accept the verdict, and Jackson is supposed to have said that "Marshall made the decision, now let him enforce it." Whether the president made that statement is unclear, but it surely expressed his general views that Georgia could not be forced to obey that particular decision. Also at that time Jackson had taken on one state, South Carolina, in the nullification controversy, and did not need a second confrontation. In December 1835, the Cherokees signed a treaty for the exchange of lands. Jackson's forceful behavior had again prevailed, and the near genocidal consequences of his policies remain a commentary on the darker side of his presidency.

As Jackson faced increasing difficulties, he began to tighten his control over the Democratic party and the cabinet. He replaced the *United States Telegraph* editor Duff Green with Francis P. Blair who would head up a new party organ. Blair's *The Globe* was clearly a Jacksonian paper, and its motto reflected those laissez faire economic views, "The world is governed too much." The president also began to focus on the abolition of the Bank of the United States, and his newspaper organ followed suit. Jackson and some of his closest advisors had come to see the bank as a monopolistic threat to liberty, a monster lined up against decent working people. In his private letters and communications and in his annual message to Congress, he expressed varying sentiments of disapproval.

In the Senate, Benton presented his views in a sharp debate with bank supporter and Senator Daniel Webster. Bank advocates reassured the president of the Bank of the United States that Jackson, after huffing and puffing, would still sign the bank's renewal bill. But Benton knew the general better; Jackson, he wrote, "aims at the destruction of the Bank." The administration's opponents were also startled by Jackson's sudden announcement that he would run for a second term despite his earlier protestations. When attempts at a reconciliation between the president and Calhoun failed, Van Buren's star rose—the heir apparent was coming into view.[15]

In the midst of this controversy, Van Buren offered his resignation as secretary of state; his initiative gave Jackson the opportunity to change other secretaries and thus purge his cabinet of disloyal members. Van Buren probably had not seen his gesture to help Jackson as being some sort of master stroke. But his resignation led to his departure from Washington and his subsequent nomination as minister to London. To humiliate him, his enemies eagerly blocked Senate approval. This action forced him to come back home, back to the vice presidency on Jackson's ticket!

The resignations and terminations in the cabinet startled the nation. Never before had a president engaged in wholesale dismissals. Clay called it a revolution and wondered, "Who could have imagined such a cleansing of the Augean stable in Washington? a change, almost total, of the Cabinet." As Remini has noted, the controversy reduced Democratic party loyalty to one question—are you for or against Andy Jackson? In that perspective, the party promoted freedom and the will of the majority, and Jackson alone represented the people. It was a giant step in transforming the limited republic of the Founding Fathers into a nineteenth-century plebiscite democracy.

Critics attacked this "executive tyranny," as they called it, and they denounced the growth of a personal coterie of advisors, which was tagged the "kitchen cabinet." Outside advisors such as Amos Kendall, William B. Lewis, Andrew Donelson, and Van Buren were seen as the real powers behind Jackson. The president had heard the accusations and dismissed them out of hand. He was, as his closest supporters knew, a strong executive who surrounded himself with a wide network of advisors, editors, friends, members of Congress, and regional party leaders.

THE MONSTER BANK

Jackson's strong-willed determination, however, is best seen in his epic battle against the Bank of the United States. Secretary of Treasury Louis McLane at first tried to push Jackson toward renewal of the bank's charter. Meanwhile, Clay garnered the Whig nomination and sought to use the bank issue in his coming campaign. He urged Nicholas Biddle, the bank's politically assertive president, to push for a recharter earlier than necessary in order to make it a campaign issue. Daniel Webster apparently concurred, and Biddle, fearing he would alienate his friends in Congress, agreed.

The president and his allies argued that the bank was "a monster"—a threat to liberty, and that it corrupted congressmen with easy loans and regular retainer fees. Jackson concluded that the bank's friends were attempting to kill him politically, but he instead would kill the monster. When he heard about the Senate vote supporting renewal, he roared, "By the Eternal! I'll smash them!" and smash them he did. Van Buren had counseled caution, as did other prominent Democrats, but the New Yorker realized that his fate was tied irrevocably to Old Hickory's moods.

Despite the popular presumption that Van Buren was the main advisor on the bank veto, Jackson mainly consulted Attorney General Roger B. Taney who had a long history of distrust of the national bank. When Biddle increased his public appearances and put political pressure on Congress, Jackson's darkest suspicions about the bank were confirmed. On June 1, 1832, the bill for recharter passed the Senate 28 to 20, and on July 3, the House of Representatives concurred 107 to 85. Like many Democrats from Jefferson on down, Jackson had reservations about the bank. But he saw the battle in a more passionate and personal way—as a direct threat to liberty and as a concentration of power in the hands of a few. "It is to be regretted that the rich and powerful too often bend the acts of the government to their selfish purposes," Jackson argued.[16]

With his veto, Jackson not only ended the hydra-headed bank, as it was called, he reasserted a presidency that had been dormant in many ways since Jefferson. In the past, presidents had used the veto only nine times total and usually for constitutional scruples. Jackson clearly was dealing with social and economic policy questions, and his veto was grounded in the laissez faire tradition of a minimal state and its fear of concentrated power.

In July, Webster openly attacked the president, arguing that "no president and no public man ever before advanced such doctrines in the face of the nation. There never was a moment in which any president would have been tolerated in asserting such a claim to despotic power." Clay added his own observation that Jackson's action was "a perversion of the veto power." When the pyrotechnics were over, Congress could not override it and the veto stood.[17]

Thus, the election of 1832 revolved around Jackson and the bank controversy. Amos Kendall became a sort of national campaign manager, and Francis Blair used his newspaper as an effective propaganda tool for the party. Biddle, for reasons known only to himself, not only reprinted Clay's and Webster's attacks, but also paid for thirty thousand copies of Jackson's original veto message. The bank president's activities only reaffirmed the Democrats' fears as to how the Bank of the United States could be used for partisan purposes.

Jackson's positions on executive power, patronage, the tariff, and internal improvements were all attacked by the Whigs. He had supported a more moderate tariff schedule, but not one that would satisfy the deep discontent in the South, especially in Calhoun's home state of South Carolina. The president was in many ways a states' rights and limited government man, but he despised the "nullifiers," as he called them. He believed that such people were simple traitors and should be hung. The president hoped that the dissension would quiet down, but he prepared for any emergency. He ordered that steps be taken to protect forts near Charleston, South Carolina. It was the beginning of what was to be later a long war of nerves between Jackson and nullifiers.

Armed with hickory sticks and Jackson's popularity, the Democrats prevailed in the election. The Whigs charged that the republic was being undone by "King Andrew I," but the masses did not seem to be swayed. The president won reelection by carrying the electorate 688,242 votes to Clay's 473,462, with the Anti-Mason candidate William Wirt and Independent Democrat John Floyd getting some scattered support. Jackson thus carried 55 percent of the popular vote and took 219 electoral votes to Clay's 49, Floyd's 11, and Wirt's 7. His base was the South (except South Carolina) and the West, although he did well in the Middle Atlantic states and carried Maine and New Hampshire in New England. Even though the election registered a clear Democratic triumph, the president's popular margin dropped by more than 1.5 percent—a rare occurrence for a second-term president. Still, his contemporaries saw his victory as a personal triumph over great, entrenched forces. It was a victory for "Jackson and Democracy," and Wirt concluded that the general might be "president for life if he chooses."[18]

THE PROGRESSION OF BATTLES

In his second term, Jackson had to confront directly the consequences of his bank veto and also the threat of secession. First, he moved to isolate South Carolina from Georgia. The latter state's leaders were prepared to defy the Supreme Court decision in the

Worcester case, which dealt with the Cherokees. As noted, Jackson and his supporters decided not to take on two recalcitrant states at once, and the Cherokees were told that they would have no support in federal quarters to fight removal, a policy Jackson supported anyhow.

Calhoun, with his brilliant conceptual mind and uneasy commitment to the Union, had proposed a full-blown theory of state nullification against federal legislation. To Jackson it was clear and unvarnished treason, but he was shrewd and bold in his handling of the crisis. In the process he won the support of many of his previous Whig enemies and lost the allegiance of some of the southern wing of the Democratic party.

The South Carolina legislature authorized a special convention, which passed an Ordinance of Nullification on November 24 that denounced the tariff laws of 1828 and 1832 as "null, void, and no law, nor binding" on that state. Jackson's public statements were strong, but he proceeded remarkably cautiously. First, he concentrated his forces on the harbor forts and avoided confronting the South Carolinians in installations on the mainland. He appealed to the people of South Carolina and to the moderates in the South, citing the advantages of Union. Jackson was clear: nullification was "incompatible with the existence of the Union, contradicted expressly by the letter of the Constitution, unauthorized by its spirit, inconsistent with every principle on which it was founded, and destructive of the great object for which it was formed." In language that Lincoln would echo a generation later, he argued, "I have no discretionary power on the subject; my duty is emphatically pronounced in the Constitution." Nullifiers and Unionists in South Carolina took up arms, but no abrupt actions were taken, although it was clear that tensions were rising in Charleston.[19]

Meanwhile, the president pushed for a revision of tariff schedules, which was introduced in the House of Representatives on June 8, 1833. Jackson insisted on a Force Bill, which would give him the power to close any port of entry and open others. Brilliantly the president would force the nullifiers to go out of their way to resist the government if they so dared. Jackson noted that the federal government's law of 1792 (amended in 1795) already gave the president the right to call up the state militia and to use federal ships and troops when its authority was challenged.[20]

Unlike in the secession movement in 1860–61, slavery was not an issue, and many Southern moderates were willing to support the

Unionist sentiments of Jackson. The progress of the tariff reform bill also helped to cut the ground from under the nullifiers when Clay and Calhoun agreed on a compromise. Webster challenged Calhoun's arguments and defended the president and the Union, as the Senate supported the Force Bill 32 to 1 with some nullifiers walking out. The president was obviously less concerned with the tariff rates than with the turmoil in South Carolina, but he did insist that the Force Bill had to pass before the tariff bill. It was a matter of principle to him. South Carolina nullifiers repealed their ordinance in part because of Jackson's stand and also because of the tariff reductions. In addition, the support they expected in the Southern states did not materialize. Prophetically Jackson warned, "The next pretext will be the negro, or slavery question."

Wherever he went, Jackson generated intense emotions. On one occasion, he was struck by a naval lieutenant, Robert B. Randolph, who was dismissed from service on Jackson's orders for theft; later the president was fired on by a would-be assassin who missed his target and was nearly caned by an angry Jackson. In 1833, the president decided to emulate his successors and undertake a tour of New England. Remarkably he was greeted with generally enthusiastic crowds, and he was seen as a true nationalist—which indeed he was. He acknowledged the cheers, charmed the ladies, and kissed some babies. One critic described it as "The degeneracy of the age in taste, feelings and principles." Jackson mixed freely with the crowds and in New York City, he bluntly declared, "Nullification will never take root HERE." One newspaper in Connecticut concluded that he seemed like a father surrounded by his happy children, the type of image Jackson loved.[21]

To the chagrin of the Brahmin caste, he received an honorary degree from Harvard College. Alumnus John Quincy Adams called it a disgrace to confer such honors "upon a barbarian who could not write a sentence of grammar and hardly could spell his own name." Legend has it that the president accepted the degree, which was conferred in Latin, and responded "Ex post facto; e pluribus unum; sic semper tyrannis; quid pro quo." Whether he did string together such common expressions, mattered little. He had conquered New England without firing a shot. Even a disgusted Adams had to conclude, "And so ends this magnificent tour."[22]

Jackson was rather ill at the end of his grand tour, but he once again recovered, ready to do battle with his enemies. Uppermost in his mind was the need to finish off the hydra-headed monster bank.

After some hesitation, he dismissed his secretary of treasury, William J. Duane, who refused to cooperate in removing the government's deposits from Biddle's institution. This firing marked the first time a president had dismissed a Senate-confirmed cabinet officer, and the question came up did the president have the right to remove him unilaterally. Replacing Duane with Roger Taney of Maryland, Jackson prepared to sign an order on October 1 that would place all future government deposits in selected state banks and use the remaining funds in the Bank of the United States to pay operating expenses. Originally, there were to be twenty-two selected banks in 1833, by 1836 over ninety were added to the system, all friendly to the Democratic party and Jacksonian ideology, causing them to be labeled by critics "pet banks."

Biddle moved to curtail loans throughout the system and squeeze especially the Western banks and economy. His conclusion was simple, "This worthy president thinks that because he had scalped the Indians and imprisoned Judges, he is to have his way with the Bank. He is mistaken." Some Democrats who had supported Jackson on the veto now bucked on removing the deposits, but Jackson, with a single-minded determination that is rare in politics, pushed ahead fully confident in his cause and in popular sentiment.

The curtailment of credit led to a sharp recession and a new public outcry. Biddle's strategy was "nothing but the evidence of suffering abroad will produce any effect in Congress." If there were any doubt about the dangers of a centralized bank and the political arrogance of its operating officer, Biddle's very reactions proved the Jacksonians right.[23]

The president's major opposition, however, lay in the Senate where the forces of Webster, Clay, and Calhoun mobilized to check what they saw as executive usurpation. Jackson feared that Congress would pass a joint resolution ordering that public deposits must stay in the Bank of the United States. In the House, Jackson allies led by James K. Polk, fought a more evenhanded battle against the bank forces. In the Senate, Clay introduced a resolution asking for a copy of Jackson's statement that he had read to his cabinet members when he discussed the removal question with them. The resolution passed, and Jackson dismissed it out of hand as an inappropriate intrusion in the business of the executive branch. But Clay persisted and he offered two resolutions: the first censured Jackson for his dismissal of Duane and the removal of deposits, and the second concluded that Taney's explanation for the removal action was unsatisfactory. In the debates, Clay argued at length against Jackson's view that he was the real spokesman of the people. Webster and Calhoun followed with their own denunciations. It was at this time that Webster privately wrote Biddle asking that his customary "retainer" be "renewed or *refreshed* as usual."[24] As this controversy was occurring, labor violence broke out in Maryland on the Chesapeake and Ohio canal in January 1834. Jackson, in response to the appeals of state officials, sent the military to stop civil disorders, another precedent for this strong president. This was the first time troops were used where defiance of the federal government was not directly involved, and further charges were leveled against "King Andrew."

In his major preoccupation, Jackson and his closest followers not only sought to destroy the bank and remove U.S. deposits, but also demanded a return to specie money only. They wanted the deposit banks to stop issuing or receiving bank notes under five dollars. Thus silver and gold would flow. Jackson believed that specie would protect the laboring classes and end economic exploitation by the rich. The epic battle brought life back to the ailing general. One of his associates approvingly observed, "You would be surprised to see the General. This Bank excitement has restored his former energy, and gives him the appearance he had ten years ago." Senator Benton also noted that he "never saw him appear more truly heroic and grand than at this time. He was perfectly mild in his language, cheerful in his temper, firm in his conviction."[25]

The opposition to Jackson began calling itself the "Whigs" after the English coterie that had opposed the abuses of the king and his ministers. For the American Whigs, Jackson had abandoned the careful republican balance of the Founding Fathers for an increasingly plebiscite democracy. In the House, one congressman proposed a resolution of impeachment against the president. In the Senate, the Taney nomination was rejected 28 to 18, and on March 28, 1834, that body voted 26 to 20 to censure the president for having "assumed upon himself authority and power not conferred by the constitution and laws, but in derogation of both." Jackson responded with a formal protest reasserting the powers of the presidency and the sanctity of democracy. The resolution had stopped short of impeachment.

The Whigs attacked the idea of even accepting Jackson's statement for the record. Years later, Benton would move that the censure be wiped off the records of the Senate, and a more mellow upper body agreed to do so before Jackson's retirement from the White House. As for the Whigs, they were in the peculiar situation of denouncing Jackson's democratic theories while at the same time appealing to the very people Jackson so praised.

As the bank controversy mounted, the president called for mass meetings and conventions by which the public's views could be directed at Congress. One senator, Hugh Lawson White of Tennessee, concluded that as the years passed, Jackson "became more and more open and undisguised in his interference to influence and control public opinion." Meanwhile as economic problems mounted, criticism of the bank was heard even in business quarters.

On April 4, 1834, the House voted not to recharter the bank, or restore deposits in it, and to support instead the pet banks. When the House sent an investigating committee to Philadelphia to examine Biddle's books, he arrogantly refused to provide the information requested or even to testify before Congress. Jackson had won. Taney followed up with a revaluation of gold and the establishment of a full deposit system throughout the nation.

Jackson had delayed Taney's nomination as secretary of treasury fearing it would be defeated, which it eventually was. By the time congressional adjournment came, the president had a long list of appointees who were not confirmed, and he continued to have problems with the Senate. The Whigs denounced his "spoils system" and saw it as a mechanism to bring in the newly enfranchised masses. Jackson's views were simply that frequent rotation in office promoted democracy and that no person had a special right to hold office, tenets that added to this leveling impression.

Despite his own passionate expressions in favor of states' rights, Jackson strengthened the presidency and consequently the central government. To continue his policies, he anointed Van Buren as his successor, and the party named Richard Johnson of Kentucky as its nominee for vice president. Johnson was a controversial choice, but his supposed killing of the Indian chief Tecumseh added to his appeal.

To Jackson, the great issues in the campaign should be the issues of economics and democracy. But increasingly the matter of slavery was becoming important. As the American Anti-Slavery Society started sending its abolitionist tracts across the nation and especially into the South, slaveholding apologists in Washington, D.C., tried to censure the mails. Jackson stayed away from the controversy at first, but on December 7, 1835, he asked Congress to enact legislation to prohibit the sending of "incendiary publications" to the South. Calhoun and his allies in Congress went further and demanded a law forbidding abolitionist material in any state or territory where local law prohibited it.

Jackson's second term also saw more successes. The Cherokees finally accepted $5 million for all their lands east of the Mississippi, which totaled approximately seven million acres. The president turned a deaf ear to the pleas of his "red children" and he warned that without removal, the Indians would be extinguished. They could not live side by side with "a civilized community." The treaty was approved by a Cherokee vote of 79 to 7, showing how few Indians chose to vote. Later, fourteen thousand Cherokees signed a petition opposing the treaty, but after a long debate in the Senate, the treaty was ratified there by a single vote. Removal was to take place within two years of the ratification date, May 23, 1838. The Indians were finally rounded up, forced into prison camps, and removed in what was to be called "The Trial of Tears." Some eighteen thousand Cherokees were displaced, of whom four thousand died in the process.

The Creeks were not treated much better. Their lands were taken so fraudulently that even Jackson was angry, and he ordered an investigation. But when the tribe took up arms in protest, the government sent in over ten thousand troops, and blood flowed on the frontier once again. Over 14,600 Creeks were removed in the summer and fall of 1836. The same strategies were used against the Seminoles, and the president, an old Indian fighter in the First Seminole War, entered into the conflict with renewed zest when violence resulted. Jackson watched closely as the war continued, and his greatest regret was that the conflict was not won sooner. He was disgusted at the performance of the Floridians, hoping the Indians would kill them so that their "women might get husbands of courage, and breed up men who would defend the country." The war continued until 1842 and cost the government $10 million.

In the end, the five major Indian nations of the South—the Choctaw, Chickasaw, Creek, Cherokee, and Seminole—had been removed to the West. Elsewhere, the Indian tribes had been pushed from parts of Illinois, Michigan, Wisconsin, Iowa, Arkansas, Louisiana, Kentucky, Indiana, Ohio, Kansas, Minnesota and Nebraska. After eight years, over forty-five thousand Indians had been expelled beyond the Mississippi River. For $68 million and 32 million acres of western land, the United States gained control over 100 million acres of land—another massive expansion of the white democratic empire. Jackson's justification was that he had saved the Indians from extinction.[26]

OLD HICKORY'S FOREIGN POLICY

While Jackson may have seemed embroiled in domestic controversy, he was also interested in the role of the United States in the world. His primary concerns were to further American commercial interests and to assert vigorously national honor and pride. In general, Jackson's foreign policy was similar to his predecessor's policies, but unlike Adams, he combined bluster, unaccustomed patience, and often good timing to further rather successfully American causes. As the historian John M. Belohlavek has concluded, Jackson "eagerly pursued a policy of promoting commercial expansion, demanded worldwide respect for the American flag, restoring American prestige and national honor, and fostering territorial growth." Jackson believed in "Manifest Destiny," long before the term was coined, and championed U.S. control of the continent from the Atlantic to the Pacific Ocean.[27]

His foreign policy was plagued, however, by the uneven quality of his diplomatic personnel and by the quick rotation of public officials in and out of government. In two terms in office, Jackson had four secretaries of state and five secretaries of treasury. He reduced the once powerful cabinet to a group he rarely consulted, meeting with them only sixteen times in eight years and discussing foreign affairs at only six of those meetings. In its place grew up a "kitchen cabinet," a group of friends, confidants, and obscure partisan officeholders who advised the headstrong president. Jackson rode his subordinates on a tight rein, delegating little authority, and on one occasion even chastised a cabinet officer for appointing a clerk without his prior approval. As he once said, a cabinet officer was "merely an executive agent, a subordinate, and you may say so in self defense."[28]

The president and his various secretaries of state did agree on the need to reform the State Department and the consular service. Too few Washington officials supervised the nearly 140 consular posts, and incompetence and corruption were rampant in the consular service. But while the State Department was being reorganized, Congress neglected to increase its staff or its salary levels. Jackson worsened matters by some of his appointments. Most consuls were really commercial agents, and the president often appointed individuals whose skills revolved around party loyalty more than demonstrated competence.

In dealing with Europe, Jackson accepted the primary importance of maintaining good relations with England, despite his youthful conflicts with British officials. The president's policy objectives in Europe were to settle American claims against various nations for allegedly violating U.S. shipping rights during the Napoleonic Wars and to encourage commercial relations in the region. By 1836, U.S. exports increased by more than 75 percent and imports by 250 percent over the first year Jackson was in the White House. In the import-export balance, Britain was central to American commercial and shipping interests, and Jackson at times would overlook its policies and even bend the Monroe Doctrine a bit to accommodate that nation.

The administration focused on restoring the lucrative trade with the British West Indies. As talks on this subject moved slowly, a patient Jackson publicly saluted, "With Great Britain, distinguished alike in peace and war, we may look forward to years of peaceful, honorable, and elevated competition." After much deliberation, the nations agreed on a reciprocity agreement in 1830 that revoked the British Orders in Council of 1826 and allowed U.S. vessels to enter Canadian and West Indian ports provided they were trading only American goods. The president also agreed to arbitration on the Maine boundary question, but intense opposition from that state and partisan attacks led to the issue being unresolved until 1842 when the state of Maine accepted a much less advantageous settlement. Overall, Jackson exhibited a remarkable ability to compromise with the British, despite his reputation as an Anglophobe over the years.

In his dealings with Spain, the president was less successful especially in his primary objective—the reduction of duties with Cuba. The weakness of the Spanish government and upheaval in neighboring Portugal led to little progress as far as American interests were concerned. Elsewhere the administration also attempted to work out stronger commercial ties, especially in the Black Sea with the czarist regime. Unfortunately, the president sent to Russia John Randolph of Roanoke, the erratic former congressman, who on one occasion referred to the czar as "a genuine Cossack, implacable, remorseless and blood-thirsty." He left his post soon after being appointed and was replaced by James Buchanan who proved to be a superb minister and who concluded a favorable treaty in 1832.

Far more difficult was the administration's attempt to get the French government to pay millions of dollars owed to American shipowners and captains for violations of neutral rights during the Napoleonic Wars. During the pre-1812 period, Napoleon seized more than three hundred U.S. ships and cargo valued at over $7 million. Previous administrations had made little progress on the reparations issue, and Jackson had hoped that by settling with Denmark on similar claims, he might set a useful precedent for negotiations with the French and with the Kingdom of the Two Sicilies (southern Italy and Sicily). Some of Jackson's advisors urged him to resort to trade reprisals, but the president rejected that approach concluding, "I cannot recommend a war thro' the Customs House." But he did promise that if the French continued their recalcitrance, "You will find me speaking to Congress as I ought."[29]

As negotiations bogged down because of the continuing instability of French politics, the president got irritated and told his advisors, "I know them French. They won't pay unless they have to." Finally, the president decided that if the Chamber of Deputies did not authorize the funds to implement the treaty, he wanted congressional authorization to confiscate French ships and property in the United States.

In the Senate, the Whigs led by Clay had a field day thrashing the president for another manifestation of his autocratic inclinations when he asked for more money for fortifications. Most trying to Jackson, their ranks were augmented by many regular Democrats who resented his aggressive leadership. When the House approved a special fortifications bill, the Senate checked the proposal after massive rhetorical assaults by Webster and Clay. Clay argued that it was a blank check for the executive; Webster called it an excuse for seizing more power; another senator, Benjamin Leigh of Virginia, concluded that the nation would become a military monarchy, "They might as well say that the president should be made consul for life or Emperor of the American people." The measure was defeated by a margin of two to one.[30]

The French Chamber did approve the appropriations, but insisted on an amendment that demanded that Jackson explain the purpose of his critical remarks to Congress on the negotiations. The president, with some justification, regarded the request as insulting and a violation of his right to address a separate branch of his nation's

government. France should pay—"without apology or explanation,"
the president demanded. Yet Jackson resorted to moderation on the
matter. He refused to apologize, but indicated that he did not intend to "menace or insult the Government of France." The treaty
resulted in $7 million in claims payments and led to other agree-
ments with Naples, Spain, and Portugal. With a mixture of patience
and bluster, the administration had achieved an enviable record of
success where others had reaped only failure.

The president also submitted a commercial treaty with the Ottoman empire, which included a provision that would have had the
United States help rebuild the sultan's navy. The Senate rejected
the ship-building article, and several senators attacked the president
for appointing commissioners without that body's consent in the first
place. The administration also ran into delays in its negotiations with
the Kingdom of the Two Sicilies. The Neapolitan diplomats insisted
that their nation was too poor to pay reparations for American losses
during the Napoleonic period. Consequently, the Americans moved
more ships into its naval fleet contingent in the Naples harbor to
underscore U.S. determination. A treaty was finally signed, and even
Jackson's long-standing critics were compelled to support ratification.

On the other side of the globe, the administration sent its agents
to the Orient to further American commercial designs. However,
when the president dispatched naval forces to Malay to investigate
an attack on Americans, he was subject to considerable criticism in
Congress and the Whig press. An overanxious commander attacked
the suspected assailants and the reports coming back led to controversy. The president, in the midst of his battle over the bank, was
hit by more charges of abuse of executive power. In the House, a
resolution demanding that the president turn over his instructions
to the naval captain was pressed, and Jackson complied with the
request the next day. Then it became clear that the captain had over-
stepped the president's orders, and criticism of Jackson on that score
died down. In other regions of the world, the president had instructed
an agent to visit Cochin China (Vietnam), Siam (Thailand), Muscat
(a sultanate on the Gulf of Oman), and Japan—travels that led to
minor and mixed results.

The main area of interest for the administration was South
America. By the time of Jackson's election, the British had created
a network of agreements and understandings in that region that resulted in investments totaling £40 million, loans to new nations there

of over $110 million, and overall trade of $32 million. In comparison, U.S. commerce with South America, excluding Cuba, was less than $10 million. In setting out its overall policies toward that region, the administration uncharacteristically accepted a very limited interpretation of the Monroe Doctrine that accentuated British power there. The president, for example, generally ignored the British takeover of the Falkland Islands off the coast of Argentina, and when Brazil asked what the U.S. position would be in case of a Portuguese takeover of that former colony, the administration vaguely supported independence, but shied away from any tough reaffirmation of the Monroe Doctrine. Jackson even refused to mediate a conflict between Peru and Colombia, fearing it would lead to interference in the internal affairs of those nations.

The most difficult challenge to that expressed policy of nonintervention arose over the Mexican situation. The United States desired to add Texas to its enlarging destiny, and John Quincy Adams had tried to purchase the territory for $1 million, an offer Jackson upped to $5 million in 1829. Jackson saw the acquisition of Texas as helping to secure U.S. control over New Orleans and the Mississippi and firming up a clearer boundary with Mexico. At that time, Spain was threatening to invade Mexico and the government there was clearly unstable.

However, the president oddly refused to encourage the strong Texan sentiments for self-government. Despite the fact that Sam Houston was an old Jackson lieutenant in the War of 1812, the president opposed any drastic action likely to lead to war there—believing that diplomacy would still work. There is some disagreement among historians as to whether Jackson was willing to resort to bribery to get Texas. If part of the $5 million ended up being used in that way, he did not care, but Jackson insisted he would not employ "means of an equivocal character" to deal with the issue. When the Mexican government tried to tighten its control over Texas, a war erupted, which led the president of the Mexican Republic, General Santa Anna, to move his army into Texas where he was defeated by Sam Houston in the battle of San Jacinto on April 21, 1836. Santa Anna, who was captured, signed a treaty acknowledging Texan independence, which he later repudiated. The Mexican government then and historians since have insisted that Jackson encouraged the Texans, but in fact he refused Stephen Austin's appeal in 1836 for U.S. aid to defeat Santa Anna. He even labeled the rebellion "rash and premature." Citing the Neutrality Act of

1818, he stayed out of the conflict, but the opinion of Americans in general was clearly supportive of the new republic. Tensions between the United States and Mexico increased, and the Texans openly lobbied in the American capital for their cause and eventual annexation.

The president remained cautious, arguing that the United States had a treaty with Mexico, and that he did not want to seem to have violated it by openly supporting the ambitions of the Texans. He also worried about abolitionist charges that any recognition of slaveholding Texas would open up the sectional question again. Uncharacteristically, Jackson observed that Congress was the "proper power" to advise on the propriety of acknowledging the independence of Texas. A resolution to recognize Texas, however, resulted in a deadlock in Congress, and the issue was bucked back to the president as he publicly sought to find out if the Texans were really interested in being annexed to the United States—which he knew they were. He continued to urge prudence on the recognition issue and even saw Santa Anna on January 19. He and the Mexican leader went on to discuss $3.5 million in compensation for Texas and for lands west to California. No agreement ultimately resulted, though. The administration with the support of Congress finally recognized the independence of the Texas nation, but it would take Tyler and later Polk to fully integrate that Republic into the United States with its present borders and the addition of some lands west of Texas.[31]

Thus, although Jackson had no real experience in foreign policy except as a military conqueror and had acquired a reputation for undiplomatic brashness rather than patience, his administration gained some major triumphs in commercial treaties and reparations. Some of his appointees were poor choices and had hurt his efforts and caused embarrassment, but overall Jackson proved to be flexible and rather understanding. His foreign policy was aggressive and self-confident, like the very executive he was. Jackson became a war hero who eschewed war and concentrated on promoting American interests and zealously guarding her republican virtue in a setting of Old World diplomats, cynical adventurers, and despotic regimes.

As Jackson's second term came to an end, his political strength in the Senate grew to the extent that not only was Benton successful in removing the earlier censure, but also some of the president's nominations were approved: Taney as chief justice of the Supreme

Court, Barbour of Virginia as associate justice, Kendall as postmaster general, and Andrew Stevenson as minister to Great Britain. Jackson also continued to stand in the way of Clay's attempts to sell public lands and funnel the proceeds to the states. To the president, such largess would only encourage the states to depend on the federal government and enlarge the scope of the limited polity he so envisioned. "Money is power, and in that Government which pays all the public offices of the States will all political power be substantially concentrated," Jackson thundered.

Democrats in Congress, though, tried to propose a compromise that would link up a distribution scheme for federal revenues with a proposal to regulate deposit banks. The party leaders also tried to quiet the charges that the executive had usurped powers in his unilateral actions on deposit—a favorite Whig charge. The new law sought to recognize the deposit banks, curtail Taney's discretion in the selection of them, and require specie in major transactions, a favorite theme of the president.

Jackson decided to sign the bill, probably because he feared that a veto might hurt Van Buren's election chances. The president received some criticism from his own ranks, but he was especially pleased by the increasing prominence of specie. Also, he was concerned about speculation in land sales and wanted to insist that only gold and silver could be accepted for the purchase of public lands. The majority of his cabinet initially opposed the president's policy, but once again he prevailed. Congress had adjourned when the secretary of treasury issued the Specie Circular on July 11, 1836. His critics were to see this stand as another example of executive abuse of power. The reaction was swift and vociferous, but Jackson stood firm again.

As Jackson aged, he became even more of a voice for democracy, advocating more popular control of government, the abolition of the electoral college, more rotation in office, popular election of senators, and even the election of federal judges. When a laborer from Brooklyn, New York, sent him a hat he had made, Jackson responded characteristically, "I shall wear [it] with prouder feelings than I would a crown."[32]

As few presidents in the nineteenth century, Jackson had created a public persona that appealed to the populace in a directly emotional way. This aloof warrior, wealthy slaveholding planter, and irascible politician had become a living symbol of the democratic impulse, despite the fact that the men who served in his administration were often recognized leaders in their home communities already. Jacksonian Democracy, as it was later called, seems at times to have little to do with the Jacksonian administration's practices or even many of its battles. But the president clearly transformed the debate into democratic terms and changed the nature of the presidency itself in the process. He restored the office by making it the focal point of action within the limited context of nineteenth-century politics and gave his successors, in various ways, a model that was more direct and passionate than the Federalists and more active and involved than the Jeffersonians.

VAN BUREN'S MISFORTUNES

Martin Van Buren was not only the most astute practitioner of the new professional politics, he was clearly the heir to Jackson's legacy and the recipient of Old Hickory's legions of friends and admirers. But like many heirs, Van Buren was to find that the estate included debts as well as assets. The four-year term of Van Buren would be almost totally preoccupied with the banking controversy and with the economic depression, and in the end, even his considerable skills were no match for the press of circumstances.

Born into a modest Dutch family in rural New York, Van Buren became a successful lawyer who exhibited equanimity and good manners to make up for his lack of formal education. Most of his political life, he had been tagged as a "trimmer," a man who would compromise on any issue for the sake of party loyalty and personal ambition. Actually Van Buren was rather constant in his support of what he regarded as true Jeffersonian principles of limited government and individual initiative and freedom. He was one of the first of his generation to advocate cohesive political parties, strong party loyalty, and partisan tests for officeholding. In place of the old Antifederalist groupings in New York state, he forged a powerful organization called the Albany Regency.[33]

As president he was faced with a growing nation that resented constraints placed in the paths of economic or social mobility. Jackson's gifts were perfectly suited to that mood, for he was a man of intense resentments that seemed to float freely from one target to another. By the sheer force of his personality, the general had beaten Biddle and the South Carolinian secessionists and preserved the national government's authority and integrity. Van Buren ran squarely into the residues of those Jacksonian controversies, which along with the depression, ended his presidency.

Van Buren had established himself as one of the major political operators of the new machine politics. He was nominated and elected, to a large extent, because of the popularity of Jackson, and the president's insistence to the Democratic party leadership that his vice president was his only heir. When Van Buren was sworn in, Thomas Hart Benton was to observe, "For once the rising was eclipsed by the setting sun." Hate him or idolize him, Jackson was an imposing figure. Van Buren, rotund at five feet, six inches, balding and contented, posed a sharp contrast to the tall, thin, gaunt, and irascible general. The Whigs called it "a footsteps administration"—a repeat of the past.

Early in his career, Van Buren had established himself as a Jeffersonian Democrat and had even visited the aging Sage of Monticello. From that experience, he gathered succor as the old philosopher stressed the importance of the Democratic-Republican party to the preservation of liberty in the new republic. Jefferson's views were a marked contrast to what Van Buren regarded as Monroe's weak-kneed nonpartisanship. For him, the task was to provide a party structure in New York and later in the nation that resurrected Jefferson's alliance of Southern planters and Northern plain republicans. While Jefferson could never accept the need for a permanent party organization, Van Buren excelled in creating such a mechanism. His skill at partisan alliances and intrigue earned him the name "the Little Magician."[34]

Van Buren was the first president who had no real role in the Revolution, and he like other leaders stressed the republican heritage they had grown up in and the magnificent achievements of the Founding Fathers. His inaugural address stressed his illustrious predecessors' contributions and expressed concern that the second generation must be as vigilant in its stewardship of the nation.

Almost immediately, the president was faced with a challenge to that stewardship—a major economic downturn that led to the panic of 1837. In May, the banks first in New York and then across the country suspended payments of specie, which in turn led to a general contraction in credit and currency. This development seemed at first only a short-term setback after a decade of boom times. But Van Buren in responding to the crisis set the tone and the policies for his entire term in office.

Later, with the further contraction of British credit, loose banking practices at home, and the consequences of some of Jackson's policies, excessive expansion and then jarring contraction took place. When the Bank of England in July and August raised its discount rate and cut in half the volume of commercial credits to the United States, the situation was compounded by the Treasury's implementation of the Deposit Act, which spread large amounts of money to banks across the nation in order to encourage the circulation of funds that the federal government held. A credit squeeze plus the Specie Circular, which Jackson issued as an executive order, were seen as the causes of the depression in the eyes of the Whigs and many others. Some conservative Democrats even agreed, and led by Senator William C. Rives of Virginia, they tried to get Jackson to approve a bill that would instruct the Treasury to accept bank notes for payments to the government, including for land and import duties. Jackson, unwilling to compromise, pocket vetoed that proposal.

It was into this controversy that Van Buren was quickly mired. Would he abandon Jackson and live up to his critics' characterization of him as a trimmer, a man moved by "noncommitalism," or would he stand firm and face the political consequences of a dispirited economy? First, Van Buren reaffirmed his support for the Specie Circular, and then he pledged his support for the deposit banks. Eventually, the panic of 1837 subsided within a year as specie from Great Britian began to flow again, and new credit allowed banking and business activity to resume. But politically, the Whigs used the depression to attack Jackson's policies and the alleged executive tyranny that had spawned those policies. Van Buren stood firmly with the specie faction and reaffirmed his and the party's identity with Jackson and with Old Hickory's hard money policies.

But the panic had led Van Buren to a decision to ask Congress to make the Treasury independent of the banks altogether. His position was a logical outcome of Jackson's visceral war against the Bank of the United States; his proposal would be the polarizing issue of his presidency. To the Whig assault, the response of the Jacksonians was clear: the blame for the nation's economic woes lay on the shoulders of the banks themselves; the problems that these state deposit banks faced were due to their own practices. Some conservative Democrats defected on the issue, but for Van Buren that split made for a more cohesive party ready for battle.

More moderate Democrats agreed that the federal government needed some control over the general currency of the nation by providing for a sound and uniform program for exchange and by acting as a check on state banking issues. The old Hamilton-Biddle Bank of the United States had provided those valuable functions. Van Buren's supporters tried to come up with alternatives to control state banks, including driving small state notes out of circulation by placing a federal excise tax on them and by passing a new bankruptcy act to close banks that did not resume specie payment within a given period of time.

In a special session of Congress, Van Buren sent a comprehensive message that clearly outlined the overall problem, his view of the banks' share in the crisis, and a proposal to divorce the Treasury Department and the banks. He turned aside the arguments that the Treasury Department had a responsibility to provide a dependable paper medium, although he did accept the view that the federal government should exercise some control over state banks, and he supported a bankruptcy law. With echoes of Jefferson and Jackson, he rejected, however, "blending private interests with the operations of public business." But Congress held back, refusing to support Van Buren's proposals. His political strategy was clear: just as Jackson had taken the bank issue to the people in 1834 and prevailed, so too would Van Buren in the upcoming election. Proudly he wrote Jackson, "I think I see my way clear for the difficulties that beset my brief administration."[35]

This time, however, the Whigs were smarter. They refused to promote publicly their plan for a national bank. They argued, with some conservative Democrats at their side, that Van Buren's real objectives were to destroy the state banks and ensure a hard inflexible currency system. Those policies, the Whigs insisted, would destroy democracy in America, prevent social mobility, and create rigid social classes. As Clay argued, for an energetic people, credit was "the friend of indigent merit." This appeal helped to split off part of the Jackson coalition that had opposed the Bank of the United States, but which needed credit especially in the commercial centers and larger towns.

These conflicts added to the national cycles of boom and bust and led to major social unrest and deep concern over the loss of civic virtue in the new republic. By the late 1830s and 1840s, America was undergoing a profound spirit of reform that spilled over into many areas of public and private life. Van Buren, by pulling the Treasury out of currency controversies, was partially attempting to preserve a pristine notion of government, one separated from the compelling power of money, which so often corrupted republican virtue. Faced with the dynamics of a growing commercial and market economy, the Democrats, however, were fighting a rear guard action. As Marvin Meyers has observed, the Whigs spoke to the hopes and the Democrats to the fears of the people. As for Van Buren himself, he was by temperament and history a cautious man who knew the virtues of delay and procrastination. His banking policy was in large part dictated by his desire to save his presidency and keep the Democratic political base and Jacksonian legacy together. Quite probably he would have compromised even more if he could have reached a consensus.

The Whigs, in turn, stressed their continuing fear of executive tyranny, as exemplified by Jackson. One elderly Federalist, Harrison Gray Otis, urged Van Buren to rise above party, reject Jackson, and read Viscount Bolingbroke's work, *Idea of a Patriot King*. Clay added to that classical touch by portraying the United States as a "two currency" nation, one in which the Treasury paid officeholders in specie or hard money, but which would not accept paper currency from the people. "A hard money Government and a paper-money People! A government, an official corps—the servants of the People—glittering in gold, and the People themselves, their masters, buried in ruin, and surrounded with rags," he ranted.[36]

The election results in 1837 showed a Whig trend emerging, including in Van Buren's home state of New York. The president had made a career out of reading the returns; ruefully he called it the "New York tornado." With the major banking issue before him, he still tried to strike a compromise that would represent some progress toward separating the government from the banks but not upset more moderate business elements. In response to his concessions, New York banks in April 1838 resumed specie payments and most other banks followed suit. Congress, however, proved to be more recalcitrant, and as Van Buren reached for a compromise, he seemed once again both a trimmer and a passive leader. One critic at this time was to conclude, "Contrary to all pre-conceived opinions of his character, Mr. Van Buren has rendered himself the most inaccessible both to friends and adversaries of all the chief magistrates that ever filled his station."[37]

The president's supporters, led by Silas Wright in the Senate, groped for compromise language, and Wright came up with a fine distinction between what he saw as two major points—the handling of funds and the kinds of funds to be handled. He insisted that only the first was important. There had to be, he concluded, separation between the public treasury and the business of corporations and individuals. The Treasury Department would be independent on the deposit side by handling its own funds, but on the specie issue Wright signaled more flexibility by asking that it be phased in over six years.

The administration received some support oddly enough from Calhoun who departed from the Whig strategy of Clay and Webster. Clay sharply criticized Calhoun's deviation, sarcastically concluding that the Southerner had cast his lot with the "sly fox," another Van Buren nickname. But Calhoun responded in good sectional rhetoric that the administration's policies would end up promoting Southern interests, and he then went on to praise ritualistically the virtues of slave labor.[38]

Webster responded in familiar rhetoric also, defending the republic of old and the "fathers who formed it for us, and who bequeathed it to us." He attacked the administration's bill and concluded, as Clay had previously, that credit was a poor man's capital. By April, the New York banks had resumed specie payments, easing up the pressure on the administration to repeal Jackson's Specie Circular. The final outcome of the long controversy was that Van Buren on July 4, 1840, signed a bill that divorced the federal Treasury and all state banks; the Treasury would handle its own funds. The Democrats hailed the act as a second Declaration of Independence. Kendall concluded that the first declaration freed the American people from the British king, the latter one delivered them from the power of British banks. Unfortunately for the president, late 1839 brought new bank failures, a strict tightening of British credit, and the beginning of a major depression that lasted for four years. To Van Buren, such cycles before and after 1839 proved even more the importance of guarding the independence of the Treasury from the influences of both state banks and British credit.

During his term, Van Buren witnessed the growth of the two-party system in the South with the Whigs becoming more prominent. And most importantly, in November 1838, Whig William Seward captured the governorship of New York, overturning the Van Buren Regency. The president insisted that the victory was really the product of voting frauds and the corrupt influence of the banks. But his associate, William L. Marcy, who had lost the election, believed that the Whigs had successfully exploited opposition to the Treasury bill to garner public support especially in the commercial areas. Added to those political woes were the deepening sectional tensions epitomized in the debate over slavery. The Democrat-controlled House of Representatives supported a resolution to reestablish a gag rule that prevented that body from even considering antislavery memorials. In the Senate, Clay moved closer to the slaveholders' position by criticizing those who wanted to meddle in their affairs. Calhoun called Clay's change "epoch," while the Great Compromiser probably saw it simply as an expedient step toward gaining Southern Whig support for his next presidential bid.[39]

Van Buren did regard Clay as his major opponent in his campaign for reelection, and he hoped to rerun the 1832 election when Jackson defeated the Kentuckian on the bank issue. Smugly Van Buren wrote to Jackson, "A better candidate we could not desire." But both Van Buren and Clay overestimated Clay's strength in his own party and underestimated the Whig lust for victory and spoils. Preparing for the campaign, the president began to tighten control over the administration and insisted on loyalty to his Treasury policies. In his first two years in office, he had removed 3 postmasters; in the next year and a half, he removed 364. Jackson approved, concluding that officeholders "ought to correspond with the Executive in all of his important measures."[40]

Van Buren then used the second downturn in the economy to push through his Treasury bill and to reaffirm the importance of a laissez faire policy of government toward economic activity. On top of depressed conditions, he added a policy of government retrenchment—probably the last thing in Keynesian hindsight the nation needed at that time. The Democrats also opposed assuming the debts that the states had incurred to Britain in order to finance internal improvements. It was time to take the bitter medicine needed to foster republican simplicity and American independence. Benton concluded that the president's Treasury bill was the logical conclusion of Jackson's policy to restore government to "its primitive and constitutional course." Calhoun was also effusive in his praise, seeing the Treasury bill as a restoration of the Constitution and a step toward the nullification view of a limited Union in which cotton, freed from the domestic and foreign credit system, would control trade even more.

Oddly enough, though, Van Buren had not entered the fray to free banks from regulation. His goals were more moderate and modest, but the consequences of his policies were to promote the deregulation of state banking, a condition that existed until the North mobilized under the Lincoln administration for war. His main con-

cern was to preserve the Jackson legacy and to further party cohesiveness in the conflict. The issue took on the ideological colora-
tion of a restoration of the values of the founders, a purgation of
the moneyed interests, a reaffirmation of the laissez faire gospel
that the government that governs least governs best. Van Buren's
policies were a blend of Jeffersonian ideology, Jacksonian resentment, and "country" or the opposition politics of old England.[41]

The Whigs picked at the soft side of the Van Buren policies.
They abandoned Clay's position of pushing for a national bank, and
instead emphasized the dire consequences of a contraction of credit,
the rigidity of a specie-based Treasury in a country in love with
commerce, expansion, and speculation. To many Americans, especially those in the economically growing areas and in the cities
linked to a more international economy, the essence of liberty was
making money, not preserving the pristine values of the Founding
Fathers.

So it was that when they came to nominate a president, the Whigs
passed over their great sentimental favorite, Henry Clay, and choose
General William Henry Harrison, the hero of the Battle of
Tippecanoe and a figure not identified in the public mind with the
controversies of the Jackson period. The general avoided the issues
and supported the principle of credit for the growing republic in a
depression. Another general, Andrew Jackson, back at the Hermit-
age, pronounced that the passage of the Treasury bill would yield a
"death blow to Whiggery, and Harrisonism."[42] He was wrong on both
counts. Caught up in a depression and the popular sentiments of
the "Log Cabin" campaign, Van Buren was overwhelmed. The great
master innovator and astute party tactician that he was, Van Buren
was more comfortable with the quiet machinations of the backroom
and the careful organization of the precincts than with the populist
hubbub that so characterized the campaign of 1840.

To garner popular support, some of his adherents asked that he
lead the nation into war, but Van Buren's instincts were more modest and his policies less bellicose than his predecessor. Van Buren's
presidency marked a pause in the steady search for territorial expansion. Before him, the foreign policies of the Federalists, the
Jeffersonians, and even Andrew Jackson were ones of enlarging the
"empire of liberty" and spreading the eagle across the North American continent. After Van Buren, especially with his fellow Jacksonian
heirs, that pattern was continued. But Van Buren on this issue proved
to be more cautious. He shied away from the ambitions of Mani-

fest Destiny, as it was later called, in his dealings on the U.S.-Canadian boundaries and on the southwest borders with Mexico. His major reservation was the difficulty that the slave controversy posed for the Democratic party; he was correct as Polk and his successors found out when those tensions were accentuated by the acquisition and development of the new lands. Van Buren would delay Texas's joining the Union and sidetracked Mexican claims disputes as best he could. The solidarity of the Democratic party was his major concern.

The cabinet secretaries supported the president by concluding that the United States could not annex Texas while Texas was at war with Mexico, since that step would violate American treaties and might actually lead to conflict with that latter nation. When the war was over, the administration and the Mexican government tried unsuccessfully to resolve American claims against the Mexicans, an issue that was referred to an arbitration commission. In his dealings with Great Britain, Van Buren tried the same moderate position, although at times tensions were pronounced. When there was a rebellion in lower Canada in late 1837, the administration refused to recognize the groups and actually assisted the British government and its troops in crushing the resistance. Van Buren's problems were compounded by the desire of some Americans near the northern border to come to the aid of the Canadians. Publicly, the president exhibited neutrality and Congress approved such a policy; eventually American opinion on the border supported Van Buren as he cooperated with the British and granted them the right to transport troops through U.S.-claimed territory.

A second problem with the British occurred over the long disputed Maine-New Brunswick boundary, and once again Van Buren opted for diplomacy and peace over bluster and war. Some members of Congress and even his friends in the New York Regency advocated a tougher line, as if they had not learned from the War of 1812 how difficult it was for the federal government to be directing armies on the Canadian border against British forces. An arbitration settlement was rejected by the political leadership of that state, and Van Buren was unwilling to alienate them. Tensions grew, and officials on both sides of the border began to mobilize troops to settle what was becoming known as the "Aroostook War." Eventually the administration took a direct role in the negotiations, and the boundary was finally drawn in the Webster-Ashburton Treaty of 1842.

But the quiet successes of diplomacy were overwhelmed by the machinations of the presidential campaign of 1840. The Whigs celebrated the ticket of William Henry Harrison and John Tyler, "Tippecanoe and Tyler too," a ticket that Clay followers called a rhyme without reason. Harrison and Tyler both received a letter notifying them of their selection at the Whig party convention. Harrison expressed his gratitude, although he maintained that he was not the equal of other leaders of "most distinguished talents." He avoided any discussion of the issues and pledged not to run for a second term. As for Tyler, he concluded that he was honored to serve on the ticket with such an "eminent patriot."

Actually, Harrison spent his time in the campaign swapping tales of his service in the War of 1812, while Democrats tried to drive a wedge between the general and his running mate. They insisted on recounting Tyler's opposition to a national bank, a position not shared by Clay and a substantial wing of the Whig party. Tyler's sentiments on slavery in the District of Columbia, internal improvements, and the tariff issue were also scrutinized. By training and inclination, Tyler was a Jeffersonian, and he shared the traditional views of his Virginia neighbors toward states' rights, limited government, and low tariffs. Harrison's opinions were vague and less developed on those issues. He had said that he believed the Constitution did not give any express grant of power for the establishment of a national bank, and concluded that it was not constitutional to exercise that power except if the power granted to Congress "could not be carried into effect without resorting to such an institution." Tyler responded that he too embraced that formula—whatever it meant.

The Whigs went on the offensive, chanting across the nation, "Van, Van is a used up man," charging he was a democrat by profession and an aristocrat in principle and life style. Whigs claimed that Van Buren had spent public funds lavishly by living in regal splendor in the White House, walking on fine British-made carpets, sleeping in a French bedstead, dining with golden spoons, and drinking imported wines.

When the Democrat-run *Baltimore Republican* charged that all Harrison needed to be happy was a barrel of cider and a government pension as he sat in his log cabin, the Whigs turned the criticism to good advantage. Harrison became the candidate of simplicity—log cabins were erected all over the nation. Actually, the general was the descendant of one of the most well-to-do families in Virginia, had studied medicine, and lived in a rather fine house. Tyler came from an even more comfortable background. Still the slogan of "Log Cabin and Hard Cider" caught the public imagination to the extent that perennial candidate Daniel Webster apologized for not having been born in a log cabin. Ironically, it was Van Buren who was actually the self-made man in that campaign; now he was portrayed as a dandified fop eating off silver plates with golden spoons.[43]

As the Whigs ran the first successful image, nonissue campaign for the presidency in American history, Van Buren tried to buttress his support by appealing to the South and taking a more positive view of slavery. But sectionalism was not as strong as concern over the depression, and the Whigs made major inroads into first-time voters and those stirred by Harrison's war record. The general swept the electoral college 234 votes to Van Buren's 60 and had an edge of 1,275,016 to 1,129,102 in the popular vote count. Harrison won 19 states, doing well in New England, the Middle States, and the new West and even carrying Georgia, Mississippi, and North Carolina. The Jacksonian period seemed to be finally over, or so the new Whig loyalists thought.

TIPPECANOE AND TYLER TOO

The inaugural of the first Whig president and vice president took place on a chilly March day as William Henry Harrison and John Tyler celebrated their installation along with satisfied party followers. The new president came from a highly regarded and familiar family; his father was active in the First and the Second Continental Congress, signed the Declaration of Independence, and had been governor of Virginia. As for the president, he had attended Hampden-Sydney College, and studied medicine but abandoned it for the military. In 1800, he became governor of the Indian Territory, where he negotiated treaties that extended the U.S. government's reach by millions of acres. As whites pushed into the region, Indians under the inspired leadership of Shawnee chief Tecumseh and his brother, the prophet Tenskwatawa, resisted. In 1811, Harrison led an armed force against a Shawnee settlement near Tippecanoe Creek, and thus a legend was born from that modest engagement. In an America that loved military men and military exploits, Harrison attracted widespread, popular attention.

After the war, he returned to his farm near Cincinnati and later served as a congressman, senator, and minister to Colombia. Still he began to move away from the Democratic party when other major positions he coveted did not come his way. When his name began to circulate in 1836 as a possible presidential candidate, he was the clerk of the Cincinnati Court of Common Pleas. But he was still, in the eyes of many admirers, "the hero of Tippecanoe," and by 1840, that remained his real claim to fame.

His running mate also came from a distinguished lineage, and his father had also been a governor of Virginia. Tyler was a graduate of the College of William and Mary, a respected lawyer, who had won praise as a thoughtful Jeffersonian and an opponent of Jackson's aggressive government. He cast the only vote in the Senate against the "Force Bill," which was aimed at South Carolina secessionists. Partly because of his opposition to Jackson, he became associated with Old Hickory's Whig critics, even though he retained much of his states' rights philosophy all his life and was not enamored with the idea of a national bank. Because of his standing in the important state of Virginia, Tyler was seen as a real asset to the ticket, although there was no rush to the vice presidential slot on the Whig side.

In the month Harrison served as president, he moved easily through Washington's social life. He was a pleasant and amiable individual, able to make people feel comfortable. Even Van Buren found him one of the most extraordinary men he had ever met, saying, "He talks and thinks with . . . much ease and vivacity. . . . He is as tickled with the Presidency as is a young woman with a new bonnet." However, the president quickly clashed with Henry Clay, who assumed that he was the real leader of the Whig party, and Harrison is supposed to have said early on, "Mr. Clay, you forget that I am the president." Although he espoused the traditional Whig preference for a weak executive, he also made it clear he was unwilling to be anyone's pawn.

Inauguration day drew large crowds despite the chilly weather, and after the swearing in ceremonies in the Senate chamber were over, Harrison without coat or overcoat went to address for over an hour and a half a crowd of fifty thousand people outside the Capitol, giving his views of the presidency and pledging to serve only one term. He promised not to intrude on the legislative branch, shared his thoughts on the limited use of the veto, and indicated that he opposed a major purge of government workers for patronage purposes. He spent the month in a whirlwind of activity, but on March 27 he was diagnosed as having bilious pleurisy which led to pneumonia. On April 4, he died.[44]

Tyler quickly left Virginia and made his way to the nation's capital. On April 9, he issued a statement of his principles and policies, which was meant to be a sort of inaugural address. Tyler insisted that he was now the "president" and not the "acting president," and while there was some criticism of his decision, Congress eventually acceded to his view. Thus an important precedent was established. One dissident voice was the grumpy John Quincy Adams who regarded Tyler as only serving in an acting capacity despite popular acquiescence to the contrary. He declared Tyler to be a

> politician sectarian, of slave-driving Virginian, Jeffersonian school, principled against all improvement, with all the interests and passions and vices of slavery rooted in his moral and political constitution—with talents not above mediocrity, and a spirit incapable of expansion to the dimensions of the station upon which he has been cast by the hand of Providence, unseen through the apparent agency of chance. No one ever thought of his being placed in the executive chair.

Clay had a calmer disdain: "I can hardly suppose that V.P. Tyler will interpose any obstacle to the adoption of measures on which the Whigs are generally united. Still, his administration will be in the nature of a regency, and regencies are very apt to engender faction, intrigue, etc." Clay quickly assumed the leadership of the Whig party and captured control of Congress in order to press his views of partisan orthodoxy.[45]

The circumstances of Tyler's accession were soon complicated by the new president's differences with the very party that selected him for the ticket. The first great issue that divided the party and its nominal leader Tyler was what should replace the Independent Treasury Act. Should there be a new central bank, as Clay was advocating? The election of 1840 and the Whig campaign had not laid out specific commitments on many of the issues that Clay was trying to line up support for in the legislative branch, including the issue of the bank. Tyler did attempt to put together a bank proposal that avoided the objections of states' righters, but Clay would not compromise. Finally, the president is supposed to have declared to Clay that he should go to his end of the avenue and do what he thought was proper, and Tyler would do the same at the other end.[46]

In June, Congress passed Clay's repeal of the Independent Treasury Act. Tyler signed it, but the battle for a substitute was to split the president from his party. The secretary of treasury, Thomas Ewing, tried to meet the challenge by constructing a compromise that would set up in the District of Columbia a central bank with offices of discount and deposit to be located in several states that gave their consent to that arrangement. This formulation was meant to overcome the constitutional objections about whether the federal government had the authority to create such an institution. Since Congress governed the District directly this would not be an issue, and since the establishment of branches would be voluntary, some other concerns would be muted as well.

Clay would not agree to the compromise, arguing that the consent of the states was not necessary for recharting a national bank. On July 27, he agreed to an amendment that presumed a state's approval unless that state's legislature in its first session after the passage of the act by Congress disapproved. Tyler, however, had decided, after remaining silent on the matter, to adhere to his states' rights proclivities and vetoed the bill.

The Democrats were as delighted by Tyler's action as the Whigs were dismayed. A mob marched to the White House to chant for Clay and against Tyler, and the Whig press in the North began a drumbeat of criticism against the president. Meanwhile, former president Jackson added his statement of approval to Tyler's stand. The lines were once again drawn on the bank issue. Tyler's action quickly severed him from the Whig leadership, but it was also clear that segments of the party were looking for any issue to discredit the unelected president in order to lay the groundwork for Clay or for others who caught their fancy. Tyler added to his problems when he seemed at first to welcome a reformed second bill, and then vetoed it. On September 13, more than fifty Whig members of Congress held a caucus in Washington and read Tyler out of the party. As Clay put it, Tyler was to be "a president without a party." As the controversy heated up, the president began to receive what eventually were hundreds of letters threatening assassination.[47]

When Tyler became president, he inherited Harrison's cabinet, and everyone except Webster was a Clay follower. Early on, Tyler made it clear that he had no intention of being dictated to by any of these secretaries, and he told them so. To supplement their advice, Tyler—like Jackson—surrounded himself with a "kitchen cabinet," personal advisors with no major government titles. After the second veto, every one of the cabinet officers resigned in protest, except Webster at the State Department. Tyler moved quickly appointing replacements, but stayed with Whigs, not going over publicly to the Democrats. Later, Tyler began adding supportive Democrats to the cabinet as vacancies opened up.

In November 1841, the president came forth with a financial plan he called "Exchequer." Under that proposal, public monies were to be placed under the control of a board in Washington, D.C., with agencies in different cities. This board would buy and sell domestic bills and drafts, receive individual deposits of gold and silver, and issue certificates redeemable in those metals. Tyler's proposal was similar to one presented in Jackson's message of December 1830, and the new bill drew opposition from the Clay Whigs and also from some Democrats as well. The president's initiative went nowhere.

Tyler had dealt also with the perennial problem of the tariff, and his position was that no new bill should violate the basic settlement incorporated in the Compromise Tariff Act of 1833. However, the administration came to realize that there was a need to raise duties somewhat to cope with the deficit then estimated to be $11 million at the end of 1841. There was also a movement in Congress to distribute the proceeds from the sales of federal lands among the states. Clay, the architect of the Compromise of 1833, advocated higher tariff rates in order to protect American manufacturers, and he and his supporters argued for the distribution of land revenues so as to divest the federal government of these reserves and compel newer and higher duties and taxes. Tyler, however, was mainly concerned with using tariff receipts for revenue and was not willing to see these funds siphoned off. He vetoed Clay's bill, and his veto was upheld. The breach between the president and Congress, and between Tyler and the Whig party thus widened.[48]

In the House, the Whig majority sent his veto message to a committee headed by John Quincy Adams, which attacked not just the tariff veto, but the president's conduct as well. The majority of the committee supported impeaching Tyler, but did not recommend such a step to the full House. When Representative John Minor Botts did propose the creation of a committee of nine to review the impeachment charges he himself had drawn up against Tyler, the president filed a protest against the report which he viewed as simply character assassination. The resolution was rejected 127 to 83, but the Whig newspapers increased their attacks on him. One of them, *The Daily Richmond Whig*, concluded, "Again has the imbecile, into whose hands accident has placed the power, vetoed a bill passed by a majority of those legally authorized to pass it." Other newspapers labeled him "His Accidency," and the "Executive Ass." When influenza swept the nation, the outbreak even was termed "Tyler Grippe"! Partly due to this divisiveness, the Whigs suffered substantial defeats in the congressional elections as the House of Representatives returned to the control of the Democrats. After all the debate, the Whigs yielded to Tyler's view, and Congress passed a bill without the distribution clause. The tariff, focusing on the need to raise more revenue, upped the general level of duties to that of 1832.[49]

Like many presidents frustrated in domestic affairs, Tyler turned to foreign policy to make his mark, and he was rather successful in furthering the expansionist agenda. He started off trying to repair relations with Great Britain, which disagreed with the United States on several issues: the location of the northeastern boundary, the right to stop and search ships to suppress the slave trade, and the culpability in the death of an American citizen from the burning of the American vessel *Caroline*. Tensions were further aggravated by the Canadian rebellion in 1841 against British authority. The British did make some moves to allay criticism by sending Alexander Baring, the first Lord Ashburton, who was married to the daughter of an American and who himself admired the United States, to negotiate outstanding issues of contention. Ashburton, working with Secretary of State Webster, undertook to settle the boundary problem between Maine and New Brunswick, and with Tyler's intervention, the talks led to an agreement whereby the United States gained seven thousand of the twelve thousand square miles under dispute.

On the issue of suppressing the slave trade, the administration could not agree with the British request to stop and search vessels to look for slaves. Strong Southern opposition and a remembrance of the impressment of free seamen prevented American approval. Instead, the two nations agreed to send a naval force to the coast of Africa to help suppress the trade. Tyler was especially proud of the steps he had taken to encourage American trade in China as well. The treaty to which he agreed opened up five ports to U.S. trade and granted to American citizens the right to live and trade in those areas, while they were exempted from local Chinese administration and law. In the Northwest, the administration was less successful in settling on a border for the Oregon Territory, although Tyler was personally willing to accept the forty-ninth parallel. The administration also tried to improve relations with Mexico, but that overture was cut short by the abrupt seizure of the city of Monterey by a U.S. naval commander, a dispute that ended with an apology from Secretary of State Webster.[50]

Of course, the major foreign policy accomplishment in the Tyler administration was the acquisition of Texas, clearly the president's greatest success. For the five years before Tyler became president, the Texas republic existed as a separate country. The United States, and most of the European powers, had recognized Texan sovereignty, while a majority of its inhabitants voted in September 1836 for annexation to the United States. Twice the Texas government was rebuffed in Washington when it raised the issue of annexation, and in May 1845, a frustrated President Sam Houston withdrew the offer. There the issue rested until Tyler came into office. Tyler, like Jackson, was mainly concerned at first with antagonizing Great Britain by such a move and raising a storm of protest in the Northern states by reopening the slave territory question.

Houston decided then to court Great Britain as a way of raising American anxieties and getting them to move toward closer association. In addition, poor economic conditions led to some concern in the United States about how long Texas could really remain freestanding. With these developments in the background, negotiations between the United States and Texas finally resulted in a treaty of incorporation signed on April 12, 1844. Texas's public lands were ceded to the United States, and its debt of $10 million was assumed. On May 15, Tyler moved U.S. warships into the Gulf of Mexico and sent troops to Fort Jessup on the Texas border in the event of a Mexican attack while the treaty was being discussed. As expected, opposition to the treaty came from several quarters in the United States, especially from those who feared it would affect adversely relations with Mexico and those who thought it would encourage the advance of slavery. The Whigs under Clay's leadership opposed the treaty, while the Democrats in Congress led in the House by Polk supported it. Jackson entered the fray charging characteristically that any Southerner who opposed the annexation was a traitor. The final vote in the Senate was 16 yea, 35 no, clearly reflecting the strength of the Whig party.[51]

Tyler then turned to the idea of a joint resolution of both houses of Congress as a way of accomplishing his objective. As he explained it, "The great question is not as the manner in which it shall be done but whether it shall be accomplished or not." On June 10, 1844, he notified the House of Representatives that he was sending to that body the treaty and all correspondence and documents he had sent to the Senate in executive session. He stated that Texas was an independent republic, and therefore the United States was not violating any treaty obligations with Mexico. The president proposed admitting Texas to the Union as a state under Article IV, Section 3 of the Constitution, which implied that a simple majority of both houses could admit it, rather than go through the treaty route, which requires two-thirds majority in the Senate. It was a brilliant move strategically. Opponent John Quincy Adams called the passage of the joint resolution "the apoplexy of the Constitution." The election of pro-annexation presidential candidate James K. Polk added a public imprimatur to the annexation cause, and on January 25, 1845, a joint resolution for annexation was passed. Texas could be admitted as a state without going through the normal territorial stage. Up to four states could be carved out of Texas territory if Texas later agreed. Those areas north of the 36°30' line were to be admitted without slavery; those south of that line would come in with or without slaves as the inhabitants decided. Texas turned over its public lands to the federal government, but had to pay off its own debts.[52]

However, to complicate matters, Congress passed by joint resolution a provision that allowed the president either to admit Texas as a state or to reopen treaty negotiations with it, a proposal that came from a Tyler critic, Senator Thomas Hart Benton. Each side expected that Polk would favor its approach. What they did not count on was that the sitting president, with only three days left in his term, would make the decision. And so Tyler did—he admitted Texas as a state. In one quick stroke, Tyler added the large southwest territory of Texas to the United States and ended his last days in office with stellar parties thrown by his new young wife. At one party, he laughed and observed, "They cannot *say now* that I am a president *without a party.*"

Tyler had given some consideration to running for another term, but he lacked any real power base. He had been criticized, as John Quincy Adams was, for not using patronage to advance his cause. But his real problem was that he had no party to call his own. He tried to form a third party to advance his case in 1844, and he made overtures to the Van Buren-Jackson wing of the Democratic party, even offering a Supreme Court seat to Van Buren and a cabinet post to Polk. A pro-Tyler convention was held on May 27 in Baltimore and some one thousand delegates attended, but in the end, nothing came of their efforts. At the Democratic convention, Tyler also had some advocates, but the party regulars supported a Jackson disciple, James Knox Polk. After the convention, some party leaders asked Jackson to get Tyler to drop out of the race. The old general refused to address a public statement to Tyler or promote the idea of guarantees of favorable treatment for Tyler followers in the next Democratic administration. Such a step would smack of a deal, like the one Adams and Clay struck against him. But in a private letter, Jackson did urge Tyler to step out of the contest in order not to hurt Polk, which is what Tyler finally did on August 20. Tyler did have one final consolation: he had stopped Van Buren from getting the Democratic nod, and he helped to defeat his old Whig enemies, especially Clay. Sometimes in politics, revenge is the most comfortable balm available.

POLK AND MANIFEST DESTINY

If it is the objective of nations to increase their power and influence in the world, then the United States in the period between Jefferson and Polk is surely a candidate for the honors of expansionism. And if the standard of presidential success is the ability to extend the republic's boundaries, then Polk's conquests must rank with Jefferson's Louisiana Purchase as major triumphs in acquisition and imperialism. The Polk administration is the high water mark of United States expansion, of what became known in the 1840s as "Manifest Destiny," that constellation of ideology, self-interest, religious fervor, and economic lust that sought to project the United States as a continental power that would establish its hegemony in the Western Hemisphere.

James Knox Polk was born in 1795 in Mecklenburg County, North Carolina, and attended the state university there, although his family had moved in 1806 to Tennessee. Polk was a congressman from 1825 to 1839, serving the last four years as speaker of the House of Representatives. He was identified as a serious, hardworking Democrat who supported the policies of fellow Tennessean Andrew Jackson and was the floor manager in the titanic bank battle. From 1839 to 1841, he was his state's governor, and three years later he was encouraged to run for president by Jackson who had given up on Van Buren because of his reservations on taking Texas. At the 1844 convention, Polk was nominated on the eighth ballot. Whigs generally attacked his low profile by asking "Who is James K. Polk?" But fortified with Democratic party support and General Jackson's blessings, and standing tall on annexing Texas and claiming Oregon up to the fifty-second parallel, Polk narrowly defeated the better-known Clay. James G. Birney, running on the Liberty abolitionist ticket, which opposed the extension of slavery, drew off 62,300 votes, which may have cost Clay New York and possibly Michigan and, thus, the presidency.[53]

Probably no president worked harder at the job than Polk, and surely no president was better able to articulate his objectives and achieve them. On inaugural day, Polk told the historian George Bancroft that his four great objectives would be: the reduction of the tariff, the reestablishment of the independent Treasury, the settlement of the Oregon question, and the acquisition of California. Polk was to prove to be a determined executive, a strong civilian commander in chief, and a man immersed in detailed control of the government. But he was also a leader who lacked charisma, had no personal following, and had few close friends. He once observed, "I prefer to supervise the whole operations of the Government myself rather than entrust the public business to subordinates, and this makes my duties very great." No wonder that he concluded, "With me it is emphatically true that the Presidency is 'no bed of roses.'"[54]

He tried to maintain balance between the wings of the party, curtailed the Van Buren faction, and exercised control over congressional Democrats on the major issues he faced. Polk pushed for cabinet responsibility, but insisted that cabinet members were his appointees and subject to his oversight and control. As his diary shows, he was continually concerned about disloyalty in the cabinet, especially on the part of Secretary of State James Buchanan who intended to run for the presidency in 1848 since Polk was committed to serving only one term. One major innovation in the administration was the handling of the budget. Before Polk, the president really had no responsibility over department estimates, which were sent directly to Congress. Polk insisted that all budget requests had to be submitted first to him for his review; an executive budget was then sent on to Congress. Polk did more than collate budget requests; at times he insisted on cuts in those proposals.

He ran a tight administration, in general, and mandated that neither he nor his wife would accept gifts from well-wishers. At one point, he even refused to accept the profits due on bonds he owned for fear of being called a war profiteer. Unlike Jackson, Polk was involved in policy-making and in detail on a day-to-day basis, and not just sporadically in particular and singular controversies. Polk's strongest achievements came from his foreign policy and from the territorial fruits of the war he waged. Three days before his inaugural, Polk witnessed the success of Tyler's joint resolution inviting Texas into statehood. As noted, the bill was passed in the House by a vote of 120 to 98 and in the Senate, 27 to 25, and the outgoing president was able to bypass the treaty-ratifying process in the Senate. Polk's electoral victory was a sign to Congress that popular sentiment favored Texas's admission. In fact, Polk may have also helped to move the resolution along through his personal influence and quiet lobbying just before his inauguration, thus eliminating his need to have to face the problem of Texas right after taking office.[55]

On another controversial expansion issue, Polk had taken, during the campaign, a hard line on dealing with the British in settling the boundary of the Oregon Territory. Expansionists had coined the slogan "54°40′ or fight," referring to the map coordinates of the fifty-fourth parallel, fortieth degree, which embraced all of Oregon. Actually though, American administrations and diplomats before Polk had pretty much accepted the boundary line as the forty-ninth parallel which was the old division between British Rupert's Land and French Louisiana west of the Lake of the Woods.[56]

Polk's response was rather ingenious. In his first annual message to Congress on December 2, 1845, he reported that British-American negotiations had broken down, and he recommended that Congress give notice to the British of the end of their convention of joint occupancy. The tone of his message was bellicose to the delight of Democrats who believed that the British had no rights in that area in the first place and were in violation of the Monroe Doctrine. Actually though while Polk was forcing the issue, he also pushed for a diplomatic settlement at the forty-ninth parallel, arguing that he was simply following that line out of deference to his predecessors.

While the Democrats controlled both houses of Congress, there were strong feelings among the Southern wing that the Oregon issue should be settled peacefully, and they were joined by a cohesive Whig sentiment. Led by a Southern Whig, Senator John J. Crittenden of Kentucky, the Senate adopted a rather conciliatory posture toward Britain, and the House followed suit. As for the British, they too favored a settlement. Faced with the prospect of famine in Ireland and a revolt in his own party on the issue of protectionism, the great British Prime Minister Robert Peel preferred to find a way to reduce tensions with the Americans. In the end, the settlement was at the forty-ninth parallel, and the Senate, on June 12, 1846, accepted the treaty 38 to 12.[57]

Polk's compromise with Britain was wise and easy compared to his policies with Mexico which ended in war and exhibited his talents as a powerful civilian chief executive. As has been seen, relations between the United States and Mexico had not gone well since the former recognized the Republic of Texas as an independent nation, and matters obviously worsened when nine years later the United States annexed Texas with its consent. Also, there remained a series of claims by U.S. citizens against the Mexican state and a long-standing dispute over whether the Texas border ended at the Nueces River or at the Rio Grande. Polk adopted an aggressive and confrontational position, hoping to get the land between the Nueces and the more southern Rio Grande and also adding California and New Mexico to the Union.

The president sent a special agent to urge the Mexicans to sell California and New Mexico to the United States, using in the process American claims as leverage in the bargain. When the Mexican government refused to negotiate, the president moved American troops into the areas between the two rivers. Polk called the cabinet together on May 9, 1846, to consider his request for a declaration of war, which would be forwarded to Congress; he argued, "in my opinion we had ample cause of war, and . . . it was impossible that we could stand in *status quo*, or that I could remain silent much longer."[58] Four hours later, Polk received news from General Zachary Taylor that the Mexicans had attacked U.S. forces. It is not unfair to conclude that the president's strategy was designed to foster a belligerent act and thus pave the way for a declaration of war. A young Whig congressman, Abraham Lincoln, introduced a series of resolutions demanding to know on what spot the attack took place. The implication was clear that the U.S. forces had provoked the

attack. Polk did not even record Lincoln's inquiries in his extensive diary reflections of the period. And Lincoln would not hold
office again until elected president himself in 1861.

On May 13, Congress declared war. When Secretary of State
Buchanan pushed in a cabinet session for a statement from the president to assure Britain and France that the United States really had
no territorial designs on Mexico, Polk bristled. While the United
States had not gone to war for conquest, "it was clear that in making war we would if practicable obtain California and such other
portions of the Mexican territory as would be sufficient to indem-
nify our claimants on Mexico, and to defray the expenses of the
war which that power by her long continued wrongs and injuries
had forced on us." The president went on to explain that he would
go to war with Britain, France, or any other nation that sought to
interfere with his policies. At a minimum, he insisted that any peace
treaty had to include U.S. control of upper California and New
Mexico.

To promote a favorable settlement with Mexico, Polk allowed
private negotiations with Santa Anna who promised the Americans
that if he were allowed to return to Mexico he would conclude all
boundary questions with the United States for a sum of $30 mil-
lion. The Mexican leader living in exile was allowed to pass from
Cuba through U.S. lines in the Gulf and permitted to return to his
homeland. Once Santa Anna controlled the country, Buchanan was
ready to begin peace negotiations, but the general promptly refused.
Thus, through American intervention, an able and astute military
commander was allowed to take over the war against the United
States.

The president was also hindered by his decision to dismiss his
own agent, Nicholas P. Trist, who was genuinely trying to negotiate a settlement, and by Polk's distrust of his military commanders,
especially Taylor and Winfield Scott, who were both Whigs and
prospective candidates for the 1848 presidential election. While Polk
was upset with Trist's apparent arrogance, the administration accepted the Treaty of Guadalupe Hidalgo, which he negotiated. With
the cabinet divided on the issue, the president forwarded the treaty
to the Senate, and he observed blithely that it had never been his
objective to conquer the Republic of Mexico or destroy her separate existence. Privately, he accepted the treaty because of growing
opposition to his war policies in Congress, increasing problems with
the U.S. Army in Mexico, and the prospect of losing control of New

Mexico and upper California. On March 10, the Senate approved the treaty 38 to 14.[59]

Polk's war had several major consequences: it further antagonized Mexico, created several visible Whig military heroes out of mediocre military men, and added more territory in the South. In the end, the Mexican War laid down straw on the tinderbox of slavery and helped lead to the Civil War. As for Polk himself, his aggressive foreign policies had added so much land that it rivaled the purchase of the Louisiana Territory. The apostle of Manifest Destiny became the father of the states of Oregon, Washington, Idaho, California, New Mexico, Arizona, Nevada, Utah, and parts of Colorado, Montana, and Wyoming.

Unlike Madison, Polk proved to be a strong and decisive commander in chief, unconcerned with the debate on inherent powers that would figure so prominently in the Civil War. Ironically, while Lincoln opposed the administration's policies in the Mexican War, there is considerable evidence that he emulated Polk in taking an even broader view of the wartime powers of the presidency, one at variance with the Whig philosophy Lincoln held throughout most of his adult life. Whether Polk was a role model for Lincoln is unclear, but there are great areas of resemblance in their vigorous and personal prosecution of the war.

As with Polk's decision to send the troops into disputed territory, Lincoln would be criticized for allegedly having provoked the Confederate states into attacking Fort Sumter. Polk refused to call Congress into session when it appeared likely that Mexico would move against the U.S. Army. Lincoln also did not call Congress back into session for three months as the Civil War was beginning, apparently fearing legislative interference. Later, each Congress declared that a state of war had already existed and gave legislative approval for a president's actions as commander in chief at the time.

Polk, however, in fighting his war, did not ask for an immediate increase in the regular army, preferring at first to rely on volunteer regiments of state militia. When he finally changed his policy and asked Congress for ten regiments, he had to wait from December 1846 to February 1847 for approval. The administration's strategy in the war was to seize the northern provinces of Mexico, capture New Mexico and its critical commercial gateway Santa Fe, move its naval forces toward California, and conquer Mexico City by landing at Vera Cruz and conducting a forced march to the capital city. Unfortunately for Polk, General Taylor on September 25 captured

Monterey and later granted the Mexican forces an armistice. Polk ordered an end to the truce and commanded General Taylor to continue the fight. Then fearing that Santa Anna would send reinforcements to the Mexican forces, Polk ordered Taylor to halt. The general, however, ignored the command and moved on toward Buena Vista where he won a widely renowned victory. The president was incensed at Taylor and concluded, "he is evidently a weak man and has been made giddy with the idea of the Presidency." Polk had the same disdain and suspicion of General Scott who was in charge of the march from Vera Cruz to Mexico City. In his diary, Polk confided, "The truth is that I have been compelled from the beginning to conduct the war against Mexico though the agency of two Gen'ls highest in rank who have not only no sympathies with the Government, but are hostile to my administration."[60] Finally, he replaced Scott after a controversial move by the general to court-martial three other officers. Like Lincoln, Polk grew weary of the inactivity of professional soldiers, and he even got involved in supply problems and purchasing decisions. But unlike Lincoln, Wilson, and Franklin Roosevelt, Polk consistently remained involved in tactics and details while overseeing the strategies of the conflict.

Having been a leader in Congress in a way that no president before him had, except Madison in the 1790s, Polk had a real understanding of the legislative process and the personalities in the legislative branch. Jackson had been able to assert the primacy of the presidency by stressing polarizing issues and by the sheer force of his magnetic personality. Polk had no such personal appeal for the mass of the citizenry, but he was fairly successful in dealing with congressional leaders by stressing the ties of party. He insisted that it was the president and not Congress who represented the national will of the people, and he acted accordingly.

The major domestic piece of legislation the president pushed was the passage of a lower tariff schedule. As a congressional leader and as governor of Tennessee, he had been an advocate of a lower tariff and supported Jackson and Van Buren in their positions. Most of the Democratic party, except in Pennsylvania and in some other industrial areas, had adopted a low tariff plank. Polk appealed to party loyalty to sway wavering Democrats in the Senate, and the new tariff schedule passed that body by only a one-vote margin before it was approved by the House.[61]

Like any good party leader, Polk counted noses and let wayward Democrats know of his disappointment at deviations. His ire was especially fueled by Calhoun and his followers who seemed to take pleasure in joining with the Whigs in opposition. As noted, there was increasing criticism of his war policies, especially in the House, which went Whig in the 1848 elections. On January 3, 1847, that body voted 85 to 81 that the war had been "unnecessarily and unconstitutionality begun by the president of the United States." The year before, a Democrat-controlled House had voted for war by a count of 174 to 14.[62]

New territory raised again the issue of sectional balance and slavery. Polk used his persuasive powers to convince Representative David Wilmot of Pennsylvania not to push his resolution banning slavery in the territories to be acquired from Mexico. He assured him that he did not wish to extend slavery, and that the provinces of New Mexico and California were not suitable for slavery. Wilmot held back on introducing his proviso, but eventually it became part of the congressional debate. Prophetically Polk warned, "The movement . . . will be attended with terrible consequences to the country, and cannot fail to destroy the Democratic party, if it does not ultimately threaten the Union itself."

As with the Louisiana Purchase, there were questions of territorial governments that had to be addressed in those newly acquired areas. Polk supported the extension of the Missouri Compromise, fearing that leaving the slavery question undecided would encourage "ambitious political aspirants & gamblers" to establish parties based on geographical divisions that would imperil the Union. By August though, the subject of a territorial government for Oregon was separated from the fate of California and New Mexico. Since the president had accepted the Missouri Compromise line, he had no problem with the bill even though it prohibited slavery in Oregon. Southern opposition, led by Calhoun, mobilized to stop the bill before adjournment. Polk, in response, threatened to reconvene Congress the next day, and eventually the Oregon bill was passed and Polk signed it.

Polk, though, remained concerned about the problem of territorial governments for New Mexico and California. Senator Benton had issued a public letter to Californians that implied they should form a government with his son-in-law Colonel John C. Frémont as governor. Polk wanted to counter that letter with one of his own, but he was uncertain at first if legally the president and the military could govern the area before Congress passed appropriate legislation. His own attorney general had upheld the right of the people to choose their own government in the absence of congressional legislation.

Finally after a long cabinet session, the president concluded that the inhabitants should obey the existing government there, and Polk opposed any convention being called to form a new government. He was concerned that a Whig victory in the 1848 election would mean that California would simply go its own way. Polk then decided to throw his support behind Senator Stephen Douglas's bill to admit California into the Union and allow the people in that territory to decide if slavery should be permitted. When Calhoun sought to mobilize the Southerners of both parties in opposition, Polk, himself a Southerner and a slaveholder, used the powers of his office to oppose what he saw as growing agitation. He then even courted Whigs to support the Douglas bill. Concerned about sectionalism, he explained, "I regarded the subject above mere party considerations, and wished it settled, I cared not by whose votes."[63] But the bill did not pass in his term.

Polk was clearly a party leader who was sensitive to the legacy of Jefferson and Jackson and astute enough to press the case for loyalty and regularity. He insisted on establishing a new newspaper that would carry his message and curtail the admirers of Van Buren, and he was the last president to have an effective administration-controlled newspaper. After his term, individual entrepreneurs established their own papers, which were more critical and later sensationalist in spreading the word to a more literate citizenry.

He also tried to use his patronage powers to satisfy the various wings of the party, but concluded that the demands were insatiable. Still, he removed in one year more than seven hundred individuals in the Post Office alone. In four years, over 13,500 postmasters were replaced out of a total of 16,000 such positions available. When some New Yorkers and others joined the Free-Soil party with Van Buren, those former Democrats were cut off from the public trough. The loss of this so-called Barnburner element of the Democratic party, as it was called, was to prove most significant to the outcome of the next presidential election.[64]

Polk was also conscientious about avoiding congressional intrusion with its use of investigative powers into the workings of the executive branch. Several times he refused to respond to requests for information, calling it a dangerous precedent. In other instances, such as a diplomatic incident concerning Ireland, he edited the correspondence he had on the matter. These claims of executive privilege, as they came to be called in the 1950s, were seen by Polk as based on his predecessors' actions and on his constitutional duty and sense of public interest.[65]

Although Polk remains a little-known president today, he emerges by the sheer force of his will and determination as one of the nation's strongest chief executives. Except for Lincoln, he is surely the most able of the nineteenth-century executives, and as with Jefferson, he left an incredible record of territorial gain and expansion. Less than a year after he left office Polk died at the early age of fifty-three, burned out from the pace and intensity of his duties.

What makes Polk's accomplishments all the more arresting is that he lacked a broad personal following or strong public support that he could count on. He was the first "dark horse" candidate, underestimated and little known—a Harry Truman of his time. In terms of his administration's stated objectives, it is clear that he was an ardent expansionist who would counsel peace, wage war, tolerate negotiations to spread the eagle across the North American continent. James K. Polk was the greatest and most successful American imperialist of them all.

Thus, the Jacksonian presidents changed the very nature of the presidency and the character and reach of the republic. The chief magistrate style of Washington and Adams gave way to the subtle directions of the Jeffersonians, and then was eclipsed by the direct, personal, and vigorous exploits of Jackson and his successors. The major intellectual and political opposition to this new model of the presidency came from the Whigs, who articulated a philosophy that emphasized a clear division of powers between the legislative and executive branches, and a presidency that was not to be as direct and as powerful as it was during Andrew Jackson's terms in office. The Whigs were never able to field a candidate who stayed in office long enough to implement that philosophy, but their views of the office were to become an important part of the American political tradition.

What followed the Jacksonian period was a presidency hamstrung by the divisions of sectionalism and the decline of the once-effective party system. And the consequences would be a terrible civil war that would bring forth initially a former Whig as president, and then in turn spawn an executive and an administration of unparalleled authority in a period of unparalleled danger.

5

The Decline of the Executive
(Taylor, Fillmore, Pierce,
and Buchanan)

The period from Polk to the emergence of Lincoln witnessed a decline in the ability of executive authority to meet the increasing sectional problems plaguing the nation. For several generations, the American people had canonized the principle of the separation of powers, and in the process had curtailed the ability of government to act without substantial consensus. But slavery and sectionalism prevented such a consensus from occurring, and the weaknesses of the American political system were apparent and dangerous in their consequences. The early models of the presidency from Washington to Jefferson to Jackson were irrelevant as the Union moved toward immobilization and finally total collapse. Still, in the late 1840s and 1850s, these problems were obvious but not yet critical. There still seemed time to play politics as usual.

ZACHARY TAYLOR AND THE UNION

Faced with a tradition of being the out-party and remembering fondly Harrison's victory, the Whig party leaders looked around for another war hero to head up the ticket. Attention turned to Winfield Scott and Zachary Taylor, the latter eventually being touted as the "Hero of Buena Vista." Secretary of War William L. Marcy had concluded early that Taylor's victories in the Mexican War would make him a leading candidate, and Thurlow Weed, New York editor and Whig politico, counseled Taylor's brother to tell the general that he should write no letters dealing with politics and should avoid discussing the issues.

171

Across the nation, clubs pushing Taylor's candidacy were springing up, although some questioned whether he even was a Whig. In fact, there was no record that Taylor had ever voted. But as one of Taylor's biographers, Holman Hamilton, has concluded, "Across the nation most Whigs were factionists first and partisans later. This was Whiggery's heritage."[1]

Taylor's main advisor was the distinguished Kentucky senator, John J. Crittenden, who apparently had given up on Henry Clay's perennial campaign for the presidency. Taylor, though, was unsure of his own intentions, arguing that he had "always been against the elevating of a military chief to that position," and then going on to propose General Scott as an alternative. In December 1846, a group of young Whig congressmen formed a Taylor club; some of its members included Alexander H. Stephens and Robert Toombs of Georgia and Abraham Lincoln of Illinois. Most of these members had at one time or another supported Clay in past elections.

By February 1847, Taylor had won his campaign at Buena Vista and his candidacy skyrocketed. One problem for Taylor was the so-called Conscience Whigs who insisted that candidates accept the Wilmot Proviso, which demanded that slavery be prohibited in the territories acquired from Mexico. In the vocabulary of the times, the Conscience Whigs were totally opposed to slavery and insisted that the party's nominees be pledged to end that abuse; Democrats who also opposed the extension of slavery were called Barnburners, after the farmers who would burn down their barns to drive out the rats; the Whigs in turn labeled all Democrats "Locofocos" after an anti-Tammany group who used friction matches (locofocos) for illumination when Tammany Hall regulars turned out the lights on them; more conservative Democrats were called Hunker Democrats, that is people who "hankered" or "hunkered" for patronage jobs. The latter group had supported James K. Polk, and its members were pledged to Cass or to Buchanan.

In Congress, however, another view was gathering support: Vice President George M. Dallas and then Senator Lewis Cass pushed for a settlement called "popular sovereignty." Under this proposal, the inhabitants of each territory would decide whether to permit slavery or not, thus getting the issue out of Congress and supposedly out of national politics. It would be a position that was most closely articulated by Stephen Douglas in his campaigns for the Senate and later the presidency.

Meanwhile, the political bandwagon for Taylor rolled on. In

Pennsylvania, Democratic support gathered for the general, and rumors circulated in the South that the ailing Calhoun would accept Taylor. In 1848, the controversial Native American party offered Taylor its nomination, which he deftly sidestepped. Still its party leaders would later promote his name and provide him with important support in Pennsylvania without his having to embrace publicly that much criticized group. By 1848, General Scott had become enmeshed in a bitter controversy with several other generals and had made remarks that had offended some immigrants. As for Taylor, he was becoming increasingly angry with the Polk administration for what he viewed as a politically motivated attempt to curtail his command and force him into retirement. That anger was making him more prone to announce his candidacy, even though he naively insisted on a nonpartisan nomination.

Taylor informed his supporters that he was a follower of Jefferson, whatever that meant in the 1840s, and that he would have voted for Clay if he had voted at all, which he did not. He regarded the national bank as a dead issue, favored a modest increase in the tariff for revenue, saw the Wilmot Proviso (which would limit the reach of slavery) as "a seven-day wonder," and stressed the need to protect the rights of slaveholders by the sword if necessary. Yet he put that defense of Southern rights within an important context that was publicly overlooked at the time by his advisors from that region. He remained like many military men a nationalist. "I will not make myself unhappy at what I cannot prevent; nor give up the Constitution or abandon it because a rent had been made in it, but will stick by & repair it, & reuse it as long as it will hang together,"[2] he asserted on one occasion.

He held the traditional Whig view favoring a weak executive; in part, this belief was the party's reaction to the legacy of Jackson and Polk. Taylor believed that while no president should hesitate to veto any law that conflicted with the Constitution, "on matters of expediency great forbearance should be used and only after the most mature consideration" should that check be employed. He opposed the centralization of power in the hands of "the chief magistrate," fearing that it "is rapidly swallowing up the other two [branches of government]."

As Taylor sought to lay out his beliefs on the great public issues of the day, his advisors were aghast when some of his letters were made public, and they asked him to stop responding to inquiries. One influential opponent, Horace Greeley, stated the case against the general by citing his proslavery views, his opposition to the Wilmot Proviso, the concerns of Old Whigs about his steadfastness, and his probable weaknesses when he would have to deal with patronage and political demands. However, when Clay's candidacy collapsed and Webster's ambitions were quickly checked, the general emerged as the most available man. As for Taylor, he summed up his credo with the declaration, "I am a Whig but not an ultra Whig."[3] That meager reassurance was enough for a party denied so often the fruits of victory, and Taylor was nominated on the fourth ballot with solid Southern support. For vice president, the party turned to Millard Fillmore from Buffalo, New York, who had been chairman of the House Ways and Means Committee and a candidate for the second slot four years before. The party adopted no platform, seeking to avoid the issues. Characteristically, Taylor received the news of his nomination in a peculiar way. The official notification came by mail, but since Taylor had a policy of not accepting letters with postage due, the letter was returned. Thus, an unprepared and rather limited military man, who entered the race partially out of pique with the Polk administration and later General Winfield Scott, accepted a major party's nomination in an almost diffident way. "Old Rough and Ready," as he was called in military circles, now was on the verge of assuming the highest position in the land.

As his advisors counseled silence, and as he remained on active duty as commander of the Western Division, Whigs expressed their delight with their candidate. Even Abraham Lincoln concluded, "We shall have a most overwhelming, glorious triumph." Meanwhile, the Democrats had turned to Lewis Cass, a well-known political figure and a hero in the War of 1812. In addition, the Free Soil party joined with elements of the Conscience Whigs (mainly abolitionists), Liberty party, and Barnburner Democrats to nominate Martin Van Buren for president with Charles Francis Adams for the second position. Lincoln sarcastically compared their platform at one point to the pantaloons a Yankee peddler once offered for sale, "large enough for any man, small enough for any boy."[4]

In the election, about 77.1 percent of the eligible voters (only 13.1 percent of the population) went to the polls, and Taylor carried the nation by 1,360,099 to 1,220,544 in the popular vote and 163 to 127 in the electoral college. Taylor ran well in most areas except in the West where he did not carry a single state. Overall, he benefited from the backing of many independent Democrats, and took four important states that Clay lost in 1844: Georgia, Louisiana, New York, and Pennsylvania. Because March 4 fell on a Sunday, Taylor waited until the next day to be officially inaugurated; some historians have whimsically concluded that Senate President Pro Tempore David R. Atchison was legally the acting president from noon of March 4 to noon of March 5. Apparently he slept through his twenty-four-hour term, making him both a curious footnote in history and also one of the few presidents, if he was one constitutionally, who caused no damage to the republic and left no enemies during his term.[5]

In any case, Taylor as president carefully balanced his cabinet geographically and turned over patronage matters to his subordinates, finding the whole practice annoying. Democrats charged that appointees were picked by secret ballot in the cabinet, with the president's own vote being only one in eight. In a few cases, this criticism appears to be so, but Taylor was also extensively involved in patronage removals. As the first Whig to serve more than a few weeks as president, Taylor found that there was considerable pressure to reallocate jobs to the hungry faithful. Removals, were, of course, not unheard of. Although the figures are incomplete, historian Holman Hamilton has concluded that Jefferson had removed 69 officeholders, Madison 27, Monroe 27, Adams 12, and Jackson 252. Van Buren had gotten rid of 80 officeholders, Harrison and Tyler 458, and Polk 342. Taylor's record was more extensive than any of his predecessors. In Taylor's first year in office, when the civil service embraced some 17,780 officials, 3,400 were removed and 2,800 resigned. The most famous removal was, of course, the American man of letters, Nathaniel Hawthorne, who had been customs surveyor at Salem, Massachusetts. After his firing, Hawthorne went on to write *The Scarlet Letter*, *The House of the Seven Gables*, *The Blithedale Romance*, and a less-memorable biography of Franklin Pierce. The most famous oversight by Taylor of a Whig politician in the patronage morass is usually identified as Abraham Lincoln who was supposedly denied the positions of commissioner of the Land Office and then governor of the Oregon Territory. Actually, Lincoln may have turned down the latter position, choosing to remain a well-paid corporate attorney and eventually becoming a candidate for higher office.

Generally, the new president was considered an outsider in the capital, an obstinate, but forthright man who overall made a rather commonplace impression. Former Vice President Dallas concluded,

"If he has any intellectual greatness, physiognomy is a cheat." Polk glumly judged that his successor was "exceedingly ignorant of public affairs, and . . . of very ordinary capacity." Physically, he did not exhibit a very commanding presence. Taylor was about five feet, eight inches tall, muscular, big boned, broad shouldered, and heavily tanned from the Mexican sun. At times he seemed embarrassed or almost shy, he chewed tobacco, and he worked hard to curb his temper. He and his wife were comparably well born and linked by family ties to some of the best-known families of the old South including Robert E. Lee, John Taylor, and the Barbour, Pendleton, Strother, and Dabney clans. His Mississippi neighbors said he was a humane slavemaster, and Taylor euphemistically referred to his slaves as "servants."[6]

Taylor believed in a strongly well-defined delegation of authority, as befitted a military man. He made no real attempt to create a bloc of congressional supporters and stressed his nonpartisan profile as a president above politics. A not very objective Clay complained in 1850, "I have never before seen such an administration. There is very little co-operation or concord between the two ends of the avenue. There is not, I believe a prominent Whig in either House that has any confidential intercourse with the Executive."[7]

In terms of his activities, Taylor countenanced moderate foreign and Indian policies. When panic over the Seminole Indians struck south Florida, Taylor ordered some reinforcements into the area, but refused to call up the militia, correctly seeing it not as a situation comparable to 1818 or to 1837 when Andrew Jackson and Taylor himself led American troops into that swampy region. In foreign affairs, the president generally deferred to his secretary of state, John Middleton Clayton of Delaware. The administration was involved in several minor but frustrating episodes with the French government and Portugal, and the Taylor administration welcomed British and French intervention in Hispaniola to halt a conflict between Haiti and the Dominican Republic. The United States government also refused to support uprisings against the Spanish to liberate Cuba, long an object of envy among Southerners who saw it as a definite addition to slave state ranks. Most importantly though, the administration approved the Clayton-Bulwer Treaty.

Concerned about British moves in Central America, the secretary of state embraced the idea of a treaty governing the construction of a proposed transisthmian canal across Nicaragua. Previously, the British had extended a protectorate over the Mosquito Indians and used that leverage to take possession of the city of San Juan. Now, the two nations mutually pledged to avoid unilateral control over any canal that might be built, supported the neutralization of the route, and pledged to be guarantors of the waterway, assuring free passage in time of war. They would extend their pledges as well to any other canal built in the south of Mexico or in Panama. Construction of the Nicaraguan canal was to begin within a year. Thus, the administration rejected the romantic expansionism of Manifest Destiny into the Central American area and also accepted British influence in the Western Hemisphere, an abridgment of the Monroe Doctrine. The treaty produced few results, however, in furthering closer Anglo-American ties.

Foreign policy matters consumed little of President Taylor's time or interest. His major concern was the mounting domestic controversy over the fate of the territories, especially California and New Mexico. Despite Taylor's Southern power base and his slaveholding record, he was a dedicated nationalist whose whole professional military career was devoted to the integrity of the republic. Like Jackson, and unlike Robert E. Lee, he identified his military service with an indivisible Union, and he threatened to lead the troops himself to thwart any secessionists. Taylor pushed for quick statehood for both California and New Mexico as a way to dampen congressional acrimony, and the administration was willing to check Texas's intention to claim vast areas of the New Mexico Territory. Under Polk, the administration had generally supported Texas Governor Sam Houston's assertion that the boundary of that nation was the Rio Grande from mouth to source, which would include large areas of what is now New Mexico, including the capital Santa Fe. Taylor refused to accept those grandiose claims and backed up his view with tough talk and the threat of troops. In addition, the administration was seriously considering extending admission to the Mormon state of Deseret (later Utah), giving some support to those inhabitants' desire for an ocean outlet at what is now San Diego.

The Southern leaders in Congress, spearheaded by Calhoun, realized that the balance in the Senate would be permanently ended by the admission of more free states. The president was increasingly alienating himself from Southern elements in his own party, and turned more to the Seward-Weed faction in the Northeast and to the tariff protectionist elements in Pennsylvania for support. In late 1849 and early 1850, the Whigs controlled neither house of Congress, marking the first time a popularly elected president's party was totally in the minority in the legislative branch.

Taylor's recommendations to that Congress included admission of California and New Mexico, adjustment of the tariff, surveys of railroad routes to the West Coast and of gold areas of California, and a revamping of military recruitment. He refused to support the notion of "open" territories where slaveholding was unlimited. Unlike Jackson and Polk, he informed his audience that the president was not a direct representative of the American people, but a part of a balanced form of government. He then reiterated his commitment to the Union, saying, "Whatsoever dangers may threaten it, I shall stand by it and maintain it in its integrity."[8]

The focal point of debate then changed to the Senate where Clay called for organizing the territories without regard to slavery, granting California the right to choose on the issue, proposing that the federal government assume the debt of the Republic of Texas in return for ending its claims to New Mexico, abolishing the slave trade (but not slavery) in the District of Columbia, and supporting a stronger fugitive slave law. Clay warned of secession unless the outstanding tensions between the sections were pacified. He even called on the memory of the revered first president, and dramatically held high a fragment from Washington's coffin, which had somehow come into his possession. However, when he finished, Clay was able to carry only two Northern Whig senators with him, Daniel Webster and James Cooper of Pennsylvania. The rest stayed with Taylor's harder line. Most of Clay's support then came from the Democrats, and in the end, it was Stephen Douglas who finally put the compromise over after an aged and weary "Harry of the West" retired from the field of battle.

In the debate that followed Clay's speech, Calhoun barely referred to Clay's resolutions, but attacked Taylor's plans as an "executive proviso" that was unconstitutional, unjust, and meant to destroy the equilibrium between the sections. He judged that at least the Wilmot Proviso, which prohibited slavery in newly conquered Mexican lands, was open and direct in its true intention. Calhoun called for a constitutional amendment to restore balance in the federal government in order to protect the slave states, and he warned that the admission of California would prove that "your real objects are power and aggrandizement." The finest and most memorable response, though, was Webster's magnificent declamation on

March 7 exclaiming that he was not a Northerner nor a Massachusetts man, but an American, and pleading for a triumph of national spirit over sectional bitterness.[9]

The debate also saw William Seward's response, which was initially aimed at supporting Taylor's plan. In that address, the New York senator concluded that "there is a higher law than the Constitution, which regulates our authority," a natural law, which prohibited slavery in all its forms wherever men of conscience gathered. But after these brilliant speeches were given, few votes changed.

The differences of opinion had taken their toll on party loyalty. With a split in the Whig ranks, Taylor increasingly felt more at home with the Northern Whigs than with the Southerners of his own background and class. Stubbornly opposed to compromise on the territorial status of California and New Mexico and deeply committed to the defense of the Union by arms if necessary, Taylor began to sound more like Andrew Jackson in the Nullification Controversy in 1833. He not only threatened to lead the troops against any Texans who dared to move into New Mexico, but also warned secessionist elements meeting in Nashville in June that he would institute a blockade of Southern ports and set up an embargo of their goods—contingency plans that were implemented by Lincoln in 1861.

At the same time, Sam Houston charged that the president had defamed Texas during the Mexican War and still retained those derogatory attitudes in the current controversy. From February to July, nothing changed much in the Senate despite the speeches and parliamentary maneuvers. Cries of impeachment against the president were heard, and the Southerners began to support Texas's belligerence in the New Mexico controversy. Taylor insisted that he would lead federal troops himself if Texas attacked the United States. He had sworn an oath to protect the Union against all assaults, an oath that the old soldier would honor.

As the summer progressed, the president stood firmly against "open" territories where there would be no limitations on slaveholding. When Southerners presented their compromise proposals, which included the "open" territory plan, Taylor opposed it; when they warned of secession, his anger exploded at the threats. The real impetus for a settlement was Senator Douglas's ingenious alliance between House Whigs and Democrats and his own efforts in the Senate to hold on to a Clay-Cass coalition. The major obstacle to such a settlement remained—the threat of a presidential veto, and there was no likelihood of overriding Taylor. The compromise that was taking shape contained the following terms and showed Clay's earlier influence: California could enter as a free state, the territories of Utah and New Mexico were to be created without reference to slavery, and Texas's claims were to be paid. The fugitive slave law was strengthened and the shipment of slaves to the District of Columbia was forbidden.

As for Taylor, his feelings of alienation toward Clay and his movement toward Seward and the Northern Whigs were accelerating. However, opposition to his position was also mounting; even Vice President Fillmore informed the president that he would personally support the compromise. Then on July 4, the president sat through a long ceremony at the Washington Monument, eating cherries and drinking cold milk, and, according to legend, ending up contracting Asiatic cholera. More likely he suffered an attack of acute gastroenteritis, aggravated by the sun and a long history of ailments. On July 9, he died.

The practical result was that the main executive bottleneck to the Compromise of 1850 was removed. Taylor had proven to be a much stronger nationalist than anyone could have anticipated. Still he embraced a quasi-Jeffersonian inclination against expansive government and reaffirmed his commitment to a narrowly defined Constitution. He also held the traditional Whig view that limited the scope of the presidency, except in military and foreign policies, and he insisted on reserving the veto for only the most egregious legislative transgressions of the Constitution. In general, he seemed to have few views on many main issues, and was probably developing his own positions at the time of his death.

The Whigs had desperately wanted to capture the presidency and resorted to a replay of the Harrison strategy—with the same results. As has been noted, the Whig legacy ended up in the White House only when it entered under the aegis of the Republican party in the person of a true follower of Clay and Taylor, Abraham Lincoln.

FILLMORE'S COMPROMISE

In the late evening of July 9, the vice president received formal notice of Taylor's death. The situation Fillmore inherited was a very tense one indeed. A few days earlier, the rumors had reached Washington that Texas intended to send 2,500 men into the disputed territories, and President Taylor was determined to resist with U.S. troops any challenge to federal authority if necessary. Southern congressmen swung behind Texas, in part as a rebuke to Taylor's intransigence on the compromise; on July 6, ninety-one congressmen supported a motion to censure the president, using a Treasury scandal as the immediate reason. Two weeks before, 180 leaders of the South met in Nashville to assert their rights to bring slaves into the Southwest.

Fillmore had to face the compromise issue immediately after taking office. He was committed to a quieting solution to the sectional controversy, but he reaffirmed his personal disposition against slavery. Yet Fillmore sought an end to agitation and political acrimony, and was willing to risk severe criticism for his decision to compromise. The new president accepted the resignations of the cabinet secretaries and then asked them to stay on temporarily. In dealing with them, Fillmore turned most often to Daniel Webster for advice on appointments, and he applied the criteria of Whig orthodoxy and common sense in choosing future nominees.

In terms of Douglas's compromise plan, the new president quickly concluded that such a broad collection of proposals presented problems. Employing Webster as a go-between, Fillmore encouraged Douglas to agree to support separate measures if the large single compromise proposal failed. When Clay allowed the issue of New Mexico's border to be clouded, Fillmore pushed for a clearer statement on the issue even if the Omnibus Bill would be the victim of that decision. Congress finally adopted several measures to enact the Clay-Douglas agreement into law; the president then warned Texas, as strongly as Taylor had, about the federal government's title in that region. Working with Webster and Douglas, he agreed to enlarge Texas's boundaries enough to win the approval of its senators.

Publicly, the new president appealed to Congress to act quickly and decisively in order to further domestic tranquility. For moderate people of influence and means and for committed Unionists, Fillmore's tone was reassuring. The Senate, almost as if taking its cue, passed the Texas boundary bill and then approved the California, New Mexico, and fugitive slave measures. After some hesitation, it abolished the slave trade in the District of Columbia. By mid-September, the House of Representatives followed suit. The president added his approval to the general package, although he wavered on the fugitive slave law; out of deference to Northern public opinion, he concluded one should "avoid the imputation of hasty and unconsidered action."[10]

One of Fillmore's objectives in restoring public peace was the desire to further the Whig party's fortunes. Ironically, the party would be split by the compromise and would never again come to power after his term ended. The ambitious Northern wing, led by Seward and Weed in New York, turned against the compromise and then abandoned the idea of a party that would bridge the sections on the divisive issue of slavery. The Northern wing moved toward an alliance with free soil Democrats, Know-Nothings, and other splinter groups that founded the Republican party in 1856. One element of that new party would be the Weed-Seward faction, which used the compromise in New York as a way to undercut its fellow New Yorker Fillmore's political fortunes and limit his presidential influence in that state.

Fillmore was generally a calm and decent fellow, a self-made man, one who sought prestige and respect, but who rarely used the full powers of his position to push himself or what he believed in. The president insisted instead on promoting party unity with the same intensity he promoted national unity—in both cases with very limited success. As Fillmore expected, the greatest problem that emerged from the compromise was the fugitive slave law, which tugged at the hearts of many otherwise compromising people and earned him history's enmity among abolitionist authors and orators. A fugitive slave law had been passed in 1793 and signed by President Washington; the enforcement of it and other statutes dealing with the same question had depended over the years on the cooperation of state and local officials. As resistance increased, the responsibility for implementation fell more and more on federal officials. After the passage of the 1850 law, two Pennsylvania judges asked the president for a general order to support the law. Fillmore was a good enough politician to see the request as "a grave and delicate question," although he was sworn to uphold the act. His cabinet unanimously agreed that he had the duty to use military force to aid civil officers in enforcing the new act. A wary president wrote Webster that while he personally detested slavery, he felt that it had to be endured and protected since it was guaranteed by the Constitution.[11]

The president was especially aware of agitation in the South. Southern governors began to complain about the federal government's attitude toward their problems, and a second Nashville Convention was called on November 12, 1850. Fillmore was informed of some plans to seize federal forts in Charleston as the first step to general secession. The U.S. attorney and other federal officers in the state resigned in order to impede the U.S. government, and the president groped around for replacements. Fillmore finally called in General Scott to prepare for the defense of Charleston, and troops were sent into South Carolina and stationed at critical points elsewhere. When the governor of South Carolina demanded to know the president's intentions, a determined Fillmore replied that as commander in chief, he had the right to place troops where he thought it was necessary for the public interest.

What saved the president from a major confrontation was the general economic prosperity and the election results in Georgia. There, influential leaders supported the compromise, and thus undercut the impetus of secessionists in the South. The second Nashville Convention fizzled out. As for Fillmore, he continued to press for political peace and opposed any modification of the fugitive slave law, noting "time and experience shall demonstrate the necessity of further legislation to guard against evasion or abuse."[12]

Ever the practical man, Fillmore stressed economic ties that fostered national unity and prosperity: railroads, canals, new industry, and international commerce. His administration celebrated the expansion of the railroad network with Canada, the link between the Great Lakes and the Atlantic Ocean, and the establishment of a steamer run between New England and Liverpool. By 1850, American traders had increasingly focused on the Orient—new and exotic markets for the import/export trade. Following Taylor's example, Fillmore supported a Nicaraguan canal route to join the two oceans, and with Secretary of State Webster in poor health, Fillmore took up the direction of his own foreign policy at times.

In the end, however, Fillmore was unsuccessful in getting a canal, and the Mexican Congress was unwilling to approve the establishment of a railroad in the Tehuantepec region. The president was reluctant to pressure the Mexicans on the issue concluding, "I am not willing to see the nation involved in war with Mexico to gratify . . . the cupidity of any private company." The same sort of moderation was exhibited in American policy toward the Hawaiian Islands and China as well. The United States pushed for an early version of an "open door" policy for Hawaii, although there was some domestic support for the annexation of the islands even at that time.[13]

In terms of Japan, though, the administration was more assertive and sent Commodore Matthew C. Perry to open up that nation
to Western trade—whether it wanted to be opened or not. Perry was
instrumental in pushing for an agreement that would protect American citizens; previously the commodore had been informed that since
the "president had no power to declare war," his mission was to be
a peaceful one, and he was not to resort to force except in self-
defense or in dealing with an act of personal violence against the
commander or crew. Perry entered the Bay of Yedo with four warships and presented in a dignified demeanor the president's formal
address to the shogun of the emperor. Then he bluntly informed them
that in ten days' time he would return with an even larger force.
When he did return, that nation was to be opened up to Western
commerce, ideas, and ambitions.[14] Thus began one of the most fate-
ful voyages in American and Japanese history.

Elsewhere, in his dealings with Peru and its territorial claims
for a nearby archipelago, and in judging the continuing turmoil in
Cuba, Fillmore gave up the grandiose rhetoric of Manifest Destiny.
Like Taylor, he refused to support attempts to overthrow the Spanish regime in Cuba or to annex that island to the United States.
Under pressure on the latter issue, the president advised Congress,
"Were this island comparatively destitute of inhabitants, or occupied by a kindred race, I shall regard it, if voluntarily ceded by
Spain, as a most desirable acquisition. But under existing circum-
stances, I should look upon its incorporation into our Union as a
most hazardous measure."

The same sort of cautious attitude was expressed in his cool
welcoming of Lajos Kossuth, the Hungarian aristocrat, who fought
for independence against the Austrians. The administration, led by
Webster, presented the United States as an example to freedom-lov-
ing peoples of the world, as a nation that both abstained from the
turmoils in Europe and wished success to countries struggling for
independence. Yet, in this case, the president personally distrusted
Kossuth, proclaiming him "not a statesman," and refused to grant a
personal endorsement for his efforts.

Fillmore overall was a steady and dignified person, who seemed
to mute the sharpness of obvious personal ambition. His colleagues
wrote that he was always open to discussion, but once he made up
his mind, he stuck with his decisions. One of his cabinet officers,
John Crittenden, concluded that in three years of working closely
with him, he had never heard Fillmore "utter a foolish or unmean-

ing word." But as his term ended, Fillmore seemed to be unclear about seeking reelection. He privately indicated a desire to retire from the field, but let his name be placed in nomination; however, Fillmore was unable to win enough votes and General Winfield Scott received the nod.[15]

The Whig party was left with little leadership. Its sitting president seemed unsure of his own intentions and ambitions, and Webster, past his prime, continued to search for his lost dream. He concluded to a friend that the presidency was "the greatest office in the world; and I am but a man, sir, I want it, I want it." But he did not get it. And so, the party again turned to a military man, the ultimate prescription of a bankrupt political party. The Democrats nominated another son of Andrew Jackson, and won with dark horse Franklin Pierce, a Northern man who sympathized with Southern fears. Scott ended up carrying only four states—Massachusetts, Vermont, Kentucky, and Tennessee, while Pierce carried the other twenty-seven states and received 51 percent of the popular vote to Scott's 44 percent.

As he concluded his term, Fillmore prepared a long statement warning that slavery would bring race warfare, political disruption, and continued agitation. He proposed that deus ex machina, the recolonization of blacks out of the United States into Africa or the West Indies—an idea that held a peculiar fascination for Lincoln and innumerable opponents of slavery over the years. The cabinet opposed publication of the message, however, urging the president to avoid exciting public passions, an argument telling to him. Fillmore thus concluded his presidency as he began it—on a cautionary note aimed at curtailing sectional fires and passionate outbursts of political animosities. It is commonplace to portray Fillmore as a dignified-looking mediocrity, but he was a cautious political leader who had modest expectations for himself and his nation. He avoided the stirring calls to Manifest Destiny and annexation so characteristic of his time and position. Fillmore not only supported the Clay-Douglas compromise, but he also helped refashion it to meet his and Taylor's concerns about New Mexico and achieve a conclusion to the controversies about the lands and wealth of the Southwest.

But the Compromise of 1850, which congressional leaders and Fillmore pushed, did not end the sectional rivalry. And the admission of California, New Mexico, and eventually Utah as Taylor had proposed did not calm the public mind. The Whig party was torn apart in the process of reconciliation; soon the Democratic party would become a casualty as well. Then the Republicans would come to power, and the impetus for secession and war would overwhelm all. The Whig administration of Taylor and Fillmore was an Indian summer of peace, whose hues and tints barely camouflaged the storm ahead.

THE PIERCE PRESIDENCY

To hold their diverse party together, the Democratic kingmakers looked for a Northern politician acceptable to the South and chose Franklin Pierce. Pierce was the son of a respected New Hampshire war hero and governor, and almost immediately after completing his study of law, he entered public service. A handsome, articulate, and studiously polite young man, Pierce was elected to the state legislature and then served in the House of Representatives and the United States Senate. His record was a modest one of limited achievements in which he established himself as a loyal Jackson Democrat and was acknowledged as a strong opponent of federal support for internal improvements. Pierce respected the constitutional rights of Southerners and strongly criticized the agitation of the abolitionists in his own region. Like most successful Democrats of this period and many Whigs, he was an ardent nationalist, a strong supporter of expansionism, and a public figure committed to Unionism and moderate compromise. A reformed alcoholic, he became intensely involved in the temperance movement, and reoriented his life even more around hard work, diligence, and divine revelation. Some observers commented on his genuine sympathy toward people, his clear presentations in law cases, and his intense powers of concentration, which seemed to create at times a halolike glow around his countenance. However, under the baneful influence of his morbid wife, he left Washington for New Hampshire, and continued his law practice while helping to manage local Democratic campaigns from 1842 to 1847.

In 1850, he threw his support behind the compromise and attracted Southern attention when he sought to invoke party loyalty to support the fugitive slave law. In the 1852 national convention, none of the major front-runners were able to command the necessary two-thirds vote for nomination, and Pierce's friends presented him as an available compromise. They tagged him as Jackson's true successor, as "Young Hickory of the Granite Hill," and Granite Clubs across the nation sprang up to celebrate his candidacy. To further his cause, his personal friend and classmate at Bowdoin College, the novelist Nathaniel Hawthorne, wrote a campaign biography. A reluctant Pierce accepted the nomination and carried the general election, but before his inauguration took place, his only son died in a freak accident before his eyes. Pierce's wife attributed the death to her husband's new position and personal ambition, and neither of them ever recovered from the terrible loss.[16]

Pierce's strategy as president was simple: he would insist that slavery and the territorial issues had been permanently solved by the compromise, emphasize the tendency toward party loyalty, and concentrate the fierce acquisitive energies in the United States on a more assertive foreign policy. In many ways, his prescriptions were vintage Andrew Jackson, but unlike the general, he lacked both the force of character and the more lenient times to carry them out. His first major overture toward Democratic unity was in his choice of a cabinet. He chose a broad-based, but young and inexperienced group, representing all sections of the nation: William L. Marcy of New York, James Guthrie of Kentucky, Jefferson Davis of Mississippi, Caleb Cushing of Massachusetts, James Campbell of Pennsylvania, James C. Dobbin of North Carolina, and Robert McClelland of Michigan. His major biographer, Roy Franklin Nichols, has chronicled at length Pierce's honest attempt to distribute patronage equitably among all sections and factions, which brought him neither gratitude nor political support.

The president recorded his own plea for party unity by observing publicly "if a man who has attained high office cannot free himself from cliques and act independently, our constitution is valueless."[17] As with most nineteenth-century presidents, including Lincoln, Pierce spent an inordinate amount of time with his cabinet on patronage matters. Unfortunately, his policy of recognizing the various factions of his party raised considerable opposition, especially in the South, after he reached out to join the Free Soilers with the New York Democrats. Other critics attacked the appointment of so-called Young Americans, men who were fired up by dreams of further territorial expansion in a nation already choking on the bounty from the triumph of the Mexican War.

To counter some of these discordant sounds, the administration began to pay more attention to publicity and to using friendly newspapers as instruments to mold partisan opinion. In addition, the president was being scheduled for a speech-making swing through New York, Baltimore, and Philadelphia to build public support. His themes were characteristically centrist: the glory of the Union, the compatibility of states rights and federal authority, and the legacy of the great Revolution. As befitting a presidential trip, speeches and festivities abounded as the populace turned out for a rare visit of a reigning chief executive. One admirer found him to be "a great man . . . the best president we have since Jackson." But Buchanan's old friend John W. Forney who traveled with the president most of the way wrote, "Pierce has had a fine reception but I deeply, deeply deplore his habits. He drinks deep. My heart bleeds for him for he is a gallant and generous spirit."[18]

After less than a year in office, the president's evenhanded patronage policies were proving to be a disaster. Some Southerners believed he was a Free Soiler at heart, while Northerners felt he was too subservient to their sectional rivals. Critics said he seemed to favor the extremists of both areas, that he neglected the moderate elements in politics, and that he did not really support the Compromise of 1850. In his November message to Congress, the president looked for common national ground and stressed the resourcefulness of the American people and the great legacy of republican institutions. He emphasized his policy of protecting U.S. rights against all aggressors and his desire to extend U.S. trade into the world marketplace. Pierce quixotically noted that the nation was now "exempt from any cause of serious disquietude" because of the general recognition of the wisdom of the Constitution and the securing of rights. He went on to propose revising the tariff, upgrading the armed forces, revamping the judiciary, and supporting in a guarded way land grants for railroad interests. In addition, Pierce reaffirmed ritualistically the wisdom of the Founding Fathers, pledged himself to the Compromise, and underscored his support for states rights in a spirit of "mutually forbearance, respect, and non-interference."[19]

Like most presidents of the middle period, including Lincoln, Pierce had little control over the legislature, either formally or informally. The role of the Senate had been greatly accentuated during the time of Taylor and especially Fillmore, but those giants in that body were gone, and the party system they had come out of was breaking down. The Whigs were giving way to a rising array of groups embracing the Know-Nothings, Free Soilers, and eventually Republicans—men who were less conservative politically, and politicians who were more willing to express and exploit the sectional differences of the nation. The Democratic party also was beginning to be affected by the tensions of severe sectional differences and the ambitions of new leaders heading up more volatile coalitions. Pierce, and Buchanan after him, were figures of the past—the past with a party that was Unionist and compromising, a party that had preached the virtues of expansion and conquest, and that destroyed more quickly than anticipated the political balance between the Northern and Southern regions.

Pierce's attempt to refashion a united party was also hurt by instability in Congress. In the House, there were fewer men of stature than in 1850, and only 80 of the 234 had been reelected to office. The Democrats controlled that body by a two to one majority, but because Southerners stayed longer in Congress and thus acquired more seniority, they controlled the major committees. For example, no eastern Democrat congressman had more than six years seniority and only one from the West was entering his eighth year.

Pierce had served in both houses of Congress, but he was never a major figure in Washington, and he had finally left to return home. Once elected president, he found that he lacked personal allies in Congress and had no real faction of strong supporters. He avoided rewarding only his friends, and as one of his biographers has concluded, "no one had a vested interest in his welfare, for if he triumphed, their enemies triumphed as well." The party discipline of the Jackson era was gone, and Pierce's strategy reflected an outdated sense of what had happened before, rather than an understanding of the more complex contemporary world around him.

The president's fantasy of a united party and a quiet public life was to be wrecked on the rocks of sectionalism. While he celebrated the Compromise of 1850, Pierce felt confident that he could turn his attention to foreign policy, economy, and party consolidation. But, like so many of his colleagues, he misunderstood the dynamics unleashed by the unorganized lands gained from the Mexican War, the rise of abolitionist outrage, and the economic dynamism of Northern development. The political initiative remained in the legislative branch and not with the president. Bills to organize the Nebraska Territory were introduced in Congress, and the able Stephen Douglas was the floor manager in the Senate for the proposal. He saw the land speculation possibilities of the area and the future of a Pacific railroad. What his own personal motives were is unclear. Probably, he desired to deal with the matter quickly, thus furthering his reputation as a man of the future and solidifying his status as front-runner for the presidency in 1856.

To get any bill through the Senate, however, Douglas needed Southern support, and the price was the repeal of the Missouri Compromise with its restrictions against slavery in the Nebraska Territory. In New Mexico and Utah, Congress in 1850 had left the issue of slavery to the courts and had affirmed that those proposed states were to be admitted to the Union with their constitutions intact. Thus, the slavery issue was to be decided by local opinion, subject to review by the judiciary. Congress clearly sought to get away from the matter as a national issue. Douglas, in dealing with the Nebraska Territory, tried the same approach and thereby eviscerated the prohibitions of the Missouri Compromise.

Pierce had always thought the Missouri Compromise unconstitutional, so he had no interest in defending it. But by concurring with Douglas, he helped reopen the very controversy that had been proclaimed closed. In fact, he warned Southerners, "Gentlemen, you are entering on a serious misunderstanding, and the ground should be well surveyed before the first step is taken." Yet Pierce was unwilling to challenge the Senate, especially since it would be passing on his appointments and on treaty matters. Facing a division in his own cabinet and in Congress, Pierce went on to insist publicly that the Compromise of 1850 had made the Missouri Compromise "inoperative and void."

As the president was inadvertently helping to reopen the bitter controversy, his administration was moving to lay out an aggressive foreign policy to promote national ambitions and unity. Pierce and Secretary of State Marcy were concerned that Britain and France were working together to curtail American interests; one area of special concern was the fate of Cuba, still under Spanish rule. Rumors increased that the British were pushing the Spanish regime to free the blacks in Cuba and thus forestall an American takeover of the island. Pierce asked Congress to grant him power to "obtain redress for injuries received, and to vindicate the honor of the flag." At about the same time, Marcy approached the Russian minister about selling the United States the territory of Alaska, a transaction Seward would consummate years later.

While no quick triumphs were opening up in foreign affairs, the president's attention was redirected to the sectional issue. He insisted on an expression of support and party loyalty from New England Democrats; he pointedly reminded Hannibal Hamlin of

Maine of the fate of Calhoun and Hugh L. White who had crossed Jackson. Later, the party newspaper announced that while the president would not regard those who opposed details of the bill as his enemies, he would allow patronage to be used against the bill's opponents. On May 30, the president signed the measure, insisting again that it would end slavery agitation forever.

In the congressional elections of 1854, opposition to the repeal of the Missouri Compromise mounted. Independent Democrats began to turn their backs on Pierce and the administration's territorial policies. Unfortunately in May, the president was faced with a controversial request to enforce the hated fugitive slave law in Boston. The response was predictably hostile, and Pierce had to provide a revenue cutter to transport the slave safely back to Virginia. Protesting Pierce's response, one letter writer said he thought he should address his communications: "To the chief slave catcher of the United States."

The results of the elections were disastrous for the Democratic party as it lost every Northern state except New Hampshire and also California, with thirty-one congressional seats leaving the party's control. Opposition ranks included a variety of new faces—disenchanted Democrats, Know-Nothings, old Whigs. Even in New Hampshire, some Democrats were repudiating the president and his policies, and several party leaders were encouraging Sam Houston of Texas to run for president in 1856. Facing his second Congress, Pierce had less leverage than he had with his first, except now he had to deal with even more complex and indecisive foreign policy issues and the shattering explosion in Kansas.

Pierce and Marcy continued to insist that Great Britain honor the American interpretation of the Clayton-Bulwer Treaty and leave Nicaragua and Honduras. They also pushed for a settlement of the Newfoundland fisheries disputes and sent James Gadsden to Mexico to purchase land for a right-of-way to build a southern railroad to the Pacific. The administration also sought to acquire Hawaii and a naval base at Santo Domingo to further extend the American domain. But U.S.-British relations floundered over an insult to an American minister in Nicaragua, and negotiations over Cuba became public. Northern fears of adding another slave territory, Cuba, and maybe risking a war made it difficult for the administration to gain popular support. By late 1855, the president requested the recall of the British minister John F. Crampton, citing his attempt to recruit troops in the United States for service in the Crimean conflict. Finally, Great Britain agreed to evacuate most of Central America and signed the Dallas-Clarendon Convention to leave the Bay Islands and Mosquito protectorate. But when the Senate insisted on amendments, the British government rejected them, and the president by that time had little political support for further initiatives.

In the second half of his term, Pierce seemed to become more assertive in his executive activities, even as he was confronted by a domestic controversy that narrowed his options. He involved himself in endless administrative details, used the veto to curtail expenditures and raids on the Treasury, and directly attacked the growth of Know-Nothing strength. In a critical test in Virginia, the Democratic party defeated the Know-Nothings' Southern thrust, and thus stopped it at what became its high water mark. The Know-Nothings were also to flounder on the slavery question, and their leadership went into the new Republican party. Pierce contemptuously called this new group "coalitionists" and "abolitionists."

To administer the Kansas-Nebraska Bill, the president appointed a Northerner governor of Kansas and a Southerner as governor of Nebraska. Unfortunately, the first appointee in the Kansas Territory was Andrew H. Reeder, a lawyer from Pennsylvania who boldly supported the Southern position. Before his appointment, Reeder had made a fortune by entering into illegal land operations; once in power, he quickly alienated segments of the populace by his bluntness on the slavery issue. When the Emigrant Aid Company in Massachusetts sent money and people into Kansas, proslavery Southerners from Missouri invaded the territory and helped elect a proslavery legislature. The president, under considerable political pressure, decided to remove Reeder, then vacillated and allowed Reeder to return to the governorship. Finally, Pierce removed the governor and two judges, and had an army officer court-martialed, all arising from land speculation abuses.

By late 1855, Pierce had also decided to run for reelection, and he exhibited increasing strength in office. Appointees suspected of Know-Nothing sympathies were routinely fired, and the president staked out the high ground of nationalism and Unionism against the rising tide of what was becoming the Republican party. When the House of Representatives was deadlocked in December over the choice of a speaker, the president pushed for an alliance of Democrats and Southern members of the American (Know-Nothing) party to stop the Republican candidate. To further his ambitions, he praised the South for its historical willingness to accommodate the

North, criticized the old Missouri Compromise, and warned that it made no sense to destroy the Union for "a fanatical devotion to the supposed interests of the relatively few Africans."[20]

But in Kansas, civil war was beginning, as a Free Soil group organized a rump government (under the so-called Topeka Constitution) opposed to the state proslavery administration that Pierce had recognized after the election there. Missourians were beginning to make plans to invade the territory; by February, the president issued an executive proclamation that ordered the free state group to disperse and the Missourians to go home. He went further and placed federal troops in the hands of the new governor, Wilson Shannon.

Congress gave the president little support on the Kansas dispute. Pierce's determination both to stand by the proslavery (or Lecompton) group, which had been elected in a controversial contest, and to treat the Topeka Free Soil group as traitors furthered the impression that the president was simply pro-South and a prop of the slavery oligarchy. Then, in March, Senator Stephen Douglas introduced a bill to admit Kansas into the Union when its inhabitants numbered ninty-three thousand (the number of people that justified one seat in the House of Representatives). Since the territory had only about a third of that population, statehood would be effectively postponed for years, and the region would be governed in the interim by its territorial legislature.

Roy Franklin Nichols has pointed out how Pierce's Kansas policy of neutrality and law enforcement helped lay the groundwork for a new anti-Democratic alliance. The president, however saw the antislavery agitation as the product of Northern politicians grasping for power. But the agitation was tied to a great source of moral energy and a reform movement that was sweeping the Western world. At first, the repeal of the Missouri Compromise brought forth a splintered response. However, as Know-Nothing strength declined and the Free Soil movement ebbed, the possibilities of a unified opposition party became more apparent to professional politicians. In the elections of 1852 and 1854, about 1.2 million people voted against the Democrats in the Northern states. In 1852, 1,022,757 voters called themselves Whigs and 157,745 Free Soilers. By 1854, about 520,000 were Free Soilers and the rest Whigs or new Know-Nothings. These factors could have led to a national Know-Nothing or American party, a new Whig party bridging both sections, or a Northern party based on Free Soil principles. The first alternative ran into the same sectional divisions that destroyed the Whigs and which would split up the Democrats eventually. By June 1855, the Know-Nothing party did indeed divide, and the Northern wing moved toward a union with the Republicans, bringing with it an antiforeign, anti-Catholic bias. To those new Republicans in Congress, the Kansas issue was ready-made for exploitation. Pierce became the perfect foil for the new crusade that would lead to a more powerful sectional party and feed the paranoia of the Southern slaveholding oligarchy.

As the convention approached, Pierce's neutrality was being portrayed as hostility to the North and a belated conversion to Southern rights. He was a candidate for reelection, but it was not to be his. The very availability and usefulness that brought him the nomination in 1852 was now spent, used up in the sectional controversies that voided the careers of many moderate Union men. Also, to some observers he seemed at times weak, indecisive, unable to provide a strong sense of direction. One Southern critic, Alexander Stephens, concluded that Pierce's policy in the Kansas-Nebraska affair was characterized as "Fickleness, weakness, folly and vacillation." Another critic concluded that Pierce's problem was that he "had no real strength but there is so much weakness in him personally, for instance you may hear it often said 'anyone but Pierce.'" In addition, his laissez faire economic policies, veto of special interest bills, and nondiscriminatory patronage practices did not add to Pierce's political strength during his term in office.[21]

The Democratic leaders then turned to an old hand, a well-known party man from the important state of Pennsylvania, James Buchanan, who had spent more recent times abroad as minister to England. Throughout the summer, turmoil increased in Kansas, and tempers flared in the Senate where Senator Preston Brooks caned Senator Charles Sumner. And in late May, news filtered back to Washington of the Pottawatamie Creek massacre in which abolitionist John Brown and his allies went on an indiscriminate killing spree.

Repudiated by his own party, denied meaningful support in the Congress, and favored by neither section, Pierce persisted in trying in 1856 to reach a settlement on the Kansas issue. In June, the Republicans nominated the exciting but unstable explorer, John C. Frémont, on a platform that castigated the president for his ineffective leadership on "Bleeding Kansas." Meanwhile in Congress, the Democrats attempted to provide guidelines to allow Kansas to take a census and hold an election for members of a constitutional convention. The bill provided for five commissioners, appointed by the president, who would assume immediate supervision and responsibility. But once again, Congress could not agree on giving the president strong support to deal with the continuous controversies there.

In fact, Congress could not even agree on a military appropriations bill, and it adjourned without providing funds. A troubled Pierce called the body back into session, trying to impress on Congress the need for troop strength to deal with the Kansas problem, Indian troubles, and the remote possibility of war with Great Britain. Finally, a chastised legislative branch approved the military bill.

Still, rumors of conflict in Kansas arrived in the capital, and the cabinet met to deal with the controversy. The president continued to support the regular proslavery government in the territory, replaced the controversial governor, and buttressed troop strength in Kansas. A modicum of peace prevailed throughout the remaining period of his term. He welcomed Buchanan's election so effusively that Lincoln commented it was "like a rejected lover making merry at the wedding of his rival."

Pierce ended his stewardship and returned home to New England, remaining an unpopular figure and dying in obscurity in 1869. When the Civil War came, he supported the Union cause, but denounced Lincoln for his violation of constitutional rights. He saw the Emancipation Proclamation as the triumph of the abolitionists and judged Lincoln to be a man of "limited ability and narrow intelligence" who had become their willing instrument. Emancipation would lead to barbarism and the killing of white men, women, and children, he predicted.

Lincoln's secretary of navy, Gideon Welles, later judged "Pierce a vain, showy, and pliant man . . . by his errors and weakness [he] broke down his administration and his party throughout the country." Nichols, in his biography, has concluded that Pierce had a reputation for moral weakness, possessed an average and undisciplined intelligence, and was a small town lawyer with little preparation for the problems he faced.[22] His initial inclinations were formed by his Jacksonian past and his thrifty New England heritage. Pierce's prescriptions were party unity and a spread-eagle foreign policy. But as the regional divergence of the social and economic systems grew, no political party was able to bridge the gap and probably no president could have provided strong consensus leadership. Pierce was overwhelmed by those dynamics, as would be the more experienced Buchanan; even the stronger and wilier Lincoln would be nearly consumed.

There is a tide in human events that people may master and take into harbor. But there are inexorable currents that cannot be ridden or channeled, social circumstances that grow and multiply beyond the capacities of leaders or followers to control, compromise, or reason. Slavery, sectionalism, raw ambition, fading Unionism were those currents, whose strengths increased as Pierce rode home to a sullen reception, and Buchanan achieved his lifelong dream of sitting in the White House.

BUCHANAN'S LAST STAND

For most of his adult life, James Buchanan had been interested in politics and had considerable experience in the common intrigue and high statesmanship that so characterizes life in that nebulous profession. He entered the Pennsylvania House of Representatives in 1814 as a Federalist, but within a decade it was clear that the old party was dying, and Buchanan finally aligned himself with the Jacksonian wing of the Democratic party. In 1827, Jackson insisted that Buchanan had visited him with a bargain from Clay—a bargain he spurned and John Quincy Adams supposedly accepted. Buchanan denied the assertion, but in a way that did not totally alienate the volatile general.

All his life, Buchanan remained a bachelor, surrounded by a stream of nieces and nephews over whom he fussed and assumed a patriarchal pose. During his youth, Buchanan's fiancée broke off their engagement, departed from town, and soon after died, leaving him brokenhearted and the subject of cheap gossip and romantic legend. Later, Buchanan was elected to the House of Representatives, served five terms, and established himself as a loyal party man, a strong defender of the constitutional separation of powers, and a supporter of the rights of the judiciary. In 1830, his name was mentioned as a possible vice presidential candidate on the Jackson ticket, but he was offered instead the ministry to Russia. There he was finally successful in opening up the czarist regime to American interests and commerce; in 1833 he returned home and was elected to the United States Senate. He established himself as a strong supporter of Van Buren and later turned down the president's grateful offer of the attorney general position.

By 1844, Buchanan was one of the major contenders for the Democratic presidential nomination, but his own critical state did not provide the support he needed, and James K. Polk got the call. Polk, in turn, named Buchanan his secretary of state, although he distrusted him and often quarreled with him over major policy issues in front of the rest of the cabinet. Buchanan was less combative and assertive in his version of Manifest Destiny than Polk, and he had reservations about the policies that led to the Mexican War. On occasions, however, he did forcefully encourage Polk to reassert the Monroe Doctrine and move toward the annexation of Cuba.

In 1852, the party turned away from the front-runner and nominated Pierce, leaving Buchanan again at the gate. But he loyally supported the choice, and received the post of minister to Great Britain. Four years later, his time had come, and he led the Democrats to a victory over the Republican nominee, John C. Frémont, and Millard Fillmore who was running on the American and Whig tickets in some states. Being out of the United States for four years and not associated or implicated in the repeal of the Missouri Compromise or the Kansas controversy, Buchanan had both the experience and the absence of open scars, which spelled to the party, availability. He was from a Northern state, opposed slavery, respected the South, shared Pierce's hatred of abolitionism, and genuinely appreciated the Constitution and political union. In a sense, he was a more experienced and worldly version of the younger Pierce, and like his predecessor, he hoped to get this unnecessary antislavery agitation behind him so as to concentrate on American foreign policy and party rehabilitation.[23]

After his term was over, his enemies would call him weak and vacillating, but in fact, he was neither. Martin Van Buren, who knew him well, called Buchanan "a cautious, circumspect and sagacious man, amply endowed with those clear perceptions of self-interest and of duties connected with it that are almost inseparable from the Scottish character." At sixty-six, he was white-haired, distinguished looking, bachelor fussy, and nosy about the affairs of others. He surrounded himself with a cabinet full of slaveholders and friends of the South and formed personal attachments with many of them. His major objective, he said in 1856, was to stop the slavery agitation in the North and destroy sectional parties. Unlike Pierce, he decided not to balance his appointments and clearly rewarded that wing of the party that agreed with his Unionist, pro-South inclinations.[24] As his biographer, Philip Klein, has observed, the cabinet was a group of Jacksonian Democrats, representative of the old America and not the new. Conspicuous by his absence was the most appealing Democrat of his day, Stephen Douglas. A rival at the 1856 convention, Douglas had married a beautiful woman who had in fact caught Buchanan's eye at one time.[25]

As Buchanan got ready to assume office, he confidentially urged his friends on the Supreme Court to issue a clear opinion on the whole slavery question, hoping to settle the controversy once and for all. The case before them involved a sixty-two-year-old Missouri slave, Dred Scott. Scott had spent four years with his master in the free state of Missouri, and eventually the family of the owner tried to set him free. The argument they used was that Scott was a free man because he had resided in a free state and the Missouri circuit court agreed. However, the state supreme court overturned the decision, finding that the precedents did not apply and meriting the criticism that their opinion was based not on law, but on the rankest political calculations. Meanwhile, Scott's owner's widow had married an abolitionist who was going to free the slave regardless of the opinion.

In his inaugural address, the president pledged his support for the Supreme Court's decision "whatever it may be," even though he secretly knew the decision already. The final disposition set off a storm of protest, more far-reaching in its implications than John Brown's later marches or "Bloody Kansas." The Court, led by Chief Justice Roger Taney, found that Scott as a Negro (in the language of the time) could not sue in court because blacks, free or slave, were not citizens. Furthermore, the due process clause of the Constitution protected slaves as property in all territories and states. Thus, the Missouri Compromise was unconstitutional, and slavery was a national and not a sectional institution. The advocates of popular sovereignty and local option went down with the abolitionists in total defeat. As for Taney, the sensitivity of his opinion was best expressed by his conclusion that blacks were "unfit to associate with the white race . . . and so far inferior that they had no rights which the white man was bound to respect."[26] The decision for which Buchanan had surreptitiously encouraged and slyly counseled respect would lead to agitation that would sweep past the abolitionist ranks into Northern and Western society, eventually fueling sectionalism and aiding the rise of the Republican party.

Almost immediately, the new president had to face the controversies continuing in Kansas with its two territorial governments, one pledged to slavery and sitting at Lecompton and the other established at Topeka and committed to a free-state constitution. Although the Lecompton government had federal support from Pierce and later Buchanan, the actual number of slaves brought into the territory numbered under two hundred. Seeking to restore calm, Buchanan appointed Robert J. Walker of Mississippi, a diminutive and shrewd administrator who had served in Polk's cabinet. After some confusion about whether to submit the whole constitution or only the slavery issue to popular referendum, Governor Walker called an election, and after charges of fraud, approved what amounted to the election of a free-state legislature. The angry Lecompton delegates responded with a constitution of their own forbidding the emancipation of current slaves and pushing for the ouster of Walker.

Douglas, under pressure from Illinois constituents, demanded that the president support Walker, but Buchanan refused. In turn, he reminded the ambitious Douglas that Jackson had crushed Democrats James Tallmadge and William Rives who had opposed him. The Senator bluntly responded, "General Jackson is dead." And so he was. Buchanan in late 1857 insisted that Congress had to uphold the Lecompton constitution, and he urged Kansas citizens to express their views on the slavery question, which was on the ballot. Douglas attacked the whole approach, and several days later Walker resigned in protest.

At Buchanan's insistence, the voters could not pass on the whole constitution, but only on the issue of slavery—a distinction that caused many free-state advocates to boycott altogether the election. The result was that the slavery provision won by a margin of ten to one. To add to the confusion, the state legislature approved a referendum allowing for a vote on the whole constitution, which led to the overwhelming defeat of the document. As the United States Senate took up the admission of Kansas, Douglas's opposition hardened. Southerners praised the Lecompton constitution, and one senator, James H. Hammond, celebrated slavery because it provided an ideal race designed by nature to be a permanent servile class, a mudsill upon which white civilization could rest. Under strong administration pressure, the Kansas bill passed the Senate, but in the House (whose members were all up for reelection), Republicans balked at the controversial proposal. When Kansas citizens were asked to ratify a congressional land grant proposal, they refused—

thus indirectly killing the Lecompton constitution and its slavery proviso. In addition, the results of the spring elections of 1858 showed that the Republicans had done well in the North and in some large Democratic cities, such as Chicago, Cincinnati, St. Louis, and Toledo, using antislavery appeals.[27]

Thus, after all his machinations, Douglas ended up being despised by many Southern leaders, while Buchanan was heavily assailed in the North, and the Republicans were gaining popular strength. Most importantly in the election of 1858, Stephen Douglas on his way to the presidency and a place in history was nearly waylaid in the Illinois senate race. In a series of debates with his Republican challenger, Douglas insisted that popular sovereignty was still possible despite the *Dred Scott* decision, since slavery required positive local support and law enforcement—a remark that further alienated Southern Democrats. Because of the apportionment of the Illinois legislature, Douglas won a majority of votes in that body despite having narrowly lost the popular vote. In that election, Buchanan had expressed his mounting disdain for Douglas, and in the senatorial campaign, a new star was becoming fixed—Abraham Lincoln.

The basic political and moral agitation against slavery was fired up by a major economic downturn in the economy in late 1857 vividly seen in the bankruptcy of the Ohio Life Insurance and Trust Company and the collapse of 1,400 state banks, 5,000 businesses, and some major railroads in the West. During Buchanan's term, a series of controversial books were printed that added to the slavery controversy. The most important and popular was Harriet Beecher Stowe's novel, *Uncle Tom's Cabin*, which treated in a fictional but graphic way the themes of master brutality and slave despondency. Later, Lincoln insisted that Stowe had really started the war, an overstatement but an indication of the power of her presentation. In addition, in 1856 the great landscape architect Frederick Law Olmsted published several books outlining his travels throughout the South. Most important, he concluded that slavery was economically self-defeating for all involved. A more critical view was presented by Hinton Rowan Helper who indicted the slaveholding aristocracy in his work *The Impending Crisis*. The book sold over one hundred thousand in a paperback, and Buchanan concluded that it also was a cause of the Civil War. Southerners responded with equal fervor, and another volume, this one by George Fitzhugh, glorified slavery and attacked the wage "slave" system of Northern capitalism. His title was appropriately *Cannibals All; or Slaves Without Masters*, published in 1857.[28]

Whether slavery was economically profitable or not is an issue still being discussed and debated by historians and economists over a century after its demise. But what is clear is that slavery did support, encourage, and underscore the development of a very different way of life, social structure, and political culture in the South. A few slaveowners and their proponents sought to liken the slave system to medieval manors and wrapped it in the romantic patina of Sir Walter Scott's fiction. But there was too much of the lash, too much calculated breeding of human souls, too much studied paranoia about the "peculiar institution" to turn raw bondage into Christian feudalism. Even if masters were generally businesslike, prudent, and patriarchal, the buying and selling of human beings created a different ideology—one alien to the celebrations of free soil, free labor, and free institutions.[29] To Buchanan, ever the party man, the slavery controversy was mainly the creation of the abolitionists, radicals who were buttressed in their efforts by well-meaning but emotional women. After his election, he summarized his aspirations, "If I can be instrumental in settling the slavery question . . . and then add Cuba to the Union, I shall be willing to give up the ghost."

In terms of his foreign policy, he believed wholeheartedly in the dream of Manifest Destiny and was even inclined to wage war against the dissident Mormons, a crusade that was fortuitously avoided by more moderate political leaders surrounding him. In terms of Central America, Buchanan's ambition was to rid the region of European influence, and he resented what he judged as British backpedalling on the Clayton-Bulwer Treaty of 1850. In dealing with czarist Russia, Buchanan expressed some interest in acquiring Alaska, a territory that had been offered to Pierce and toward which he expressed, in the end, no interest. Buchanan offered $5 million, which the Russians rejected, and the issue stayed dormant until Seward's purchase in 1867.[30]

The president continued to support American commercial ties with China and Japan, and treaties were signed with both nations. Buchanan's major objectives in Cuba and in Mexico, though, were less successful. Deep hatred of slavery in the North stopped any proposal to annex Cuba, and in dealing with Mexico the administration was concerned about the policies of Louis Napoleon and the

French. Buchanan advocated in December 1858 a temporary U.S. protectorate over the northern states of Chihuahua and Sonora, but the Senate refused to concur. A year later he requested authority from Congress to invade Mexico and obtain an indemnity for past claims and security in the future. By then, however, John Brown's raid at Harper's Ferry and the whole slavery controversy had seized congressional attention.

Early in 1860, the Mexican government agreed to a treaty in which the United States would pay $4 million for transit rights from the Gulf of Mexico to the Pacific and the right to police the route. The Senate in May rejected that agreement, the McLane-Ocampo Treaty; the North opposed acquiring any more Mexican territory, and the South was less than enthusiastic since that nation had already abolished slavery. In an important sense, the rejection of the treaty marked an end to Manifest Destiny in Latin America for decades to come. In terms of the siren lure of Cuba, the administration wanted to offer $30 million, a proposal that also became entangled in the slavery controversy. To some of his colleagues, Buchanan's aggressive foreign policy was a calculated attempt to divert the nation's attention away from the slavery issue; but in fact, he sincerely pushed for expanding the American domain, even though that very expansion had created the social dynamics that were leading to increasing antislavery sentiments and Southern reaction.

The elections of late 1858 had showed rather clearly that the Democratic party's only dependable base of support was in the South, and Buchanan moved to underscore his personal fealty to that region and to its Washington representatives. And as Buchanan became more frustrated, he buried himself in administrative details and was even more nosy and possessive about the lives of his cabinet members and their wives. In Congress, Southern Democrats led by Jefferson Davis demanded that Northern Democrats support their proposal for a federal slave code for all territories. As historian Elbert Smith has argued, "In the name of states rights and local power they had long argued that the federal government had no power to bar slavery from a territory. Now they would insist that the same federal government had both the power and the duty to impose slavery on territories even if the inhabitants already there objected to it."[31] The argument was clearly aimed at Douglas and his nascent presidential candidacy, and Southern assertiveness would finally break up the party and end any chance of a compromise candidate in 1860. The Southerners started off the session by stripping Douglas of his chairmanship of the Committee on Territories. Rumors soon spread that Southern partisans were looking for an opportunity to kill Douglas, and he hired a well-known sharpshooter as a bodyguard. But as the emotions dampened and commercial prosperity coincidentally increased, tempers seemed to cool and the Unionist elements in the South picked up support.

Earlier in 1856, the turbulent shadow of John Brown had fallen across the nation. In the midst of the troubles of "Bleeding Kansas," Brown and some followers had killed and mutilated the bodies of five proslavery men, none of whom even owned slaves. He had received considerable moral support and some money from New England abolitionist groups for his special vengeance. Privately, Brown had speculated among his family and a few friends about creating a new state in Virginia for escaped slaves. Then in July 1859, Brown and twenty-one men rented a farm near Harper's Ferry, Virginia, and prepared for a general uprising to free and arm slaves with the guns from the nearby arsenal.

The slaves did not rise up, indeed few had heard of Brown, and the attack failed almost from the beginning. The president sent Colonel Robert E. Lee and Lieutenant J. E. B. Stuart to crush the rebellion. The rump revolt sent shudders throughout the South, however, and even Republicans put quick distance between themselves and the Brown insurrection. For reasons of his own, the governor of Virginia, Henry A. Wise, insisted on an immediate trial and exaggerated publicly Brown's threat. Brown was found guilty of murder and conspiring with slaves to rebel, and he was sentenced to die. At his trial, Brown was lucid and articulate, a martyr giving up his life to end the vilest of institutions. Overnight, Brown became a hero to the abolitionist movement. Ralph Waldo Emerson called him, "The Saint, whose fate yet hangs in suspension, but whose martyrdom, if it shall be perfected, will make the gallows as glorious as the Cross." Thoreau went even further and linked Brown up with Jesus Christ, and the well-known Unitarian clergyman, Theodore Parker, gave his stamp of approval to Brown's revolt.[32]

To Buchanan, Brown symbolized the type of abolitionist fervor that disturbed the body politic and drove moderates out of the field. In the early 1860 congressional session, the president was faced with increasingly bitter references to John Brown and rising sectional hostility in the Congress. For nearly two months, a deeply divided House of Representatives could not agree on a speaker, and some congressmen actually carried weapons for self-protection. As the Republicans fell all over themselves to repudiate Brown, Southerners insisted on seeing the raid as the logical outcome of the types of charges the new party was making. To add to the president's problems, he was being accused of improperly using patronage to push the Lecompton constitution. An angry Buchanan defended himself and challenged the House to impeach him if they found any irregularities. When no action was initiated, he pronounced, "My vindication is complete."

The real vindication that Buchanan wanted was a second term, an objective no president since Jackson had reached. On his way to the nomination, he saw the short, squatty, imposing figure of Stephen A. Douglas. The administration with its federal officeholders, newspapers, and patronage connections sought to sidetrack Douglas's candidacy, and while those attacks were unsuccessful, they did help to discredit the senator and hurt his chances in the general election in 1860. Meeting in April in Charleston, South Carolina, the convention came to loggerheads with many Southern delegates walking out, and finally adjourned before its business was completed. A second session was scheduled for June in Baltimore.

At Baltimore, the Douglas delegates insisted that no individuals could be seated unless they were pledged to support the platform and the final ticket. In the end, many Southern Unionist and border state delegates again left, and Douglas and Georgia Governor Herschel J. Johnson were nominated by the remainder of the convention. Some of those who had left now formed their own coalition and nominated Senator John J. Breckinridge of Kentucky for president and Joseph Lane of Oregon for vice president. Buchanan and former president Franklin Pierce supported Breckinridge, and the administration put its efforts behind that faction. A third ticket came in May when confirmed Unionists such as John J. Crittenden of Kentucky, John Bell of Tennessee, Edward Everett and Amos Lawrence of Massachusetts, William C. Rives of Virginia, and others pushed for a Constitutional Unionist party ticket to be headed by Bell, a former speaker of the House, a leader of the Whig party, and former secretary of war under William Henry Harrison.

In May in Chicago, the Republicans nominated Abraham Lincoln who heeded William Cullen Bryant's advice to "make no speeches, write no letters as a candidate, enter into no pledges, make no promises, nor even give any of those kind words which men are apt to interpret into promises." Douglas, on the other hand, waged an active campaign with a personal trip through the South pleading the cause of Union and outlining the horrors of secession—a step some of the Southern governors were planning even before the election was done. An anxious Jefferson Davis proposed that Bell, Breckinridge, and Douglas all withdraw in favor of Horatio Seymour of New York as a compromise candidate to stop Lincoln, but Douglas refused. The division led to a Republican victory in the presidential race and helped the party gain five seats in the Senate even as they lost nine seats in the House. The party however would not control either branch of the legislature as long as the Southern delegates stayed in Congress.

As secession support increased after Lincoln's election, Buchanan tried to work out some compromise that would reassure the South or at least forestall the rupture until his term was completed. The Southern members of his cabinet generally stayed in office, many of them using their influence over Buchanan and informing their own states' leaders of the president's feelings on various confidential matters. Between December 20 and February 1, a group of states announced their desire to secede, but the representatives and senators remained in Congress up to the end and even beyond those decisions. Even after Jefferson Davis was inaugurated as the president of the Confederacy, he still tried to keep open negotiations with Buchanan. But while Buchanan was effusive in his support of the South and its claims, he refused to compromise on the legality of secession.

Despite the popular view that Buchanan in this period was weak and overwhelmed by events, in fact, his position remained fairly clear and in many ways paralleled what Lincoln would adopt until the attack on Fort Sumter. The president asked his cabinet what specific powers he had to collect duties and imports charges and what authority he had to defend federal property if it were attacked. Could he use military force if local federal officials were absent and how could he execute laws usually administered through the federal courts? Essentially, he wanted to know the legal standing and practical problems of enforcing federal laws and regulations where the usual channels and officials were absent.

The response of his attorney general was that the executive had both an obligation and a right to collect the duties, defend public property, and execute the laws. With these strong findings in hand, Buchanan in his message to Congress in December 1860 chose instead to reinforce the South's sense of persecution and blamed the crisis on the "long continued and intemperate interference of the Northern people with the question of slavery." The agitation had led to a "malign influence on the slaves, and inspired them with vague notions of freedom," a condition that led to many a white matron throughout the South dreading what might befall her and her children. Buchanan asserted that no Congress had ever restricted slavery, except for the Missouri Compromise provision, and he reaffirmed his own pledge to execute only the laws on the books. Ambiguously, he insisted that certain grievances might justify secession but reaffirmed that secession was unconstitutional. Reaching back to Jackson's response in 1833, he asserted that the Union was perpetual. Historian Elbert B. Smith has concluded, "Thus the president defended the Southerners' own excuses for secession, denied them any such right, announced his unwillingness to coerce them, and declared that secession could be prevented only by concessions that every Southerner knew would never be made."[33]

Buchanan was not alone in his fear of disunion and war. On December 18, the Senate created a special committee of thirteen of its members to deal with the imminent crisis; its membership included such notables as Crittenden, Davis, Douglas, Toombs, Seward, and Wade. Under Crittenden's statesmanlike chairmanship, six amendments were proposed to the Constitution. As historian James M. McPherson has concluded,

In their final form these amendments would have guaranteed slavery in the states against future interference by the national government, prohibited slavery in territories north of 36°30′ and protected it south of that line in all territories now held or *hereafter acquired* [emphasis added]; forbidden Congress to abolish slavery on any federal property within slave states (forts, arsenals, naval bases, etc.); forbidden Congress to abolish slavery in the District of Columbia without the consent of its inhabitants and unless it had first been abolished by both Virginia and Maryland; denied Congress any power to interfere with the interstate slave trade; and compensated slaveholders who were prevented from recovering fugitives in northern states.

In a practical sense, the most important proposal was the extension of the Missouri Compromise line; the pledges on the District of Columbia were not important, and the fugitive slave proposal was clearly unenforceable. In fact, only the territory of New Mexico was left under the 36°30′ line, and it had a grand sum of twenty-two slaves after twelve years of having a slave code in place. Clearly then, the Crittenden plan was more aimed at assuaging Southern sensibilities by giving them what they wanted most: federal approval for slavery as an institution in a society increasingly critical of it. Still, thousands of Northerners, desiring peace and concerned over the financial consequences and loss of trade if secession occurred, flooded Congress with petitions of support.

Jefferson Davis insisted that no proposal be reported to the Senate unless a majority of both Republican and Democratic committee members approved. The Republicans, led by Seward, were willing to move toward conciliation, but they had reservations and sought advice from the president-elect, still sitting quietly in Springfield, Illinois. Lincoln's overall position seemed to be that he would not touch slavery where it existed, would enforce the fugitive slave laws, and would oppose any dismemberment of the Union under any guise. But on the sticking point—the expansion of slavery into the territories—he stood firmly opposed. To compromise on that issue would "shift the ground" upon which he was elected, divide his party, and in the end still not satisfy the Southern hotheads. To the moderate Southerner Alexander H. Stephens, Lincoln summarized his view: the South had no reason to be troubled that he would upset slavery where it existed, but the president-elect added, "You think slavery is *right* and ought to be extended; while we think it is *wrong* and ought to be restrained. That I suppose is the rub. It certainly is the only substantial difference between us." Stephens's response was equally informative: the South resented having its beliefs "under the bar of public opinion and national condemnation." The result was that the Republicans in the Senate committee refused to approve extending the Missouri line to the Pacific Ocean.[34]

Watching all of these events, Buchanan was upset at Lincoln's supposed intransigence and what he clearly foresaw as the consequences. In late December, he sent General Duff Green to Lincoln to ask if he would approve a national convention or a popular referendum on the Crittenden compromise. Lincoln apparently had some reservations about Southern intentions, but decided to support the view that the popular will should prevail. He offered to send a letter of support, but then changed his mind. Lincoln insisted that his statement could be released only if half of the senators from Georgia, Alabama, Mississippi, Louisiana, Florida, and Texas would sign a pledge that their states would suspend secession efforts. That letter sent to Senator Lyman Trumbull of Illinois was not delivered or published, however, and Buchanan decided instead to send to Congress a special message on January 8.

In his message, he once again celebrated the blessings of Union and warned that Congress had to find a way of reassuring the South that its grievances would be dealt with fairly. The president also lent his support to a peace conference called by the Virginia legislature to be held in Washington. Some twenty-one states sent delegates, including former president Tyler, who met and approved resolutions similar to the Crittenden Compromise, which the Senate rejected.

With a settlement out of sight, Buchanan was faced with one difficult issue in the closing days of his presidency—the status of federal forts and properties in the South. The president was clearly startled by a letter in late October 1860 from his army chief, General Winfield Scott, which recommended that the federal government allow secession in certain areas and which sketched out how four new nations could be created. The proposal probably grew out of Scott's realization that the Union army was a paper force of sixteen thousand men, mainly policing the Western frontier against Indian raids. Most of the federal forts were in fact manned by only a skeleton staff, and at that time, South Carolina was pushing for the return of federal forts with attention focused on Fort Moultrie, Castle Pinckney, and Fort Sumter.

Buchanan stood firm on the forts, partially in response to Northern public opinion. He warned his secretary of war, John Floyd, in November 1860, that if the forts were lost because of neglect, "it were better for you and me both to be thrown into the Pacific with millstones tied about our necks." In late 1860, attention focused on Charleston harbor fortifications, commanded by a Southern unionist, Major Robert Anderson. Anderson grew concerned about South Carolina's mobilization, and he moved to repair Castle Pinckney and arm the forces at Moultrie. Anderson was ordered by the administration to hold the forts, but avoid any act that might "needlessly tend to provoke aggression."[35]

Meanwhile the president lost his most important subordinate, Howell Cobb, the secretary of treasury, who returned to his beloved Georgia, and also Lewis Cass, the ineffective secretary of state, who protested Buchanan's alleged vacillation in the crisis. Buchanan, still hoping for a compromise and trying to avoid antagonizing the South, refused to send reinforcements to Anderson. Criticism of Buchanan mounted when Cass resigned and charged that the president had approved Secretary of Interior Jacob Thompson's visiting North Carolina to discuss secession at the suggestion of his home state of Mississippi. Then to add to Buchanan's troubles, on December 20 the governor of South Carolina, Francis W. Pickens, demanded that the United States turn over Fort Sumner. The president had previously received assurances that the fort would be left alone if the federal government undertook no aggressive actions in the area. Buchanan's response was that only Congress could decide on the relationship between the federal government and South Carolina, and he could not surrender Fort Sumter or recognize the dissolution of the Union. Meanwhile, South Carolina began to establish shore batteries near the forts and sent three commissioners to Washington to negotiate.

On December 22, the president received evidence that Secretary of War Floyd had spent money without congressional authorization. As the details of the situation became clearer, the president wavered about whether to ask for his resignation. Buchanan received further complaints from Pittsburgh residents that with Floyd's approval cannons were being shipped to Texas forts—obviously on their way to secessionist elements. The president quickly canceled the order.

As Buchanan waited for the South Carolina commissioners, Major Anderson decided to move his forces to reinforce Fort Sumter. The Southern cabinet sympathizers saw this as an unnecessary provocation, and even Buchanan swore that it was against his orders. The sympathizers insisted on forcing Anderson back to his previous position, and Buchanan was uncertain what to do. The president reviewed Anderson's orders and supported his decision after all, leaving Floyd to resign using the decision as a pretext. By the end of the year though, the president indicated he was willing to order Anderson back if South Carolina would again promise to leave the federal forts alone. However, the Northern cabinet members refused to support such an overture, and Buchanan backed down fearing a rupture in his own cabinet. On December 31, the president approved sending additional troops and supplies to Fort Sumter, but the ship encountered hostile fire in the Charleston harbor and retreated. Now Buchanan was attacked in the North for weakness and in the South for provocation. By then the last two Southerners in his cabinet had resigned.

As matters cooled down, South Carolina approached Buchanan about "buying" the fort, a ruse he rejected. Fortunately, Anderson

had indicated to the administration that he did not need reinforcements and continued in place until Lincoln took over. Congress,
however, seemed even more paralyzed by the problem and refused
to give the president any authority to call up the militia or to raise
money for defense. It is little wonder that Lincoln, watching all these
twists and turns, refused to call Congress back into session until
nearly three months into his presidency.

Buchanan did strengthen Fort Taylor at Key West, Fort Jefferson
on Tortugas Island, and Fort Pickens at Pensacola. When the South
Carolinians tried to move against Sumter before Lincoln's inaugural, it was Jefferson Davis who stalled. By March 4, Buchanan's
burdens were over. As he rode with the tall president-elect, Buchanan
concluded, "My dear sir, if you are as happy in entering the White
House as I shall feel on returning to Wheatland, you are a happy
man indeed." Graciously, Lincoln chose to respond, "Mr. President,
I cannot say that I shall enter it with much pleasure, but I assure
that I shall do what I can to maintain the high standards set by my
illustrious predecessors who have occupied it."

Now the Union, after four years of concern and struggle, was
someone else's problem. Buchanan finished his term under the historical pale of charges of vacillation, timidity, misjudgment, and even
treasonable sympathies. He was compared unfavorably with Lincoln
after him and with Jackson before him. Why did Buchanan not
imitate Old Hickory's threats in 1833 to hang the secessionists?
Partly, the presidency had gone into a period of marked stupor if
not major decline, and Buchanan lacked the aggressive personality
and magnetic popularity that the general had. Despite the fact that
Buchanan had spent nearly all his adult life in public service, he
was frequently out of the country and did not fully sense the magnitude of Northern sentiment that had grown since 1850. Hatred of
slavery and, more importantly, hostility toward increasing Southern
demands had filled the ranks of slavery opponents with more Northerners than the New England abolitionists and impressionable women
that Buchanan sneered at.

The Jacksonian past with its small farms, cottage artisans, and
Western expansionists had spent its energies and given the nation
the very territories that led to more lands and more antislavery
agitation. The party of Jackson and Van Buren and Polk came undone, just as other national institutions went awry on the rack of
sectionalism. The presidency since Jackson, with the possible ex-

ception of Polk, was filled by men whose individual performances and composite records provided a poor accounting of executive effectiveness. But it was Polk's seeming successes that helped lay the groundwork for the Civil War.[36]

The democratization of politics, the rise of mass participation, the death of the closed caucus, and the introduction of the convention system gave the nation a presidency of military heroes and professional party functionaries. It is hard not to judge them as markedly inferior to what had gone before, to the chief executives schooled in a more elitist political world, given to occasional and enlightened philosophical reflection and awarded the presidency more often by deference than by intrigue. Indeed, the great men of the "middle period" of the early republic did not achieve the presidency; in the antebellum era, the Clays, Websters, Calhouns, Bentons, Douglases reached for, but never achieved, the highest office.

Americans like to believe that the strength and essence of the republic lies not in the governing class but in the rank and file, in the common sense and initiative of average citizens. But the lessons of this antebellum period are clear and so are those of the Civil War—the collapse of leadership led the nation into drift, indecision, and war, and resoluteness preserved the Union in the end. That collapse of leadership occurred not just in the presidency, but in many areas of community life and in many institutions of American society. Some historians have charged that the war was a product of a blundering generation; however, the failure was not one of technique but of vision. The men who came into American political and social positions of repute in the 1840s and 1850s were climbers, devoid often of a sense of history and brought up in a world of ballyhoo and political chicanery. Politics was mass spectacle, just as it is now mass entertainment, and the great moral issues were avoided as being inflammatory as they are now avoided for being inconvenient. The presidency was simply lost in that national vacuum, and when it was reconstituted, it moved to center stage in ways no one fully prophesied, with consequences more profound and at a cost more gruesome than the American national character could comprehend.

6

The Presidency Goes to War: Abraham Lincoln as Commander in Chief

The acrimonious national disputes of the 1850s over states' rights, territorial expansion, the status of slavery, and the right of secession took their toll on the ties that bound the North and South. By the election of 1860, the heterogeneous Democratic party could no longer bridge the gap across the Mason-Dixon line, and it was rent into three factions. The mainstream Democrats, after a confusing and divided convention, nominated Stephen Douglas; the Southern states' rights adherents put forth John Breckinridge; and a group of moderate constitutional Democrats rallied around John Bell.

In the Republican councils, it became obvious that this division might lead their party to victory, and the powerful bosses and state chairmen looked for a probable winner. Going into the Chicago convention, the Republicans had only a single presidential contest behind them with the 1856 campaign of explorer John C. Frémont. In May 1860, they came together to debate the merits of the major contenders, one of whom might very well end up in the White House. The forerunner was William Seward, the nationally known senator, a former governor of New York, and the candidate of the powerful machine run by Thurlow Weed. Seward had considerable strength in Maine, Michigan, Wisconsin, Minnesota, California, and Massachusetts, as well as in New York. He was a man who was profoundly conservative, and yet was identified with his radical remark that there was a higher law than the Constitution—the moral law that prohibited slavery. He had argued that the battle between the forces of freedom and those of black bondage would lead to an "irrepressible conflict."

Pitted against Seward were a variety of opponents. From Pennsylvania came Simon Cameron, a long-time Democratic leader who changed his party affiliation and became a Republican United States senator. Cameron had established a record as a shrewd political operator and as a rich and successful industrialist. His name was associated with partisan intrigue and backroom deals, but his role as a major figure in the important Pennsylvania delegation gave him considerable leverage in the national convention. However, in his circuitous route to the Chicago convocation, Cameron had welcomed Know-Nothing support, and thus alienated the powerful German-American element that was strong in the Republican party of that period.

A third principal was Salmon P. Chase of Ohio, an antislavery advocate who had been associated in the 1840s with the Liberty and Free Soil parties. Elected governor of Ohio in 1855, he had strong local support for the nomination, but little national visibility. A respected and responsible public official, he had distinguished himself during his period of public service in his home state.

An additional contender was the sixty-eight-year-old Missouri Whig, Edward Bates. Bates was a Southern planter, a sensible conservative, a man of conscience who had freed his slaves and provided for them later. Horace Greeley called him a fine candidate, and the powerful Blair clan in Maryland had declared their support for his candidacy.

And last, there was Abraham Lincoln of Illinois, a highly regarded local lawyer who had run for the nomination for the Senate in his state twice and had been defeated both times, but whose name was prominently mentioned in early 1860 as a possible vice presidential candidate. Many delegates at the convention were seeking a Westerner, one who opposed the extension of slavery in the new territories, who was conservative in speech and in bearing, a candidate who was not associated with the Know-Nothings, and who could command German-American support. On the third ballot, the Republican convention stopped Seward's bid and turned to an available alternative, Lincoln.

OUT OF THE WILDERNESS

No American political figure is as complex as Lincoln; none has been elevated to legend so firmly. In all popular polls and in nearly all historical judgments, he has assumed the designation of America's greatest president. Such a conclusion would have been greeted with disbelief by his colleagues and contemporaries, and probably even by Lincoln himself. His background is the American dream come true.[1] A dirt-poor boy, with no more than one year of formal education in total, knowing no influential patrons, Lincoln had moved aimlessly across the lonely farms and desolate plains of Kentucky, Indiana, and Illinois. After several years in the state legislature of Illinois, Lincoln got his turn to go to the U.S. Congress—the very term that marked Polk's entry into the Mexican War, a war Lincoln opposed. He was a strong supporter of economic development and insisted for years after the Mexican War that his basic political concern was internal improvements and not the expansion of slavery. As a good Whig and an old admirer of Clay, Lincoln worked hard for the party and waited for some reward, only to find that it was usually denied. He practiced law, met people, gave speeches filled with cracker-barrel humor and shopworn adages. Over the years, he established himself as an early opponent of slavery but not a New England abolitionist. Disappointed by politics, Lincoln turned more toward building a lucrative law practice and was a corporate counsel retained by railroads and the McCormick Reaper Company. Then in the 1850s, Lincoln's attention was refixed on the issues of slavery and its expansion into the territories of the Kansas-Nebraska region and the newly obtained Southwest.

Indeed as noted, twice he ran for the Senate and twice he was defeated. But in the second race, he won national attention in a series of debates with Stephen Douglas in 1858. Although there were fewer differences between the two candidates than is generally supposed, those debates cast Lincoln into the forefront of Republican leaders. In 1859, he made a lecture swing through New England and New York City and was well received. Despite the fact that he was to retreat from the logic of his position, Lincoln, like Seward, gave the nation a phrase that would be used to identify the magnitude of the new conflict.

In an address at the Republican state convention that nominated him for the Senate in 1858, Lincoln delivered a riveting address, attacking the *Dred Scott* decision, Douglas's doctrine of popular sovereignty, and Buchanan's policies. He argued that slavery agitation had increased and would increase even more until the crisis had been resolved. Then in words that would cause Southerners to shudder, he warned, "A house divided against itself cannot stand. I believe that this government cannot endure permanently half slave and half free. I do not expect this Union to be dissolved—I don't expect the house to fall—but I expect it will cease to be divided. It will become all one thing, or all the other."

Under attack by Douglas, Lincoln maintained that he did not support racial equality, and that he believed that the white race should be in ascendancy. He was insistent, especially campaigning in southern Illinois, that he was not in favor of black citizenship, and he concluded that the federal government lacked the constitutional authority to touch slavery in those states where it was recognized and supported. He even upheld the enforcement of the controversial fugitive slave law passed by Congress. The Lincoln of the 1858 debates has disturbed many modern-day liberals and lent some credence to the view that he was simply—by today's standards—another white racist politician.[2]

Such a characterization is understandable, but it is just incorrect. Lincoln all his life opposed slavery, hated what it did to the dignity of the slaves and the character of the masters. Legend has it that he first saw slaves being bought and sold when as a young boy he ventured down the Mississippi River to New Orleans, and he never overcame that sense of horror. In Congress, he introduced a bill to end slavery in the federal capital—an act in advance of his times and one of singular courage. He favored white ascendancy, but warned that he did not believe that the "negro should be denied *everything*." He opposed the "tendency to dehumanize the negro, to take away from him the right of ever striving to be a man."[3] Lincoln, the poor boy who made good, looked upon the United States as the last best hope of mankind. He welcomed the upwardly mobile and ambitious, and denounced the view that every society had to have a "mud-sill," a lower class confined forever to a place on the bottom of the heap. But in the end, the Union he so celebrated was a white man's world. Lincoln was a practical politician, not an abolitionist, although he genuinely hated slavery more intensely and more consistently than almost any other mainstream political leader. As a boy who grew up in states characterized in part by Southern culture, as a man who married into a slaveholding family, Lincoln retained many of the racial attitudes of his youth even as president. What made him different from the average politician on the race issue was, first, his genuine hatred of the institution of slavery and his deep personal sensitivity toward human suffering; and second, the unique cataclysmic events that turned a conservative Whig into the Great Emancipator. Thus it was that Abraham Lincoln, who claimed he was more controlled by events than the master of them, became the greatest revolutionary of them all—the commander in chief who brought about the demise of slavery forever in a land where it had seemed firmly entrenched.

Lincoln was nominated for the presidency for several reasons that are quite different from what would become his destiny. Lincoln was seen by the convention delegates as more moderate than Seward and as more acceptable to the South and border states. With his Western background, he was the epitome of the "new man"— the embodiment of the frontier spirit. His supporters regaled the nation with the legend of the log cabin (that had helped Harrison in 1840) and passed around rails supposedly split by Honest Abe himself. Lincoln, while not ashamed of his frontier past, never really exploited it. He was, he said, of undistinguished background; the story of his family was "the short and simple annals of the poor," he told an early biographer. In the campaign of 1860, he said little, stayed at home as was the custom, and bided his time as the Democrats divided up the vote. The results gave Lincoln 1,866,452 votes to Douglas's 1,376,957, Breckinridge's 849,781, and Bell's 588,879. While Lincoln received only about 39 percent of the popular tally, he polled 180 electoral votes to Breckinridge's 72, Bell's 39, and Douglas's 12. Douglas's popular support, while extensive, was spread across the nation and not concentrated in the major states. Lincoln had carried all of the free states, except New Jersey, which he split with Douglas. Breckinridge captured the lower South, plus Arkansas, Delaware, Maryland, and North Carolina. Bell also did well in some of those states and carried the border states of Kentucky, Tennessee, and Virginia. Douglas received all the electoral votes of Missouri and three in New Jersey.

Lincoln thus won a large electoral vote victory with less than 40 percent of the popular vote. But his victory was somewhat troubling; it was a clear sectional victory, one likely to further fuel the forces of alienation and secession in the lower South. In the area later to become the Confederacy, Lincoln received not one popular ballot except in Virginia, where he polled some 1,929 votes, most of them in the Northern panhandle area around Wheeling. Even Breckinridge, the candidate of the Southern states' rights forces, received over 278,000 votes in the Northern states. Clearly, the Republicans had not moved much beyond Frémont's level of support in 1856, except that under new circumstances victory emerged.

The usual explanation was that the Democrats, by dividing up the vote, allowed Lincoln to creep in. But in fact if there had been a common anti-Lincoln ticket, he still would have won the presidency because the Republicans would have held onto enough of the electoral vote. Unlike Douglas, who had wide national support, Lincoln's votes were concentrated, and he wasted no votes in futile states. He had no popular support in the South at all and very little in Kentucky, Virginia, and Maryland. Thus where he did garner popular support, he usually won, and therefore carried the total state electoral vote, except in Missouri and New Jersey. Although voting statistics are confusing and incomplete for this period of history, it appears that Lincoln's victory was due to his ability to join New England and the older Northwest region with the free states of the Midwest, California, and Oregon. Despite the popular view that it was the German-American Republicans who brought victory, it appears that Lincoln's success, at least in the Great Lakes states, was due more to the old Yankee stock that had migrated from New England than to foreign-born voters; the only exception was in Illinois where the German-American vote was indeed critical to the Republican ticket.[4]

The election of Lincoln on November 6, 1860, then, was a clear-cut sectional victory, one likely to infuriate Deep South secessionist supporters. To those agitators, the presidential election marked the final insult, even though the Democrats still controlled Congress, and the Supreme Court had supported slavery without restriction. As Lincoln celebrated his unique personal triumph, and as his party marked its first great campaign success, the forces of dissolution were unleashed once again, this time not to be contained.

EARLY SECESSION MOVES

The election of Lincoln led to Southern cries in more radical quarters for secession from the Union. The moderates in Virginia and Kentucky, however, pushed for a border state convention to slow down the disunion movement. President Buchanan and Lincoln both favored the idea, but hotter heads in the Deep South, especially in South Carolina, wanted to end the Union altogether. Some Northerners, such as Horace Greeley of the *New York Tribune*, urged that they be allowed to leave in peace. As Greeley editorialized, "We hope never to live in a republic whereof one section is pinned to the residue by bayonets." Even Winfield Scott, the head of the U.S. Army, proposed four unions of the states, a rearrangement whereby the slave states would be trustees of the territory south of 36°30'.[5]

Others suggested that the Lincoln electors should vote instead for Breckinridge, and support a statesman-like compromise with the South. Breckinridge's selection would save the Union, it was argued, while Lincoln's formal election by the electoral college in February 1861 would end it. But as so often happens in political crises, events flow from the actions of the extremists. On December 20, 1860, South Carolina passed an ordinance of secession—it was now a separate nation, at least in the eyes of its own partisans. The impetus for disunion swept through the lower South and by early 1861, South Carolina was joined by Alabama, Florida, Georgia, Louisiana, and Mississippi. Gathering in Montgomery, Alabama, the delegates from those states met to form the Southern States of North America. In February, the secessionists elected Jefferson Davis of Mississippi and Alexander H. Stephens of Georgia to be provisional president and vice president, respectively. In March, the forces of secession banded together to depose the Union-oriented governor of Texas, Sam Houston, and consequently that important state entered the Confederacy. Among the states of the Deep South, only in Texas was the ordinance of secession submitted to a popular vote, and there that was done after its adoption by the state's delegates.

As for the Buchanan administration, it permitted this new government to be established without any interference. The border states, especially Virginia, were not a part of the early secession movement, and it was unclear what type of support the Confederacy would have there. The crisis atmosphere was accelerated by the seizure of federal military establishments in the South; once again South Carolina took the lead. By the end of December 1860, secession leaders controlled post offices, customshouses, the federal courts in Charleston, and Castle Pinckney and Fort Moultrie in the harbor region. Elsewhere, this step was repeated as federal arsenals, forts, and customshouses changed hands. By the middle of January 1861, forts in Savannah, Mobile, and Pensacola were seized, and Southern agents were in the North buying munitions and war materials.[6]

Yet in the border states and even among large segments of the Deep South, secession was not greeted with uniform support. Stephens, who knew the president-elect, praised Lincoln as a "good, sound and safe man," and argued that slavery would be protected under his administration. In December 1860, President Buchanan had denounced secession and advocated "peaceful constitutional remedies" to deal with the problem. As noted before, Congress in response had created a broad-based committee in both houses to deal with the mounting crisis. But the Senate, a body once marked by the great compromises of Clay, Webster, and Calhoun, failed after eleven days to come up with a formula for peace. In the House of Representatives, the same fate resulted as Republicans refused to agree to Southern demands to protect and extend slavery. Yet both houses passed a proposed constitutional amendment by two-thirds majorities, which would guarantee that Congress would never amend the Constitution to abolish or interfere with slavery. And in the House, John Sherman of Ohio introduced a resolution that neither Congress nor the nonslaveholding states had a right under the Constitution to interfere with or regulate slavery in any state. That resolution was passed 161 to 0. Another compromise came from John J. Crittenden of Kentucky, the successor to Clay's mantle in the Senate, who favored extending the Missouri Compromise line (36°30') to the Pacific coast—thus creating a national Mason-Dixon line and protecting slavery below it and prohibiting it in the territories and states above. Republicans attacked his proposal, but in fact it was more restrictive than the Supreme Court's policy in the Dred Scott case, which made slavery an unregulated national institution.[7]

Part of the confusion of the period was due to the internal disorganization of the new Republican party. Many prominent Republicans, including Seward and Weed, were given to compromise. Despite Seward's popular reputation as a radical, he was quite willing to enact a stricter fugitive slave law and to allow the admission of still more slave states. Even when the Southern representatives were absent from Congress in February and March, the majority of Republicans in that body supported the admission of the territories of Colorado, Dakota, and Nevada without having them prohibit slavery, a provision they had previously insisted on when they attacked Douglas. It was, as Douglas pointed out sarcastically in 1861, the exact principle he had proposed in 1854—popular sovereignty.

And what of Lincoln, himself? As we have seen, in this period, the president-elect watched carefully what was happening, kept his own counsel, wrote confidentially to a few trusted colleagues, and was preoccupied with the demands of patronage seekers. He felt it would do no good to speak out publicly and might even encourage the secessionist elements. Privately, he favored a fugitive slave law moderately enforced, promised not to recommend the abolition of slavery in the District of Columbia, indicated that he would not support the end of the slave trade in the United States, and said he did not care if slavery were extended into New Mexico (where it was thought the institution would not be economically viable). To his old acquaintance and Georgia politician, Alexander Stephens, he promised no interference with slavery where it existed, and assured him that, "the South would be in no more danger in this respect than . . . in the days of Washington." He even asserted that he would not discriminate against the South in terms of patronage appointments in its region, nor allow Northerners to come in and take over administrative posts there. But on one point, Lincoln refused to yield—he would not accept the expansion of slavery into the new territories. This step, he concluded, would "lose us everything we gain by the election."[8]

On secession he had said little, but he expressed the view that no one state could leave without the consent of the others, and that he thought the federal officials should "run the machine as it is." He would support a constitutional amendment to reassure those who feared that slavery would be interfered with, but on the territorial question, he wrote to Republican leaders: no compromise; it would lead to "a slave empire." His position was clear, but it by no means commanded universal support in his own party. Even in Massachusetts, probably the most antislavery state in the Union, twenty-two thousand citizens signed a petition to Congress urging the adoption of the Crittenden compromise.

In terms of the economic realities, it is doubtful that there would have been much migration of slaveholders into the new territories. There were 22 slaves in New Mexico (which included present-day Arizona), and even in "bleeding Kansas" in 1860, there were fewer than 200 slaves out of a population of 100,000 people. The Republicans had already let into the Union Dakota, Colorado, and Nevada with no preconditions. In terms of fugitive slaves, which so upset the Southern planter class, the 1860 census numbered them at 803 or about one-fiftieth of one percent of the total slave population. These two great issues—territorial expansion and fugitive slave laws—were symbolic concerns far out of proportion to the actual conditions of the time.

But those issues were not unimportant, for they became litmus tests concerning how one felt about the peculiar institution. The

South demanded not just protection, but a vote of approval for its way of life. Lincoln's election did not threaten its domestic institutions, but it did signify that the South would no longer be able to check the growing dominance of free soil northern and western America. It must be remembered that, except for the Adamses, Lincoln was the first president who was not a slaveholder or a Northerner somewhat sympathetic to the Southern planter class. Lincoln's stand on the territories was clear, and it enabled his party to define itself in contrast to both the Douglas Democrats and the slaveholding interests.

Between the election and the inaugural, Lincoln stayed in Springfield, listening and watching. He realized that some Southern leaders had begun preparations for military operations and he was concerned about the loss of federal installations. On December 21, 1860, the day after South Carolina's secession, he confidentially wrote General Winfield Scott that he should be prepared "to either hold or retake the forts, as the case may require."

Lincoln carefully worked on naming his cabinet, dealing with the major party leaders and fulfilling agreements made by his managers at the party convention. As his inauguration approached, he bid farewell to his neighbors in a touching tribute,

> My friends. No one, not in my situation, can appreciate my feeling of sadness at this parting. To this place, and the kindness of these people I owe everything. Here I have lived a quarter of a century, and have passed from a young man to an old man. Here my children have been born, and one is buried. I now leave, not knowing when or whether I may return, with a task greater than that which rested upon Washington.

As he left Springfield, he traveled by train through Illinois and western Pennsylvania to the upstate cities of New York, down to New Jersey, Philadelphia, Harrisburg, Maryland, and on to Washington, D.C. His speeches were frequently somber and often melancholy. He characterized himself as "the humblest of all individuals that have ever been elevated to the presidency," and he reassured the South of his conservative tendencies and moderate inclinations. The crisis was artificial, he concluded.

On reaching the capital on February 23, Lincoln was warned of possible assassination attempts and, at the insistence of the authorities, he arrived early in the morning. His enemies quickly spread the rumor that Lincoln came into town in a long military cloak and a Scotch plaid cap, and cartoonists spread the tale of his allegedly sneaking into the capital. Soon a barrage of criticism would be hurled at this man: they called him a simple Susan, a gorilla, the ape from Illinois. They insisted that Lincoln spoke in a crude way, had grown a shaggy beard at some girl's insistence, and was unused to the social graces of the capital. He was simple, stupid, and quite homely.

In his inaugural address, on March 4, Lincoln struck two themes: his guarantee that the South should not feel threatened by his election and his devotion to maintain the Union. Yet he promised that where there was hostility to the United States in a locality, "there will be no attempt to force obnoxious strangers among the people," and that while the government had the strict legal right to control its federal officers, he deemed it "better to forego for the time the use of such offices." Thus, despite his policy of firmness and fraternity, the new president spoke of temporizing rather than of asserting forcefully the federal government's authority. The speech was generally not well received in the South, and the new administration entered office facing the same problems that the previous one faced.

FORT SUMTER

The first order of business for the new president was patronage. For a party out of power, the acrimonious election of Lincoln still meant offices, positions, and newly found opportunities. Much of the public reaction to Lincoln's balanced cabinet was unfavorable, and Republican stalwart James G. Blaine recorded that Buchanan's final cabinet had more strong defenders of the Union than the new one. The president managed those patronage chores, but spent most of his time deciding what to do about the future of federal establishments in the South. As has been noted, Buchanan allowed Southern occupation of many federal installations in the South. He has been strongly criticized for this lack of leadership, but he insisted with some justification that to have replenished the forts in December 1860 would have been "little short of madness . . . with the small force" at his disposal. Lincoln was not unsympathetic to this realistic compromise at first, but compromise was not what he ended up with as the crisis approached.[9]

Once again the focal point would be South Carolina. There in the harbor, two of the three forts had fallen under secessionist control. Only Fort Sumter remained in federal hands. The fate of Sumter was a subject of early negotiations after the inaugural and, at times, the new administration did not speak with one voice. The federal government had to confront the fact that Major Robert Anderson, the fort's commander, could not remain at Sumter beyond six weeks because of a shortage of food; April 15, 1861, became the day of decision.

Lincoln and his cabinet discussed the matter, and the president found his major advisors nearly unanimous in opposing reprovisioning the fort. At this time, the South sent three commissioners to negotiate with Lincoln on the fate of the fort, and while the president at first refused to see them as representatives of an independent nation, indirect contact was established. The administration's position was confusing as Seward, acting on his own, gave the commissioners the impression that the fort would be given up after all.

The president had seriously pondered the question, fearing that a tough stand would alienate Southern moderates, especially in Virginia, and drive them into the waiting arms of the Confederacy. He had concluded, "If you will guarantee to me the State of Virginia, I shall remove the troops. A state for a fort is no bad business." With the nonsecession delegates at Richmond holding the state in the Union, the president realized that military conflict would force Virginia to choose between its Southern neighbors and its historical attachment to the Union. Fearing the consequences, Lincoln as late as April 4 was still considering whether to withdraw from Fort Sumter.

As he pondered the issue, a conference of Northern governors met at Washington and demanded that Lincoln stand firm on Sumter. In addition, Lincoln's old friend and political confidant, Francis P. Blair, visited him and warned that withdrawal would be treason and would not sit well with the people of the North. Faced with these pressures and increasing secessionist belligerence in Virginia, Lincoln moved toward a tougher line.

Cautiously, he worked out a policy to reinforce the less-visible Fort Pickens in Pensacola, Florida, in order to emphasize his overall policy, but also to "better enable the country to accept the evacuation of Fort Sumter as a military necessity" if it came to that. The Buchanan administration had concluded in the last weeks of its term an agreement that it would not reinforce Fort Pickens if Florida promised not to attack it. Lincoln's Pickens expedition ran into problems, however, and his subtle plans were checked as any possibility for a Sumter compromise was ended. The president faced a stark choice: give up Sumter and ignominiously surrender federal authority, or send an expedition knowing it might mean conflict and war.

Lincoln ordered Fort Pickens reinforced and, in a confusing chain of events, he also had the Sumter expedition go ahead. The administration then informed Governor Francis W. Pickens of South Carolina of its intention to send the fort provisions, but not men, arms, or ammunition. South Carolina, however, refused to bend, and with Confederate President Davis's approval, attacked the fort. After thirty hours of steady shelling of the fort, Major Anderson surrendered Sumter.

Some critics of Lincoln's policy have argued that he shrewdly maneuvered South Carolina into firing the first shot, and thus in assuming the blame for starting the war. One of the president's friends recorded that on July 3, 1861, Lincoln said, "The plan succeeded. They attacked Sumter—it fell, and thus, did more service than it otherwise would."[10] Yet, even if that remark were faithfully recorded and really reflected his view at the time, Lincoln could not have taken comfort in what he saw happening. The conflict ended the neutrality of several border states and drove an unprepared North into war. Perhaps, he misjudged the intensity of Southern feeling about the issue and the results that the defense of Fort Sumter would have on the Southern mentality.

Historian James G. Randall has summarized the Sumter crisis in a balanced judgment: "When war came it turned out that he had kept the non-aggressive record of his government clear, which assuredly is not to his discredit; but to say that Lincoln meant that the first shot would be fired by the other side *if a first shot was fired*, is not to say that he maneuvered to have the shot fired. That distinction is fundamental."[11]

The Sumter crisis showed the extent of the South's alienation from the Union, and the power of the secessionists increased as confrontation led to full-scale war. Whether Lincoln knew what the consequences would be is unclear, but his government's handling of the problem was muddled and indicated that the new president lacked control over members of his own administration, especially Secretary of State Seward. Concerned about saving the Union, pledged to nonviolence against the slave states, faced with a politi-

cally balanced but unstable cabinet, the president began to mobilize the country for a war he kept saying need not have come.

THE EIGHTY-DAY DICTATORSHIP

To many of his colleagues at the time, Lincoln seemed vacillating and indecisive during his early weeks in office. It may be that
he was moving cautiously through a minefield of hazards, any one
of which would have stymied even a more experienced executive.
Some of his biographers find that he exhibited many of the symp-
toms of a nervous breakdown, a diagnosis not out of the question
for a man who faced a very stressful situation and had a history of
melancholia and some unstable emotional periods.[12]

But if Lincoln did seem unsure of his way and was suffering
from doubts at times, he retained a certain surety of purpose that
was often lacking in those who at first questioned his capabilities.
He weighed compromise at Sumter, but insisted on asserting federal authority in the most nonbelligerent way possible. Oftentimes,
caution and prudence are seen as vacillation, just as action and
movement seem impulsive to the fainthearted.

Once South Carolina fired on Fort Sumter and the Confederacy
lined up behind it, war was inevitable. That development was not
remarkable, but the metamorphosis of the man in the White House
was. In weeks, a new Lincoln emerged, one fortified with such
determination that his strengths seem so unexpected and so mystifying. How did it happen that Lincoln almost immediately began
asserting an interpretation of the presidency that rested on no previous example? How did it happen that this conservative Whig, this
corporation and neighborhood lawyer, came to assume near dictatorial powers in the nearly three months when he mobilized the
nation for war?[13]

The presidents under whom Lincoln grew up were modest men
with much to be modest about, to paraphrase Winston Churchill.
Some were competent; most were weak; all suffered, except for
Jackson and perhaps Polk, from the consequences of the ascendancy
of Congress in the 1815 to 1850 era. Many of the most successful
presidents of the late eighteenth and early nineteenth centuries, especially Washington, Jefferson, and Monroe, worked through indirection and not by asserting their powers vis-à-vis Congress. Only
Jackson, and his protégé Polk, neither of whom was Lincoln attracted

to, were exceptions. Lincoln, as president, is clearly outside of that dominant tradition, and it is especially strange since his lifelong political allegiance was to the Whig philosophy of limited executive power, constitutional rights, and balanced government. That he would assert such a different view after years in the crucible of war would be explainable; that he did so after only weeks in office is truly baffling.

Perhaps one explanation is that his deep affection for the Union as an almost religious ideal was the driving force. He seized power to save what had been given to him, and all his forceful initiatives were somehow infused with a passion that only responsibility could compel. But he surely disproves the adage that great presidents must be men experienced by years in public office, for though he was good politician, he was not a regular in the public eye. And Lincoln disproves also the supposition that strong presidents pattern themselves on strong predecessors. There were no Roosevelts before him; indeed, they built on his foundation. The Whig Lincoln was by no means a Jackson admirer, and while he respected Jefferson, he did not think him a strong executive. He revered Washington as the premier Founding Father, but the patriarch's problems were not similar to his own. Lincoln, the epitome of the self-made man in so many mythic American ways, is also the self-made president. Before him was little in the way of example, after him would be the severest reaction in American history to the use of executive power. Lincoln stands out in the nineteenth-century American landscape as an anomaly as an executive, a stranger in what was up to then a rather familiar and untroubling political scene.

What made him so different in the early period? From April 12, 1861 to July 4, 1861, the president assumed far-reaching powers, some in violation of the Constitution. The political scientist Clinton Rossiter has called it a "constitutional dictatorship" and concluded that the unusual powers Lincoln assumed in those early months were fairly established by the time Congress reconvened, and that despite congressional attempts to pare them down, Lincoln's powers were virtually intact throughout the war. Thus, he set the pattern that would characterize his behavior for the next four years.[14]

Just what Lincoln believed in April 1861 about those extraordinary powers he assumed is unclear. He said that he had sworn an oath registered in heaven to defend the Constitution. As a young man and as president he was deeply committed to the Union as an historical entity and as "the last best hope on earth," as he phrased it. On April 15, 1861, he issued an executive proclamation in which he announced that since the laws were being obstructed in the seven states of the Deep South, he would use constitutional and statutory powers to call up seventy-five thousand men in the state militias to put down the insurrection. The Militia Act of 1795 gave the president the authority to call up those units if he found "combinations too powerful to be suppressed by the ordinary course of judicial proceedings or by the powers vested in the marshalls." The president also called Congress into special session, but set the date on July 4. Probably, Lincoln thought that the war would be short and that he could avoid congressional meddling by setting the date three months into the future.

On April 19, the president ordered a blockade on the coast lines of the seceded states, and the next day he ordered nineteen vessels to be added to the navy. By May 3, Lincoln took the extraordinary step of adding over forty-two thousand volunteers to the military and enlarged the regular army by twenty-three thousand and the navy by eighteen thousand. He had already instructed Secretary of Treasury Samuel Chase to furnish $2 million to pay private citizens in New York for military acquisitions. Thus in contradiction to the Constitution, the executive branch of government and not the legislative had raised up armies and appropriated public funds.

On April 27, the president went further. He ordered the commanding general of the U.S. Army to suspend the writ of habeas corpus in the Philadelphia-Washington corridor in order to contend with mob violence and sabotage on the railroads, and by July 2, Lincoln extended the order from Philadelphia to New York as well. When Chief Justice Taney, sitting in a circuit court case, protested the order, the president ignored the decision. Lincoln went on to close the post offices to treasonable correspondence and ordered those suspected of disloyal and treasonable practices to be arrested and detained in military custody.

When Congress convened on July 4, Lincoln's message laid out the steps he had taken and justified them in terms of "the war powers of the Government"—a novel phrase for that time. He maintained that no government should be asked to forgo the right of self-preservation and concluded that this right was centered in the presidency. He argued that his actions, whether strictly legal or not, were necessary and that none of these steps were beyond the "constitutional competence of Congress." Thus, he concluded that Congress should ratify after the fact what he had done and that, under circumstances of grave emergency, the government, headed by the executive, could commit actions outside of the law to preserve the greater fabric of government. In his defense, Lincoln asked, "Are all the laws *but one* to go unexecuted, and the Government itself go to pieces lest that one be violated? Even in such a case, would not the official oath be broken if the Government should be overthrown when it was believed that disregarding the single law would tend to preserve it?"[15]

On August 6, 1861, the Congress retroactively approved all acts, proclamations and orders of the president concerning the army, navy, and militia call-ups. Later, in 1863, the Supreme Court in the *Prize* Cases upheld the blockade and concluded that the president was the true judge of the type of response the crises demanded in dealing with domestic insurrection.

EARLY WAR MOVES

In issuing these proclamations after Sumter, Lincoln was faced with some major practical difficulties in a nation of decentralized military power. For example, how should he use those regiments— as a national army or organized by state? Who paid the costs for the war effort? Were the Confederate privateers to be treated as pirates? Were their soldiers traitors rather than belligerents because they were in rebellion?[16] With all of this uncertainty, the president also was faced with demands from the various states to promote their own local sons to major military positions. And in the capital, the War Department was not able to handle the first wave of enthusiastic volunteers, who had to be fed, clothed, and armed before they could fight.

To add to Lincoln's burdens, the Southern states that had tried to stay neutral began to secede after Sumter. On April 17, 1861, Virginia started its movement, and on May 7, Arkansas and Tennessee followed, even though in the latter an initial popular referendum went 3 to 1 against secession. A second referendum in June yielded the desired results for the Confederate sympathizers and Tennessee left the Union. North Carolina soon followed Tennessee and even those border states that stayed in the Union, except for Delaware, refused to send any regiments to defend the U.S. government until after July 4.

Meanwhile, prosecession mobs prohibited Northern troops from

passing through Baltimore toward Washington. Lincoln at first had
to agree with Maryland officials to send the troops around the city;
finally Brigadier General Ben Butler moved in and established military control over the city.

Northern newspapers continued their criticism of the weak
administration and patronage pressures mounted on the beleaguered
president. Indeed, in the critical months of 1861, half of Lincoln's
letters dealt with patronage requests. One old acquaintance, Lyman
Trumbull, concluded that "there is a lack of . . . positive action &
business talent in the cabinet. Lincoln though a most excellent &
honest man lacks these qualities." That impression of general incompetence was only confirmed by the outcome of the first major
battle of the war, the confusion called Bull Run. Washington society drove out to the battlefield to watch the event, and at first it
seemed that the Union commander, Irvin McDowell, had defeated
the Confederate forces of P. T. G. Beauregard. But by evening, Lincoln received the discouraging news: McDowell was in retreat, and
a disorganized army was beating its way back to the capital, leaving Washington exposed and vulnerable to a Confederate attack.

Although he did not force McDowell to confront the Confederate armies, Lincoln and his cabinet had rejected General Scott's
request for a delay until August. Political considerations required a
quick victory, and one that would make use of the ninety-day volunteers whose enlistments would soon be up. Faced with this debacle, Lincoln sat down on the night after Bull Run and wrote out
a military plan. He wanted a tighter blockade, a strong force at Fort
Monroe and its vicinity, control over Baltimore, a strengthening of
the Union position in the Winchester, Virginia area, movement in
Missouri, a reorganization of forces in the District of Columbia, a
discharge of the three-month volunteers, and a raising of more forces
with longer terms of service. Lincoln insisted that the strategic ports
in Virginia be taken, and he wanted a coordinated attack in the West.
In July, after the Union debacle at Bull Run, the president named
George B. McClellan, the victor in a modest campaign in western
Virginia, to be commander of the Union army. The dream of a short,
happy war was dashed at Bull Run. McClellan came in with plans
for extensive retraining and strategic planning—a prelude, he said,
to the major campaigns ahead.

At first, not all the states were anxious to enter the fray. The
state of Lincoln's birth, Kentucky, initially worked out a policy of
neutrality between the two major armies and promised to respect

federal authority and ban Confederate troops in its state if the Union pledged not to move troops through Kentucky. Lincoln dealt with the situation rather gingerly at first, remarking, "I think to lose Kentucky is nearly . . . to lose the whole game. Kentucky gone, we cannot hold Missouri, nor, as I think, Maryland. These all against us, and the job on our hands is too large for us. We would as well consent to separation at once, including the surrender of the capital." His cautious policy seemed to pay off as the Unionists carried nine out of ten of the congressional districts in the June 1861 elections. By the fall, the state was still tenuously in the Union camp.[17]

A very different development took place later in Virginia as the forty-eight counties in the western part of the state opposed secession and were finally reorganized in 1863 as a separate state. In Tennessee, the eastern part of that state stayed pro-Union despite the decision of the governor and the legislature to enter into a military agreement with the Confederacy. Farther west, Missouri was also bitterly divided on the issue of secession. Lincoln inadvertently added to the volatility of the situation by sending General John C. Frémont into the region. Frémont immediately generated controversy by issuing a proclamation assuming all administrative powers in the state, ordering persons found with arms to be court-martialed and shot, and confiscating all property held by those in rebellion. In the process, he declared that their slaves were free from then on.

To Lincoln, Frémont's abrupt actions challenged his own executive control of the war and created a hornet's nest on the emancipation issue. Fearful of the reactions of the pro-Union, slaveholding border states, Lincoln refused to upset the delicate balance of sentiments by emancipation. He informed Frémont as politely as possible that no one should be shot without the president's consent and that no confiscation should proceed outside of the confines set by the Confiscation Act of 1861. That act provided that seizures of assets should be done through the courts and would involve only property used in aiding rebellion. However, Frémont generally ignored Lincoln's orders and proceeded on his own until finally he was brought down by publicized charges of favoritism, corruption, incompetence, and graft. Lincoln eventually removed Frémont as commander of the Department of the West, and consequently incurred the wrath of the abolitionists who approved of the general's order.

By the end of the year, the president faced a difficult balancing act in the border states and had given conservative General McClellan his public support in revamping the newly named Army of the Potomac. To the abolitionists, Lincoln was definitely not a kindred spirit, and to conservative critics he seemed a less-than-imposing executive. Even his own attorney general, Edward Bates, confided to his diary, "The Prest . . . is an excellent man . . . but he lacks *will* and *purpose*, and I greatly fear he had not *the power to command.*"[18]

BEGINNING A FOREIGN POLICY

Lincoln's first priority in office was the prosecution of the war, and he was involved in foreign affairs only as they might affect that effort. Observing the new president's displays of caution, his secretary of state, William Seward, thought he saw a vacuum and attempted early to move in and fill in. In an April 1, 1861 memorandum, the secretary laid out a foreign policy that included evacuating Sumter, defending the Gulf of Mexico ports, and demanding explanations from Spain and France on disputed issues with the United States. If their responses were not satisfactory, Seward wanted to call Congress back into session for a declaration of war. Supposedly, this foreign threat would rally the discordant parts of the Union together, and thus avert the possibility of civil war. Seward also proposed that the United States toughen its position toward Great Britain and toward czarist Russia. He bluntly concluded that the president should either take control of foreign policy or assign a cabinet minister, that is Seward, to do it. "I neither seek to evade nor assume responsibility," Seward pronounced.[19]

Lincoln, with characteristic patience, simply informed Seward that he saw no drift in his policy, and that he had already communicated publicly his objectives in a variety of messages. In terms of establishing foreign policy, the president firmly concluded that such responsibilities were his alone. Working with Seward and some rather capable American ministers abroad, Lincoln from the beginning steered clear of confrontations that might divert resources and attention from the war effort. Some major obstacles were quickly apparent, however. Segments of the British upper class were talking in approving terms of the Southern cause, and Prime Minister Palmerston did not seem friendly to the Union. In fact, except for the Russian minister to the United States, nearly all of the major foreign ambassadors and ministers were favorably disposed to the South.

The Confederates tried hard to push for foreign recognition of their new government, and Jefferson Davis devoted a considerable amount of effort to that cause. Consequently, he also vigorously objected to Lincoln's April proclamations establishing a naval blockade. By that step, though, Lincoln had in fact complicated matters by deciding not to treat the secessionists as pirates or traitors, thus lending support to the view that the Confederacy was a belligerent power. The British insisted on remaining neutral in the dispute for the time being—a step that drew complaints from the Lincoln administration, but which in the long run worked against the Confederacy.

The Lincoln government and the British had several major disputes with which the president had to deal. In late 1861, an American captain stopped the British steamer *Trent* and arrested two Confederate leaders on board. The British, quite correctly, regarded that seizure as an insult and demanded the release of the prisoners. While many Union leaders saluted the captain's daring, the administration was more prudent. Lincoln's attitude was consistent: he did not want two wars on his hands. The president received unexpected help when the queen and her husband modified a tough note that Palmerston had originally intended to send, thus giving the Americans a face-saving opportunity to settle the controversy. Finally, the envoys were released and the administration closed the book on a particularly difficult episode. Lincoln overall insisted on not becoming preoccupied with foreign affairs. In late 1861 and early 1862, his primary concerns were the weaknesses in the Union war effort and problems in his own cabinet.[20]

THE POTOMAC COMMAND

Lincoln had serious reservations when he appointed Simon Cameron to be secretary of war, but commitments made by his convention managers and the need for a broad coalition cabinet led him to bow to pressure. It was a bad decision, one that became all the more obvious as the early phases of the war ended. Congressional oversight and public opinion became more critical of the inefficiency, graft, and corruption in the War Department. By the beginning of 1862, the president offered Cameron a way out, the

U.S. ministership to Russia. Like Frémont, Cameron had embarrassed the president by advocating in a report that slaves be employed as soldiers—a difficult issue that Lincoln had tried to sidestep. With characteristic magnanimity, Lincoln defended Cameron against some of the congressional criticism of mismanagement and pointed out that the early phases of the crisis required quick action in order to protect the integrity of the Union. Lincoln insisted that he and other members of the administration were at least equally responsible for whatever errors or wrongs had occurred.

In Cameron's place, Lincoln named Edwin M. Stanton of Pennsylvania, a Democrat and prominent lawyer whom Lincoln had met on less than favorable terms before the war. Stanton had served briefly as attorney general in the Buchanan cabinet and had privately been critical of Lincoln and his abilities. The president's nomination for that post came without much consultation and apparently was due to his sense that Stanton, as abrasive as he was, could rein in the chaos of the War Department.

Stanton immediately indicated his sympathy for the newly created Congressional Committee on the Conduct of the War—a joint House-Senate group that was to plague the president during his term in office. The committee conducted lurid investigations of the war effort, attacked Democratic generals such as McClellan, and pushed the radical Republican cause and its military partisans—Frémont, Ambrose Burnside, John Pope, Joseph Hooker, and Irvin McDowell. Since Lincoln was committed to McClellan at this time, he too incurred the committee's wrath.

When McClellan was called to take command of the Army of the Potomac in late July 1861, he found a military mess. Even Stanton said that after Bull Run the overall situation was a national disgrace and attributed that plight to Lincoln's running the war effort for five months. Washington was unguarded, and McClellan had before him an ill-equipped, demoralized, and disorganized force. Rather remarkably, McClellan reorganized the troops, improved discipline, moved to protect the capital, constructed a communications system, and won the admiration of his troops, who called him "Mac" and "the American Napoleon."

But McClellan was not as well thought of by radical Republicans and by some of the more moderate cabinet secretaries. He could be rude to congressmen, inflated in his self-estimation, curt to the president, and often too slow in his responses to situations that required decisive leadership without long drawn-out planning.

When on one occasion, McClellan, having gone to bed, refused to receive Lincoln and Seward, the president simply passed it off by observing it "was better at this time not to be making points of etiquette & personal dignity." As he observed, one bad general was preferable to two good ones; unity of command, he thought at that period, was crucial to victory. Not everyone was as magnanimous as he.

But as summer passed and winter, fall, and spring came, McClellan had not begun the campaign that he had promised. Pressure was building on the administration for a Union offensive. Even Attorney General Bates urged Lincoln to become the real commander in chief of the armed forces, and when McClellan fell ill of typhoid fever, Lincoln actually considered taking to the field himself to lead the troops. The president began to give closer scrutiny to the operations in the West and became involved in military affairs in Columbus and east Tennessee. He read Henry Halleck's *Science of War* and studied strategic works for military advice. On January 10, 1862, Lincoln seemed especially agitated over the lack of movement, and two days later called together a council of several generals and some cabinet officials to discuss the war effort. An ill McClellan made plans to leave his sick bed and defend his strategy before the council. But at the meeting, he pointedly refused to discuss his strategy, citing the possibility of someone disclosing his plans.

On January 27, a weary Lincoln issued General Order No. 1 which mandated a forward movement by February 22. Four days later, the president followed up with another order that an expedition should seize a railroad point southwest near Manassas Junction. McClellan formally requested permission to debate the order, and consequently, it was not put into effect. Lincoln was a man gifted with intense powers of concentration, but he was no military strategist and his military experience was a minimal duty in the Indian Wars of which even he made light. Under intense pressure from Congress and public opinion leaders, he pushed for, demanded, insisted on, and pleaded for action. McClellan's caution frustrated even the normally cautious Lincoln. The president admitted that no Union general was better able to organize and train an army, but he complained McClellan suffered from "the slows." In his cabinet, Chase and Edwin Stanton were consistently opposed to McClellan, and Lincoln was exposed to stories of the general's alleged disloyalty toward him and of his own political ambitions.

In frustration, Lincoln apparently did take to the field himself in May 1862. While on a visit to Fort Monroe, the president with Stanton and Chase conferred with naval and military leaders. There is evidence that the president actually led some troops in the capture of Norfolk and sent three gunboats up the James River. Thus Lincoln became for a brief moment the commander in chief on the battlefield that Bates had counseled.

Historians favorable to the legendary Lincoln have generally agreed with his decision to transfer part of McClellan's command to John Pope in June 1862, and then in November 1862 to remove McClellan altogether. They have indeed accepted almost on faith the president's judgment that while the general was a great organizer, he lacked the will to fight decisively. Yet, it is quite possible to argue that Lincoln, inexperienced in military matters and unsure of his political position, overreacted by curtailing McClellan the first time, in overruling his military strategy, and in interfering with the timetable the general created. McClellan was the best general in the Union army in 1861, and his replacements stumbled from one defeat to another.[21]

McClellan needs to be judged in a broader perspective. He turned a ragtag mob into a fighting force after the debacle of Bull Run. His military objective was to move down the peninsula, while Lincoln and his cabinet insisted on establishing a buffer between the capital and the Confederate forces. McClellan argued, quite rightly, that it was his army and the threat it posed to Richmond that served as the real focus of Confederate attention. In the time he had control of the Army of the Potomac, McClellan never suffered a major defeat, and he prevailed in what may have been the most important battle of the war—the checking of Robert E. Lee's invasion at Antietam, although he did not defeat the Confederate forces. That victory, although too limited in the eyes of Lincoln and his cabinet secretaries, enabled the president to issue the Emancipation Proclamation, and it proved to interested European nations that the South could not win the protracted conflict. One of Lincoln's most able and balanced biographers, James G. Randall, has concluded, "Had McClellan collapsed at Antietam as Pope had done at Second Bull Run, it is hard to see how the Lincoln government and the Union cause could possibly have survived, to say nothing of launching an ambitious emancipation policy, which occurred directly after Antietam." In retirement after the war, Lee remarked that McClellan was the most formidable foe he had faced, a telling compliment in and of itself.[22]

But in early 1862, Antietam was still far away, and McClellan lay ill and buffeted by radical Republican pressures. The general's plan was to move the army down the Chesapeake, up the Rappahannock to Urbana, Virginia, and then across land to the Manassas line above Richmond. The president, who supported a land invasion instead, indicated his disapproval. While McClellan began to modify his plan, the Radical Republicans continued their attacks in public and their character assassination in private against the general. Radical congressmen met with Lincoln and demanded a "reorganization" of the Army of the Potomac—in effect, a move to strip McClellan of his authority as general in chief. On March 8, 1862, Lincoln capitulated to the political pressure, and McClellan lost vital authority just before his major offensive was to begin.

To achieve his objectives, McClellan needed a large, unified army, assets he was denied by the time he began his movement south. As McClellan confronted Lee and Johnston in the Peninsula campaign, General Irvin McDowell was slow in moving his First Army Corps Union forces to assist him. The Confederates at the same time sent Thomas "Stonewall" Jackson through the Shenandoah Valley, inciting fear in Washington that the Confederates would take the capital. Lincoln asserted military control over the railroads, and Stanton demanded that the governors send all the militia and volunteers they had to protect the area. A worried Lincoln wanted McClellan to give up his campaign and come back to Washington.[23]

The president, in fact, tried at times to run the war from Washington. He commanded Frémont, for example, to move against Jackson at Harrisonburg immediately. But Frémont, after promising to go ahead, did not do so, leaving Lincoln to ask, "I see that you are at Moorefield. You were expressly ordered to march to Harrisonburg. What does this mean?"[24] By June 1862, Lincoln was still concerned about McClellan's concentration of forces on the peninsula and Jackson's presence in the Shenandoah Valley, even though the latter had actually left. Under increasing attacks from the Radical Republicans in Congress and pressure from Stanton and Chase, Lincoln made Pope commander of the army in Virginia; McClellan was demoted and his title was changed to commander of the Army of the Potomac.

On July 8, Lincoln visited McClellan in the field at Harrison's

Landing. The president was clearly thinking about moving the army instead of allowing it to advance on Richmond. McClellan opposed that step and took the occasion to hand the president a letter in which he laid out his own policy about how the war should be run. He picked the wrong time to be audacious, and the president read the letter and handed it back to him with no comment. In the letter, the general had argued that the war was a battle between armies, and that confiscation, the abolishing of slavery, and other punitive actions on civilians were unnecessary. He concluded with a personal pledge to serve Lincoln forthrightly as his position might require.

The president, returning to the capital, found even more anti-McClellan intrigue, and on July 11, he ordered Henry Halleck to become general in chief, head of all the land forces of the United States. On August 3, Halleck took the step that the president had contemplated; he ordered McClellan to move his troops closer to the capital. McClellan, with his army only twenty-five miles from Richmond, protested that the order would result in a disaster. But Halleck prevailed, and Lincoln had proven himself to be a mediator, rather than a leader in what was the most important military decision he had made up to that time.

In late August, Lee and Jackson did with Pope's army what they could not do with McClellan's. They soundly defeated the Union forces at the Second Battle of Bull Run. Pope was soon relieved of his command and returned to the army in the West. Then two days after the defeat, McClellan was asked by Halleck to command the defenses of Washington, a position with no real control over the armed forces. Lincoln, desperately fearful about the capital, met with McClellan, and according to the general, asked him as a personal favor to take command of the city's defenses. In his diary, Secretary of the Navy Gideon Welles recorded that the president was "greatly distressed" and turned to McClellan because of the confidence the army itself had in him. Welles added that the War Department was bewildered and proposed nothing and did nothing.

It was at this point that Lee made his major move. He advanced toward Maryland, directly threatening Baltimore, Philadelphia, and as Lincoln feared all along, Washington. At Antietam, on September 17, 1862, the two forces met in the most ferocious battle of the war. It was, McClellan wrote, "the most serious ever fought on this continent." For over fourteen hours, the battle waged; in the end, there were over twenty-three thousand casualties. McClellan did not definitely defeat Lee, but he stopped the latter's advance and proved that the Union army was the match of the Confederate forces. Lee moved back to the lower side of the Potomac. McClellan had saved the capital and probably Lincoln's ability to continue effectively as president and commander in chief.

Instead of giving McClellan his due credit, his critics pressed on. He should have pursued Lee and brought the war to a quick end, they insisted. The president again visited McClellan, calling him his best general and then counseling him to move against Lee quickly. Finally, Lincoln ordered McClellan to cross the Potomac and seek out the Confederates, hoping to beat them to Richmond. But McClellan insisted on regrouping and reworking his strategy. He unfortunately expressed to the president his concern for his weary horses, which led to a rare caustic response from Lincoln, "Will you pardon me for asking what the horses of yours have done since the battle of Antietam that fatigues anything?"

On October 26, 1862, McClellan crossed the Potomac and slowly mobilized his army for an offensive. Then on November 7, he received notice that he had been replaced, this time by Ambrose Burnside. Again Lincoln had bowed to Chase and Stanton and the Radical Republicans. Later in 1864, the president defended his decision by saying that he had repeatedly tried to get McClellan to move but to no avail. The general had waited nineteen days after Antietam before he decided to cross the river and another nine days before the actual move took place, and made very slow progress even after that. The president concluded, "I began to fear he was playing false—that he did not want to hurt the army. I saw how he could intercept the enemy on the way to Richmond. I determined to make that the test. If he let them get away, I would remove him. He did so & I relieved him." Lincoln had also received a torrent of rumors and false accusations about McClellan's loyalty, patriotism, and political aspirations. The Radicals in Congress and in the cabinet had their way—McClellan was forced out again.[25]

EMANCIPATION . . . IN A WAY

Lincoln had also incurred the animus of the abolitionists by his cautious handling of the slavery question. They attributed his lack of leadership to a misguided fixation with keeping the border states in the Union and to the unfortunate influence of Seward. Lincoln's attitude toward slavery, as has been seen, was a consistent policy of personal detestation and political conservatism. In his inaugural address in 1861, he had pledged not to touch slavery where it existed and to recognize that the Constitution, which he swore to uphold, sanctioned the institution in oblique language. When the war came and Unionist generals such as Frémont and Ben Butler attempted to free those slaves held by owners in rebellion, the president at first demurred. The decision on emancipation, any form of emancipation, was one he would face in his own time.

But events progressed quickly as runaway slaves moved toward Union army encampments. Partially in response, Congress passed a series of measures that provided for the confiscation and emancipation of slaves under various provisions of law. The first Confiscation Act, approved on August 6, 1861, provided that when slaves were engaged in hostile military service, the claims of owners to such labor were forfeited. A second act passed on July 17, 1862, declared that the slaves of anyone who committed treason or was supporting the rebellion were "forever free." Another act, passed on the same day, freed slave soldiers and their families held by the enemy and, later in the war, freedom was extended to include slave soldiers of loyal owners who were to be granted bounties. In addition, on April 16, 1862, Congress abolished slavery in the District of Columbia and provided for compensation to the owners; by June 19, emancipation came to the territories but compensation was not provided. Thus, in some ways the legislative branch had enacted a more extensive policy of emancipation than the president's controversial proclamation did.

Lincoln's attitude toward emancipation was strongly influenced by his pessimistic view about racial harmony. At one meeting, the president told a committee of blacks that both races had suffered from slavery and that equality was impossible. He bluntly concluded that "on this broad continent not a single man of your race is made the equal of a single man of ours . . . I cannot alter it if I could. It is a fact." He felt that without the presence of blacks in the United States, there would have been no war, even though he acknowledged that "many men engaged on either side do not care for you one way or the other." Only the physical removal of the black race and its colonization in some spot like Chiriqui on the Panama isthmus or Liberia in Africa would bring peace. In addition, the president remained committed throughout his term to compensation for the owners. In March 1862, Lincoln asked Congress to support gradual emancipation to be completed sometime before 1900. This gradual process would be voluntary and controlled by the states, rather than by the federal government. Compensation to the slaveholders, however, would be paid for by the federal government. Lincoln's plan angered abolitionists, convinced few border state leaders, and left him without a realistic policy on an issue of increasing importance.

By the summer of 1862, Lincoln apparently moved sharply on the slavery question. Senator Charles Sumner of Massachusetts had tried to persuade Lincoln in December 1861 that emancipation must come, but the president put him off, promising action in a month to six weeks. By July 1862, Sumner pushed again, warning that the Union needed the freed slaves to augment its own armed forces. Lincoln listened, but concluded that he was afraid that half of the Union officers would leave the army and three more states would join the Confederacy if he heeded Sumner's advice. Finally, as he described it, he had to act. Lincoln concluded, "things had gone . . . from bad to worse, until I felt that we had reached the end of our rope . . . we . . . must change our tactics, or lose the game." He quietly worked on an emancipation proclamation, and on July 22, he presented it to the cabinet, not asking their advice on the matter but simply informing them of his intentions. Seward suggested that the president postpone his proclamation until some military victory was secured, and Lincoln saw the wisdom in such a postponement.

As he waited, Lincoln listened as advocates of emancipation called for action, a step he had already decided upon. His general attitude toward slavery was publicly aired in a letter on August 22, 1862, to the editor of the *New York Tribune*, Horace Greeley:

> My paramount object in this struggle is to save the Union, and not either to save or to destroy slavery. If I could save the Union without freeing any slave, I would do it; and if I could save it by freeing all the slaves, I would do it; and if I could save it by freeing some and leaving others alone, I would also do that. What I do about slavery and the colored race, I do because I believe it helps to save the Union; and what I forebear, I forebear because I do not believe it would help to save the Union. . . . I have here stated my purpose according to my view of official duty; and I intend no modification of my oft-expressed personal wish that all men everywhere could be free.

Finally, the president met with his cabinet on September 22, 1862 and after some preliminary levity, announced that he had made a promise to himself and to his Maker to issue the proclamation. He then went on to observe that there might be others who would do better as president, but "I must do the best I can, and bear the responsibility of taking the course which I feel I ought to take." The proclamation, issued by Lincoln as commander in chief of the armed forces, notified the nation that on January 1, 1863, all slaves held in rebellious areas would be free. As a conciliatory gesture, the president indicated that after the war, he would recommend to Congress that all loyal citizens should be compensated for loses incurred by acts of the United States, including the loss of slaves.

A charge frequently made is that Lincoln freed the slaves in states where he had no power to do so and did not touch them in states where he could have. The statement is factually correct, but totally misleading. The proclamation was an important step in the destruction of slavery on this continent. In terms of the loyal border states, the president warned that they should accept compensation while it was still an option, but their leaders refused to heed his advice.

Although the moral issue of bondage reverberated throughout the nation, especially in the rhetoric of the abolitionists, Lincoln avoided that approach. He insisted that his decision was based on grounds of military necessity. The president argued that action normally forbidden or deemed unconstitutional could become lawful in emergency times, and that the Constitution invested the executive as commander in chief with the law of war.

Between September and January, Lincoln still talked of compensated emancipation so often that some felt that he was backing off from the radical consequences of true freedom. Lincoln's Emancipation Proclamation became confused, in part, because of his own personal ambivalences. In December 1862, a month before the proclamation was to provide for immediate freedom in rebel states, Lincoln was still advocating that each slave state be given the chance to develop its own plan of gradual, compensated emancipation, which did not have to be completed until January 1, 1900. Those states would get federal assistance in the form of interest-bearing government bonds. If a state decided to restore slavery, the only penalty Lincoln would levy would be that the state had to refund the bonds. In August 1864, he seemed to depart from his early insistence that rebel states had to recognize emancipation. He told conservative critics, "To me it seems plain that saying re-union and the abandonment of slavery would be considered, if offered, is not

saying that nothing *else* or *less* would be considered, if offered. . . .
If Jefferson Davis wishes . . . to know what I would do if he were
to offer peace and reunion, saying nothing about slavery, let him
try me." Thus, if at times Radical Republicans in Congress and
abolitionists outside of it questioned the president's commitment to
the cause, they could hardly be called men of little faith.[26]

But when the new year came, Lincoln went ahead proclaiming
emancipation throughout the rebel states, except in Tennessee and
certain parts of Virginia and Louisiana, which were occupied by
Union troops. He cautiously urged the freed slaves to avoid violence and "labor faithfully for reasonable wages." Newly freed male
slaves were inducted into the armed services, and the president
characterized his policy as "an act of justice, warranted by the
Constitution upon military necessity."

The response was mixed, even among abolitionists. Wendell
Phillips called for greater support for these newly freed people, and
William Lloyd Garrison demanded emancipation in all the states.
In the South, the response was, of course, hostile; Davis saw the
move as leading to gruesome racial warfare and the old fears of
slave insurrections were revived. In segments of the North, the idea
of a future containing millions of freed blacks was not well received
either. Yet all knew that something significant had happened by
Lincoln's dry and formal declaration.

In Britain, demonstrations of support took place across the island. At Birmingham, over ten thousand people signed a scroll vow-
ing their support to the president on behalf of "all Men who love
liberty." In Manchester, a similarly warm address was sent to the
president hailing his action. In a touching response, Lincoln recip-
rocated their sentiments, and in another letter to the working people
of London, he cited the glory of free institutions throughout the
world. Diplomats reported favorable responses toward the proclamation in France, and even in Spain among the clergy and conservative leaders.

Lincoln was to say later, "I admit I have been more controlled
by events, than I have controlled them." Events had indeed controlled much of Lincoln's response to the monumental tragedy before him. He made war to save the Union, to restore a nation of
opportunity for the white race. But by the turn of the wheel of fire,
he had transformed the very nature of the war and then the character of the Union. Lincoln would be remembered not for his hesita-

tions, his uncertain displays of leadership, his delicate balancing acts. By 1863, he was in deep trouble, politically and militarily. He announced emancipation as a way of tipping the scales in what was becoming a long and bloody war. Freed slaves would fight for the Union, would leave the plantation system feeding the rebels, would prove to foreign nations that the South could not win and should not win, and would keep the abolitionists and Radicals in Congress at bay for a while. But by ending slavery, first in the South and later in the rest of the United States, Lincoln changed the moral complexion of the war. He became the Great Emancipator and not the great equivocator, the liberal world statesman, not the perennial candidate for public office. Watching the events unfold, his personal secretary John Hay concluded, "While the rest are grinding their . . . organs for their own glorification, the old man is working with the strength of a giant . . . to this great work."

Yet despite the proclamation, the emancipation of millions did not happen with the stroke of the pen. These blacks had no income, no clear legal status, no protection on the plantations where the overwhelming majority of them resided. Because they were declared politically free did not mean that they were economically independent or citizens of the Union. Even in the army, black troops found themselves commanded by whites, subject to prejudice in the Union army, and plagued by late-arriving and unequal pay. Lincoln himself at first was leery of arming ex-slaves and postponed the systematic use of black troops. But the impetus of war rushed ahead, and by the end of the conflict nearly 180,000 blacks had served in the Union ranks.

Still, in 1864, a committee of inquiry established by the War Department found that emancipation had not come, that the proclamation "cannot free a single slave." The committee wondered whether there would be sufficient guarantees to protect the freedom of the former slaves and urged that emancipation be extended throughout the United States. While some slaves filled the camps of the Union armies, the vast bulk of them did not experience emancipation until the demise of the Confederacy and the eventual occupation of the South by the Union armies. There is little evidence of black riots or violent upheavals on the plantations, yet contemporary observers recorded that Lincoln's proclamation was well known and well received within slave quarters throughout the Confederacy. Nevertheless, slaves must have asked what many whites asked at the time: what would it mean after all?[27]

ASSAULTS ON THE PRESIDENT

To many of his contemporaries in 1862, Lincoln did not appear to be a great president, not even a competent one. In Congress, many of his troubles came from a group of senators and representatives that history has labeled "The Radical Republicans." This loosely drawn coalition pushed for emancipation and demanded severe punishment for the secessionists. Some were influenced by that brand of American Protestantism that revels in retribution and casts political events into moral crusades. Others were truly horrified by slavery and lent their might to advancing the cause of freedom. Still more were concerned with the future of their party, the continued cohesion of their political alliances, and the availability of federal patronage. They recognized that a reunited America would bring back Democratic congressmen who would join with their Northern allies and reestablish control of the national government by their party. The Republicans could lose the peace, even after they had led the nation through a successful war. To prevent this restoration, the Radicals wanted to change the nation, to destroy slavery, to cripple the Southern aristocracy, and to enfranchise eventually the only new voters they could count on to vote Republican: the freed slaves. These Radical Republicans had different views on many aspects of these issues, but together they made Lincoln the focal point of much of their animosity. The Committee on the Conduct of the War became one of their tools for extracting retribution, and that group plagued the moderate generals, especially McClellan and his two chief subordinates, Fitz-John Porter and William B. Franklin, and harassed the wartime president in a way no other legislative committee has ever dared.

In the Senate, the Radicals included Zachariah Chandler of Michigan, Benjamin F. Wade and John Sherman of Ohio, Charles Sumner of Massachusetts, Lyman Trumbull of Illinois, Henry Lane of Indiana, and James Lane and Samuel Pomeroy of Kansas. In the House, the most prominent radicals were Thaddeus Stevens of Pennsylvania, Owen Lovejoy of Illinois, Schuyler Colfax and George Julian of Indiana, James Ashley and John A. Bingham of Ohio, Roscoe Conkling of New York, Henry Winter Davis of Maryland, and John Covode of Pennsylvania.

On the other side of the aisle, the Democrats were generally in opposition to what they perceived as the abuse of civil liberties by the administration. Some prominent Democrats, especially Stephen

Douglas before his premature death in 1861, strongly supported the Union and Lincoln. A second segment was committed to the Union, but was critical of the government's war policies. A third group did not support the war, advocated a compromised peace with the South, and was soon tagged as "Copperheads," that is, Southern sympathizers, by their enemies.[28]

No major American president has been less successful in leading his party than Lincoln. One reason was that the Republicans were still not a cohesive group, but rather an unstable coalition that had just won its first national victory. All American parties are by their very nature loose coalitions, but in Lincoln's time, this lack of cohesiveness was even more apparent than before or after his era, such as in the periods of Jefferson and Jackson or the Reconstruction and the New Deal. Lincoln used patronage to build a personal faction, but still lacked a broad base throughout his term.[29] Second, Lincoln had little experience on the national level and had no background in leading Congress. He strongly exerted his executive powers, but did it outside of congressional guidelines and not in league with the legislature. Unlike Woodrow Wilson, who saw himself as a "prime minister," or FDR who redefined his party as the vehicle of the liberal New Deal, Lincoln did not take Congress into his confidence; perhaps, he realized he could not do so reasonably. Third, the presidency was cast in a different light in the nineteenth century, especially for old Whigs such as Lincoln. They had not learned the art of subtle and invisible leadership that Jefferson, Madison, and Monroe exercised on Congress through their cabinet and close acquaintances. They did not understand the strong executive model, used by Washington and Hamilton and later by Jackson. Whigs respected balanced, efficient, and orderly government. Such a prescription did not lend itself to managing a civil war. Lincoln ran the war with as little congressional support as he could get away with without causing a rupture. In dealing with its leaders, he was polite, patient—and even deferential—at times.

Richard Neustadt, the political scientist and presidential expert, has argued that presidential power is a product of professional reputation and personal popularity. In the grim days of 1861–63, the president was not seen as a shrewd political operator; alleged inadequacies were frequently commented on, cursed, admonished, and reported. His popularity was low, as best one can tell. The war was going poorly with the controversial draft, high taxes, and political imprisonments, and the allies of Lincoln were hurt by the performance of the Union armies. Lincoln was the leader of the war effort; he never chose to disassociate himself from it.

Lincoln's stock then was not high in 1862. When he informed Congress of his quite legitimate objections to the Confiscation Bill of 1862, his message was greeted with hoots and laughter from Radical elements. Then in September 1862, a group of Northern governors met and decided to force changes in the administration's war policy. Some indicated that, in fact, they wanted the president's resignation, and a few even demanded that Frémont head up a military dictatorship instead. Lincoln allowed the governors to visit the Executive Mansion, but turned the tables on them by praising their advice. He had them sit with his cabinet, while he monopolized the conversation, and later escorted them out.

A second more serious challenge though took place in December, which threatened Lincoln's control over his own cabinet. A group of senators demanded Seward's resignation and forced the president into an untenable position. In a masterly display of adroitness, Lincoln called the cabinet together and indicated that Seward had offered his resignation. He reported the Senate group's remarks and then expressed shock and dismay, noting that he was not aware of any serious disagreements in the cabinet. Having stressed the theme of unity, the president invited the Senate group in later and before the cabinet, minus Seward, the secretaries supported the president's conclusions.

Rumors spread that the whole cabinet had resigned. Actually, Chase, the favorite of the Radical element, had been embarrassed by the public confrontation and offered his resignation. Lincoln then had Chase and Seward's letters—a balanced victory and a net loss for the congressional Radicals. As he phrased it with some glee, "I have got a pumpkin in each end of my bag." Now, he sent both men identical statements requesting them to stay. For the first time in his administration, it was clear to all that the president was the master in his own house. Radical attacks continued, but they never came as close again to the heart of the presidency.[30]

THE FIERCENESS OF BATTLE—1863

In the West, Union forces had been on the move in 1862. Military and naval leaders coordinated a series of inland river battles as the Union took Fort Henry and Fort Donelson, and occupied

Nashville and the railroad terminus at Columbus, Kentucky. But during April 6–7, 1862, the armies of Pierre Beauregard and Albert Sidney Johnston nearly defeated Ulysses S. Grant's troops; with reinforcements, however, the Union won a major battle and drove the Confederates toward Corinth, Mississippi. Lincoln's spirits were also refreshed when the navy under Admirals David Farragut and David Porter prevailed in New Orleans in April. Soon Ben Butler began his controversial occupation of that city, and once again the president had to intervene, finally removing him in December 1862. After the victory of New Orleans, the Union forces went on to seize Memphis, and by the spring of 1863, Grant had decided to move against well-fortified Vicksburg, a Confederate stronghold.

But in the major theaters of action, the picture was dismal. As noted, Lincoln had bowed to Radical pressure and his own misgivings about McClellan, and appointed Ambrose Burnside, who led the Union forces on December 13 at Fredericksburg to one of its worst defeats. Confederate artillery and infantry ripped the Union lines to shreds and filled the field hospitals to capacity. The outcome, as expected, was blamed on the president, and more than one critic agreed with the abolitionist James Sloan Gibbons who implored, "May the Lord hold to rigid account the fool that is set over us. . . . What suicide the administration is guilty of! What a weak pattern of Old Pharaoh! What a goose!"[31]

After more controversy within the War Department circle, Lincoln named "Fighting Joe" Hooker to be the head of the new Army of the Potomac. Still, the president was uncertain about Hooker and wrote him a letter that contained a rather blunt warning, "I have heard . . . of your . . . saying that both the Army and the Government needed a Dictator. . . . What I now ask of you is military success, and I will risk the dictatorship. . . . Beware of rashness, but with energy, and sleepless vigilance, go forward, and give us victories."[32]

Hooker prepared for his much awaited battle against Lee and mobilized a force twice the size of his Confederate opponent's. However, under Lee's superb strategy and Stonewall Jackson's maneuvering, the Confederates dealt Hooker a sharp setback at Chancellorsville, just west of Fredericksburg. Unfortunately for the South, Jackson was mortally wounded in the confusion of battle, by some of his own men. Lincoln, dismayed once again by his generals, ordered Hooker to move quickly against Lee. Lee, however, had ambitions of his own; concerned about the uncertain forces of the war and the fate of the Confederacy, he decided to bring the war northward again and strike close to the Union capital.

Meanwhile, Hooker and Halleck had an altercation, and the administration used that incident as an occasion to remove Hooker from his command. Once again, Lincoln had to reach into his bag of officers and come up with a replacement for the hapless Potomac army: George Gordon Meade. The president concluded that the native Pennsylvanian, Meade, would fight well on his own dung hill, as he put it. At this point, support was building to recall McClellan, and rumors spread that the New York State Democratic party leaders would raise an army under his command, which would advance on Washington and remove Lincoln and his administration. However, the president had seen enough of McClellan and the opposition fires that he attracted.

In early July 1863, the two great armies in the East met in combat at the little-known town of Gettysburg, Pennsylvania. The result was one of the most costly and clearcut victories for the Union in the East during the war. At the same time in the West, on July 4, 1863, Grant finally had captured Vicksburg. The Confederacy had seemingly reached its zenith, and the collapse was beginning. To Lincoln, the excitement was tempered when he found that Meade actually did not pursue Lee's army following the battle of Gettysburg and destroy it before it recrossed the Potomac. Lee's forces thus were able to reenter Virginia on July 13 and 14. Once again the president lamented the generals destiny had willed him.

A disgruntled Lincoln chastised Meade in a letter, "He [Lee] was within your easy grasp, and to have closed upon him would . . . have ended the war. . . . Your golden opportunity is gone, and I am distressed immeasurably because of it." And then, thinking twice on the matter, the president folded up the letter and left it unsent. As expected, the Radicals quickly added Meade—another Democrat— to their enemies list; his important victory at Gettysburg was due to the corps commanders and not his leadership, they argued.[33]

Chancellorsville, Gettysburg, and Vicksburg were marked by high casualties that taxed the crazy quilt of conscription measures Congress and the president had put into place. In July 1862, a group of governors had urged Lincoln to call for more men and crush the Confederacy once and for all. The president then called for three hundred thousand men to volunteer for up to three years. By July 17, 1862, Congress approved a militia act, which granted to the executive additional powers of conscription for the federal militia, but which used the administrative agencies of the states. Lincoln followed that step with a draft of three hundred thousand men for nine-month service. By March 3, 1863, Congress finally had approved a centralized conscription system with a large national network put into place. The act, however, allowed a draftee to provide a substitute in his place or to contribute $300 in commutation money. These calls to arms were not well received in many of the loyal states; the manpower shortage was compounded by the fact that over two hundred thousand men eventually deserted from the Union army during the war. In major cities such as Troy, Albany, Newark, and areas in Ohio, Wisconsin, Indiana, Kentucky, Pennsylvania, and Missouri, dissatisfaction spilled over into violence against the draft.

The worst disturbance was in New York City during July 13–16, 1863, where thousands rioted to protest the draft and Lincoln's war policies, and hundreds were killed. Many less-belligerent citizens questioned the constitutionality of the 1863 Conscription Act, and the Supreme Court stayed away from reviewing the legislation. The confusing and unfair administration of the draft also made it susceptible to severe criticism; learning those lessons, the federal government in World Wars I and II would abandon any initial hope of voluntary enlistments and go to a national draft run by the War Department, using regulations that the military, and not the Congress, would establish.

As he struggled with the musical chairs of command and put patches on the inefficient war machine in Washington, the president received an invitation to commemorate the fallen patriots at Gettysburg on November 19, 1863. By doing so, he took a simple occasion and consecrated the confusing war into a national sacrifice for expiation. In the process, Lincoln imprinted his mark on the nation in a strong symbolic sense, and became immortal. Legend has it that the president wrote his famous address on the back of an envelope on the trip to the cemetery and that his remarks were poorly received by the audience. In fact, Lincoln worked on his address several times before it was delivered, and it was well regarded by those who could hear him. His words were recognized once they were printed as an eloquent statement on the war aims and the demands of democratic patriotism.

The presentation followed a long, classically eloquent speech by Edward Everett of Massachusetts, the chief speaker for the occasion. The president spoke in a high-pitched voice in the characteristic Midwest twang of the time. Those words invoked the work of the Founding Fathers, respectfully praised the glorious dead soldiers, then rededicated the nation to a new birth of freedom under God, and concluded with the prophecy that "that government of the people, by the people, for the people shall not perish from the earth." Lincoln had been criticized throughout his term for banal utterances and undistinguished oratorical performances, but this time he captured the public mood in a way no statement had since the Declaration of Independence. Moving through the chaos of war, the mishaps of uncoordinated military strategy, the collapse of a train of generals, and the hesitations of emancipation, Lincoln had by late 1863 come to etch himself on the Union imagination.

Unlike the Emancipation Proclamation with its cool appeal to military necessity, the Gettysburg Address provided the passion and the vision that seemed to animate the harried commander in chief. The issue was not just war, but the very future of self-government on earth. Later, Lincoln began to extend the real meaning of the conflict: "This is essentially a people's contest. On the side of the Union it is a struggle for maintaining in the world that form and substance of government whose leading object is to elevate the condition of men—to lift artificial weights from all shoulders; to clear a path of laudable pursuit for all; to afford all an unfettered start, and a fair chance in the race of life."

THE OTHER PRESIDENT

While Lincoln was struggling with the burdens of war and defining anew the meaning of the gruesome, costly conflict, he had a counterpart who was also facing similar problems—Jefferson Davis. By comparing those two men one can get a better understanding of presidential leadership in this period. Davis was born a year before Lincoln, less than a hundred miles away in a log cabin not much better than the one Lincoln knew as a boy. Unlike Lincoln, Davis's family sent him to a Catholic school in Kentucky, even though his family was Baptist, and then on to Transylvania University. Through the influence of his father and an older brother, Davis received an appointment to the United States Military Academy. After a successful stint as a soldier, which included distinguished service in the Mexican War, Davis entered politics from the state of Mississippi and became a congressman and later a senator. He also served with distinction in Pierce's cabinet as secretary of war, and when the secession movement gained full strength in early 1861, Davis looked forward to a military appointment, instead of the singular honor of being the first and, as it turned out, the last president of the Southern nation.

There have been many reasons given for the South's defeat in the Civil War: the far-reaching economic superiority of the North, the willingness in the latter part of the war for Union generals to abandon old nineteenth-century European military strategies, the ability of the North to prevent Britain and France from recognizing the Confederacy, the lack of Southern civilian discipline during the war, and a host of accidents and strokes of misfortune in battle or in intelligence gathering. The respected historian David Potter has argued however that Davis's deficiencies as a military and civil leader, as compared to Lincoln, really made the difference.[34] And because the South lacked, and discouraged overall, the rise of a well-organized opposition party, there was no real challenge to this mediocre performance. Davis failed then in three critical ways. First, he was a proud, at times haughty, individual, rather sensitive to slights and put off by the give and take of politics. Even his wife, Varina, concluded, "I thought his genius was military, but that as a party manager, he would not succeed. He did not know the arts of the politician and would not practice them if understood, and he did know that of war." Second, Davis had a fundamental misconception of his job as president, spending an incredible amount of time on details to the neglect of the larger picture and the need to mobilize his people for a long protracted war. Also, he was deficient in handling the political and military role of commander in chief, placed too much emphasis on personal friendship, and did not have the foresight to appoint early in the war a general in chief.[35]

Davis's position, though, was somewhat different from Lincoln's, and the war strategies he supported necessarily reflected that reality. Interestingly, both faced many of the same situations—a reflection of the decentralization of American life, the relatively low level of experience among professional military men, and the pressures for patronage, status and recognition—the true engines of duty and patriotism.

When the Confederacy drew up a constitution, it retained most of the basic elements of the United States Constitution with certain provisions to protect more explicitly states' rights and slavery. There were some other changes as well: the president was elected for a single six-year term, the president had the item veto over appropriations, cabinet members could be given seats in Congress (though this was not implemented), a budget system was created, and two-thirds instead of three-quarters of the states had to concur for an amendment to pass. At his inaugural on February 18, 1861, Davis compared the South's secession to the Declaration of Independence and cited the "right of the people to alter or abolish them [their governments] at will whenever they became destructive of the compact for which they were established."

Like Lincoln, Davis was a loose administrator and some of the criticism of his term in office rested on what one of his cabinet members called his lack of prompt business habits. In addition, Davis was a poor judge of character, and frequently appointed and held on to weak individuals. One of his closest friends, General Josiah Gorgas, wrote, "The President seems determined to respect the opinions of no one; and has, I fear little appreciation of services rendered, unless the party enjoys his good opinion. He seems to be an indifferent judge of men, and is guided more by prejudice than by sound discriminating judgment."

Yet, in the crucial first decision that led to the beginning of the war, it was Davis, for better or worse, who made the judgment not to let the North send supplies to Major Anderson at Fort Sumter. The second important event in which he was involved concerned dictating the strategy that ordered General Joseph E. Johnston's army to join Beauregard's forces at the Battle of Bull Run. When Beauregard took credit for the victory, an angry Davis wrote the general that his report seemed "an attempt to exalt yourself at my expense."[36] Unlike Lincoln, who was willing to give his generals even undeserved credit if they would only advance, Davis maintained at times a less than magnanimous attitude in dealing with his subordinates, and he seemed preoccupied by some need to gain on the political front what had been denied him on the battlefield.

But like his counterpart in the North, Davis spent much of his time on the draft and command problems. He saw that after the first enthusiasm of volunteering, even the South experienced a decline in the willingness of young men to enter military service. The Confederate president also went before his Congress and advocated longer enlistments: three years or the duration of the war, and not the sixty days that the legislature had enacted. Pushed by Generals Lee and Jackson, Davis on March 29, 1862, recommended the passage of the first conscription act in American history, and on April 16, the Confederate Congress approved it.

Able-bodied white males between the ages of eighteen and thirty-five were called up for three years' service; but the act allowed substitutes, as the North would do, and permitted draftees to elect their own officers in the ranks below colonel. Fearing slave insurrections, the Confederate Congress approved an exemption for overseers of twenty slaves or more—a step that was much criticized. As the war progressed, the draft was extended to those men eighteen years of age and those between thirty-five and forty-five in 1862, and by 1864 to ages seventeen to fifty, though those in the forty-five to fifty category and those seventeen years old were to be confined to the reserves or home guards. Critics, such as Governor Joe Brown, charged that Davis overmobilized the states, stripping them of manpower to produce food, and denying expertise to the industrial and transportation sectors.

Davis did insist on maintaining the code of war in dealing with prisoners and noncombatants. He wrote to Lincoln on July 6, 1861, that if captured crewmen were treated by the North as pirates and thus executed, he would order similar penalties. He also denounced Ben Butler's treatment of the women of New Orleans and proclaimed that Butler should be shot upon capture. Davis seemed especially outraged at the Emancipation Proclamation, arguing that it was meant to encourage slave insurrections; he therefore threatened death to any ex-slave soldiers and their white officers; yet within fifteen months, the Confederacy would be seriously considering the enlistment of black soldiers also.[37] Like Lincoln, Davis was reluctant to approve the death sentence for deserters. Lee, however, had some deserters shot before the cases went to Davis for review, knowing of the president's leniency.

With pride, Davis also pointed out that the Confederate government was not engaged in the suppression of liberty the way the Lincoln administration was, although the Confederate Congress also suspended the writ of habeas corpus. Davis, too, was plagued by military rivalries, personality conflicts, and legislative intrusion. Although he did not have a Committee on the Conduct of the War with which to deal or a real opposition party, the Confederate Congress still contained strong critics of Davis, and when New Orleans fell in August 1862, there was an inquiry into the loss.

In managing the war, Davis, in general, was less interested in naval operations and not convinced of their importance—an unfortunate attitude in a rebellious nation divided by the Mississippi, surrounded by an ocean and gulf, and heavily dependent in its foreign policy on using cotton exports as a lever on Britain to gain recognition. Like Lincoln, Davis at times seemed overly preoccupied with the defense of the capital city, often at the expense of major strategic war aims. The symbolic value of losing the capital was extremely important to both men, but unlike the North, the South chose to move its capital closer to the enemy lines. Lincoln could not move Washington, D.C., without admitting defeat, but early on, the South had decided to acknowledge Virginia's importance by transferring its seat from Montgomery, Alabama, to Richmond.

When McClellan began his first march toward Richmond, Davis took to the field, visiting the Southern generals, rallying the troops in the rain, and inspecting defensive works. It was by all accounts a most impressive and heroic display of leadership. While Lincoln searched for a fighting general in the East, Davis had wisely decided to release his military advisor, Robert E. Lee, for field action some fourteen months into the war after Joseph Johnston's wounding at Fair Oaks.

Lee has become so canonized in the South and so respected in the North that it is sometimes difficult to realize that in the early months of his command, he too was learning his craft. He had never commanded a large body of troops—indeed, none of the leading generals on either side had ever commanded a division, or even a brigade. Americans had not been to war except in the Mexican conflict some twenty years before and in occasional Indian campaigns. At the time of his resignation from the U.S. Army, Lee was only a lieutenant colonel. In his early battles, he left too much to his subordinates and often gave imprecise orders. Indeed, over one-third of his army was lost in the battles to defend Richmond, and Lee suffered from shortages of men and matériel throughout most of his campaigns.

Still, Davis had what Lincoln lacked—two generals, Lee and Stonewall Jackson—who were in the Eastern theater a powerful combination. After the Second Battle of Bull Run, Lee asked Davis's approval for an invasion of Maryland and then Pennsylvania. If he had been successful, he would have been in a position to threaten Washington and Baltimore, which would have encouraged peace sentiment in the North. He urged Davis to follow up military successes with a call for peace that might in turn affect the 1862 elections in the North. But that victory never came; faced with a restored McClellan and some bad luck, Lee was stopped at Antietam.

For Davis, the war required that he turn his attention to foreign diplomacy as well. His strategy and that of his secretary of state, Judah P. Benjamin, was to induce Britain and possibly France to recognize the Confederacy. Their central assumption was that European mills would grow desperate for cotton, and this would force those nations to come to the aid of the South. But like most economic sanctions and international trade strategies, it was unsuccessful. Cotton was not king, and in fact, Europe began to import cotton from other sources, especially India and Egypt. The United States furthermore threatened to break off relations with Britain if it recognized the South and, despite the predictions of leaders like William Gladstone, Confederate military victories did not come with any regularity. After Antietam, European sympathy toward the Confederacy, where it had previously existed, generally disappeared.[38]

Later Davis and his cabinet severely injured the South's chances by approving Lee's march into Pennsylvania. The defeat at Gettysburg, coupled with the fall of Vicksburg, crippled the Confederacy. At Gettysburg, Lee lost twenty-five thousand out of the seventy-five thousand men he had commanded and retreated into the South. At Vicksburg, Davis refused to approve his secretary of war's plea to send reinforcements, arguing it violated his prerogative as commander in chief, and would wreak havoc on the military department system. Davis insisted that units be maintained separately and had no chief of staff between himself and the military leaders to manage day-to-day matters.

Again like Lincoln, Davis had to deal with the sensitivities of fighting generals, although he was less willing to listen to their self-serving complaints, a woe even the patient Lincoln tired of. In the case of the contentious General Sterling Price of Missouri, Davis finally said he would accept his resignation and would be happy if he went to Missouri and raised a new army of state forces to support the Confederacy in his own way. The next day, Davis backpedaled, and Price decided not to resign after all.

War brings out strong executive leadership, and Davis also was accused of being too powerful, of being a despot. When he invoked the Impressment Act of 1863 and seized one-half of the cotton supplies, Davis instigated a stir of protest among the planters. Other criticisms came from his handling of the homefront, especially finances and transportation difficulties. The Confederate Congress was unwilling to tax its people, in part because its region of the nation was used to low taxation and was unwilling to meet the demands of mobilization. It has been estimated that the Confederacy raised about 1 percent of its income in taxes; thus, paper money with no backing financed the war. Still, at least until the battle at Gettysburg, the currency system did not collapse, although it was teetering.

In terms of transportation, the South had 104 railroad companies with varying gauges of track and few connecting cities. When in 1861 Davis urged the Congress to connect the Danville-Greensboro gap, delays and a lack of cooperation prevented even that minor adjustment. By May 1863, the Confederate government had passed a railroad control act, but its tough provisions were not used as Davis stressed cooperation instead. He also was reluctant to interfere with speculation and hoarding, adhering to a Whiggish laissez faire economic theory much longer than Lincoln.[39]

Although Davis did not have as much organized opposition in Congress as Lincoln had, he did have to be concerned about some discontent in the legislative branch. And like Lincoln, he had problems with some state governors, although in Davis's case the states' rights ethos of the Confederacy ran counter to his need to centralize some activities in the war. Because the South also stressed the importance of a show of unity, there was no real opposition party during the war. Whigs and Democrats were generally expected to work under a unified government. There were, of course, opposition leaders who demanded more activity, less activity, or more patronage. Still, the Confederate Congress was much less effective and intrusive than the United States Congress. In part, many able leaders left the legislature and went to war rather than accommodate themselves to simply debating the war. In addition, alcoholism, absenteeism, and florid old-time rhetoric were prevalent in the Southern Congress. Like Lincoln, Davis rarely took the legislature into his confidence or exerted much legislative leadership. But unlike Lincoln, Davis was often cool, aloof, and autocratic rather than flexible or even noncommittal. He disliked dealing with people motivated by self-interest rather than by patriotism, a fatal flaw in a political leader, especially in that period of history.[40]

As in the case of Lincoln in the North, there was some sentiment in the Confederacy for dumping Davis and putting Lee in his place as a dictator. Still, Davis retained strong control over the Congress, having his vetoes overridden only once. His base of support was the more moderate and yet deeply concerned representatives from the border and occupied states, and his major opponents came from the Georgia delegation. As criticism mounted at the end of the war however, some 40 percent of the Congress could be counted on to oppose the president on occasion.

And as was also true with the U.S. Congress, the Confederate Congress sought to control the president's cabinet selections. In 1864, Davis confronted head-on an attempt to limit the terms of cabinet members to two years, a move intended to increase the influence of the Senate. The bill was never voted on; still, Davis was warned that he had to reorganize the cabinet if he expected to keep Congress's confidence. He eventually rejected that advice in the sharpest terms.[41]

With the state governors, Davis ran into some concerted opposition, which was even more contentious than Lincoln experienced. The Northern governors usually pushed their president to be more forceful in his leadership; the Southern governors interposed themselves to object to Davis's attempt to provide such leadership. A confederacy of seceded states was brought into existence to underscore states' rights; much of the institutional weakness of that loose union was due to the exact nature of its birth. Judah P. Benjamin wrote, in late 1861, "The difficulty lies with the governors, who are unwilling to trust the common defense to one common head— they therefore refused arms to men who are willing to enlist unconditionally for the war and put their arms in the hands of a mere militia who are not bound to leave home."

The most difficult governor for Davis was Joseph E. Brown of Georgia, a Yale Law School graduate, born in the red hills of his state. He protested that conscription was unconstitutional because it violated state sovereignty. Davis's response was a defense of the role of the central government and the "war powers" of the Confederate Constitution. He also cited the strength of the opposing army and the critical nature of conscription. Since there was no Supreme Court, the state's higher courts were relied upon for guidance. Georgia's supreme court declared that the conscription laws were constitutional, and so did other state court judges, while the chief justice in North Carolina found them unconstitutional.

Brown, along with Davis's vice president, Alexander Stephens, and others combined to attack the president on his power to suspend the writ of habeas corpus. Davis had suspended the writ only three times and for limited periods to deal with spies and traitors. Brown called his state legislature into session on March 10, 1864, to protest the law and warned against dictatorship. The governor even tried to bypass Davis's regulations dealing with blockade running.

Davis faced another problem with the young governor of North Carolina, Zebulon B. Vance, who criticized the president's promotions policy and also engaged in blockade running activities. Vance's uncooperativeness was matched by Governor Andrew Magrath of South Carolina, who complained about the expansion of the central government under Davis.

As the war difficulties mounted, Davis became more eloquent in the defense of the cause and in his concerns over Southern honor and the perils of invasion. Despite the criticisms of his tenure, a series of state legislatures led by South Carolina and followed by Mississippi, Georgia, Virginia, and several military units as well passed resolutions of support for Davis. Yet, like Lincoln with the North's "Knights of the Golden Circle," Davis had to be concerned about secret organizations that were not loyal to the cause, such as the "Heroes of America," with rituals, handshakes, and special passwords. These groups were especially strong in the pro-Union areas of western Virginia, North Carolina, and northern Alabama.

Overall though, the criticisms of Davis's leadership focused on his penchant for detail, his insistence on appointing West Point graduates to leadership posts, his rigid departmental organization, his zealous concern about the prerogatives of his office, his aloofness and poor judgment of men, his loyalty to personal favorites among the generals, and his defensive strategy. The organizational system of the army left each department reporting to Davis rather than to a general in chief as with Lincoln. The result was inflexibility, and an inefficient use of manpower. When Lee surrendered on April 9, 1865, and his 27,800 troops laid down arms, there were still another 175,000 men scattered about in other sections of the Confederacy.

A comparison of the war presidents indicates that they faced many of the same problems: a nation without experienced military leadership, a decentralized government with little national infrastructure, a legislative branch that was less than supportive, criticisms of alleged arbitrary exercise of constitutional authority, and often a lack of diplomatic skill in their state departments. The South was a traditional agricultural society, bound to slavery, lacking a strong industrial and financial base. Yet, in our own time, such "underdeveloped" nations have defeated better organized and equipped foes in long protracted wars of attrition and endurance. By Antietam, Gettysburg, and Vicksburg, it would seem that the course of the war should have been obvious to the South. But the Confederacy pushed on, and the war once again accelerated in a series of bloody battles that taxed Davis as surely as it taxed the other president across the river.

THE FORCES OF DISSENT

One remarkable aspect of Lincoln's personality and presidency was his ability to suffer abuse, criticism, and general nastiness without striking back or turning sour. Despite his genuine sense of humility, Lincoln had the assertiveness and self-confidence of a successful self-made man, without exhibiting the usual, slightly veiled defensiveness so often characteristic of such individuals. His attitude toward the presidency was best summarized in a story to which he resorted when asked how it felt to be the chief executive of the nation. Lincoln told the tale of a man who was tarred and feathered and ridden out of town on a rail. When someone asked him how he liked it, he responded, "If it were not for the honor of the thing, I'd much rather walk."

For Lincoln the presidency was not a pleasant task. He was an enormously ambitious man. Indeed, his one-time law partner, William Herndon, wrote that Lincoln's ambition was an engine that knew no rest. But the presidency and the prolonged war brought with it a lasting disappointment, tempered by a sense of duty and stewardship. In the end, Lincoln would reflect, "I dreamt of power and glory, and all I have are blood and ashes."[42]

The president returned from Gettysburg with a mild form of smallpox; characteristically, he joked that now he had something to give all the office seekers who plagued him. Continuing to deal with a hypercritical Congress, the president showed some resentment toward the Committee on the Conduct of the War and its attacks on his judgment. He argued convincingly that while he never doubted his ability to suppress the rebellion and of reuniting the Union, the Committee, however, was "a marplot, and its greatest purpose seems to be to hamper my action and obstruct the military operations." As with other presidents before and after him, he was reluctant to accede to legislative requests for information. The president on one occasion actually cited George Washington for having established the precedent of withholding documents requested by the legislative branch, arguing it would be "incompatible with the public interest."[43]

As the war continued in 1863, the Supreme Court finally gave the president some support. By a vote of five to four, the Court in the *Prize* cases upheld the executive's war policies that established procedures for seizing vessels that violated the blockade. The contention of Lincoln's opponents was that those war measures—taken between April 15, 1861, which was the date of the president's proclamation of insurrection, and July 13, 1861, when Congress recognized the existence of the insurrection—were illegal. What was at stake was the president's leadership during the first eighty days of the war. Fortunately Lincoln had appointed three of the five judges who voted in the affirmative that his action was valid.

The most controversial and disagreeable problem was the president's suspension of the writ of habeas corpus and the use of what can justly be called arbitrary arrest. In Baltimore, for example, the administration had ordered the arrest of the mayor and the police chief; in another case, Chief Justice Roger Taney challenged the arrest of John Merryman in Maryland, who had allegedly expressed his hostility to the United States while holding a commission as a second lieutenant and possessing arms belonging to the United States.[44] Taney flatly stated that the president did not have the power to suspend the writ of habeas corpus. When Stanton tried to appeal the case to the Supreme Court, Attorney General Bates warned against it. A negative decision would "do more to paralyze the Executive . . . than the worst defeat our armies have yet sustained," he argued.

In September 1862 and then a year later in 1863, Lincoln issued proclamations suspending the habeas corpus during the conflict. By 1863, however, Congress had passed an act that allowed the president to suspend the writ, indemnified officers who engaged in searches, seizures, imprisonments, or arrests, and exempted military officers from having to answer court writs. Lists of prisoners were to be sent to federal courts, and judges could discharge suspects upon grand jury findings after those individuals took a loyalty oath.

Meanwhile, the president extended his sway by issuing a set of regulations dealing with the militia under an act passed on July 17, 1862. Those regulations covered not only routine military matters, but also the treatment of prisoners of war, noncombatants, spies, runaway slaves, and a host of other problems. The executive branch of government assumed, especially in occupied areas of the South and in several regions of the North, the functions of the judiciary branch. In addition, special courts were established by presidential order in such occupied areas as Louisiana, and they had unlimited powers. These courts had jurisdiction over not only men in the military, but also civilians accused of military offenses and even those arrested for disloyal acts. It was only after the war was over that the Supreme Court in the *Milligan* case (1866) ruled that military courts could not supersede civilian courts in regions where civilian courts were still operative.[45]

Lincoln faced other sources of dissent within the Northern ranks besides so-called Copperheads, or Southern-sympathizing Northerners. Secret societies, such as the Knights of the Golden Circle with its private army and esoteric rites, were also major opponents of the administration. The Knights of the Golden Circle were eventually absorbed into the Order of American Knights; in New York state, a secret society called itself the Sons of Liberty and chose Clement L. Vallandingham of Ohio as the supreme national commander.

Vallandingham was to be one of Lincoln's most controversial critics, a quixotic Copperhead who directly challenged the Union government during its most trying period. Lincoln's response to his challenge was a characteristic mixture of forbearance, firmness, and later simple neglect. Vallandingham was a well-known lawyer and legislator in the ranks of the Democratic party in Ohio. He had been an officer in the militia and a congressman, and he was an articulate opponent of the war. He attacked the president for violating civil liberties and refusing to work out a peaceful compromise. On April 13, 1863, General Burnside, without the War Department's approval, ordered an end to agitation in the Ohio region; he stated "the habit of declaring sympathy for the enemy will not be allowed in this department."

On May 1, Vallandingham defied Burnside and at a mass rally of the Democratic party in Ohio, he attacked the administration again. Vallandingham was roused from his bed in the middle of the night, arrested, tried before a military commission, and found guilty of expressing disloyal opinions aimed at weakening the government. He asked a federal court to issue a writ of habeas corpus, which it eventually refused to grant, because it ostensibly lacked jurisdiction. Realizing the embarrassment he had caused the administration because of the controversy, Burnside offered his resignation. Lincoln's response was to the point, "When I wish to supersede you I will let you know. All the cabinet regretted the necessity of arresting, for instance, Vallandingham—some perhaps, doubting, that there was a real necessity for it—but, being done, all were for seeing you through with it." Refusing to commute the sentence, the president decided to ship Vallandingham off behind military lines in the South.[46]

To continue his strange odyssey, Vallandingham persisted and found his way beyond those areas and returned eventually to the Union by surreptitiously entering through Canada. Disguised with a thick mustache and having a pillow tucked under his coat, Vallandingham reemerged from exile to run later unsuccessfully for governor of Ohio. Although the Vallandingham case is often treated by historians as a sort of comic relief amidst the tragedy of the war, the challenge to the administration was of some importance. The controversy has to be seen in the larger context of the extensive criticisms of what were perceived as gross violations of American civil liberties by the administration.

Lincoln had designated first Seward and later Stanton to administer the arrests policy. Initially, Seward set up a passport system for those going abroad, created a network of confidential agents, and pushed for expedited punishments. Stanton used an even more extensive detective bureau and a secret service, which were viewed by some as overzealous. It has been estimated that over 13,500 people—and probably more—were arrested and confined to military prisons between February 1862 and the end of the war. Among those people who were arrested were editors and political leaders who had opposed the war effort, including members of the Maryland state legislature.[47]

Lincoln was aware of the early and continued criticisms of this part of his war policy. He defended it on one occasion, pleading, "I am a patient man—always willing to forgive on the Christian terms of repentance; and also to give ample *time* for repentance. Still I must save this government if possible. What I *cannot* do, of course, I *will* not do; but it may as well be understood, once and for all, that I shall not surrender the game leaving any available card unplayed." Yet he realized that the arrest of innocent people raised the level of opposition, which helped the Confederate cause.[48]

In Congress, the controversial issue of arbitrary arrests also surfaced, and attacks on Lincoln continued—even among some Repub-

licans; Lincoln's proclamation of September 24, 1862, on the habeas corpus was probably one factor in the party's losses in several
border states elections. Still, the president defended his actions and
dealt with the supporters of Vallandingham in a particularly telling
response. To a petition from an Albany meeting of pro-Union Democrats who protested the Vallandingham arrest, Lincoln's position was
clear. The president described the irony of those enemies of the
Constitution who used its protections while they sought to destroy
the Union it created. He argued the arrests were preventive and not
vindictive, and informed them that Vallandingham had tried to prevent the enlistment and recruitment of troops. Then the president
asked, "Must I shoot a simple-minded soldier boy who deserts, while
I must not touch a hair of a wily agitator who induces him to
desert?"[49]

By February 1864, the Supreme Court had its chance to rule on
the Vallandingham controversy. The majority concluded that since
the military commission was not a court within the definition of
the law, the high court could not issue a writ of certiorari to review the proceedings. Later in the *Milligan* case, the Court did insist that, "Martial rule can never exist where the courts are open."
Interestingly, Burnside, who had precipitated the original controversy,
decided on June 1, 1863, to suppress the publication of the Chicago *Times* for its support of Vallandingham. Stanton's response was
quick: he informed Burnside that the president wanted the order
reversed and expected to be notified before "administrative" decisions such as the arrest of civilians or actions against newspapers
were taken. To add to the president's problems, General Milo Hascall
issued a similar order in Indiana against the Columbia city *News*.
His order was revoked and Hascall was sent elsewhere.

Overall though, despite the firestorm of opposition in 1862, the
Republican party did fairly well in the 1863 elections. On September 15, 1863, the president had issued a tightly drawn proclamation
that suspended the writ of habeas corpus throughout the United
States. Its basis was a congressional statute that had been passed,
rather than his own definition of executive power. However, Lincoln faced hostility from other important quarters, especially on the
draft, as has been noted. The Democratic governor of New York,
Horatio Seymour, who was elected in 1862, became publicly identified with those opposing the draft, and was mentioned quickly as
a prominent possible candidate for the presidential election in 1864.
Fearing more disturbances in his state, Seymour asked for lower

draft quotas and complained about the calculations being used by the War Department.

Overall, Lincoln looked at the dissent from all sides, which plagued him day after day, and concluded, "I am president of one part of this divided country. . . ; but look at me! I wish I had never been born! . . . With a fire in my front and rear; having to contend with the jealousies of the military commanders, and not receiving that cordial cooperation and support from Congress which could reasonably be expected; with an active and formidable enemy—in the field threatening the very life blood of the government—my position is anything but a bed of roses."[50]

But such sentiments were a luxury that Lincoln could ill afford. He was calm, calculating, self-effacing, and above all patient—patient beyond almost human endurance. By mid-1863, the South had suffered crushing defeats in two important theaters, and Union armies were moving toward Chattanooga to gain control of eastern Tennessee. However, the Army of the Cumberland led by Major General William Rosecrans and the Confederate Army of Tennessee under Braxton Bragg reached a stalemate. By September 20, 1863, after two days of concentrated attacks on his left flank at Chickamauga, Rosecrans blundered by redeploying units from his right flank and thus opened the way for the destruction of the right wing of his army. Only Major General George Thomas's forces held the line, earning him the nickname of "Rock of Chickamauga."

Lincoln fretted as his generals moved too slowly and indecisively for him. He avoided, as best he could, trying to dictate strategy, but he surely questioned what was happening to an advance he saw often as being excrutiatingly slow, and victories that melted too quickly into delays. His chief of staff, Halleck, at times ignored the president's inquiries, but after Gettysburg, Lincoln insisted that General Meade should attack Lee. He caustically commented, "the honor will be his if he succeeds, and the blame may be mine if he fails." As for Rosecrans, the president tried to assure him of his support, even though he had discussed removing him from command; on top of that, a weary Lincoln wondered why Burnside had not sent the assistance he had promised to Rosecrans.

Then in September and October 1863, major changes in command were made, probably instigated by Stanton rather than Lincoln. Grant, as commander of the newly created "Military Division of the Mississippi," was put in charge over Rosecrans; Grant quickly relieved him and gave Thomas command of the Army of the

Cumberland. In an impressive turnaround, the Union forces prevailed at Missionary Ridge near Chattanooga, and finally defeated Bragg's army in a major encounter there and at Lookout Mountain. On November 25, a delighted Lincoln wired Grant, "Well done! Many thanks to all." Lincoln had finally found his commander.

WINNING REELECTION

While the Union was chalking up some notable victories in the West, the campaigns in the East seemed costly stalemates that fed the ranks of the Peace Democrats and called down on Lincoln the wrath of the Radicals. Indeed, in many ways, the string of difficult victories in the West, while the Union armies seemed stalemated in the East, may have saved Lincoln and the Union cause. The president indeed had found a general, but he was one who incurred incredible losses as he waged his battles of attrition. By midsummer of 1864, the campaigns that Grant instigated had not brought clear-cut victories, only more bloodshed and conscription. Lincoln realized all too well that his reelection depended on the military situation more than anything else.

As the Republicans entered the new year, the party was divided between the Radical elements and the conservative Whig group. The Radicals looked for a candidate to stop Lincoln, and they toyed with the prospects of Frémont, Chase, or General Ben Butler. Horace Greeley in his *Tribune* columns added Grant's name to the list, and anti-Lincoln partisans pushed to have the convention postponed beyond its June date in order to gather more support for a viable alternative. The major figure being considered was Lincoln's secretary of treasury, Salmon P. Chase. Chase claimed that he was at first unaware of the growing movement to replace the president with him. Yet he was unhappy with what he perceived to be Lincoln's poor leadership; the president seemed too often listless, inefficient, indecisive, and in general inadequate to the great burdens of the office. A quickly written Chase biography, based on information supplied by the secretary, began to appear in public. In major cities, Chase clubs began to spring up in late 1863, and the secretary's name was now prominently mentioned.

Then in February 1864, a group led by Senator S. C. Pomeroy of Kansas sent out a letter proclaiming that Lincoln could not be reelected and that even if he were, the war effort would continue to languish. As an alternative, the "Pomeroy Circular" suggested Chase as a man who possessed the qualities that a president in this crisis needed. Throughout all of this, Lincoln and his secretary of the treasury worked together, without speaking of the campaign. Finally, Chase insisted to Lincoln that he had not encouraged the movement and he offered his resignation. The president refused the offer, simply stating that he perceived no need for a change.

The conservative wing of the party, led by the Blairs of Maryland, was not content to let the matter drop. Francis Blair, Jr., on the floor of the House of Representatives, launched a series of assaults on Chase and his record, from which Lincoln was quick to disassociate himself. Chase's support came from the large number of patronage appointments the Treasury Department controlled, and some officials claimed that they were being asked to align themselves with the secretary over the president. The situation was especially critical in newly occupied Louisiana. Then in early March 1865, Chase announced in a letter to an Ohio supporter that he was pulling out of the race. Actually, the week before, Ohio had held a Republican party caucus in the state's general assembly, and the leaders supported Lincoln's renomination.

But Chase's withdrawal did not mark the end of the challenge to the president. A group of Republicans, calling themselves the "radical Democracy" met at Cleveland and nominated John C. Frémont for president and the attorney general of New York, John Cochrane, for vice president. The delegates charged that Lincoln had proven to be untrue to the cause of human freedom, and that a new chief executive was essential to the salvation of the nation. Frémont, the Republican standard-bearer in 1856, argued that it was Lincoln and not he who had caused the split in the party. The attorney general attacked the administration for its violations on constitutional liberties, its weaknesses, its disloyalty to its true friends, and its overall incompetence.

Other prominent men criticized Lincoln's record. The great orator and abolitionist Wendell Phillips saw the president's reelection as being disastrous to liberty and to the rights of blacks. Another group of Republican leaders argued for a postponement of the convention, and the Cincinnati *Daily Gazette* reported that prominent leaders were demanding the president's resignation. While these were important pockets of dissent, the Lincoln forces controlled the party machinery, and many of the state and county committees throughout the nation. Lincoln and his supporters were not reluc-

tant to use the full resources of his presidency, including patronage
and government contracts to solidify his strength.

In early 1864, the president began to receive the support of some
of the major delegations. In New Hampshire, the state Republican
committee supported him publicly; the Republicans in the Pennsylvania legislature followed suit; so did supporters in New Jersey,
Indiana, Maryland, Colorado, California, Rhode Island, Ohio, and
Kansas. By June, the party convention followed the Lincoln bandwagon. The Radicals, seeing the probable outcome, pressed, as convention losers often do to shape the platform to their liking. The
final draft contained a call for an antislavery amendment to the
Constitution, a railroad to the Pacific coast, and renewed support
for redemption of the national debt. The platform stressed the need
for "harmony" in the government—a code word for getting rid of
cabinet conservatives like Seward and Blair. The convention nominated Lincoln and added Andrew Johnson of Tennessee to woo war
Democrats to the "Union" ticket, as the Republicans called their
party that election.

The president apparently opposed at first dumping Hannibal
Hamlin as vice president and even considered Ben Butler as a running mate, a choice the general unwisely rejected as it turned out.
Some of Lincoln's advisors urged him to move rapidly on introducing new states to the Union in order to increase his Western electoral tally, but the president for some reason chose to proceed slowly,
probably desiring a genuine mandate and not simply a stacked electoral decision.[51]

His ambivalences in the election were apparent. On the one hand,
he refused to get involved in running the political machine, as he
called it. "I have enough on my hands without *that*. It is the *people's*
business—the election is in their hands." But Lincoln was too astute a politician to neglect the most important contest of his time.
He interfered where he saw problems, as in the critical state of
Pennsylvania, when he directly organized speakers for the party's
cause and used the patronage powers he had to solidify his base.
When it was suggested to Lincoln's secretary, John Hay, that perhaps the editor James Gordon Bennett of the New York *Herald*
might lessen his criticism if he had a promise of a foreign ministry
later, Hay disagreed, saying that Bennett was "too pitchy to touch."
But Lincoln did not think so, and he offered him the post in France.

In Missouri, John Nicolay arrived bearing Lincoln's instructions
to mediate the factionalism there. And although the president was

forbidden by custom to "campaign," he did sit for a long interview in August where he spelled out how emancipation meant two hundred thousand former slaves for the Union army. To those who attacked his abolitionist policy, the president argued, "no human power can subdue the rebellion without the use of the emancipation policy and every policy calculated to weaken the moral and physical forces of the rebellion." And it was probably Lincoln who came up with, or first used prominently, the words that became the unofficial slogan of the campaign: "No time to swap horses in the middle of the stream," a plea for continuity of leadership during the war.[52]

Lincoln's major opponent, though, would not be Frémont, but the Democratic nominee, General George McClellan. It is likely that Lincoln had tried to get McClellan to disavow the nomination by offering him a military command once again, including an adjunct position with Grant, or perhaps the command of the Army of the Potomac. But McClellan sought and received the Democratic nomination, and then struggled with his position on the party's platform. Vallandingham and his followers had pushed through a plank that called the war effort a failure and demanded an end to hostilities and a convention of the states or some similar mechanism to restore the Union. After hesitating on the issue, McClellan insisted on a guarantee of union before peace negotiations began—the opposite order spelled out by the Peace Democrats. Thus entering the election, McClellan too was faced with internal splits in his party's ranks.

Lincoln said little about McClellan's candidacy either publicly or privately. He knew in one sense that the race was his to win or lose, and that his fate depended on the military situation. He had, though, aggravated his problems by vetoing the Wade-Davis bill, the Radical Republican plan for reconstruction of the Southern states. The two Republican sponsors of the bill then issued a statement published in the New York *Tribune* that charged the president was guilty of "grave Executive usurpation" of authority. They attacked his reconstructed governments in Arkansas and Louisiana as "mere creatures of his will." And they labeled his actions as sinister, rash, and a violation of the rights of humanity and republican government. Concerned by the charges from men in his own party, Lincoln observed, "To be wounded in the house of one's friends is perhaps the most grievous affliction that can befall a man." As the president had guessed, the manifesto was the first step in an effort to get him to give up the nomination he had just won. Republican

Radical Henry Winter Davis issued a call for a new convention in September, and a group of party leaders met surreptitiously in New York and included some important figures from that state and Massachusetts. Thurlow Weed, who attended, informed Lincoln that his reelection was an impossibility, and the president's campaign manager, Henry J. Raymond, agreed. Raymond advocated a publicized peace offer to Jefferson Davis—a concession that obviously would not please the Radicals who were the source of Lincoln's opposition.

On August 23, 1864, Lincoln wrote out a long memorandum outlining special overtures that he would make to McClellan if the latter was elected. He would urge McClellan to raise as many troops as he could for the final trial, and Lincoln, in turn, would devote all his efforts to assisting and finishing the war. Then Lincoln sealed up the letter, and strangely had all his cabinet members sign the outside of the document, without telling them what was in it.

Another group of Republicans continued the assault on the president and called for a new convention on September 28 in Cincinnati. Before issuing the statement, they polled the Republican governors to see if the president could win in their states in the coming election. But by the time the statement reached the governors, the tides of war had changed. Major General William T. Sherman, Grant's successor as commander of the Military Division of the Mississippi, had captured Atlanta, and the fate of the Confederacy was clear, even to Lincoln's critics. On September 22, Frémont dropped out of the race, apparently as a result of a less than honorable deal on Lincoln's part. In order to soothe the Radicals, the president requested the resignation of his conservative ally and longtime friend, Postmaster General Montgomery Blair. Blair and his family had become a lightning rod of the Radicals' animus. The president's lame response to Blair was, "You very well know that this proceeds from no dissatisfaction of mine with you personally or officially." Just before his action, Lincoln had assured Blair's father that his son was a good and loyal ally and should not be sacrificed for false friends.

As the campaign progressed, the president and his campaign leaders used the full patronage at their disposal to foster his reelection. In New York, Lincoln removed Chase's associate, Horace Binney, from the New York customshouse and replaced him with his own man; later he chose a new surveyor of the port and named a new postmaster in New York City. He threw his full support behind the Seward-Weed machine in order to carry that crucial state; and in Philadelphia, Chicago, and Indiana, the president firmed up his control over the patronage network. When he received word that one official was not supporting a regular party nominee, Lincoln bluntly replied, "Your nomination is as binding on Republicans as mine, and you can rest assured that Mr. Halloway shall support you, openly and unconditionally, or lose his head." One newspaper in Indiana complained that hundreds of government clerks were mailing out Lincoln literature instead of conducting the nation's business.

Federal employees were expected to work for the ticket and also to contribute to the Republican war chest; a 3 percent levy as salary was in many cases standard, and postmasters were expected to contribute personally from $2 to $150 each, depending on the size of the post office, to the congressional campaign. The party also expected and obtained campaign contributions from those who were receiving government contracts during the war, and the quartermasters provided the names of those who were favored with government largesse.

Most importantly, the Republicans counted on the soldier vote. Over one million documents were distributed by the party to soldiers, and the president and his campaign managers insisted that troops from critical states be furloughed in time to go home and vote. It has been estimated that the soldier vote, three-quarters of which went for Lincoln, helped the Republicans win six vital states without which the president would not have been reelected. On election day, November 8, 1864, Lincoln received 55 percent of the vote and carried the electoral vote 234 to 21. He swept every state in the remaining Union, except Delaware, New Jersey, and his own birthplace of Kentucky. His victory was strongest in Massachusetts, weakest in New York. He did well among the German-American population, but poorly in the cities and among Irish-Americans. Lincoln had earned the right to characterize his own victory: "It had long been a grave question whether any government, not too strong for the liberties of its own people, can be strong enough to maintain its own existence, in great emergencies." To him, the decision was clear: he had asserted the power of the government and had received in the end a mandate from the people to continue the war.[53]

THE TRIALS OF ATTRITION

Lincoln's electoral victory was mainly due to successes in the field. But he knew all too well, the armies were extracting a terrible toll in life and treasure. In February 1864, the president had promoted Grant to lieutenant general, a rank that only George Washington and Winfield Scott (as brevet) had held. A small, quiet, and sloppily dressed man, Grant became the new American hero. The general had decided on a series of offenses in the East designed to end the war. Lincoln seemed unsure of what was being contemplated, writing as late as August 1864 to Grant, "The particulars of your plans I neither know nor seek to know." In fact, Lincoln had submitted earlier his own strategic plan to Grant, one the general found to be unsatisfactory.

On May 5, 1864, Grant began the bloody forty-day "Overland Campaign" that took his armies from the battle of the Wilderness, through Spotsylvania, to the North Anna River, on to the slaughter of Cold Harbor, and finally the seige of Petersburg. Each was a bloodbath, and the terrible Union losses gave credence to Grant's nickname, "The Butcher." The total Northern casualties from the Wilderness campaign through the harrowing battle at Cold Harbor reached 54,000 men—7,621 of whom were killed. At Cold Harbor alone, there were 12,000 casualties, killed and wounded. Later, Grant was to write, "Without a greater sacrifice of life than I was willing to make, all could not be accomplished that I had designed north of Richmond." Many soldiers pinned their names on their own uniforms for identification of the dead later. Legend has it that following a battle, Grant's army moved on, not even bothering to bury its own men.

Lincoln visited the general in late June and expressed concern about the siege of Petersburg. He had written Grant, "I do hope you may find a way that . . . shall not be desperate in the sense of great loss of life."[54] As the North was registering shock over the course and cost of the war, Horace Greeley floated another peace feeler to the president. He had received word that Jefferson Davis had authorized two emissaries to present peace terms. Lincoln agreed to meet with them if Greeley himself escorted them from Canada where they were staying to Washington. Lincoln's terms were clear: the restoration of the Union and the end of slavery; the president sent John Hay in mid-July 1864 to Niagara Falls with that message. The peace initiative fell through, but another would follow.

The war continued through the summer. Lincoln had already called up more troops, and opposition to the draft increased. The administration also faced financial problems by this time. Earlier, in 1862, Congress had issued "U.S. Notes," or "greenbacks" as they were called—government paper not backed by gold and which greatly depreciated in value. Congress, faced with the problem of wartime inflation, had tried in 1863 to set up a national banking system to stabilize the problem. That system, planned by Secretary of Treasury Chase, created federally chartered banks, which would purchase U.S. bonds and which could use the bonds as security for issuing banknotes guaranteed by the federal government. The banknotes were accepted at par value and could be exchanged for gold. By June 1864, Congress attempted to control speculation by restricting gold trading. In order to fund the war, Congress had voted a federal income tax of 3 percent on all incomes over $800, a rate that was graduated in 1864 on a scale that went from 5 to 10 percent. Congressional Republicans were anxious to redeem their campaign promises to important constituencies, and so in the president's first term they supported a high tariff, subsidized the railroads, passed a land grant college bill, and created a homestead policy. Lincoln, preoccupied with the war, simply signed these measures and avoided anymore confrontations with his own party. Yet, another arduous battle was still in front him at this time—Reconstruction.

PRELUDE TO RECONSTRUCTION

Lincoln had pretty much run the war in his own way, despite the obstruction of Congress. He intended to do the same with regard to Reconstruction. That decision, made somewhat abruptly, may have been a mistake on his part; surely, it was disastrous to his successor. The president believed that the necessities of war gave him, as commander in chief, extraordinary powers to wage that war, powers that were superior to those of Congress. He had confronted immense opposition, and still he had mandated measures in his early months that were extraconstitutional at best, and so he had Congress ratify them later. He had usually stymied the legislative branch in its attempts to interfere with his choice of cabinet officials and generals. He had declared slaves to be free in rebellious states, again citing military authority. Civilian courts were ignored or superseded, much to the horror of even conservative Union men. Now, the president faced reconstruction, and he recognized two facts: first, that his powers to move in such extraordinary ways were due to the circumstances of war, and that when the conflict was over, his scope of authority would be surely circumscribed. Second, Lincoln realized that his objectives and those of the Radicals would lead to very different types of reconstructed governments.

As has been noted, Lincoln was by birth and by family ties a Southerner and despite his general tolerance, he shared even during his presidency many of the racial attitudes of that region. The Union, he had said, was the issue, but slavery was in some way the cause of secession. To save the Union, he became an abolitionist; to live up to his conservative inaugural oath, he took on the mantle of Great Emancipator. Still, by 1864–65, only about 5 percent of the slave population had been freed. Most slaves were behind Confederate lines in the South and still held in bondage.

The president desired a speedy end to the war and a quick rehabilitation of the secessionist states. If one theme comes out in his correspondence on the issue, it is the need to move fast on restoration. Why the haste? In part, it was probably just a desire to get back to normal, to peace and to harmony. But Lincoln's plans ran into opposition from the Radicals in Congress, and some of their concerns were valid.[55]

The war for secession had been supported by most of the Southern leadership classes and any restoration would bring them back to power. In addition, those states would return to the national government with their senators, their representatives, and their electoral votes; probably very soon a Democrat president and a Democrat Congress would result. Black freedom had yet to be secured; there were serious constitutional doubts about Congress's Confiscation Acts and even more about Lincoln's Emancipation Proclamation. Lincoln seemed firm on abolition by 1864, but still he insisted on discussing colonization, compensation to slaveholders, and a phased-in plan for emancipation—even after he had "freed" slaves in rebellious territories in January 1863.

The Radicals believed, not without some justification, that speedy reconstruction would result in a return to the status quo before the war. What would be the political and economic consequences of millions of freed blacks without jobs and without civil rights? Would they simply be exchanging their status as slaves for a new nominal wage bondage that left them on plantations still run by overseers?

All the sacrifice and energy would have been spent in vain. And incredibly, their party—the party of Union and emancipation—could be cast out of power. At stake were not simply the humanitarian goals that came out of the terrible war, but also that network of patronage and privilege that war had brought.[56]

A reconstructed South would not support the same economic interests the Republicans had favored, and a South-West alliance would have dismal consequences, especially for supporters of a high tariff. The Radicals demanded retribution and called it justice. Besides their philosophical concerns were the pragmatic problems that success in the war would bring. Lincoln seemed at first interested primarily in a speedy reconstruction, and he created the nucleus of early "restructured" governments in some Southern states to move the process along. In December 1863, the president established a policy of general pardon and a restoration of state governments. The president offered a pardon (except in specific cases) and a full restoration of rights (except for slaveholding) to anyone in a seceded state who took an oath of allegiance to the U.S. Constitution, the Union, and all valid congressional acts and presidential proclamations. For restoration purposes, Lincoln decided that if one-tenth of those voting in 1860 would reestablish a republican form of government loyal to the Union, he would recognize it as the true government of that state.

This 10 percent formula was to be the foundation upon which pro-Union governments were to be built, and Lincoln decided to use this formula in several occupied states in order to create models as to how reconstruction under the executive's control could proceed with minimum dislocation and without lasting bitterness. He strongly opposed bringing in outsiders to run these states—a policy later changed and characterized as "carpetbagger" rule. When Louisiana fell to the Union forces, Lincoln began to use that state as a first test. He pushed for elections of congressmen and, after a fight, the House of Representatives voted to seat Louisiana's two elected representatives in February 1863. But, matters moved too slowly for the president, and he feared that disloyal elements might preempt his objectives by creating a government that would refuse to recognize emancipation.

By 1864, a state convention in Louisiana proposed a constitution that accepted emancipation, and elections proceeded normally. The constitution was overwhelmingly approved by the loyal people of Louisiana, and it seemed as if Lincoln's plans were working well.

But Radical opposition hardened, and some of the leaders in that state refused to support the new government.

The president had also moved quickly in other occupied states as well. In Tennessee, he appointed in 1862 Andrew Johnson as military governor, and by 1865, a reorganized government was established—although not recognized by Congress until 1866. In 1863 and 1864, Arkansas, a reluctant secessionist state, was reorganized with Lincoln's approval. Local support was strong for such reconciliation, and the president pushed for immediate elections in March 1864. In Florida, the president by 1864 asked for reconstruction "in the most speedy way possible," and he sent his assistant John Hay to aid in the process. Events did not go well in that state, however, and readmission was slow in coming.

The president's formula was flexible and designed to facilitate easy restoration. Basically, the process included the building of a loyal nucleus, a constitutional convention to revamp the state government, and popular elections for state and congressional offices. Voters had to take a loyalty oath, and eventually federal troops were removed, leaving local people pledged to the Union in charge.

In Congress, opposition to Lincoln's policy grew and an alternative was put forth by the Radicals. In the House of Representatives, Henry Winter Davis introduced a bill to guarantee republican government to states where it had been "usurped or overthrown." Davis's original bill required that a majority of white male citizens had to take an oath, and that no person who had voluntarily borne arms against the United States, or given aid to such persons, could participate in the creation of a new constitution. No former civil or military officer of the Confederacy could vote or hold office under the reconstructed state government. The Senate agreed with the House version and passed it on to Lincoln, who was in the capital that day.

Lincoln argued that the bill was too inflexible, and he was unwilling to set aside the Arkansas and Louisiana governments he had, in effect, created. The president disagreed with the Wade-Davis emphasis on past loyalty; the future was his concern. He explained, "On principle I dislike an oath which requires a man to swear he *has* not done wrong. It rejects the Christian principle of forgiveness on terms of repentance. I think it is enough if the man does no wrong hereafter."[57] One of the bill's supporters, Senator Zachariah Chandler, argued that the important objective was to end slavery in the restored states, as Lincoln himself had proposed. But the president responded that Congress had no authority to act, and that he alone could do on military grounds what could not be done constitutionally in peacetime.

The president pocket vetoed the bill and continued to advocate quick and amiable restoration. But other Republicans were strong in their opposition to his actions and to his logic. Thaddeus Stevens argued that the Southern people had to "eat the fruit of foul rebellion," before they could return. He was committed to the "perpetual ascendancy" of the Republican party, and saw that its entire economic program of subsidies and privileges was at stake.

THE THIRTEENTH AMENDMENT

By 1864, Lincoln and the Congress had both proclaimed an end to slavery, and yet it remained an institution. As has been noted, the president in his proclamation in 1863 had used what he argued were his war powers and "freed" the slaves in most of the areas in rebellion. In Congress, support had grown even earlier for some drastic challenge to slavery. In August 1861, Congress passed the first confiscation act which provided that slaveowners would forfeit all slaves used in military service against the United States. In July 1862, the second such act declared "forever free" all slaves of owners who supported the rebellion or were guilty of treason, a provision close to Lincoln's later edict. Congress also abolished slavery in the District of Columbia and in the territories, granted freedom to slaves who served in the Union armies (by 1864, even if they were owned by Unionists), and ended the fugitive slave laws. Yet even though Lincoln's actions were in fact less far-reaching, still his proclamation took on more importance in the symbolic and practical world of war and abolitionism.

In 1864, Lincoln was pushing for emancipation and had by that time generally, but not totally, given up on compensation, having seen that gradualism was not possible. The question remained whether the proclamation or even the congressional confiscation acts were constitutional, and whether emancipation would continue to be national policy after the war ended. The president had insisted that the Republicans in the election of 1864 support an antislavery amendment to the Constitution and after his victory, he pushed for its approval.[58] Lincoln spoke to moderate Democrats in Congress, used some patronage to further his case, and was successful in getting the lame-duck Congress to reconsider and pass the proposed amendment in early 1865. It has been speculated that the president persuaded Senator Charles Sumner to postpone consideration of a bill to regulate the Camden and Amboy railroad in New Jersey, in return for the company's help in getting several Democratic congressmen to support the amendment. Lincoln probably backed off, knowing Sumner's general attitude to such pressure. For whatever reason, enough Democrats in the last session switched and the Thirteenth Amendment was approved. Lincoln regarded it as the fulfillment of his work, a great moral victory, a cure for many of the evils he saw before him. By the end of 1865, the Thirteenth Amendment was added to the Constitution with its provisions that prohibited slavery and involuntary servitude in the nation. William Lloyd Garrison fully credited the president with the amendment; the glory belonged to "the humble railsplitter of Illinois—to the presidential chainbreaker for millions of the oppressed—to Abraham Lincoln!"

The war was coming to an end. As his first term concluded, Lincoln again was approached by a peace commission, and this time he went with Seward to meet the group at Hampton Roads, Virginia, on February 3, 1865. Lincoln greeted Confederate Vice President Alexander Stephens and several others, and once again they explored possibilities for terminating the war. Lincoln's position was reiterated: he insisted on a restoration of the Union and refused to get dragged into a common alliance for a war against the French-controlled Mexico. Stephens, according to his recollections, asked the president if the Emancipation Proclamation would free all the slaves in the South, or only those who were actually freed during the war. Lincoln supposedly said the proclamation was a war measure and would become inoperative after the war. Seward informed them of the Thirteenth Amendment, but also viewed it as a war measure that could be defeated if the Confederate states returned to the Union in time! Lincoln instead argued that the South could postpone the adoption of the amendment for a five-year time span and held forth the carrot of compensation.

If Stephens's memoirs are correct, Lincoln was talking once again of graduated emancipation with compensation, arguments that he earlier had indicated to others he had abandoned. And if Stephens's views are faithful summaries of Lincoln's feelings, the president's record on emancipation is even more confusing. For while he was pushing the Thirteenth Amendment clearly and decisively, he was still clinging to a moderate course which he himself had made impossible. In any case, the Confederates rejected Lincoln's plan, a development that probably saved the president from intense attacks by the Radical Republicans if they had known of the alleged conversations at that time. When Lincoln came back to the capital, he presented his cabinet with a proposal resurrecting compensation; to a man they opposed his plan, and he dropped it. The war had ground too deeply for half-measures now.

By March 1865, Lincoln's second inauguration was imminent, and there even was talk of his running again in 1868. In his short inaugural address, the president blamed the war on the development of slavery, and ended in those familiar sentiments, "With malice toward none; with charity for all; With firmness in the right, as God gives us to see the right, let us strive to finish the work we are in."

Meanwhile, the war continued as Sherman's armies captured Savannah and marched on the Carolinas, and Grant finally took control of Petersburg on April 3, 1865. The president accepted Grant's invitation and went to visit his army as it reached the Confederate capital. Almost recklessly, the president watched the forces in the city, landed at Richmond, and walked up Main Street to the executive mansion evacuated by Jefferson Davis. Soldiers cheered Lincoln, and blacks sang and shouted in the presence of the Great Emancipator. Then in the main parlor, where even today one can feel a sense of eeriness, Lincoln met with Union officers and Richmond citizens. One newspaper writer noted that the president came without pomp or parade, not as a conqueror but as a friend to rebuild what had been destroyed.

In the next few days, Grant continued on, and Sherman wired that "if the thing is pressed, I think Lee will surrender." Lincoln's response to Grant on April 7, 1865, was clear—"Let the *thing* be pressed." On April 9, Lee surrendered at Appomattox Court House. The administration had made it clear to Grant that he was not to discuss any political questions, that such matters "the president holds in his own hands." Even after the capitulation, Lincoln struggled with reconstruction, most especially in Virginia where leaders had been assured that the president had sanctioned their calling back the Virginia legislature. In another change of policy, Lincoln began to talk of allowing "the very intelligent" blacks and those blacks who had served in the Union army to vote. Actually, he had earlier suggested that policy in discussions about reconstruction in Louisiana, and now raised it on April 11, 1865. He promised some new announcement concerning the South later, and had requested, probably as a gesture of reconciliation with Congress, that Senator Sumner accompany him as he delivered some general remarks to a crowd before the White House.

In the cabinet, he admitted that he may have moved too fast in reconstruction, and he instructed Secretary of War Stanton to draft an executive order setting up military governments for former Confederate states. To Stanton, this meant that the president had moved toward the Radical position; although the black suffrage question was deferred, the secretary concluded that a long cabinet debate was in order on this and other matters. The president also indicated that he did not intend to call Congress back into session, and thus from April to December, he once again would have a free hand. Those were the last decisions the president would make.

LINCOLN'S LEADERSHIP

Lincoln's murder on Good Friday, April 14, 1865, transformed him into a national martyr, and the manner of his end and his own sentiments of clemency made him the Christ symbol of the American dream. Surely, his presidency had been an extraordinary one, not just in the exercise of power but in its single-minded devotion to the Union. The "poor boy made good" had become the Great Emancipator; the wavering conservative Whig had been transformed into a man of vision and liberty. At times, Lincoln seemed to be vacillating and unsure to his contemporaries; to history, he became the prudent leader weighing all factors until he could shape events to fit his destiny. His detractors have been debunked themselves by the mainstream interpretations of history—his generals were too slow, just as he said; some of his cabinet too disloyal, just as he feared; the Radicals too vindictive, just as he charged. The Civil War, even in the South today, is seen favorably through Lincoln's eyes.

Yet the Lincoln presidency is a more varied pattern than that. He appointed some very poor cabinet officers and gave them considerable leeway. The quick mobilization in the spring of 1861 led to speculation, mismanagement and corruption. A few critics have even argued that Lincoln may have prolonged the war by his sacking of McClellan. Lincoln's flirtations with peace offers are seen now as shrewd efforts to get the Peace Democrats on his side; in fact, they may have been unnecessary confusions, especially toward the end of the war. The administration's dragnet policies of arrests did not have to be so extensively applied and extended throughout the war. The suspension of civil liberties, which Lincoln defended and modified, created immense political problems, some of which would not have been necessary if the army had been more carefully controlled. And once he freed the slaves, Lincoln needed to give more attention to their plight and what would happen to them. It was not enough to say he only freed the slaves to save the Union; once they were freed, what did the president intend to do except allow them to serve in the Union army?[59]

As Lincoln liked to say, he was confronted by facts and not by a theory; some of the Radicals recognized the facts much earlier than did the president. The greatest problem of his presidency was his inclination to exclude Congress as much as possible from the major decisions of the war. More than Jackson, whom he did not admire, and Polk, whom he criticized, Lincoln ran the government as much as possible without legislative guidance. Perhaps it was necessary considering the quality of that body, or perhaps it was a decision that led to the growth of a cohesive Radical wing. Still, the Civil War is to a great extent the Lincoln presidency writ large. His election was the immediate cause of secession, his early months set the framework of the North's response, his decisions created the war machine, his timing prevailed in emancipation, and he planned the reconstruction. When all is said and done, Lincoln stands like a colossus in that conflict, and by his words, posterity has come to give meaning to the war, the Union, and the terrible sacrifices he extolled. No president in that century, and none except Franklin D. Roosevelt in our history, so expanded the office, and transformed it into the ferocious engine of American democracy.

7

The National Clerk (Andrew Johnson, Grant, Hayes, Garfield, Arthur Cleveland, Benjamin Harrison, and McKinley)

The presidents who followed Lincoln reaped to some extent the backlash against the strong presidency he created, and most of them lived with the legacy of the war and its uncertain Reconstruction, as the period became formally known. But the dynamics of the war furthered the rapid development of the new industrial order—one in which the presidency seemed at times to be a most timid bystander. In foreign policy, the Civil War provided a respite from territorial expansion, and economic imperialism was interrupted. After the war, however, important new segments of American society wanted their nation to take its place beside the European powers in asserting its influence and global interests, although the United States lacked the military might and diplomatic leverage to become a true rival. Thus, in the latter part of the nineteenth century, executive authority seemed to have a very confined career in the American political universe.

ANDREW JOHNSON'S RECONSTRUCTION

As the draped coffin of Abraham Lincoln was shipped back home to its final resting place, politicians filled with grief and politicians filled with ambition gathered in small groups to evaluate his successor. Ironically, some Radical Republicans at first welcomed Andrew Johnson's ascension to power. George Julian, the abolitionist from Indiana, even called Lincoln's death "a godsend to the country"; and Senator Zachariah Chandler of Michigan concluded that

the Almighty had kept Lincoln in office as long as he was useful to
His work, and then replaced him with one who would do better in
the postwar situation.[1]

Johnson had given the Radicals good reason to believe that he
was one of them. Benjamin Wade in fact worried that the new president would seek to execute too many Confederates! Johnson had
made his reputation as a bitter critic of secessionists, calling them
traitors who had ceased to be citizens. In the 1864 campaign, running on the second spot with Lincoln, he demanded that "treason
must be made odious and traitors must be punished and impover-
ished." When he took over the presidency in April 1865, he posted
rewards for the arrest of major Confederate leaders, including
Jefferson Davis, and for the accomplices of John Wilkes Booth.
Johnson talked about breaking up large Southern estates, ensuring
the end of slavery, and putting some of the Confederate leaders on
trial. Little wonder that Chandler concluded that Johnson "is as
radical as I am and is fully up to the work." The president in fact
had served on the Committee on the Conduct of the War and knew
well the agenda of the Radical Republicans in Congress.[2]

But those who thought they understood Johnson misjudged his
intentions, in part because they misunderstood the making of the
man. Like Lincoln, Johnson was born and raised in the white culture of rural poverty, denied the advantages of formal education.
But Lincoln emerged into adulthood with an incredible sense of
presence, of confidence that allowed him to somehow absorb the
slights of people and the misfortunes of life, while he grew into a
mysteriously complex and forgiving human being. Johnson, on the
other hand, never forgot any slight—real or imagined—inadvertent
or calculated. He was much more successful as a politician than
Lincoln—winning every election he ran in as he made his way from
being a simple, illiterate apprentice tailor to the military governor
of Tennessee. He was a Jacksonian, a loyal party man, whose major achievement was the sponsorship of the Homestead Act.
Johnson's plebeian political philosophy was a crude mixture of
egalitarianism, economic opportunity, and personal resentment
against the rich and the wellborn. He picked up from his friends,
and later his devoted wife, the rudiments of learning, developed into
an effective and vitriolic speaker, and pledged his ambition and
talents to the cause of the Union. From local and state offices, he
went on to the House of Representatives, the Senate, and the state
governorship. When the Southern states began departing from the

Union, Johnson stood like a rock against secession and was appointed military governor of Tennessee by Lincoln. He was abrupt, arbitrary, and somewhat effective, and the harried president turned aside criticisms and supported Johnson. When the Republicans tried to broaden their base in 1864, they renamed the national ticket "Union," looked for a Unionist Democrat, and found Johnson. Lincoln may have had some reservations about Johnson because he had him quietly checked out, but he finally concurred in the nomination.[3]

Lincoln had bequeathed Johnson a confused and controversial Reconstruction policy, one that even the president was uncertain about on the very day of his death. As has been seen, Lincoln's policy was guided by the belief that Reconstruction was an executive responsibility during the war; he had proposed setting up state governments based on 10 percent of their citizens taking a loyalty oath to the Union. His policy emphasized leniency and speedy readmission (or reacceptance) into the federal government structure. Lincoln avoided the philosophical issue of whether the seceded states could be "readmitted" in what he insisted was a perpetual Union. And, despite his historic destiny as the Great Emancipator, he toyed with gradual or phased-in abolition, compensation, and colonization long after the proclamation went into effect. How Lincoln would have handled Reconstruction and a balky Congress is conjecture, but surely a victorious president with the possibility of reelection in 1868 and substantial political skills would not have ended as Johnson did at the conclusion of his disastrous term.

But in the summer of 1865, Johnson emulated Lincoln in one regard—he did not call Congress back into session and insisted on rushing through a Reconstruction and pardon policy. Consequently, he gave the impression to the Radicals and many Northern moderates that he was surrendering the very victory they had won on the field. Johnson's policies failed, and their bankruptcy was apparent almost from the start. One critical factor that led to the Radicals' assault and the president's quick political demise was the recalcitrance of Southern leaders who fulfilled the worst Northern predictions about what they would do under a lenient peace.

On May 29, 1865, Johnson issued two proclamations that granted full amnesty and pardon to all Confederates (except members of certain specifically excluded groups) who took an oath of future loyalty to the United States and promised to support all wartime edicts on the emancipation of the slaves. Those excluded were high-level civil, military, and diplomatic officials of the Confederacy, and those who had deserted the Union cause while holding federal offices. Johnson, the white plebeian hero, added another exclusion—those rebels who had taxable property of over $80,000. However, a provision in one of those proclamations allowed direct appeal to the president for a pardon, and soon Johnson was flooded with personal delegations of the wealthy and wellborn rebels—a sight he seemed to relish. To the consternation of some Radicals, the proclamations restored all property (except slaves) to the Confederates, and ended the possibilities of confiscation and the creation of a true black yeoman class in the South.

On May 29, Johnson also established a provisional government for North Carolina, which became a model for other Southern states. The procedures generally followed the pattern by which a provisional governor, with broad powers and the support of the Union occupying forces, would call a state constitutional convention, followed by the election of a legislature, regular governor, and representatives to both houses of Congress. Johnson urged that the Southern states grant some very limited concessions on black suffrage in order to curtail the cries of the Radicals. Each state was expected to void its ordinances of secession, accept the Thirteenth Amendment, recognize the end of slavery, and repudiate the Confederate war debt. Those terms of reconciliation, incredibly mild by any standard of human conduct, were resented by Southern leaders.

Some states refused to declare secession ordinances null and void, and instead "repealed" them; other states added reservations to the Thirteenth Amendment; still others seriously considered rejecting the war debt provision. Added to those complications, the officials elected from this new South were disproportionately prominent Confederates, men who could not take the Congress's "iron clad oath" if they were elected to go to Washington. By that oath, an official had to swear that he had never borne arms against the United States of America. In addition, these new governments began approving the establishment of black codes aimed at curtailing the rights and activities of the newly freed slaves.

Although those codes varied by state, their basic objectives were to create a system of segregation, prohibit interracial marriages, stop blacks from serving on juries or testifying against whites, and re-enact many of the provisions of the criminal parts of the older slave codes. Blacks, for example, could not enter into employment (except as agricultural laborers) without special permits in South Carolina, could not buy or rent farm land in Mississippi, could not leave the land in several states without permission, could be arrested if they refused to work for their employers, and in some cases could be arrested as vagrants if they were not employed and could then be auctioned off or hired to landowners who paid their legal fines. Carl Schurz, traveling through the South, concluded at the time that while individual bondage to owners was outlawed, in its place was a system whereby "the blacks at large belong to the whites at large." Through all this, during the summer and fall of 1865, Johnson said nothing. He philosophized that there would be some problems, but gradually the freed black would receive "the protection to which he is justly entitled." Thus, by the time Congress assembled on December 4, Johnson had completed, in his eyes at least, the general outlines of restoration—pardons and self-government.

In 1865 and into 1866, the Radicals never commanded anywhere near a majority of the elected and sitting members of Congress. Moderate Republicans urged cooperation between the executive and legislative branches. The Ohio Republican legislative caucus, for example, passed a resolution praising the president and stressed moderation as the best policy. The Radicals pushed for a moratorium on admitting the newly elected Southern congressmen until the Reconstruction issues had been thought out. Central to the discussion was the future of the newly freed slaves—a burden to which Lincoln had devoted little attention and with which Johnson was intellectually incapable of dealing.

Johnson's major contributions were diatribes that mixed intemperate remarks with studied racism. He insisted that the South must remain a "white man's country," and concluded that throughout history "negroes have shown less capacity for government than any other race of people . . . left to their own devices they have shown a constant tendency to relapse into barbarism." Johnson is alleged to have written Governor Thomas C. Fletcher of Missouri, "This is a country for white men, and by God, as long as I am president, it shall be a government for white men." He had a deep conviction that blacks were inferior to whites, and it is hard not to conclude that, in part, his Reconstruction policies were heavily influenced by such attitudes. He even had a disdain for black troops, whose burdens were far out of proportion to their numbers. When he heard that his home in Greenville had been used by black troops, he communicated to General Thomas, "It is bad enough to be taken by traitors and converted into a rebel hospital but a negro whore house is infinitely worse."[4]

For some Radicals, these sentiments—widely echoed in the North—were repugnant to their moral beliefs and their faith in human nature. Although it is difficult for many cynics to believe, elements of idealism and fellow feeling do animate political people and inspire at times public deeds. A good segment of the Radicals viewed slavery as a moral wrong and hated racial discrimination. In this regard, they were far in advance of their party, their nation, and much of the Western conscience. Other Radicals were less inspired; to them, the blacks had to be melded to the Republican party for pragmatic reasons. That party was still a minority party, one that did not command the allegiance of a substantial segment of the American people outside of the North. If a mildly reconstructed South were admitted easily into the Union and into Congress, the Democratic party would reunite its branches and soon run the federal government. Somehow it seemed unfair and unpatriotic to give up national leadership after the Republicans struggled to win the war and save the Union. Equally important, the Republicans had created, as has been noted, a political alliance that aided railroad, corporate, and commercial interests. A Democratic party restoration meant free trade, low tariffs, and an agrarian national perspective. For the Republicans to stay in power, their party then needed to enfranchise a new constituency. Thus, their concern over the fate of the former slaves was written in many scripts.[5]

Lincoln had assumed that the Republicans could win 40 percent or so of the Old South Whigs, and could form a national coalition that way. Thus, he had little desire to push for widespread black suffrage, and his views of that race were probably milder, but still as negative at times as Johnson's more vitriolic racial declarations. In this sentiment, the Northern states and citizenry were equally unbending. In Connecticut, Ohio, Michigan, Minnesota, and Kansas, voters had rejected proposals to give blacks the right to vote after the war.

What is remarkable about the Radical leaders is not that their idealism was frequently mixed with partisan ambition and concerns over patronage or economic interests, but rather that some of them, quite independent of or in opposition to constituent pressures, were supporters of equal rights in this period. Also astounding is that in this atmosphere, they worked hard to turn around Northern sentiment on the suffrage issue and to impose their views on the South and eventually on their own regions as well. By then, Johnson stood in their way, and they were merciless in their opposition to him and to his misguided policies on Reconstruction. Like their Protestant forebears, their wrath was righteous and knew no bounds. Against that force, Johnson threw up the defenses of an independent executive and the traditional restraints of a balanced Constitution.

The basic issues the two branches would clash over were three: the future of the former seceded states, the demands of the former Confederates to be restored to their rights, and the status of freed blacks. While Johnson had denounced the Confederates as traitors, he had little interest or personal concern for blacks and insisted on stressing states' rights instead. When Congress returned in December 1865, it considered Thaddeus Stevens's resolution for a joint committee on reconstruction to report on the condition and mood of the South, and whether the states "were entitled to be represented" in the federal legislature. Carl Schurz had already toured the South between July and October, and his balanced report noted that opposition to the Union was ended, but that there was little popular loyalty and that the freed blacks needed some measure of protection.

Concerned about Schurz's report, the president released a perfunctory review done by Grant that stated that Southerners were willing to act as good citizens and were awaiting the course to be pointed out to them. Actually, at first the Southern states' leaders expected no lenience from the federal government and were willing to accept any conditions including black suffrage to normalize relations and end military occupation. As one Confederate leader, Christopher Memminger, the former secretary of treasury under Davis, said in 1871 to Schurz, "I think you are right in saying that if we had originally adopted a different course as to the negroes, we would have escaped present difficulties. But if you will consider for a moment, you will see that it was as impossible, as for us to have emancipated them before the war. The then President held up before us the hope of a 'white man's government,' and this led us to set aside negro suffrage."[6]

As Congress began its review of the situation in the South, black leaders went to see Johnson on February 7, 1866, to press their case for federal assistance. The president told the group, led by the great orator Frederick Douglass, that the franchise would only hurt the freed blacks in the long run. When Douglass persisted in his support for giving blacks the ballot, Johnson insisted on the rightness of his cause. Later, an angry president concluded, "those damned sons of bitches thought they had me in a trap! I know that damned Douglass; he's just like any nigger, and he would sooner cut a white man's throat than not."[7]

A week later, Johnson, in much the same spirit, vetoed an extension of the Bureau of Refugees, Freemen, and Abandoned Lands. Congress in 1865 had created the Freedmen's Bureau, as it was called, to aid in the transition from slavery to freedom, but Johnson found it unnecessary and opposed providing special benefits for one class of people. In its brief period of existence, the Freedmen's Bureau issued more than fifteen million rations and provided medical care to a million people. It allocated $5 million for black schools, helped protect blacks from landowners, tried to preserve their freedom of contract, and was solicitous of their new civil rights.

Johnson also rejected allowing military authorities to punish individuals who violated black civil rights—an objection based on some legitimate concern over the proper role of the armed forces in peacetime. The president also concluded that a bill that proposed confiscating land from former owners lacked legal due process. Several days later, Johnson went even further and in a public speech honoring George Washington's birthday gave an informal talk to citizens who serenaded him at the White House. Johnson, in his old plebeian stump style, attacked the abolitionists and rebels alike, seeing both as extremists who would break up the government. He went on to accuse Radicals, such as Thaddeus Stevens, Charles Sumner, and Wendell Phillips, of laboring to destroy the republic. Melodramatically, he offered up his own life on the altar of the Union as a tribute to self-government. Critics charged that these unfortunate remarks both demeaned the presidency and alienated even further activist elements in Congress.

In late March 1866, the Congress passed a civil rights bill and sent it on to Johnson, who promptly vetoed it. The bill established a definition of citizenship ("all persons born or naturalized in the United States and not subject to any foreign power, excluding Indians not taxed"); gave citizens, regardless of race, color, or previous condition of servitude, the rights to make and enforce contracts, bring suit, give testimony, and conduct property transactions; granted equal benefits of the law and equal justice regardless of race; established penalties for those officials who violated those rights; and granted federal courts the authority to review the situation if state courts failed to enforce these rights. The president vigorously opposed federal intrusion into state disputes and issues, saying it violated the Tenth Amendment. And he insisted, "the distinction of race and color is by the bill made to operate in favor of the colored and against the white race." While Congress had upheld Johnson's veto of the Freedmen's Bureau bill, this time it rose up and even moderates moved to override the president on the civil rights bill.[8]

On April 2, Johnson declared the rebellion over (except in Texas, which had not reorganized its state government), and the Supreme Court usually used this date as the official end of the Civil War. Congress though was becoming increasing hostile to Johnson, and it passed a bill providing for statehood for Colorado and for Nebraska, and mandating a new Freedman's Bureau—measures Johnson had publicly opposed. Then in June, Congress adopted the Fourteenth Amendment, which institutionalized in the Constitution many of the principles of the civil rights bill. Although presidents are not a part of the amendment process, Johnson insisted on denouncing the proposal and urged the states to reject it. Congress had implemented ratification by insisting that "readmitted" states had to approve the amendment before they would be allowed full rights to participate in the federal government—an obvious contradiction that acknowledged the right of states to amend the Constitution while they were not acknowledged as full-fledged states for representation purposes.

In the spring of 1866, the president insisted on using his office and federal patronage to support candidates who advocated his views on Reconstruction. Between August and November, he removed over a thousand postmasters and customs and revenue agents to ensure loyalty to his principles. Working with his allies, the president went on to support the creation of a new Union party, which met in Philadelphia in August. That coalition of moderate Republican and Democrats condemned secession, supported both emancipation and states' rights, and attacked the arbitrary centralization of power in Congress.

The president added to the political fire of the summer by "a swing around the circle"—a trip from Baltimore to New York, Detroit, and St. Louis. Radicals deliberately sent hecklers to challenge and disrupt him, and he, unfortunately, responded in kind. Johnson's passionate denunciations brought forth criticism and did not aid his cause. The election results were almost totally negative for him, the chances for a new Union majority were dashed, and the president faced a hostile Congress with the ability to override by a two-thirds majority his vetoes. During the campaign, the Republicans had hit hard at Johnson's policies and at Southern treatment of the freed blacks. Their case was helped by serious race riots in Memphis and New Orleans, which provided evidence to many voters of the abdication of federal responsibility.

Johnson's secretary of navy, Gideon Welles, judged that the campaign had been mismanaged, and that the Unionists had neglected their constitutional themes. The president, on the other hand, refused to heed his advisors' counsel that he allow Congress to take the initiative on Reconstruction after the election. In January 1867, Johnson vetoed a bill to extend suffrage to blacks in the District of Columbia, a proposal that had been overwhelmingly rejected by whites in the jurisdiction in December 1865.

The most important congressional legislation of the session, though, was the First Reconstruction Act passed in the spring of 1867. Pushed by moderate Republicans and accepted by the Radicals, the bill authorized dividing the South (excluding Tennessee) into five military districts, each under the command of a military officer appointed by the president. These generals were allowed to establish military commissions to try civilians even where regular courts were operating. The bill mandated procedures for voter registration and the establishment of new state constitutions with provisions for black voting, ratification of the Fourteenth Amendment, and exclusion of former Confederate leaders.[9]

Johnson vetoed the bill, attacking its provision that allowed for military trials and castigated the "absolute despotism" of military rule. The Supreme Court, however, in the *Milligan* case, with an opinion delivered in 1866, had already ruled that martial law could not be imposed where civilian courts were functioning. Both houses of Congress passed the bill over Johnson's veto, and battle lines were drawn for the larger struggle to come.

More important, Congress approved two measures that seriously challenged the executive authority of the president. The Army Appropriations Act contained a provision that General Grant could not be assigned to duty outside the capital without his approval and that all orders to the army from the president or secretary of war had to go through Grant to be valid. Drafted by Secretary of War Edwin Stanton and pushed by the Radicals, the bill clearly was aimed at putting Grant beyond the reach of the president and under the protection of the Radicals. Johnson, concerned about the total military appropriations bill, signed the measure with a strong protest about the provision.

The second measure dealt with tenure in office and prohibited the president from removing any civil officer whose appointment required Senate approval. Such appointments were to last throughout a president's term plus one month, or unless the Senate concurred in the removal. The purpose was to protect Stanton—but he was, in fact, an appointment made by Lincoln and was not covered by the statute anyhow. The bill was vetoed and passed again overwhelmingly. The issue of removal had been discussed in the early years of the republic, especially in the first term of Washington, and the matter was less clear then than is generally assumed today when nearly every authority accepts the president's right to remove subordinates. The Tenure of Office Act, however, was not a philosophical innovation of the Radicals: it was a dagger aimed at Johnson's recalcitrance. At this time, in the spring of 1867, some members of Congress began considering impeachment of the president—the only approved method for removing a sitting executive.

At first, the prospects of impeachment were improbable. When the Radicals pushed in the House for articles of impeachment, the full body was unwilling to follow. Some of the charges were absurd—such as that Johnson was involved in Lincoln's murder or that he had incited racial violence in the South. Johnson generally ignored the charges, went about his obstinate business, and avoided attacking his accusers. Meanwhile, he vetoed the Second Reconstruction Act, citing in part its provisions allowing military supervision of state constitutional conventions.

Johnson pursued two strategies in dealing with Congress—he scrupulously observed the letter of the laws passed, and he continued to assert publicly the prerogatives of a strong executive. Faced with a disloyal secretary of war and a commanding general who was cautious and politically ambitious, the president was in a sensitive position. When in the summer of 1867 Johnson asked for and received from his attorney general an opinion limiting the powers of the five district commanders to register or disenfranchise voters, Stanton and Grant drafted surreptitiously a bill that Congress passed to overturn that opinion. The president vetoed the bill and went on to observe that within a period of less than a year, the legislative branch "had attempted to strip the executive department of the Government of some of its essential powers." He bluntly warned,

"Whilst I hold the chief executive authority of the United States, whilst the obligation rests upon me to see that all the laws are faithful executed, I can never willingly surrender that trust or the powers given for its execution."[10]

Toward the end of July 1867, the president moved to dismiss Stanton from the War Department and relieve Radical favorite General Philip Sheridan from the New Orleans command. Shrewdly, he asked Grant to take over temporarily the War Department. Stanton, who had originally argued that the Tenure of Office Act was unconstitutional, now cited it as grounds for refusing to leave office. The president, in fact, "suspended" Stanton and appointed Grant as "Secretary of War *ad interim*," thus following the provisions of the act itself. To add to the congressional fires, Johnson in September decided to extend even further his pardon policy, restoring all rights, privileges, and property (except slaves) to nearly all former Confederates who took an oath of loyalty. The only exceptions were the highest officials of the Confederate government, flag officers of the Confederate army and navy, those involved in the assassination of Lincoln, and those who had mistreated prisoners of war.

While Johnson directly challenged the Radicals and most of the moderate Republicans in Congress and positioned himself for the Democratic nomination for the presidency in 1868, the election returns in late 1867 brought him good news. Democrats did well in New York, New Jersey, Pennsylvania, Maryland, Ohio, and California; in Kansas, Ohio, and even Minnesota, black suffrage proposals were defeated. The president picked up on the popular backlash and denounced the Republicans as a party that sought to clothe "the negro race with the political privileges torn from white men." Still, though, the House of Representatives in early December 1867 refused to vote articles of impeachment since many believed that specific violations of law were necessary to take such a drastic step; a majority of Republicans registered themselves against going ahead with impeachment proceedings.[11]

Then in January 1868, the Senate by a vote of 35 to 6 refused to approve the removal of Stanton. Before this conflict reached the boiling point, Grant had quietly watched as he saw President Johnson reverting back to his strict constructionist past and engaging in vituperations against the Radicals and the black race. He privately characterized Johnson's speeches as a national disgrace, and he feared that the president might attempt to declare Congress an unconstitutional assembly; very few people knew that Grant ordered the weapons in Southern arsenals shipped north. Finally, Grant became intimidated by the whole controversy and, thinking of his own political future, literally left his office at the War Department and went back to his headquarters as commanding general, an action that signified defiance and desertion to Johnson. The president was furious with Grant's behavior, but the general noted that he had just realized that the Tenure of Office Act provided for a jail sentence and a fine for individuals who dared violate its provisions! Johnson with some justification regarded Grant as having been deceitful, and the president's criticisms made their way through the capital rumor mills. Johnson's choice to replace Grant was General Lorenzo Thomas. He proved to be timid and unsure in assuming Stanton's War Department position, and eventually he was arrested in a test case in the tenure of office controversy.

On February 24, 1868, the House of Representatives impeached Johnson; the president's response was cool and collected. Overall, many moderate Republicans had hesitated until the Stanton issue forced their hand. The case against Johnson was clearly contrived and weak. But the two branches of government had reached a logjam on the issue of Reconstruction, and the president was clearly not going to allow what he perceived as his prerogatives to be whittled away.

It is common to cite Johnson's errors up to this point, and there are many to cite. But it is forgotten that the Radicals also went after the third branch of government—the Supreme Court—and instigated legislation to curtail the power of the Supreme Court to review appeals from military commissioners. The Radicals sought to restrict the Court's power to overrule an act of Congress by declaring it unconstitutional, and the House of Representatives approved a bill requiring two-thirds concurrence in such a case; the Senate did not act on the bill but later it did agree with the House to curtail the high court's jurisdiction in habeas corpus cases. Rarely in American history has the appellate jurisdiction of the Court been limited, although that threat has been made periodically by various disaffected congressmen in the past two centuries.

There are two aspects of Johnson's estrangement from the Republican party and his near conviction that are often overlooked: the role of General Grant and the army, and the concern over the high court's new conservatism on war-related issues. Both complications are somewhat linked together in the volatile politics of the late 1860s. For the Republicans to stay in power, they needed the cooperation and support of the army, especially Grant, and the army officers in turn had to have congressional aid against the threat of civil suits brought because of official acts committed during the war. In a series of cases in late 1866 and early 1867, the Supreme Court began to challenge the use of military justice when civilian courts were open in the area, and it also stuck down the requirements of test oaths.

In April 1867, a majority of the state governors and a growing list of Confederate leaders were urging an end to resistance and encouraging full participation in the creation of new state governments required by Congress. In the fall elections of 1867, the Democrats did rather well, and Republicans began to see the vivid importance of black voters to the future of their party. In 1865, proposals to enfranchise the blacks had been uniformly defeated across the land, and only in five New England states were blacks granted full suffrage, with partial suffrage in New York. But by 1867, Republican officeholders supported a change and only California and Pennsylvania opposed blacks voting.

The actions against Johnson then came partially as a result of the Radicals' fear of the Democratic party's and the South's growing strength and the critical scrutiny of the Supreme Court toward military administration. Blaming Johnson's policies, Radicals joining with moderate Republicans were able to move the impeachment process through the House; to those who counseled an accommodation, the president insisted to Colonel William Moore that if he could not "be president in fact, he will not be president in name alone." Later he objected, "Impeachment of me for violating the Constitution! Damn them! Have I not been struggling ever since I have been in this chair to uphold the Constitution which they trample under foot!"[12]

The main charges against the president were various violations of the Tenure of Office Act and the Conspiracies Act of 1861, bypassing Grant in giving orders to a subordinate officer, unlawfully controlling the disbursement of government funds, and being unmindful of the high duties and dignity of his office. In addition, he was alleged to have challenged the constitutional legality of Congress in August 1866. The House articles were presented to the Senate by several Radical and moderate congressmen, but the rhetoric of some of the former actually hurt the case with wild charges that the president was a murderer and a robber! Johnson wisely kept quiet and did not appear before the Senate or in the galleries, despite his own desires to confront his accusers. His defense counselors were superbly capable attorneys who focused the debate into narrow legal channels where Johnson's record was the strongest. They pointed out Stanton's early objections to the Tenure of Office Act, that the secretary was not even covered by it, and how the president had tried to get a court test of the controversial bill.

During the trial, the president was approached confidentially through third parties, on behalf of a moderate Republican, Senator James Grimes, who urged that Johnson appoint an acceptable person to replace Stanton. The president forwarded the name of General John Schofield in Virginia, one of the original five district commanders and a moderate Republican also. Senator Edmund G. Ross of Kansas, to be immortalized by John F. Kennedy in his *Profiles in Courage*, cast the deciding vote against conviction. Ross had received assurances from Johnson that he would transmit to Congress the Radical-styled constitutions of South Carolina and Arkansas, which the president did. However, Johnson refused one other offer of assistance—a deal with Senator Samuel C. Pomeroy of Kansas who allegedly was willing to trade his vote for some common patronage.

Against the backdrop of Chief Justice Salmon Chase's procedural rulings, which favored the president's positions and the careful strategy of the defense, the Radical case began to unravel. In the Senate, the first charge in the impeachment resolutions failed by one vote to command the two-thirds majority, passing only 35 to 19. Seven Republicans had voted not guilty, but there is some evidence that four others would have changed their vote if it became necessary to stop a conviction. Obviously, many of the moderate Republicans opposed pushing Johnson over the brink and resorting to impeachment and conviction for political purposes. Also, since Ben Wade, who was president pro tem of the Senate, would succeed Johnson, moderates recoiled from entrusting the executive position to a person seen by some as a demagogue who favored women's rights, the interests of the working man, and inflationary economics.[13]

In the last year of his presidency, Johnson continued to veto Congress's Reconstruction policies, which that body overrode repeatedly as before. He extended his pardoning power to cover more and more Southern leaders. But while Johnson's Reconstruction policies generated the most controversy, his administration did launch important initiatives elsewhere. The United States acquired

Alaska ("Seward's folly"), checked French ambitions in Mexico, and fostered railroad expansion.

Johnson was denied the Democratic nomination for another term in July 1869. "Why should they not take me up?" he wondered. It was said that he had no party, no real organization. "Caesar had a party, and Pompey and Crassus had a party, but . . . the commonwealth had none," Johnson glumly concluded. The Democrats, however, were uninterested in classical allusions as they turned to a tried formula: a Northerner with Southern support, Horatio Seymour of New York. His opponent, General Grant, would prevail, but would carry with him into office initially with support from even some segments of the South.

Johnson returned to Tennessee, but in January 1875, he was elected as one of his state's U.S. senators and joined in March the very body that had tried him for high crimes and misdemeanors. He attacked Grant's Reconstruction policy and his sending of troops into Louisiana to support a Radical state government which Johnson saw as an attempt to subvert democracy and strengthen the military. On July 31, 1875, he died and, at his request, a copy of the Constitution was placed under his head.

GRANT'S INDULGENCES

Lincoln's uncertainties and Johnson's stubbornness led to a national policy of Reconstruction that was ambiguous and mismanaged. Grant would become the recipient of that troubling legacy, just as he was the beneficiary of the slaughter called the Civil War. Historians have generally praised his generalship, but have judged him to be the very worst of chief executives. Leaving aside the parlor game of ranking the presidents, we can see a much more complex record. Grant is surely not the Platonic ideal of a president, but neither was he a bushbum on the circuit. He trusted friends of dubious character too much and too long, often to the point of obstructing justice to protect them. But he was also at times a fairly strong executive, and one of the few presidents in the nineteenth century to make a determined effort, although often unsuccessful, to lead the legislative branch of government.

The tale of Grant's rise is cut out of American whole cloth. He was a graduate of West Point, compiled a noteworthy record in the Mexican War, and then left the army to try his hand at business.

Despite a good marriage, his personal life was disappointing, and he moved from one failure to another, often consoling himself in a haze of alcoholism. When the secession movement began, Grant quickly realized that civil war would bring the end of slavery as a system and as a way of life. With that foresight, he was remarkably ahead of Lincoln, or at least of Lincoln's public sentiments. Grant returned to the army as a commissioned officer and was one of the few major West Point graduates whose allegiances were unequivocally committed to the Union. With the continued support of his local congressman, Elihu B. Washburne, he was commissioned a brigadier general.[14]

In the morass of Union army politics and the confusion of the war in the West, Grant established a reputation as a general who would fight. Lincoln, who was desperate for victories especially before the election of 1864, kept an eye on the somber warrior, and on several occasions stepped in to prevent his career from being sidetracked by jealous superiors. Grant established through his campaigns a new style of warfare—not the flashing cuts and moves of Lee or Stonewall Jackson, or the brilliant maneuvers of Napoleon or Caesar. He was in many ways the father of the modern war of attrition, a strategy that was to reach its greatest fruition in the European wars of the twentieth century. Grant knew that the North's major asset was that it had more men to spend in battle, and he waged a series of methodical sieges that slowly drove the Confederates out of the West, away from the Mississippi, and finally down the eastern peninsula away from the Potomac River and the capital. In the process, he compiled a record of incredible bloodletting—the names of Shiloh and Cold River are still synonymous with the nightmare of conventional warfare. The Civil War was one of the most brutal wars in the nineteenth century, and more Americans died in that struggle than in all the other U.S. wars, including World War II, combined. A humane Lincoln shuddered as the casualties came in, pleading with Grant for less cost; but in the end, he concurred with Grant's strategy. The general won battles and that was what counted.

When the war ended, Grant served under Andrew Johnson, but tried carefully and unsuccessfully to avoid getting caught between the executive and Congress. At times, he seemed weak, contrived, and even less than candid in that power play. But he recognized that it was not his struggle, and he still commanded the allegiances of the North and the respect of many Southerners. When he accepted the nomination for the presidency, he added to his remarks the simple wish, "Let there be peace." The words were both soothing and electrifying. Although Grant had never held public office, he received 3,012,833 popular votes to Seymour's 2,703,249, and took 211 of the 294 electoral votes, thus becoming at forty-six the youngest man ever to hold the presidency up to that time.

The great issue confronting the new president was the status of Reconstruction. He had put distance between himself and Johnson's laissez-faire policies, and yet he too wished for an end to animosities. Deep down, he felt that the best solution would have been keeping military governments in the Southern states rather than struggling to create new civilian governments that either rested on uneducated black voters or on the promises of former traitors.[15]

The history of Reconstruction has gone through a series of revisions. The usual stereotype is that it was a time of trial and injustice for the conquered white peoples of the South. The former Confederate states are portrayed as being run by carpetbaggers, scalawags, and opportunistic and vengeful blacks who ruled the South and left it bankrupt, corrupt, and impotent. In fact, the treatment of the Confederate leadership and the people of the rebellious region is unique in the chronicle of history for its generosity. After having precipitated a terrible war and waged it for four long years, the South suffered no real revenge at all. Only a few top leaders were ever incarcerated for long, only one officer was tried for "war crimes," no property was systematically confiscated, except for human beings held in slavery. A close examination of the carpetbaggers (Northerners in the South holding office) shows that many of them came not in the 1870s to exploit the region, but usually right after the war to invest in and work in the South. Black-controlled legislatures, few and far between, did indeed run up high bills, and some corruption surely occurred. But much of the large increase in public expenditure went to build up social services, such as free public education, long neglected by the planter aristocracy. The real atrocities that greeted Grant's inauguration were not perpetrated on the whites by the meager occupation army of four thousand men in the South, but by the rising violence directed by the Ku Klux Klan and the White Councils on black voters.[16]

There were still some concerned whites who genuinely cared about the newly released slaves—the Freedman Bureau officials, some old abolitionists, and elements of the Radical Republicans. Their legacy can be seen in the Fifteenth Amendment, which granted to former slaves the right to vote, and in a series of civil rights bills that aimed to both reconstruct the South and guarantee protection to the blacks who voted almost uniformly Republican. In dealing with the problems of Reconstruction, Grant was more "radical" than Lincoln and more sympathetic to the problems of the former slaves than Johnson. He hated the controversies of Reconstruction politics, but as an old soldier, he was unwilling to see the victories of the battlefield undone so easily in peacetime. At times, he did walk away from the problems of the freed slaves in his charge, especially at the end of his second term, but compared to the racist Johnson and the accommodating Hayes he remained a figure of comparative strength. Overall though, in the period from 1865 through the 1870s and beyond, the life of the blacks in the South deteriorated rapidly. Freedom was granted without the prerequisites that would make liberation and self-sufficiency possible.

Grant started off his term by promising that he would administer the laws, all of them, even if he disagreed with them—an obvious allusion to Johnson. He avoided asking for the advice of Congress or party leaders and named a fairly weak cabinet of his own choosing. One observer of the time, John Bigelow, concluded that "His Cabinet are merely staff officers, selected apparently out of motives of gratitude or for pecuniary favors received from them. His relatives and old friends were among the first provided for . . . No president before was ever got in the family way so soon after inauguration."[17]

Grant almost immediately came into conflict with the haughty Charles Sumner who was chairing the Senate Committee on Foreign Relations. Sumner had been a problem to Lincoln as well, but the wily Illinois politician courted him with a mixture of flattery and corn syrup and had him on board—at least as much as anyone could—in the later years of his term. Grant was used to command, not persuasion. Lincoln understood better that politics is an occupation where one must feast with those you would rather not talk to under normal circumstances. Leaders in democracies practice the arts of genial acquaintanceship and hypocrisy not because of character flaws, but because of the dynamics of limited power and fickle public sentiment.

The first major foreign problem Grant faced involved outstanding claims with Great Britain that arose out of the Civil War. On that issue, Sumner was most obstreperous, and on that issue the president and his competent secretary of state, Hamilton Fish, were most successful. During the war, the British had recognized the Confederate states as belligerents and had allowed three ships to be fitted in their yards. The ships were then manned by Confederate sailors and visited havoc on Union shipping. After the war, the United States government demanded reparations. The British government finally consented, but by then American sentiment had hardened, and the Senate in 1869 rejected by a vote of 54 to 1 a joint convention on the dispute. Sumner took a major role in upgrading American claims, asking not $15 million, as had been discussed, but $125 million. He then added to the bill a $2 billion charge, which Sumner saw as Britain's share for encouraging the Confederates. Buttressed by increasing opposition to British rule in Ireland and a desire to annex Canada, foes of a moderate treaty seemed to be prevailing when Grant stepped in.

With a strong push from Secretary of State Fish, the president agreed to the Treaty of Washington, which provided for arbitration, one of the first major uses of that device in international disputes. Finally, the tribunal in September 1872 awarded the sum of $15,500,000 in gold to the United States for damages done by the three vessels fitted in British yards.

In foreign policy, Grant had no problem with expanding the U.S. boundaries, but his interests pointed not so much to conflict with Great Britain over Canada, but to the south: Cuba, Santo Domingo, and Mexico. Fascinated by the dreams of Manifest Destiny of his youth, Grant decided without much consultation to send a personal envoy, Orville Babcock, to work out a deal with the authorities in Santo Domingo (now the Dominican Republic). Grant was informed that for a mere $1.5 million, the price of the Santo Domingo debt, the United States could annex that small nation. Secretary of State Fish, however, was outraged at the proposal, and the cabinet rejected it. But Grant taking a cue from Lincoln walked to Sumner's house and there made a persuasive case for ratification. He left assuming that the senator had pledged his support. While Sumner did characterize himself in the conversation as a true Republican and an administration man, he ended up opposing the treaty, criticized the president's lobbying of the Senate, and expressed his personal opposition to ending the independent status of one of the few black republics in the world. Despite the president's heavy pressure, the treaty was defeated by a tie vote, 28 to 28. Grant returned to the issue in December 1870 and proposed a resolution of annexation as had been used in adding Texas to the Union. Both houses of Congress adopted a resolution by Senator Oliver P. Morton to create a special commission to examine the issue. That group prepared a rather factual statement about the resources of that nation, but Grant's proposal was never approved. The president's attention then turned to Cuba where Grant wanted to issue a proclamation according belligerent rights to the insurgents fighting Spanish rule. However, Fish opposed that proposal as well and insisted that the president refrain from recognizing the rebels. Once again the executive had been thwarted by less-adventuresome minds.[18]

On the domestic front, the president in his first term made clear his commitment to return to a currency based on specie and the retirement of greenbacks. On March 18, 1869, the president pledged the United States to pay in gold or its equivalent all U.S. notes and bonds, except where otherwise especially exempted. The results would be to tighten the currency flow, encourage deflation, and create problems for private debtors, especially farmers and small businessmen. Tighter currency is generally a prescription for a depression, and Grant—the failed small businessman—most surely must have known what the consequences would be.

What he did not know was the web of speculation that was being woven around him by members of his own family. At this time, two New York financiers, Jay Gould and James Fisk, were heavily involved in speculative gambles, manipulating the gold market, and trying to control U.S. Treasury reserves. To help them, Gould sought to get Grant's brother-in-law to introduce him to the president so as to express directly his views. Gould and Fisk were successful, but listened with horror as the president remarked in passing that "there was a certain amount of fictitiousness about the prosperity of the country and that the bubble might as well be tapped one way or another." The president became convinced of the wisdom of Gould's arguments and let it be known that he opposed forcing down the price of gold. Gould promptly bought gold reserves for himself, Grant's sister, the assistant treasurer, and Horace Porter, the president's private secretary. Porter repudiated the purchase when he learned of it, however.

Grant meanwhile had become suspicious of Gould and had his sister and her husband warned about the follies of speculation. The government sold quantities of gold, and the price tumbled from $162 to $135 an ounce rather quickly. Gould sensed that probability, and sold heavily, but his counterpart Fisk did not, and angry traders threatened to rip apart his offices. Wall Street analysts called that Friday, September 24, 1869, "Black Friday."[19]

The currency situation was compounded by one of those mystifying decisions that only the Supreme Court can visit on a free people. On February 7, 1870, the Court, headed by Chief Justice Salmon Chase, ruled in *Hepburn v. Griswold* that the Legal Tender Act was unconstitutional. That bill had been drawn up by Chase himself when he was secretary of the treasury, and it had authorized the creation of greenbacks, or money not backed by gold or silver. The Court claimed that this inflated money deprived people of their property by forcing creditors to accept dollars of lesser value than they had lent. On the day of the decision, Grant had coincidentally sent to the Senate the names of two proposed justices to fill vacancies on the Court. On May 1, 1871, the Supreme Court, with two new votes, overruled the *Hepburn* case leading critics to charge incorrectly that President Grant had deliberately packed the Court.[20]

The currency problems were a continuing source of concern for Grant and would play a part in the depression of the 1870s, which continued in some parts of the nation well into this century. But the most intractable issue the president faced in his first term and into the second was Reconstruction. As the rebellious states acceded to ratifying the Fourteenth and Fifteenth Amendments, conservative white politicians became more visible especially in Tennessee, Georgia, South Carolina, and Virginia. Democrat strength was growing, black voters were being intimidated, and the Klan and White Councils became a staple in those regions. In North Carolina, Governor William W. Holden declared two counties in a state of insurrection, and a hundred citizens were arrested under martial law. The state's chief justice issued a writ of habeas corpus to free the individuals incarcerated and Holden ignored it. The Democrats then appealed to the federal courts, and Grant ordered a U.S. regiment to execute the order. Meanwhile, the Democrats swept the state elections, and the governor surrounded the state capital with black troops for protection. He eventually became the first governor ever impeached and removed from office.

Faced with cries of white resistance and black repression, Congress, in a last gasp of Radical Republican fire, passed three "enforcement acts," which Grant signed. On May 31, 1870, the president approved the first act aimed at suppressing the Ku Klux

Klan, which authorized the president to use the military to aid the judiciary and enforce the Fourteenth Amendment. On February 28, 1871, a second act placed electors for members of Congress under federal protection, provided for appointment of supervisors by federal judges to ensure a fair vote, and empowered U.S. marshals to appoint deputies to prevent violations of voting rights. On April 20, 1871, a new Congress passed a third act, which gave the executive extraordinary powers to enforce the Fourteenth Amendment including the right to suspend the writ of habeas corpus until the next session of Congress ended. Grant used these powers only once when on the advice of the governor he suspended the writ in nine counties in South Carolina to curtail violence. Later the Supreme Court was to declare the so-called Ku Klux Klan Act unconstitutional. In his second term, the president confronted racial and political disturbances and sent additional U.S. troops to Louisiana, Mississippi, and South Carolina.

But on March 22, 1872, Grant in a very different mood of reconciliation signed a generous amnesty act, which removed the disabilities of all Confederates except senators and representatives who had served in the Thirty-sixth and the Thirty-seventh Congress, officers in the judicial, military, and naval services of the United States, and heads of departments and foreign ministers of the United States who had all joined the rebellion. Later, even these former officers of the United States who had turned their backs on their government were eventually restored as well. However, when Senator Sumner tried to add provisions to end racial discrimination on common carriers, in theaters, inns, schools, cemeteries, churches, and juries, his bill was voted down. He noted the irony in looking at both of these bills, and concluded, "the time has not come for amnesty. You must be just to the colored race before you are generous to former rebels."[21]

As he approached reelection, Grant dealt with several other issues as well. He and many other Republicans supported the party's tradition of a high tariff, and despite considerable agitation the "reform" Tariff Act of 1870 reduced the high Morrill Tariff by only a modest 5 percent, mainly on pig iron. Later, in 1872, Congress dropped the tariff on tea and coffee and lowered duties on other items as well.

Most unusual though was his comparatively tolerant attitude toward the Indians. Unlike most military men of his time, Grant had made his reputation in the Civil War rather than Indian fighting.

During his earlier service, he was genuinely disturbed by the treatment of the tribes and in his inaugural address, he asked for a more humane policy. This so-called Peace Policy had four major components: the end of a treaty system that supposedly dealt with each tribe as a separate nation; the treatment of Indians as individuals rather than as members of a tribal community; the predominance of reservations in tribal life; and an accentuation of educational efforts to enable Indians to gain full citizenship. Grant's policy of "civilization and ultimate citizenship" was aimed at the eventual assimilation of the Indians into the mainstream of American life. Central to this transformation was the Indian agent, and Grant clearly tried to attract a better class of men to that office before corruption caught up with his good intentions.

During his terms in office, however, some two hundred battles were fought between the government and the tribes, and the climate for reconciliation vanished. In addition, many of the tribes did not want to be assimilated. Their ways of thinking, their values and assumptions were such that they rejected the very goals Grant offered. The reservation system often left them with undesirable tracts of land, and extreme poverty resulted from their exile into these contained areas. In the end, the Peace Policy did not succeed as Grant and other white reformers had hoped. Yet it was a statement of the president's good intentions, a sentiment not widely shared in that century by presidents or common folk.[22]

Thus, as the president entered the 1872 campaign, he had compiled a mixed record. He was being systematically attacked not just by the Democrats, but also by a reform element in his own party called "Liberal Republicans." The Liberals were a strange collection of editors, intellectuals, and disgruntled politicians who were unhappy with Grant in particular and with the general drift of the party. They came from the older Protestant middle classes and supported civil service reform, free trade, hard currency, and a politics cleansed of the rough and tumble. They generally favored less government and purer politics, and cared little for the problems of the freed slaves.

The Republicans named Grant and Henry Wilson of Massachusetts on their ticket and titled them "The Tanner" and "The Cobbler." Grant had hated his years as a workingman, but now this workingman's ticket was the party's theme. The party counted on the general to hold on to the black, the soldier, and the Midwest vote. Worrying little about ideology, the Democratic party turned around and nominated the Liberal Republican candidate, Horace Greeley. Some opponents of Grant had reservations about this choice; William Cullen Bryant wrote, "We who know Mr. Greeley know that his administration, should he be elected, cannot be otherwise than shamefully corrupt. . . . There is no abuse or extravagance into which that man through the infirmity of his judgment may not be betrayed."[23]

Grant, however, had correctly judged the public sentiment. Greeley carried only Maryland, Georgia, Missouri, and Kentucky. The president received 286 of the 349 electoral votes and his popular majority was 3,597,132 to 2,834,125. Several weeks later a weary Greeley died, and Grant, in typically magnanimous fashion, showed up for the funeral. His second term, like so many presidential second terms, was markedly less successful than the first, and the seeds of corruption came out in full bloom. Grant's penchant for placing his trust in dubious associates, his tendency to name family members to public offices, and his lack of foresight in understanding the consequences of his actions led to a litany of charges of corruption and nepotism.[24]

In fairness to Grant, however, some of these charges grew out of a milieu he did not create. The Civil War was a time of graft, corruption, speculation, and shameless profiteering. We sometimes forget that the great Lincoln administration, in gearing up for war, presided over a less than simon-pure operation. The political culture of the times was a far cry from the civic virtue of the Founding Fathers or the later moralism of the Progressives. It is odd that Ulysses S. Grant, a man who was personally honest and a sworn foe of profiteering, should have his times so linked with the darker side of politics.

The speculation of Gould and Fisk had come dangerously close to his family, although not touching Grant himself. Then, in his second term, two major scandals hit—the Crédit Mobilier affair and the "Back Pay Steal." The first affair really predated in some aspects the Grant administration and was more of a congressional scandal than a reflection on the executive branch. Initially, the *New York Sun* leveled a charge of bribery against a company organized by promoters of the Union Pacific Railroad, which set up ways to divert the profits from railroad construction to themselves. In order to thwart any government intervention, the directors spread large blocs of stock among influential people. In the fall of 1867, 343 shares of stock had been distributed at a low price to key congressmen and senators, including Schuyler Colfax, Roscoe Conkling, James A. Garfield, James G. Blaine, and Henry Wilson. A congressional committee cleared most of these men later of any wrongdoing. A second indignation—last minute raises for major officers in the government (with some retroactive arrangements)—prompted a further howl. Grant signed the appropriations bill, but asked for the item veto—a proposal that has been made by various presidents and that has been consistently rejected by Congress. Eventually, in December 1873, Congress in response to public pressure repealed almost all the raises.

But on too many other occasions and in too many other ways, the stench of corruption, malfeasance, and nepotism filled Washington, and Grant was clearly responsible for mismanaging the executive branch. The president at times seemed almost to impede justice or to show more scorn for those who uncovered corruption than toward those who betrayed his trust in the first place. Most especially Grant's crucial role in crippling the prosecutions arising from the Whiskey Ring and his defense of Secretary of War W. W. Belknap are a part of a chronicle of disgrace unmatched until the Nixon administration. Even Warren Harding, who was easily fooled, displayed a true sense of righteous indignation at the rottenness around him.

The scandals were numerous and far-reaching. As he began his second term, Grant became even more careless. In March 1873, the president reappointed his brother-in-law, James F. Casey, as collector of customs in New Orleans. Casey had been involved in corrupt activities and had been the subject of a congressional inquiry. Then in September, Grant nominated Alexander Shepherd, the very symbol of boss politics, to be the head of the Board of Works for the District of Columbia. The president's appointments, suggested to him by a kitchen cabinet of private advisors, consistently showed a general disregard for public opinion. The decisive master of Shiloh and Cold Springs floundered about as he looked for a new chief justice after the death of Salmon Chase; and when the attorney general position also opened up, he named an inexperienced lawyer, George Williams, to that post.

By 1874–75, the administration was plagued by a series of major investigations that unveiled the true bankruptcy of Grant's leadership. The most famous was the "Whiskey Ring," a loose collection of distillers, revenue agents, and politicians who conspired to defraud the federal government of taxes due on alcohol. The major mover behind the ring was General John A. McDonald, a Missouri colonel and a speculator whom Grant had made supervisor of internal revenue over the region embracing Kansas, Arkansas, the Indian Territory, New Mexico, and Texas. The original intent of the ring was to raise money for the Republican party, but it was soon expanded into an engine of personal graft and embraced a large number of other individuals including Grant's secretary, Orville E. Babcock, and William McKee, the owner of the St. Louis *Democrat* and later *Globe*. In 1874 in St. Louis alone, the distillers defrauded the government out of $1.2 million. The web of corruption spread across the country, and heavy payments were extracted for political protection.[25]

Then in 1875, the young secretary of the treasury, Benjamin H. Bristow, moved decisively to bring the matter to a head, and he was quickly targeted by some of Grant's kitchen cabinet for political extinction. On May 10, he ordered a series of sudden raids to seize ledger books and papers as evidence. Only partially successful, he continued his assault. Meanwhile, Grant replaced his lax attorney general, George Williams, and his shady secretary of interior, Columbus Delano, with new men. Williams's wife had actually attempted to blackmail the president for alleged activities with "a certain lady," although Grant had not even known the woman in question. While this intrigue was taking place, Babcock sought to get the president to name Ben Butler as attorney general, a sure guarantee to end any real investigations of corruption. Grant wavered and started to defend both Williams and Delano as victims of their own bad judgment, of pernicious influences that unfortunately surrounded them, and of trumped-up newspaper allegations. Williams left, but Delano held on longer, despite charges of corruption aimed at his son, because the president hated to terminate a subordinate who was under fire. Grant finally offered the scandal-ridden Interior Department to Babcock's uncle who fortunately declined it. Then the president turned to Zachariah Chandler, another Babcock ally. For attorney general, the president did nominate Edwards Pierrepont, a well-regarded New York lawyer.

Grant continued his efforts to help friends, but it was often at the expense of the public treasury. In early 1875, the president pushed to reimburse a private person for expenses supposedly incurred in the leasing of Samana Bay in Santo Domingo. Grant's contentious secretary of state however refused to support the $50,000 pay-off and rejected an even larger request for $150,000 a year later.

Then in a strange incident, the president intervened at the request of Boss Shepherd to stop a federal district attorney from being removed. Apparently, the district attorney had been involved in the so-called Safe Burglary affair in which government officials had tried to frame a local reformer, Columbus Alexander, on charges of burglary.

While the president waded in dirty waters, Bristow persistently moved to crack the Whiskey Ring. In the spring of 1875, a grand jury returned a string of indictments, and Babcock was supposed to have discussed with General McDonald the possibilities of both of them being pardoned. The president met with McDonald and later expressed his personal sympathy for McDonald's plight. Interestingly enough, the president became increasingly resentful of Bristow for his zeal despite widespread public support for the investigation. Initially, Grant wrote Bristow, "Let no guilty man escape if it can be avoided. . . . No personal consideration should stand in the way of performing a public duty." It was good advice. In one city alone, St. Louis, the grand jury returned 253 indictments.[26]

What the president did not realize at the time was that the evidence at the trial would lead right to Babcock, and that he had sent a telegram to McDonald that lent credence to the view that Babcock was blocking the investigation. When the special prosecutor in St. Louis completed his presentation in the case, he criticized Grant, and subsequently he was dismissed by the attorney general upon order of the president.

Grant's defensiveness was accentuated when newspapers in early 1876 reported that his brother and son were implicated in the whiskey frauds. Also, the president had insisted that federal attorneys not grant immunity to suspected criminals who turned state's evidence, a move that would cripple the government's ability to bring to trial the higher-ups. It is hard to argue that the president did not know what the consequences of his order would be; indeed in 1876 in another instance, he had urged the use of amnesty to get subordinates to incriminate their superiors in order to clean up the Interior Department.

Then stepping over the line even further, the president offered to testify as a character witness in the trial of Babcock. Most of the cabinet officers vigorously protested, arguing that a president should not allow himself to be brought into a court of law as a witness, and they cited Jefferson's refusal to testify in the Burr trial. Grant instead swore out a deposition that the defense used with delight. Partly on the basis of that statement, Babcock was acquitted, and he even attempted to return to his job at Grant's side. Later he was appointed inspector of lighthouses and was subsequently indicted in the Safe Burglary incident. Grant continued to see him, believing that Bristow, the federal prosecutors, and the newspapers had persecuted him unjustly.

At approximately the same time, Secretary of War William Belknap was charged with taking payments for Indian post positions. He immediately resigned on March 2, 1876, to stop any impeachment proceedings, and Grant foolishly accepted the resignation with "great regret." Later a worried president directed the attorney general to see if Belknap would be prosecuted under civil or criminal law. The former secretary had apparently been urged by his high-living wife to receive such kickbacks from agents, and Belknap subsequently acknowledged his late wife's role in his transgressions. The president seemed undisturbed by the matter and never expressed any outrage at the breach of public trust.

The Belknap case was complicated by the question of whether a person who had resigned from public office and was no longer a civil officer of the United States could be impeached under the Constitution. The Senate by a vote of 37 to 29 decided it did have jurisdiction. Belknap was clearly guilty, but the Senate on a straight party vote concluded its deliberations with 37 for conviction and 25 against, substantially under the two-thirds required for impeachment. Of the 25 voting no, 23 insisted that the Senate lacked the jurisdiction to hear the matter in the first place since Belknap had already resigned his federal post.

On March 9, 1876, investigators for the House of Representatives cited the president's brother, Orvil, for putting agents on Indian posts who were supposed to kick back to him part of their profits. Reformer Edwin Godkin summarized those incidents with the observation, "while Belknap allowed his wife to sell traderships and apply the money to his household expenses, the president allowed his brother to steal them and keep the money himself."[27]

The real loser in all of these episodes was, of course, Ulysses S. Grant and his hopes for a third term. Even in the corrupt America of the 1870s, he had gone too far. By 1876, the administration had been discredited and was in shambles. The president became erratic in his public statements and actions. He decided to reorganize his cabinet, and for some strange reason he even took time out from preparing for his State of the Union address to make veiled attacks on the Catholic church. Many of the leaders of the Republican party, who were weary of the controversies, looked for a "reform" candidate for president and eventually settled on Rutherford B. Hayes.

More investigations were begun. In those proceedings, the cabinet supported the president in his desire to limit congressional intrusions into conversations between the executive and department heads. A form of "executive privilege" was clearly supported even by Treasury Secretary Bristow against the legislative branch's aggressive demands. Elsewhere, the American minister to Great Britain, Robert C. Schenck, was exposed as being involved in stock manipulations and returned home. The House of Representatives then charged that Secretary of the Navy George M. Robeson had amassed a fortune while in public office. In July 1876, a House committee found him guilty of malfeasance, but stopped short of charging him with corruption. Its recommendation for impeachment was never acted on because it became involved in the Hayes-Tilden election controversy later that year.

The House's inquiry into the Whiskey Ring trials not only uncovered more of the seamy details of the story, but revealed the president's hostility to the investigations and his efforts to impede their progress. Still another House committee questioned the Justice Department's use of money designated for the Secret Service. With Grant's approval, more than $40,000 was paid to a New York election commissioner to prevent fraud in that city; no accounts or vouchers were furnished, however, and it was alleged that he deserved only $10,000, not $40,000 plus, for such services. It was this transaction that Mrs. George Williams also threatened to expose when the Senate refused to confirm her husband as Grant's choice to be chief justice. She insisted that the money had been used in the reelection campaign of Senator Roscoe Conkling. Later when Grant was about to dismiss her husband, she apparently warned that she would use this information against the president. Perhaps this was the reason that Grant retained George Williams in the cabinet after it was charged Williams diverted department funds for household expenses.[28]

Other investigators uncovered massive fraud in the Freedmen's Bureau, which was started to help poor blacks and which now was connected with the Shepherd machine in the District of Columbia. Another examination of the New Orleans custom house run by Grant's brother-in-law uncovered that federal money had been spent on putting fictitious people on the payroll and on supporting partisan activities. Then the president began a series of firings and dismissals of people who helped push the Whiskey Ring trials—the last act in a chronicle of pettiness and stupidity, if not venality. Finally, Benjamin Bristow left the cabinet as did the civil service reformer, Postmaster Marshall Jewell.

In terms of the vestiges of Reconstruction politics in his last term, Grant refused to send troops into states like South Carolina that had civil disturbances and political factions vying for control. He did send troops into Florida and Louisiana to quell major disturbances and to protect legal boards of canvassers. But his days of enforcing Reconstruction and protecting Republicans and black voters were over. He had never cared much for Rutherford Hayes, and whether Tilden won the presidency in 1876 meant less to him than to the party regulars. In the whole election controversy, he could afford to be statesmanlike and detached—which was probably what the nation needed as the GOP stole the election.

When partisans in his cabinet insisted he take a stronger position in South Carolina and that it was "war and revolution," Grant abruptly countered, "No, no! It is no such thing!" He insisted this time that the federal government had no right to interfere in South Carolina as he had done earlier in Louisiana. Philosophically, he related to his secretary of state that he had opposed the Fifteenth Amendment, that it had done the Negro no good, had been a hindrance to the South, and held no political advantage to the North. Reconstruction was ready to be buried, and Hayes and the Republicans did that as part of a bargain for the White House. Blacks were to be left to their own poverty and the designs of their previous masters. The promise had been betrayed.

The Grant administration took place in an era when city machines had grown incredibly corrupt, when railroad and corporate magnates ravished the land and choked off the free enterprise system they so praised, when the easy morality of war and wartime commerce continued on unabated, and when a mixture of idealism and corruption blended in the so-called reconstructed governments of the South. It was a time of ethical miasma, and surely the roots as well as the fruit of society were infected. But Grant and his cronies were not just victims of those times and those attitudes. They came to embody those views. The president, truly in his time an honest soldier in the service of his country, became a crude spoilsman who permitted the corrupt to plunder and obstructed the cleansing process of justice. How he got to that stage is unclear.

Allan Nevins concluded that his moral obtuseness and his spiritual blindness were due to his long years of friendless hardship and misfortune, that he loved not wisely but too easily. But in a world of alienation and separate souls, such loneliness is not unique to Grant. For leaders of greatness, and for lesser mortals, pain should be a builder of character not an excuse for betraying common hopes.

HAYES AND THE END OF RECONSTRUCTION

The election of 1876 remains one of the most controversial in American history. Through various deals, extensive bitterness, and intense partisanship, Rutherford B. Hayes assumed the presidency after prevailing over Samuel Tilden. Hayes had been a brave officer in the Union army, and later served as a congressman and governor of Ohio. His supporters saw him as an attractive and available candidate from an important state, a man whose reputation for honesty and upright behavior made him a viable alternative to Grant, who desired a third term, and to James G. Blaine, the major challenger. Hayes, everyone's second choice, garnered the nomination and ran against New York Governor Samuel Tilden.

Over the years of Reconstruction, Radical Republicans had helped to enfranchise 700,000 blacks and had cut down white voting by 627,000 through restrictive legislation, but these steps were still not enough for this election. The final vote showed Tilden with a popular margin of 250,000 votes, but the Republicans challenged the electoral count in Florida, Louisiana, and South Carolina where they controlled the political machinery. The Democrats in turn challenged one elector in Oregon who was a postmaster and thus a federal officeholder and disqualified under the Constitution from being an elector. The situation was complicated by the fact that the lame-duck Senate was controlled by the Republicans and the House by the Democrats. Constitutional questions were prejudiced by partisan intrigue; finally the leaders of Congress appointed a special electoral commission composed of fifteen members: five from the Senate, five from the House, and five from the Supreme Court. The swing vote in terms of partisan affiliation was Justice David Davis of Illinois, a respected Independent who unexpectedly was elected to the United States Senate in Illinois. His place was taken by Justice Joseph P. Bradley who voted with the Republicans on every major challenge, giving them an 8 to 7 margin. Thus the Hayes supporters prevailed in the election dispute.[29]

The Democrats accepted this decision, and the explanation usually given is that a bargain was struck whereby Hayes's representatives in late February 1877 agreed that he would remove the last of federal troops occupying Louisiana and South Carolina, thus ending Reconstruction and consequently leaving the freed blacks to their own efforts and to the reemergence of white Southern control. Actually, there were a variety of events during the disputed election period that indicated a pattern of compromises and deals, including promises of aid for Southern internal improvements, a subsidy for the Texas and Pacific Railroad to connect the South to the lucrative West coast, a cabinet seat for a prominent Southerner, and some Southern influence in distributing patronage in that region. In return, Southerners promised not to support a Democratic filibuster to tie up the electoral count and not to obstruct the election of a Hayes confidant, James A. Garfield of Ohio, as speaker of the House of Representatives.

The deals fell through, however. The Southern Democrats refused to stand aside and let Garfield take over and Hayes, remembering the Crédit Mobilier scandal, decided against a subsidy for the Texas and Pacific Railroad. To make sure that Hayes delivered on the promises of his emissaries to remove the troops, Democrats in the House refused to pass the army appropriations bill until the withdrawals were guaranteed. Then, as a sign of the lingering bitterness, two Democratic justices who had also served on the electoral commission did not sit with their colleagues at Hayes's inauguration. Other critics, to show their disdain, labeled Hayes, "His Fraudulency" or "Rutherfraud B. Hayes."[30]

A weary Samuel Tilden refused to lead any crusade against the Republican-Southern Democrat deal, although there was substantial evidence that the presidency was rightfully his. As Garfield noted, "The Democratic businessmen of the country are more anxious for quiet than for Tilden; and the leading Southern Democrats in Congress, especially those who were old Whigs, are saying they have seen war enough, and don't care to follow the lead of their northern associates who, as Ben Hill says, were 'invincible in peace and invisible in war.'"[31]

Thus, as so often happens in politics, the forces of expediency and chicanery prevailed to put an honorable man in office. Hayes proved to be a man of uncommon integrity who appointed a very capable cabinet and reasserted the prerogatives and decency of his office. But he left little in the way of achievements. His inaugural address set the tone emphasizing patriotism and integrity, "he serves his party best who serves his country best." On the Southern issue, Hayes pulled out the last Unionist Reconstruction troops, earning him the title of "statesman of reunion." Actually, as we have seen, Grant had already abandoned most of the remnants of "bayonet rule." The total U.S. Army strength in 1876–77 was only about 25,000 and most were fighting Indians on the plains or protecting the Mexican and Indian frontiers of Texas. Only 3,280 officers and men were on duty in the South at the end of fiscal 1876.[32]

In his political calculations, Hayes thought of restoring the white Republican party in the South by wooing back the traditional Whig element in that region. In the presidential elections from 1836 through 1848, the Whigs polled 2.4 percent more votes than the Democrats, and in the election of 1860, the combined Southern votes of the Douglas Democrats and the Constitutional Union party exceeded the secessionist Breckinridge Democrat ticket. It was thought that if that conservative coalition could be reformed, it would eliminate the need for Republicans to rely on black votes. Overall, the national political scene was rather closely divided in the 1870s with increased party competition in the major states in the east and central areas—Connecticut, New York, New Jersey, Ohio, Indiana, and Illinois. The withdrawal of Reconstruction troops and the systematic disenfranchisement of Southern blacks did not lead, however, to a reemergence of Whig conservatism as Hayes speculated, but to a solid Democratic South that rested in part on white supremacy, white racism, and even white terrorism.

Hayes hoped for major Republican inroads in Maryland, Virginia, Tennessee, and Arkansas, and he appointed numerous Southern Democrats to federal offices to rebuild the party. But the GOP did not do well overall in the South, and the residual Whig influence was submerged under Reconstruction resentment and virulent racism. The president later candidly admitted, "In my anxiety to complete the great work of pacification, I have neglected to give due attention to the civil services—to the appointments and removals. The result is, some bad appointments have been made. Some removals have been mistakes. There have been delays in action. All this, I must now try to correct."[33]

Thus, the president alienated the radical elements, the so-called carpetbaggers and stalwart wings of his own party, abandoned loyal black voters, and was unable to add many Democrat or former Whig voters to the GOP. He realized his plight early on when, in October 1878, the Southern Democrats refused to support Garfield for speaker of the House despite their assurances to the contrary. The congressional races in 1878 also did not go well for the party; not one Republican was elected governor in the South and only three Republicans were sent to Congress from that region. Hayes's observation was, "I am reluctantly forced to admit that the experiment was a failure." Garfield concluded, "The policy of the president has turned out to be a giveaway from the beginning. He has *nulled* suits, discontinued prosecutions, offered conciliation everywhere in the South, while they have spent their time in whetting the knives for any Republican they could find."[34]

Later Hayes would see his reconciliation in a broader perspective, one more philosophical and detached, one that saw the rights of blacks being secured by law and the courts. It would be "a slow process, but the world moves faster than formerly, and it is plain that the politicians on both sides who seek to thrive by agitation and bitterness are losing rapidly their hold," he maintained. All his life Hayes had been by temperament a man of harmony and a conciliator who hated violence and disruption. And his policies rested as firmly on those sentiments as on the general public awareness that the fire and passion of the Reconstruction had been spent. At the beginning of Hayes's term, George William Curtis in *Harper's Weekly* was more complimentary when he noted that the new president was "more of a patriot than a partisan, who regarded public questions with a humane eye of statesmanship, more mindful of the general welfare than of party or personal advantage."[35]

That love of harmony and fear of disruption can been seen in the president's handling of the railroad strike in the summer of 1877. The strike began in West Virginia and spread through Maryland, Pennsylvania, New York, Ohio, Kentucky, and Illinois. Violence followed and wholesale destruction took place in different locales. Many state militiamen were sympathetic to the strikers and were reluctant to intervene. The strike had followed a severe cut in pay, while at the same time the salaries of management and dividends to stockholders were safeguarded. Pay scales to start off with were not high. Brakemen averaged $1.75 for a twelve-hour day; conductors $2.78; firemen generally earned $1.90 a day. Unpaid idle days increased in 1877, and a 10 percent wage reduction put into effect in the summer of 1877 lit the tinderbox.

The governor of West Virginia, Henry M. Mathews, under pressure from the president of the B & O Railroad, asked Hayes for troops. Hayes, however, demanded more information before he ordered two small detachments to go to Martinsburg, West Virginia, and he issued a presidential proclamation urging peace and order. After that episode, rioting broke out elsewhere, and Hayes sent troops into Maryland and then to Pennsylvania. Meanwhile, Indiana, Ohio, and Illinois became targets of the strikers, and Hayes shipped arms to Columbus at Ohio Governor Thomas L. Young's request, and to Chicago and East St. Louis. Hayes restricted the mission and authority of U.S. troops in Indiana and refused the requests of the governors of Michigan, Wisconsin, and California for further assistance, although he issued executive orders to the armed forces to protect federal buildings during the strikes.

Hayes became, in the eyes of nineteenth-century labor radicals, the epitome of a strikebreaking conservative, even though his position was more that of an executive dedicated to prudence and moderation. With Congress out of session and the possibility of disruption on a national scale, Hayes used the few troops he had at his disposal in a rather effective way. There is no question, though, that his policy was one that favored the railroad owners, men who were establishing a record for rapaciousness unparalleled in American history up to that time. Even Hayes recognized later the dynamics of what was happening around him. On May 2, 1886, he observed, "It may be truly said that for twenty-five years, at least, railroad workingmen have had too little, and railroad capitalists and managers, those who have controlled and manipulated railroads, have had too much of their earnings—or too much of the money made out of them."[36]

In another controversy, Hayes insisted on breaking the power of the Senate oligarchy and restoring some independence to the executive, probably his most important contribution to the office itself. Lincoln had ruled in spite of Congress; Johnson had been impeached and nearly convicted by the Congress; and Grant's administration added little to the luster of the office. Hayes did not inherit a position in good shape politically, but early on he insisted on asserting the authority of his office to name cabinet officers and other major appointments with minimal interference from the party bosses.

Although a loyal Republican party man, Hayes was moved by his own moral compass and his own sense of stewardship. He was, above all, a man of moderation, and he concluded at one point, "While I maintain inflexibly the authority of the Executive department against all attempts to cripple it by other departments, I must not magnify it at the expense of the just prerogatives of either the judicial or the legislative branches." Hayes's battles with the Senate oligarchy started early with his cabinet appointments. He nominated for secretary of state William M. Evarts, who ran into trouble from the Conkling faction of the New York Republican party. In addition, independent-minded Carl Schurz, slated for the Interior Department, had been anathema for years to party regulars across the country, and the proposed postmaster general was David M. Key, a Democrat and former Confederate officer—a problematic combination. Even respected Senator John Sherman, nominated for the post at Treasury, had problems in the Senate confirmation process.

In dealing with patronage appointments, Hayes responded to public outcries of waste and corruption in the New York customshouse by removing three high officials of the port, all Conkling men. Conkling countered by blocking their replacements. Hayes, supported by Sherman and his allies, prevailed in the struggle, which helped restore the chief executive's power during the postwar period. One of Conkling's allies, Senator Henry M. Teller of Colorado, remarked of Hayes, "He thinks he is George Washington." The president recorded in his dairy, "I have had great success. No member of either House now attempts to dictate appointments. My sole right to make appointments is tacitly conceded."[37] In 1881, Conkling would take on another president, James Garfield, on a similar patronage issue and lose once again. Observing the final outcome, which included a repudiation of both Conkling and Thomas Pratt by the New York state legislature, Hayes could note that he had struck the first blow against the boss system that so influenced his party.

Hayes's position in office was further buttressed when the Democrats tried to resurrect charges of electoral fraud in his much disputed election. However, a congressional inquiry and an exposé by a New York newspaper discovered that the Democrats themselves were involved in electoral irregularities in South Carolina and Florida, and that Tilden's nephew was a part of that fraud. People aware of Tilden's propensity for detail had a difficult time not believing that the candidate himself was involved, and in 1880, the party quickly passed over Tilden when it chose its next presidential candidate.

Like most of the postwar presidents, Hayes had to face the controversial issue of the money supply and the strong desire of the South and West for the free coinage of silver, which they saw as helping to create an inflationary and cheaper currency. From 1792 to 1873, the United States had a bimetallic standard in which silver and gold dollars circulated as legal tender in payment of debts. Gold was worth more, and the ratio of silver to the more precious metal was generally set at 16 to 1. In 1873, Congress officially ended silver coinage, and many farmers and debtors saw this step as a deliberate attempt to create a scarcity in money that would make their debts more expensive to pay off and cause a severe depression. When farm prices dropped in the period from 1873 to 1878, those fears seemed justified, and public sentiment forced Congress to pass the Bland-Allison Act, which committed the federal government to mint from $2 million to $4 million a month in silver dollars. A sign of the times emerged as the legislature in Illinois passed a bill making silver coins a legal tender at face value.

The Democratic state conventions meeting in the summer of 1877 advocated the repeal of the Resumption Act and the free coinage of silver. The conventions of the Greenback partisans supported the same position, and Republican state conventions in the West urged the restoration of silver to its former status. Even Ohio and Pennsylvania Republican leaders agreed. Although Hayes vetoed the free coinage bill, it was passed nonetheless. The president's response was that the bill stained the reputation of American credit, and he insisted, "We are a debtor nation. Low rates of interest on the vast indebtedness we must carry for many years is the important end to be kept in view. Expediency and justice both demand honest coinage." His position should have come as no surprise; in the 1875 campaign for governor in Ohio, he attracted national attention as a sound money candidate. Treasury Secretary John Sherman was more restrained and felt that a restoration of the silver dollar at 16 to 1 would mean a limited coinage of silver and not pose a threat to financial stability. But the president insisted on standing virtually alone on the issue. Little wonder that Hayes wrote after his silver veto message, "I am not liked as a president, by the politicians in office, in the press, or in Congress."[38]

The president also favored resumption of specie payments, another controversial step designed to tighten currency and reduce borrowing. The United States, before the Civil War, had the Treasury exchange gold and silver coins for bank notes or greenbacks supported only by the credit of the United States. During the Civil War and after 1865, the Treasury did not allow such specie exchanges. But in 1875, Congress approved redeeming legal tender notes in specie at full value starting in 1879. The purpose was to end the use of greenbacks, a move Hayes and Sherman agreed on. They were quietly effective in putting together their economic plans which emphasized the primacy of the gold standard, the accumulation of reserves, and an assurance to the financial communities of their commitment to sound money. When the Bland-Allison Act did go into effect, however, it neither impacted on the value of American securities nor provided the economic impetus the silver advocates had hoped. The American economy was more complex by then, and the causes of the approaching depression were to be more intractable.

Hayes faced two other major long-standing questions—the plight of the Indians and the growing importance of the United States in the world. His policies exhibited remarkable continuity with the past. In regard to Indian problems, the president and his new secretary of the interior, Carl Schurz, tried to show greater sensitivity, and they supported some reforms. The impetus for a different policy, though, came not from the politicians but from the publication of two major books in the field: George W. Manypenny's *Our Indian Wards* and the much-read Helen H. Jackson's *A Century of Dishonor*, which castigated the government's policies. Still despite their good intentions, the administration leaders presided over the harsh removal of the Poncas tribe from Dakota to what became Oklahoma. The president continued to advocate landownership, education, citizenship, and governmental support as a general policy—echoes of Grant's Peace Policy.[39]

The foreign policy activities of Hayes and Secretary of State William Evarts were more modest, but they involved the protection of U.S. citizens, especially near the tense U.S.-Mexican border, fostering American trade abroad, and trying to reach a moderate settlement with China on the explosive immigration question. The secretary also was involved in investigation of the murder of American missionaries in Turkey, the drafting by Germany of naturalized U.S. citizens, and the expulsion of Jewish-Americans from czarist

Russia. The administration was instrumental in promoting a U.S.-controlled canal in Nicaragua and curtailing European, especially French, influence. In addition, the president took a tougher stand than Grant did with regard to Mexico. He indicated that revolutionary governments must not only show they had popular support, but must also be able to fulfill their international obligations if they expected American recognition. The administration approved the "hot pursuit" of lawless bands by the U.S. Army beyond the border and on into the northern provinces of Mexico. Hayes was charged with wanting to start a war in the South in the same manner as Polk, a president whom Hayes had criticized for exactly that reason over a generation before.[40]

In addition, the president refused to support the Chinese Exclusion movement, which was gaining strength in California, and he opposed Congress's unilateral repudiation of the Burlingame Treaty, which permitted both extensive Chinese immigration and very lucrative American trading. Finally, a special commission negotiated a new treaty that regulated immigration from China, and the document was approved by the Senate. Evarts also pushed for better trade relations with Japan, Korea, and Hawaii and secured Pago Pago as a U.S. naval station. In forecasting a new world role, the Hayes administration furthered the building of a larger navy, advocated subsidies for merchant ships, and supported overall policies that sought to establish eventually the United States as a real force in world trade. Hayes ended his term with a series of goodwill trips through different areas of the country where he stressed the benefits of the Union and economic prosperity. Now he had a chance to praise the positive aspects of ending Reconstruction and putting aside the ways of war. He continued to celebrate the virtues of a united and prosperous American Union. On one trip, he compared the nation to the American schoolhouse, where diverse peoples could be "fused into one harmonious whole." It was harmony, above all, that Hayes seemed most drawn to during his term in office.[41]

GARFIELD, ARTHUR, AND THE GILDED AGE

As the election of 1880 approached, Hayes threw his support to his secretary of the treasury, John Sherman of Ohio, a capable but essentially colorless public figure. But the real excitement was the efforts of the Stalwarts to renominate Ulysses S. Grant. The strategy of the Grant managers was to force the delegations to cast their votes by state rather than individually, the so-called unit rule. If New York, Pennsylvania, and Illinois voted unanimously for the general, then those 170 votes added to the 176 he had in the South would give Grant 340 of the 379 he needed for the GOP nomination. In the end, the more independent Republicans, often designated as "Half-Breeds," were able to stop the unit rule from becoming adopted and Grant's chances subsequently unraveled.

One of the major figures in the Sherman drive was James A. Garfield, who delivered a splendid nominating address, which stressed party unity, but barely mentioned his fellow Ohioan's name. On the thirty-fourth ballot, the convention turned away from the major candidates—Sherman, Grant, and James G. Blaine of Maine— and nominated Garfield. To appease the important New York Stalwart delegation and Boss Conkling, the convention nominated the former customshouse chief Chester A. Arthur, who had been fired by Hayes.

Garfield presented a superb story for campaign managers. He was the son of poor parents in Ohio, was raised by a young widow, became a born-again Christian at eighteen, was a young president of what became Hiram College, and later became a Civil War hero who rose to the rank of major general. He entered politics and was aligned with the abolitionists and Radical Republicans. Garfield supported the impeachment of Johnson, opposed soft money, and generally favored a laissez faire social philosophy. He concluded that "the chief duty of government is to keep the peace and stand out of the sunshine of the people." He believed that the Granger farm movement was communist-related, opposed the development of labor unions, supported using federal troops to break strikes, and insisted on property qualifications for men desiring to vote, while he branded female suffrage as "atheistic."[42]

Although Garfield was an ambitious rising politician, he was consistent on hard money, antislavery, and the preservation of the Union. His biographers have pointed to his sense of individual destiny and deep personal morbidness. He seemed, however, to exhibit a sense of detachment and self-doubt, which might have limited his effectiveness as an executive if he had stayed in office long enough for it to matter.

Against Garfield, the Democrats nominated General Winfield Scott Hancock, a Union commander at Gettysburg and the administrator of Louisiana and Texas during the Reconstruction period. He was a man with few enemies, a respectable war record, and the right inclinations—no mean feat for a Democrat coming of age in the Civil War epoch. The Greenback party nominated a Union general as well: James B. Weaver. In August 1880, Garfield met in New York City with the leaders of all the factions of the Republican party and put together an agreement in which he promised to reward all wings with patronage. Stalwarts such as Grant and Conkling worked Ohio and Indiana, and Arthur took personal charge of their campaign tours. The prospective vice president also kept track of party assessments of public officials in order to support the GOP's war chest. Even with these well-organized efforts, Garfield received only about ten thousand votes more than Hancock with 9.2 million citizens going to the polls. Garfield carried the electoral college by a larger margin of 214 to 155, including the critical state of New York.

Immediately, Garfield ran into an avalanche of patronage demands, opposition to his balancing act among the factions, and an aggressive posture from James G. Blaine who was the new secretary of state. Only lukewarm toward civil service reform in the first place, Garfield faced the patronage pressures that he knew had so burdened past presidents. Like many Republicans, including the prewar Abraham Lincoln, Garfield held a Whig view of the presidency. He refused to lead Congress, even though that body was disorganized in its own operations at the time. He avoided controversy and leadership fights, and once wrote, "I love to deal with doctrines and events. The contests of men about men I greatly dislike."[43]

But the new president could not avoid the patronage problems that he had to confront. A first point of contention was once again the lucrative collectorship of the New York custom house, and Secretary of State Blaine came up with a convoluted plan to curtail the Stalwarts. Arthur, loyal to Conkling, protested the move and Grant concluded that his successor lacked "the back-bone of an angle-worm." But Garfield refused to back down on his right to appoint whomever he wished, and he turned the patronage mess into a principled stand defending the powers of the presidency. By mid-May, the president triumphed over the bosses on patronage issues, and it seemed as if a strong executive were being born.[44]

In addition to the handling of jobs for the faithful, Garfield dealt with a major scandal in the Post Office Department and its handling of mail route contracts. The new president also turned his attention to the plight of Southern freed slaves and the future of the Republican party in the new South. In 1878, Garfield had been a critic of Hayes's attempt to woo Southern whites, and he had been an early supporter of black voting as a way to guarantee Republican rule and the fruits of war. But like many whites, he opposed equality, found blacks generally distasteful, and advocated the catch-all escapist solution—the colonization of blacks elsewhere. As befitting a self-made man and an academician, he believed that education was the hope for the former slaves. He refused to grant patronage to Southern Democrats and instead focused on rebuilding the Republican party in the hostile new South. His objective was clear: to gain support in the region "on the great commercial and industrial questions rather than on questions of race and color." And he began to support the "Readjuster" movement of William Mahone in Virginia, a reform group that embraced blacks and also whites who had been Democrats in the past.

Then on July 2, 1881, at a Washington, D.C., railroad station, Garfield was shot by a disappointed office seeker, Charles Julius Guiteau. For several months, the crippled president, with a bullet in his spine, clung to life. On September 19, he died, and Chester A. Arthur, the very epitome of the Stalwart patronage tradition, took the oath of office.

Arthur, nicknamed "The Gentleman Boss," was a dignified practitioner of the art of governing in a political machine known for its venality. He moved easily within those circles and times, but retained a sense of goodwill and decorum, which served him well in the difficult months between the attempt on Garfield's life and his death.[45] He kept Garfield's cabinet, made changes slowly, and stayed arm's length from his former Stalwart cronies. One of Arthur's old friends remarked, "He isn't 'Chet' Arthur anymore; he's the president." And another glumly concluded that Arthur "has done less for us than Garfield, or even Hayes."[46]

The most important cabinet secretary in Garfield's brief term was James G. Blaine, the hated symbol of the Half-Breed wing and a determined opponent of Arthur's Stalwart faction. Blaine's initiatives in foreign policy have been seen as laying the groundwork for a more vigorous American imperialist period, which reached fruition in the McKinley and Theodore Roosevelt administrations. Garfield had expressed an interest in American foreign policy when he was in Congress, and he pushed for reciprocal trade, arguing in 1876, "we want all fair chances that the markets of the world can give us for selling our surplus supplies." He saw the United States as a major power in the Pacific with its transcontinental railroad and the purchase of Alaska. America would become "the arbiter of that sea, the controller of its commerce and chief nation that inhabits its shores," he maintained.[47]

During these early months in the administration, Blaine pushed for commercial treaties and reciprocity, and sought to use American influence to mediate various long-standing conflicts in Latin America. The administration following Hayes's policy even went so far as to back away from the Clayton-Bulwer Treaty, which prohibited the United States or Britain from excluding the other from any deal over building a canal through Central America. As for Europe, Blaine had to deal with attempts in Britain, France, and especially Imperial Germany to cut back on U.S. exports of pork. Blaine also pursued ties with Korea and the island of Madagascar in seeking to expand U.S. trade and influence.[48]

The Garfield-Blaine foreign policy emphasized reciprocity in trade; the president had seen that approach as especially important in building the Republican party base. He concluded optimistically that he would develop a policy more popular with "the people of this country than it has been since the day of its birth." Although many policymakers spoke of the need to find foreign markets for U.S. goods abroad—a typical imperialist theme—it is difficult to see that motive as the guiding principle of American foreign policy. From 1877 to 1881, exports accounted for only 8.2 percent of the GNP and for the years 1882 to 1886, that percentage dropped to 6.6 percent. American manufacturers in general seemed to care little about exports. The interest of Blaine and others was due more to concerns over national prestige and comparative international advantage than pleasing corporate leaders.[49]

Arthur's choice at the State Department to succeed Blaine was former U.S. Senator Frederick T. Frelinghuysen of New Jersey, a scion of one of the oldest and most respected families in that state. Even more than Blaine, Frelinghuysen placed the administration behind the search for markets and commercial reciprocity as a national policy. He and Arthur rejected the idea of interfering in foreign disputes, even in Latin America, and Frelinghuysen moved further away from the limitations of the Clayton-Bulwer Treaty and supported an agreement with Nicaragua that embraced the idea of a canal there. The Senate rejected the proposed treaty, however, and Grover Cleveland withdrew it altogether, concluding that it was an alliance that went "beyond the scope of our national polity or present means."[50]

Frelinghuysen and Arthur continued to deal with the difficult and unexciting problem of excluding U.S. pork in Europe and with the centuries-old conflict between the British and the Irish. The United States was especially concerned with naturalized Americans who were being held prisoner by the British under the Coercion Act. Elsewhere, the administration also insisted on protecting trading interests in the Madagascar region and in Liberia. But the administration and the citizenry as a whole had little political leverage or military power in a world where imperialist powers were beginning to flex their muscles. As the *Nation* concluded, "the people of the United States want as little of foreign policy as possible."[51]

American armed force strength underscored that philosophy. Since the Civil War, the U.S. Navy had rapidly declined from being one of the world's strongest fleets to one of its weakest. By 1881, every major European nation and several Latin American naval forces were superior to that of the United States, and the new secretary of the navy under Garfield, Judge William H. Hunt from New Orleans, strongly advocated an upgrading of the navy, a recommendation Arthur approved. When Hunt took over as minister to Russia, his successor, William E. Chandler, continued to foster a vigorous rebuilding campaign, and he constructed new steamboats, searched for coaling stations, and identified naval base sites. However, he did not succeed in establishing a chain of coaling stations and could not get congressional appropriations for a newly augmented merchant marine. Even with the president's support, Chandler added only three cruisers and a dispatch boat. A larger navy would have to await a larger role for the United States in the 1890s.

And although the administration toyed with contacts with Korea, Indochina, and even the Congo, the major European powers set the international pace, and the United States had to make do with only limited contacts, mild entreaties for reciprocal trade, and modest diplomacy. When the United States agreed to the Berlin Conference's guarantee of neutrality in the Congo, the treaty died in Congress, and President Cleveland later went on record opposing it.

Meanwhile on the domestic front, President Arthur moved through the landmines of corruption and civil service reform. He decisively supported prosecutions in the Post Office scandals case, incurring Stalwart criticism. He watched with dismay as Garfield's assassin went on trial; Guiteau told astounded listeners that the late president's death was a "political necessity," that he actually talked to Arthur during the presidential campaign, and that he had helped the GOP by his actions. He was found guilty after his insanity plea was dismissed, and he cried out, "I saved my party and my land, God hallelujah!" To some, the trial represented an unfortunate commentary on the legal system and its treatment of insanity; to others, his behavior was an outgrowth of the rottenness of the spoils system itself.

The death of Garfield and the conversion of Arthur to a merit system added to the political support for civil service reform. However, responding to the strong reservations of party leaders, Congress rejected changes in that area, and even respected Democratic Senator George Hunt Pendleton was unable to generate much support for any reform. Then in November 1882, the GOP suffered a series of major defeats in the congressional elections. Arthur increased his own support of the cause, coming out for competitive examinations and an end of assessments on officeholders. In December 1882, the Pendleton Act passed the Senate with unanimous Republican support, but with only one Democrat outside the South, George Pendleton himself, favoring it. Despite general support for reform, the act placed only about 11 percent of the federal government's employees under civil service. It was both a modest beginning and a major break in the patronage system—a rupture aided and abetted by the dismissed customshouse patronage chief, Chester A. Arthur.[52]

In dealing with the South, Arthur showed the same mixture of pragmatism and partisan finesse that served him well in the past. The president supported the attempt to entice Senator Mahone and his fellow Democrat defectors in Virginia into the GOP. In other states, Arthur endorsed cooperation between regular Republicans and independents, but generally the president and his allies' strategy did not work out well in major tests in North Carolina, Texas, Arkansas, Tennessee, Louisiana, and Florida. Even in Virginia, the coalition began to fall apart as the Democrats skillfully used traditional political and personal alliances, racist appeals, and fraud to take over the Old Dominion. A traditional partisan spoilsman with no real social agenda, Arthur had little interest in race relations and showed no concern when the Supreme Court emasculated the Civil Rights Act of 1875. Yet the GOP continued to hold on to the overwhelming support of black newspapers and voters, still living on the memory of the Great Emancipator.

Arthur underwent a welcome and necessary transformation from machine politician to national leader but in the process, he continued to further the split between the Blaine-oriented Half-Breed and the Stalwart factions. That division coupled with the worsening of a progressive kidney illness made renomination impossible. The Republicans finally turned to James G. Blaine, while the Democrats nominated the honest and stubborn governor of New York, Grover Cleveland. The Republican control on the White House was to end.

CLEVELAND AND THE ECLIPSE
OF BOURBON DEMOCRACY

Between the collapse of the Buchanan administration in 1861 and the reforming years of Woodrow Wilson beginning in 1913, no Democrat was elected president except Grover Cleveland who won in 1884, lost in 1888, and then remarkably returned for a second term in 1892. In his extraordinary rise and long political career, Cleveland exhibited to his fellow citizens a rocklike integrity and personal character. Like all of us, his vices flowed out of his prominent virtues. He was stubborn, inflexible, and bullheaded in staking out his principled positions and in keeping to them. His foremost biographer, Allan Nevins, concluded that Cleveland's "greatness lies in typical rather than unusual qualities. He had no endowments that thousands of men do not have. He possessed honesty, courage, firmness, independence, and common sense. But he possessed them in a degree that others did not."[53]

Cleveland began his political career in Buffalo, New York, and held a variety of local offices including sheriff and mayor. It was in the latter race that he expressed the view that "public officials are the trustees of the people." A journalist quickly changed the remark to "a public office is a public trust"—a slogan that helped to propel Cleveland into the governorship of New York and on into the White House. The formula of his success was, in Horace Merrill's words, that he would make "no sordid deals including the public purse strings; impress the voters with his independence of machine politics; quietly accept machine politics in so far as it was expedient. In short, be a politician without seeming to be one, and at the same time retain personal integrity."[54]

In the campaign of 1884, American politics reached a new viciousness. The Democrats attacked Blaine, the "Plumed Knight" from Maine. Blaine had been charged with exploiting his position in 1869 as speaker of the House of Representatives when he allegedly made a decision that guaranteed a land grant for the Little Rock and Fort Smith Railroad. He went on to use the opportunity to sell railroad bonds and obtained secretly a lucrative commission. Some of his communications were supposed to have contained the postscript, "Burn this letter," which was not done, to his later embarrassment. On the other hand, Cleveland was attacked for his probable paternity of an illegitimate child and also for the purchase of a substitute to take his place in the Civil War draft. With delight, the GOP chanted at political rallies, "Ma, Ma, where's my pa?" The Democrats, not to be outdone, would reply, "Gone to Washington, ha, ha, ha! Burn that letter."

During this mindless campaign, Blaine attended a much publicized dinner where a Protestant minister attacked the Democrats, calling them the party of "Rum, Romanism, and Rebellion." The reaction among Catholics and others was swift and sure, and Blaine lost New York state in the general election, probably due to this episode. The Republican ticket was also hurt by its association with "Belshazzar's Feast" at Delmonico's Restaurant in New York—a disgusting exhibition of wealth and conspicuous consumption that showed a good many people the silver lining of the party. Consequently, Cleveland became the "reform candidate" that many Mugwump Republicans could rally behind, and he won, although a switch of only six hundred votes in New York would have thrown the election to Blaine. The bloody shirt, the electoral efforts of Civil War veterans, and the energies of the old GOP establishment were not enough. A nation weary of corruption and governmental high jinks turned to a man who seemed to embody a sense of political gravity and steadfastness.

Grover Cleveland was a very cautious and restrained person. He came from the eastern wing of the Democratic party, which was not in that era a hotbed of liberal thought. These so-called Bourbon Democrats were conservative, business-oriented, and generally suspicious of change. In many ways, where Cleveland stood in the domestic political spectrum was not too far away from Harrison, Hayes, and Garfield, although in foreign policy he turned aside from the imperialist dreams of the Gilded Age Republicans.[55]

As expected, the first order of business was the hungry Democratic party's lust for patronage. Of the approximately 126,000 federal employees, 110,000 were political appointees chosen by the president or by his immediate subordinates. In some of those positions, a system of rotation grew up and these jobs were divided up among the party faithful. Oftentimes a certain fixed percentage of one's salary had to be given as an assessment to the party in power. Cleveland at first glance leaned cautiously to the civil service reformers' side, although he did not fully embrace their fervor.[56]

The second issue to emerge quickly was the continuing currency controversy and the fear in financial and business circles that the Bland-Allison Act of 1878 had gone too far. That act required that $2 million to $4 million worth of silver bullion be minted monthly so that the government had produced nearly $200 million in such currency. During and after the depression of 1884, gold was being demanded in place of silver or greenbacks, and consequently the government had to accept silver dollars for its debts and pay out gold to its creditors.[57]

Treasury officials feared that gold reserves would drop below the $100 million mark—a figure assumed to be the balancing line between stable and irresponsible levels. When business pressure built up to end silver coinage, the Southern and Western representatives responded with their usual vigor and outrage. Proponents of silver saw the change as a plot to hurt the poor, the debtors, and the farmers, and as a favor for well-off bankers and bondholders. They warned Cleveland that in the past six years, two-thirds of the Democrats had consistently voted together to defend the coinage of silver. But Cleveland did not respect that wing of the party, and his position was really closer to that of Hayes and Arthur than to most of his fellow partisans. In the House of Representatives, many Democrats refused to adhere to Cleveland's position, and abandoned his proposal to suspend silver coinage—an idea he floated before he took office. Interestingly, in 1892 every state convention from Virginia to Texas, though controlled often by conservatives, endorsed free silver in some form or another.[58]

In the first year of his administration, Cleveland had continued the initiatives of President Arthur to rebuild the American navy. The navy was still mired in its old traditions and comfortable procedures and was characterized by wooden ships, old shipbuilding designs, and dated weaponry. In 1883, Congress authorized construction of three cruisers and a dispatch boat; by 1885, it added four more vessels. In keeping with its decentralized traditions, the Department of the Navy was a collection of eight uncoordinated bureaus before Cleveland and Secretary William C. Whitney pushed for a reorganization. The president continued the buildup, but emphasized its defensive importance rather than seeing it as a prop for empire.

While the buildup of the navy was a pleasant task, Cleveland early on had to face major controversies over the development and use of Western lands. The opening up of the Great American West is a tale of extraordinary initiative and personal courage; it is also the chronicle of genocide against the Indians and unmistakable greed. In addition, over the years endless land disputes erupted among the homesteaders, and claim jumping and surveying frauds were common. In the front ranks of the forces of rapaciousness were the railroads. By 1871 Congress ended land donations to the railroads, but by then the companies controlled over 160 million acres. Public scrutiny in 1886 focused on one railroad in particular—the Union Pacific—which had received generous government land grants and loans and which was being poorly managed and manipulated by Jay Gould. Partially as a response to mounting criticism of the railroads, Congress passed the Interstate Commerce Act, which was supposed to deal with rate discriminations and other abuses. For Cleveland, the whole history smacked of abuse of the public trust, and he observed that "a contest waged on the one hand by wealth, represented by the most capable and accomplished lawyers, overflowing with precedents and arguments, and an overcrowded office almost buried under accumulated work and ill supplied with men to bring the delayed cases to conclusion."[59]

Concerned about the land controversies, the administration suspended the activities of the General Land Office in the trans-Mississippi West, and in August 1885, the president issued a proclamation denouncing unlawful enclosures of federal lands and waterways. Cleveland also reversed Arthur's order proclaiming certain Indian lands on the Dakota Territory in the public domain, and he supported the Davies Bill, which allowed tribes to divide up their reservations and granted them the rights of U.S. citizenship.

As he wrestled with these early policy matters, Cleveland had to face two issues that haunted executives of this postwar period— the spoils system and challenges to the president's prerogatives. He understood well the importance of party loyalty and the claims it made on appointees and elected officials. But he generally supported civil service reform and had a deep contempt for the demands of spoilsmen and the whining of their job-hungry friends. He once confided to a reporter, "This office seeking is a disease. . . . Men get it, and they lose the proper balance of their minds." He favored some rotation in office, and emphasized a four-year maximum term for minor officeholders, although he resisted removals for only partisan purposes. When Democrats complained that too few jobs were coming their way after so long a wait, Cleveland's typical response was, "I cannot rid myself of the idea that I owe so much to the country, that all other obligations shrink almost to nothingness before it."[60]

Some of the party's newspapers also attacked Cleveland for timidity. The *New York World*, owned by Joseph Pulitzer, cautioned, "Cleveland must remember the obligations which an administration elected by a great historical party owes to that party." On the other hand, some Republicans insisted that good people were being dismissed from office just because of their allegiance to the GOP. Senator Eugene Hale of Maine charged in 1888 that the president had refilled 40,000 of the 52,609 fourth-class postmasterships, changed 2,000 of 2,359 presidential postmastership positions, and replaced 138 of 219 consuls, 100 of 111 customs collectors, 84 of 85 internal revenue collectors, 64 of 70 marshals and 22 of 30 territorial judges.[61]

Republican senators used protests from dismissed officeholders as a way to confront directly the president and attempted, as they had done with Andrew Johnson, to restrict the authority of the executive. The Tenure of Office Act of 1867 had been revised, however, and it was considerably weakened when Cleveland decided to challenge it. The revised law allowed the president to suspend an officer at his own discretion, instead of only for misconduct or the commission of a crime. The Republicans were demanding some statement of reasons for these dismissals, hoping to show Cleveland's actions as meanly partisan, but the president refused to supply such statements. The Republicans, in turn, then threatened to stop ratifying appointments if he persisted in his intransigence. Cleveland had in effect invoked a form of executive privilege by refusing to give them information on removals. Finally, on March 1, the president made a formal appeal to the country and rallied weak-kneed Democrats in the Congress to his side. Several important GOP senators walked away from the battle, and the controversy dragged on. By June 1886, Congress had repealed the Tenure of Office Act altogether.

Cleveland was less successful on other major issues. Despite his opposition on the silver coinage issue, Congress was reluctant to follow his lead, if leadership it was. In fact, the president made his opinions known to Congress, and then rested on pronouncements about the separation of branches of government, and how he had no desire to legislate. He proved to be cautious on another of the great continuing tests—the tariff. Like any good Democrat, he opposed high rates, but he was more guarded than most, fearing repercussions for American industries and a split in the party on the issue. Later, Cleveland was converted to tariff reform if only because its advocates included many "good government" people especially those opposed to the spoils system. Meanwhile in the West, Republicans found that farmers who normally supported the GOP had grown restive with high railroad rates and were looking for more aggressive government action.

The congressional elections of 1886 provided no trend one way or another concerning public sentiment. The president continued his "good government" stance and presented to the legislative branch a proposed change in the tariff schedules. During all this activity, Cleveland took time out from his official duties on June 2, 1886, to marry his twenty-one-year-old ward in an elegant White House ceremony.[62] One particularly difficult issue remained, and here Cleveland was especially vulnerable politically. As the first Democratic president since before the Civil War, Cleveland could not escape the residues of the war and the suspicions that would be directed at him by veterans, especially from the Grand Army of the Republic, which had become an arm of the Republican party.

In the spring of 1886, the former Confederate president Jefferson Davis emerged from seclusion and laid a cornerstone to commemorate the Confederate dead buried in Montgomery, Alabama. Northern response was bitter in some quarters. Cleveland at this time had taken a tough stand against some veterans pension bills, which were replete with fraudulent claims—a position that could be easily characterized as a former draft dodger refusing benefits to Union heroes. No president before Cleveland had vetoed even one of these pension lists. To Cleveland, the nation had to be leery of all raids on the Treasury; as he observed, "the people support the Government, the Government should not support the people."

Cleveland added to his woes in June 1887 by ordering the return of captured Confederate flags to Southern leaders. The president thought this request a reasonable one and a good step to promote amity. Instead it raised sectional bitterness to new heights in some areas of the North. One Grand Army of the Republic commander, Lucius Fairchild of Wisconsin, proclaimed bitterly, "May God palsy the hand that wrote that order. May God palsy the brain that conceived it, and may God palsy the tongue that dictated it." The president later revoked the proposed transfer, noting lamely that he could not dispose of federal property by executive order.[63]

While political sectionalism remained important, the real impetus to nationalism came from the new economic ties that began to bring the regions together often in spite of themselves. And in this climate, powerful corporations grew up driven by the urge to control whole sections of commerce and industry and willing to engage in ruthless competition and monopolistic practices. Cleveland thought little about the long-term consequences of such developments. His view of the presidency was limited, his education deficient, and his rapid rise in politics in only three years from mayor to the White House had deprived him of any real sense of public discontent beyond the conventional issues of tariff rates, civil service, and the coinage of silver. He was to show little strength of leadership until the middle of his first term, preferring instead to take on a single issue at time, thinking about it and planting his feet firmly on one side or another.[64]

In 1886, in various locales, labor unrest began to grow. Most explosive was the lockout of 1,400 employees at the McCormick reaper plant in Chicago. Demonstrations in favor of the eight-hour workday spread, and one man was killed, several more injured. Later peaceful demonstrations turned into a confusing explosion and a riot ensued. An unfair trial led to the conviction of five labor leaders. Through all this, Cleveland became acutely aware of class tensions. He was a man of strict law and order, but he was critical of what he called "the grasping and heedless exactions of employers," and supported government arbitration of disputes and the incorporation of labor unions.[65]

In 1887, Cleveland took on, in his usually blunt way, the tariff question. The federal government was running a projected surplus estimated by the end of the fiscal year at $140 million, which added to the pressures to cut the tariff rates; Cleveland waited for the right time to present his plan, and a new vigorous executive rallied the Democratic party around a unifying issue with considerable national appeal. Opposition, however, mounted in strong protectionist areas of the country. Cleveland recognized that his stand might imperil his reelection, but characteristically he argued, "What is the use of being elected or reelected, unless you stand for something?" Leading his party, he strongly branded the tariff as a "vicious, inequitable, and illogical source of unnecessary taxation."[66]

The issue became a part of the presidential campaign as Cleveland was easily renominated, and protectionist Benjamin Harrison of Indiana headed the GOP ticket, which won the election. Cleveland's defeat in 1888 has usually been ascribed to his forceful position on the tariff, but it must be remembered that Cleveland won the popular vote by a margin of over 100,000 even though he lost the electoral college 233 to 168. Cleveland's problems revolved around the continuing internal feudings of the party organization that so afflicted the Democrats in that period. The Republicans, on the other hand, under the strong leadership of their national chairman, Senator Matthew S. Quay of Pennsylvania, were rather effective in systematically soliciting businessmen for their cause. The GOP could use the protective tariff issue to mobilize industrialists and fellow sympathizers including some workers who feared for their jobs. The Democrats overall were ineffective in getting out the vote in some critical areas, especially in New York, where the bosses still had a strong animosity toward Cleveland. This time the Republicans made a concerted effort to court Irish-American voters who generally resented the administration's foreign policy overtures toward the British government. The GOP was also fairly successful in dispensing bribes in New York and Indiana. Cleveland's response to all this was his usual, "It is better to be defeated battling for an honest principle than to win by a cowardly subterfuge."[67]

In the area of foreign policy, Cleveland did seek to effect a major change during his first term. He and his secretary of state, Thomas F. Bayard, rejected most of the expansionist emphasis that had characterized the Republican administrations that preceded them. Where Secretaries Blaine and Frelinghuysen had pushed for making Nicaragua into a virtual protectorate in order to promote the transisthmian canal, Cleveland had a very different view. He withdrew the Frelinghuysen-Zavala Treaty of 1884, generally left weaker nations alone, refused to encourage investments in foreign countries, and was an outspoken opponent of imperialist pretensions. In addition, Cleveland and Bayard pressed for the autonomy of the Samoan Islands, putting a halt on German ambitions in that region. The president denounced the conduct of German agents in the archipelago and proposed to send a formal message to Congress on the matter, but then decided otherwise. Nature intervened and a hurricane destroyed British, American, and German warships at Apia, thus averting a political confrontation.

Another problem that the president faced was fishing disputes with Canada. Under strong pressure from New England fishermen and their U.S. senators, Cleveland pushed for a new treaty to provide greater access to Canadian fishing waters. The United States and Great Britain agreed to set up a working group to prepare a draft of a new treaty. The proposed document provided for a joint commission to set the territorial limits of U.S. fishing in Canadian waters, deal with jurisdiction over estuaries and bays, and outline a compromise on the issues of U.S. duties on fish sold by Canada in the states.

The issue became complicated when New England senators pushed for retaliatory legislation in Congress aimed at prohibiting the entry of Canadian vessels and Canadian-caught fish into American ports. Cleveland instead supported a strong bill that gave the president extensive discretionary powers in this area. The treaty proposal was rejected, however, and the situation stayed as before. Cleveland then turned around and insisted on legislation to allow him more authority in the area of retaliatory action against Canada. His action was less directed at the neighbor to the north as it was at the recalcitrant Senate. The House supported the president, but the Senate, as he expected, did not. For the president, the move was a tactical foray in an area where he had previously provided little leadership.[68]

After his defeat, in 1888, Cleveland went back and practiced law in New York City, living a fairly quiet life with his young wife and their daughter, Ruth, who was born in 1891 and who according to an apocryphal legend was supposed to be the inspiration much later for the name of the popular candy bar, Baby Ruth. But like so many ex-presidents, he yearned to return—and remarkably did.

The congressional elections of 1890 led to a repudiation of the GOP, as the Democrats captured the House 235 to 86. Cleveland took to the stump attacking the high-rate McKinley tariff, but Cleveland being Cleveland grew concerned about the party's drift toward the silverite position and insisted on speaking out also against the heresy of "free silver." He issued a public letter stating his position—surely knowing that this would be a step bound to alienate important wings of his party. But he concluded, "I am supposed to be a leader in my party. If any word of mine can check these dangerous fallacies, it is my duty to give that word, whatever the cost may be to me."[69]

In his third try for the presidency, in 1892, Cleveland clearly emerged as a staunch conservative and was more associated than even before with the economic and banking interests of the East. He received the nomination and in a rather mild campaign won the election by sweeping the electoral vote 277 to 145 and the popular vote 5,556,000 to Benjamin Harrison's 5,175,000. Cleveland's victory was clearly decisive and, for the first time since Buchanan's term, the Democrats controlled the presidency and both houses of Congress.[70]

The most explosive event during the summer of 1892 was the fierce battle at the Carnegie steel works between union leaders and Pinkerton guards hired by Carnegie agent Henry Clay Frick. The violence and brutality of the confrontation hurt the pro-business Republicans and lent credence to the view that class warfare was about to sweep the nation. Cleveland attacked the attempt to crush the union, agreeing in a modest way with some of its complaints. But labor unrest spread throughout areas of the South and West, as the nature of the American economy was changing dramatically. Cleveland's second term was to prove more disappointing than his first—a not uncommon occurrence in presidential politics. Once again he was flooded with patronage requests, and criticisms followed that he was too much of a partisan spoilsman or that he was not cognizant of a particular person's unique contribution to the party. While patronage considerations abounded especially in the Treasury and State departments, Cleveland added significantly to the classified civil service totals by putting 85,000 of the 205,000 into those ranks and keeping reformer Theodore Roosevelt on the Civil Service Commission.

Cleveland pushed for an early victory in repealing the Sherman Silver Purchase Act; when the panic of May 1893 hit the nation, calls for currency reform and tougher financial practices were echoing throughout skittish financial circles and even into silverite areas in the hinterlands. Under intense pressures, Cleveland called for a special session on August 7.

During this summer, Cleveland's health became a problem, and he quietly underwent a major operation for removal of cancerous tissue in his mouth. Fearing public concern and unsure of the economic situation, the president vanished, and the surgery was successfully done on a yacht, with few people knowing about it. As currency difficulties increased, the hoarding of gold, silver, and even greenbacks occurred in different locations. Despite a brilliant speech by an up and coming William Jennings Bryan, the House of Representatives passed a bill repealing the Silver Purchase Act, and the Senate followed suit. The Democrats were clearly divided on free coinage, however, and it was the Republicans who provided the margin for Cleveland and sound money men of both parties. Senator James T. Morgan, a silverite, branded the bipartisan alliance saying, "they stick as close and affectionately to each other as a stamp sticks to a love letter." In the Senate, Democrats pushed for a compromise, but Cleveland demanded the silver law's unconditional repeal and he got it.[71]

Cleveland also continued his firm opposition to American imperialist foreign policy and he reversed Harrison's support for annexing Hawaii. The United States under Republican administrations had long desired to add the Hawaiian Islands to its definition of Manifest Destiny. When there was a revolt against the queen of Hawaii on January 16, 1893, the American minister there, John Stevens, unilaterally recognized the provincial government the next day and proclaimed an American protectorate over her realm. Although the Harrison administration finally disavowed the protectorate, it acted as if it still existed. Soon after, Secretary of State John W. Foster sent the Senate a treaty of annexation.

Cleveland recalled the treaty before it was voted on. One newspaper, the New York *Commercial Advertiser*, contrasted the dream of Seward, Marcy, and Blaine to put the United States at the crossroads of the Pacific with the timid actions of Cleveland, "the Buffalo lilliputian." The president further ordered an independent investigation of the situation in Hawaii, which revealed that U.S. companies and their local allies had helped instigate independence for commercial reasons rather than any idealistic motive to help the natives. The cabinet discussed how to put the situation right again, how to restore the deposed queen to her throne, and how to end the rebel regime. The queen wanted no compromise and insisted on prosecuting her disloyal subjects, while the provisional government refused to yield to Cleveland's desires to undo their revolution. The president finally dumped the matter into the lap of Congress asking for a legislative solution that would be consistent with "American honor, integrity, and morality." Congress, as one might expect, did nothing and the provisional government remained in power.[72]

Cleveland's basic approach in foreign policy held true in the case of Cuba as well, as he refused to recognize the rebels on that island, in large part because, in his judgment, it would have meant war with Spain. Some senators demanded that the president acknowledge the existence of an independent Cuba, and one warned of impeachment if he did not. When others insisted that Congress should declare war anyhow, Cleveland bluntly countered that as commander in chief, he would not mobilize the army regardless of the legislative branch's decision. Thus, Cleveland refused to take on the role McKinley embraced later as a war president.

As his second term moved on, the tariff remained an issue that Democrats could run on, and Cleveland once again became a reformer of the rate structure. The House was more amenable to change than the Senate, but Cleveland's attempt to rally Democrats in Congress to the party banner and remind them of the party's previous position drew a hostile reaction from the upper house. One Democrat and former Cleveland ally, Arthur Pue Gorman, denounced Cleveland as dishonest and devious in trying to repeal the tariff, and insisted that he was encroaching on the legislative branch's prerogatives. Cleveland's efforts failed in part due to his own weakness as a leader; in 1913, Wilson would face a similar situation with the Senate and prevail. A watered-down bill finally passed, but Cleveland refused to sign it. The Wilson-Gorman Act, as it was called, made few changes except in removing the duty on wool.

But as this ritual tariff battle was continuing, as it had since the 1790s, powerful forces of dissent were gathering especially in the West. Financial problems, dropping prices, and depressed conditions prompted cries for social justice. At the core of the discontent was the worldwide food surplus that was due to the mechanization of agriculture and the increase in available productive acreage. From 1880 to 1900, land under cultivation in the United States jumped over 50 percent to 305 million acres. In Canada, Argentina, Australia, and Russia, production increased markedly as well.[73]

On the farms, credit was hard to come by, mortgage rates were climbing, prices had dropped, tariff rates kept high the prices of articles of consumption, railroad charges were increasing, and debts and foreclosures mounted. Cleveland's tough stand on sound money only added to the difficulties in the hinterlands. The administration had decided to float a $50 million bond issue in order to replenish the gold stock in the U.S. Treasury, and once again the president was attacked for working with Wall Street and corporate financiers. When Congress passed a moderate silver bill, which would probably have had little impact on the economy but which would have healed some of the party's wounds, Cleveland again exercised his veto.

Cleveland's problems multiplied as economic conditions worsened. The president of the American Federation of Labor, Samuel Gompers, insisted that in 1894 some three million people were unemployed. A good number of these people became vagabonds and tramps. One Jacob Coxey gathered some of these bands together and rounded up an "army," which left Ohio to march on Washington and demand that the government issue a half-billion dollars in paper money. By the time the army reached the capital, it was disorganized and only three hundred people arrived.

Several other armies had experienced similar fates in their protests, but the point was clear that discontent could become militant, and Cleveland was becoming even more of a period piece. Nowhere was this more obvious than in the Pullman strike. During the winter of 1893–94, the Pullman Palace Car Company cut wages by about 25 percent and dismissed many employees in order to slash costs. Yet in the previous fiscal year, the corporation paid substantial profits, and to add insult to injury, the company's town rentals in Chicago, where many of the employees lived with their families, were considerably higher than those of the surrounding areas.[74]

Finally left with little disposable income for even necessities, workers led by Eugene V. Debs struck, and conflict spread across the nation. Attorney General Richard Olney pushed hard for the president to enter the strike and assert the federal government's authority against the labor unions. In the past, Olney had strong ties to railroads and had taken a tough stand against the Coxey protest march. Apparently, he hoped to get a court injunction to forbid any attempts to interfere with the mails, have the judge and marshals indicate that the order could not be enforced, and then get Cleveland into a position where he had to use troops to rescue the courts.

Cleveland did send troops on July 3, 1894, and soon extensive mob violence broke out in Chicago. Public opinion seemed to favor his decisiveness, and his attorney general warned him that he had to stop the forces of anarchy and destructive despotism. But some criticism did come closer to the truth. Governor John P. Altgeld took the president to task for sending U.S. troops into his state of

Illinois without state authorities asking for them, the usual practice
in American history. The president's response rested on the alleged
need to protect the mails and on a broad interpretation of the interstate commerce power of the federal Constitution, a strange defense
from a conservative.

A presidential commission later reviewed the strike, condemned
the Pullman Company and its manager, and defended the union from
charges of having provoked violence. In 1895, the Supreme Court
upheld Cleveland's use of emergency powers, but avoided approving the specifics of the injunction. The president had followed too
closely the assumptions and information of his attorney general and
in seeking to protect property and life had broken the strike.[75]

In a foreign dispute in 1895, Cleveland relied on advice from
the same Olney. The background was a border disagreement between
British Guiana and Venezuela, which the United States was interested in seeing settled. When the British proved to be reluctant to
arbitrate, Cleveland became annoyed. Olney, who had become secretary of state, took a hard-line view of the whole conflict and urged
a reaffirmation of the Monroe Doctrine arguing, "Today the United
States is practically sovereign on this continent, and its fiat is law
upon the subjects to whom it confines its interpretation." The response of the British to that formulation was hostile.

The administration then asked Congress for money for a commission to determine the Venezuelan boundary and insisted that the
United States maintain that border against any aggression. The threat
of war was obvious, and it unleashed the very imperialist sentiments
Cleveland so deplored. But the wheel turned as expressions of
Anglo-American friendship eventually prevailed. Finally, the dispute
was settled by arbitration.[76]

Despite the president's show of forceful leadership at times, his
general policies were not meeting many of the demands that severe
depression and continuing unrest were bringing. In the congressional
elections in 1894, the Democrats were handed a startling defeat,
causing their strength to drop in the House of Representatives from
219 to 104 while the Republicans increased from 127 seats to 244.
The Populists had polled 1.5 million votes, up 42 percent over 1892,
and elected 6 U.S. senators, 7 congressmen, 21 state executive officials, 150 state senators, and 315 state representatives. Cleveland
was becoming a leader of the past; the future would belong to Bryan.

Added to Cleveland's woes was the need to float still another
bond issue in late 1894. By then the cash reserves in the Treasury

were a little over $100 million dollars and only some sixty million or so were in gold. However, in the winter of 1894–95, economic conditions were brutally harsh and once again a drain of gold supplies took place. In less than ten weeks, the Treasury faced serious difficulties after the 1894 bond issue had been let out. Cleveland pleaded with Congress to give him authority to have the Treasury sell 3 percent long-term bonds, redeem and cancel greenbacks and Sherman Act notes, and require that all import duties be paid in gold. Western opposition predictably mounted to any tight money policies.

Faced with congressional deadlock, the president and Secretary of Treasury John Griffin Carlisle planned to float a third bond issue under the authority of the older act. The key figure in these financial negotiations proved to be J. P. Morgan, the very symbol of all that the Western populists and union leaders hated about Wall Street. The administration and the Morgan syndicate were unable to agree on terms of the sale at first. But the government floated the bond issue yielding $61,116,244, and the syndicate did well in disposing of the bonds quickly in February. This, in turn, led to criticism that the Morgan group and its associates, the Rothchilds, made $5 million for twenty-two minutes of work.

Antagonisms in the West toward the Eastern financier classes were also increasing as a result of the Supreme Court's decision striking down the income tax, which had been passed during the Civil War. In addition, the high court ruled that even the diffident efforts of Attorney General Olney to prosecute the trusts under the Sherman Act were improper. The act required proof that a trust not only possess a monopoly in manufacturing, but also that it extended into interstate commerce. Olney was not particularly disturbed with the Supreme Court's verdict, since he never approved of the law in the first place, but the intentions of the Court added to public discontent. In addition, the Court upheld the injunction against Socialist labor leader Eugene V. Debs and his associates for obstructing the mail trains that were deemed to be engaged in interstate commerce. The Court refused to look at the merits of the case and simply reasserted the power of the national government. Overall, it appeared that the courts had thrown their lot in with the wealthy classes and had made it impossible to get a fair hearing or to ameliorate corporate abuses.

To many populists and Westerners, all of these trends showed that the government was a captive of the Eastern wealthy classes, and Cleveland often became a target for their rage, even when he was not involved. As Ben Tillman said while campaigning in South Carolina for a Senate seat, "Send me to Washington, and I'll tickle Cleveland's fat ribs with my pitchfork."

As he moved toward the end of his second term, Cleveland pressed hard for his party to hold on to his sound money position and focused his efforts on the South, having given up on the West. In late 1895 and early 1896, the administration tried to float still another bond issue by public subscription instead of through the House of Morgan, and the government sold $66,800,000 of the bonds to 788 persons and $33,179,250 to Morgan. The government was able to replenish the gold reserve to a level of about $128,713,000, but the drift to silver had captured the Democratic party by 1896. In contrast, the Republicans under the strong leadership of Mark Hanna emphasized the gold standard and sound money in their campaign and contribution efforts.[77]

At the 1896 Democratic convention, Bryan's brilliant "Cross of Gold" speech earned him the nomination, and the Democratic party pledged itself to the cause of silver. Cleveland's response was to the point, "If ever there is a penitentiary devoted to the incarceration of those who commit crimes against the Democratic party, how easily it could be filled just at this time." Cleveland's two separate terms represent some continuity and departures. He vigorously opposed the drift toward empire and reasserted the faith of simple republican virtues. But in the first and especially in the second term, he staked out a strong and at times inflexible position, putting the government behind the propertied and financier classes. He never fully comprehended the immense social changes beginning around him or understood that popular discontent could not be salved with modestly lower tariff rates.[78]

THE HARRISON INTERLUDE

Benjamin Harrison, the grandson of William Henry Harrison, emerged as a dark horse choice of the Republican party in 1888 because of his strength in Indiana, one of the critical states in any presidential race in that period. He was a well-known local Civil War brevet brigadier general, a U.S. senator and a strongly religious Presbyterian. In the election of 1888, the major issue was the tariff, and Harrison waged a rather effective front-porch campaign, as he gave ninety-four speeches from his Indianapolis home. Although Cleveland carried the popular vote, Harrison won the electoral vote 233 to 168. With his collected, calm and almost icy public persona, Harrison celebrated his election with the observation, "Now I walk with God."[79]

Almost from the beginning, he ignored many of the party leaders and spent incredible time on patronage matters, favoring people with backgrounds similar to his own. Every cabinet member—like the president—was a Presbyterian, five had legal training, several were natives of Ohio, and some had risen to the rank of brevet brigadier general in the Civil War—a closet of advisors made in the image of its leader. During the campaign, he had seemed more willing to support extending civil service than Cleveland; after his inauguration, though, his ardor for reform cooled. One major appointment to the Civil Service Commission that he made was Theodore Roosevelt who ungratefully was to characterize Harrison as "the little gray man in the White House."[80]

In a period of executive decline, Harrison was remarkably attuned to the need to provide some presidential leadership in dealing with the legislative branch, and the Fifty-first Congress passed some important pieces of legislation. Harrison retained the general Whig disposition to defer to the legislative branch, but he did push for his proposals more than was usual in the period before Theodore Roosevelt. Harrison also threatened to use the veto, and insisted on having input in the bills being discussed. Faced with a very narrow majority in both houses (39 to 37 in the Senate and 166 to 159 in the House of Representatives), party cohesion was important and loyalty was stressed. Assisted by a powerful House speaker, Thomas "Czar" Reed, a Republican agenda was put forth in Congress.

The major issue was once again the tariff, and the Republican party position was clear: higher rates. The McKinley Bill, as it was called, raised custom duties an average of 49.5 percent, the highest tariff up to that time. The tariff had two important consequences: first, it gave the executive extensive leeway in negotiating reciprocal treaties, and second, it created such an uproar in some regions that it contributed to extensive GOP losses in the 1890 congressional elections. More than a dozen reciprocal agreements were approved, and the president was granted extensive powers to negotiate trade agreements and modify tariff rates without having to consult Congress.

But the Democrats had skillfully conveyed to the population that

they were being hurt economically, especially those living in the
rural areas. In his annual message on December 1, 1890, Harrison
defensively denounced the misinformation that "has been so widely
disseminated at home and abroad." on the issue.[81] The Republicans
tried to quiet some of the popular discontent on two matters: anti-
trust legislation and the silver issue. The first concern eventually
led both parties to support the Sherman Anti-Trust Act, which was
little more than symbolic reassurance on the question of monopolistic practices. The bill passed the Senate 52 to 1 and swept through
the House without a division. The law was vague and was rarely
used since economic concentration was not a great concern to the
Harrison administration. Congress did not even appropriate funds
to conduct investigations of trusts. The administration instigated a
total of seven antitrust cases, but the Justice Department prosecuted
few major cases successfully. Cleveland and McKinley, who both
followed Harrison, presided over eight and three prosecutions, respectively. Only with a new type of public outrage and a new popular champion, Theodore Roosevelt, would the Sherman Anti-Trust
Act become a law of some reckoning.[82]

The handling of the silver question was less harmonious. Divisions between the Republicans from the West and the mainstay of
the GOP in the industrial East were accentuated in the demand for
free, unlimited coinage of silver. Harrison, unlike his predecessors,
seemed more sympathetic to the silver advocates. As has been noted
before, the Bland-Allison Act passed in 1878 over Hayes's veto,
mandated that the federal government purchase $2 million to $4
million of silver billion each month and coin silver dollars. However, the government never bought more than the minimum, and
most of the minted silver was never put into circulation, since the
United States stayed on the gold standard.

Harrison knew that the silver issue was being pushed by some
Republicans, especially those from Nevada, Colorado, and the six
new states created in the West. Their endorsement of the Harrison-
supported tariff was important to the party, and their political leverage markedly increased. Congress finally settled on the Sherman
Silver Purchase Act, which had the government purchase 4.5 million ounces of silver, the total output of U.S. mines at the time.
But even that commitment was not sufficient for the silverites as
the price of silver dropped far below the $1.29 per ounce level that
Harrison and others counted on.[83] The panic of 1893 led Congress

to repeal the Sherman Act, as the Republicans emphasized even more the sanctity of the gold standard.

The GOP under Harrison's lead exhibited a final gasp of interest in protecting black rights against abuse in the South, but party discipline broke on the issue and the Senate prevented any legislative action. The same roadblock appeared as repeated attempts to provide federal aid to combat illiteracy failed. Part of the opposition came from a fear of federal interference in local conditions, but some of the criticism was due to the possibility that blacks might augment their political power.

As noted, in the congressional elections, the GOP suffered major losses, and the results further undercut the president's leadership. Some of the losses were due to state and local rather than national issues, but the GOP had also adopted positions on social issues that tended to be seen as too prohibitive and restrictive. Party loyalty was affected by popular opposition to various proposed pieces of state legislation in Illinois, Indiana, Iowa, Michigan, Ohio, and Wisconsin. Faced with squabbles over patronage, which alienated important Eastern Republican bosses, and attacked because of the high tariff and the compromise silver policy, the president was confronted with increasing problems. A loner by inclination and reserved by choice, Harrison had few advisors, and a string of deaths in his cabinet members' families cast a pale over the last two years of his administration.

The Democrats used these popular sources of discontent skillfully, and a third-party movement, the People's party, was grounded partially on those accumulated grievances. In 1892, the Populist ticket headed by a former brigadier general, James B. Weaver, polled more than a million votes offering a viable alternative to both the Republicans and the conservative Democrats.

Harrison did what many presidents do; stymied at home, he turned to foreign policy and began a series of initiatives that were belligerent, chauvinistic, and dedicated to increasing American influence in the world. To support Harrison's foreign policy, the United States continued to augment the size of the navy and to make some token nods to a growing military establishment. After the long post-Civil War deterioration of the fleet, the United States under Arthur and then Harrison made some strides to upgrade American naval forces. The United States in 1882 had too few warships and too many naval officers—one officer for every four enlisted men.[84]

Prodded by junior officers and the compelling ideas of Captain Alfred Thayer Mahan, the role of sea power in the world was recognized by the naval establishment in the United States and later in Europe. In his book *The Influence of Sea Power Upon History 1660–1783*, Mahan emphasized the importance of naval commerce in the balance of power, the desirability of an isthmian canal, the importance of acquiring bases in the Caribbean, the need for a powerful navy, and the benefits of annexing Hawaii. Partially, in response, Congress in 1883 authorized the commissioning of three steel cruisers, the establishment of a Naval War College, and the construction in 1885 of five small naval cruisers, two larger cruisers, and two second-class battleships. The administration and Congress toyed with upgrading the army as well, but there they were less successful. Changes were made in recruitment and training, however, and the rights of enlisted men were more fully recognized. At the time, the army was preoccupied with the Indian wars and after the brutal Battle of Wounded Knee, the tribes were pacified, to use the euphemism for defeat and near extinction.

In examining the administration's foreign policy, considerable attention has focused on the achievements of James G. Blaine, who had previously been secretary of state under Garfield and briefly under Arthur and who was the single best-known Republican in the United States during this period. Blaine has been portrayed by some historians as a far-sighted leader who envisioned the American nation exerting considerable influence by building and controlling an isthmian canal and having a strong presence in the Caribbean and in Hawaii—a perspective similar to Mahan's prescriptions. Actually though, Blaine was often ill during Harrison's term and after 1890, it was the president who moved vigorously if not aggressively into the foreign policy field. In confronting Germany and Great Britain in Samoa, for example, Harrison firmly pressed U.S. interests. The secretary of state's instructions to an American delegation going there spelled out the administration's position, which recognized that "our interest on the Pacific is steadily increasing; that our commerce with the East is developing largely and rapidly; and that the certainty of an early opening of an Isthmian transit from the Atlantic to the Pacific (under American protection) must create changes in which no power can be so directly or more durably interested than the United States."[85]

Harrison also pushed for a stronger U.S. presence in Latin America, working with Blaine to have the United States replace

Great Britain as the major economic force in that region. The administration ended up with eight reciprocal trade treaties in that area, proving that Harrison's rare display of extensive lobbying of Congress was a correct strategy.

The foreign policy of the administration was at times a mixture of toughness and negotiation. In another area, the president took a hard line with Chile after an internal altercation there led to threats of war. In fact, it appeared that the administration was ready to confront Chile militarily unless the latter backed down, and its minister apologized. In New Orleans, when a lynching occurred involving Italians and Italian-Americans, the president pronounced insensitively that Italy's outrage was an overreaction, and he would make no apology. In other trade issues, U.S. demands for an end to the boycott of pork by certain western European nations were reiterated, and Harrison insisted on a quick end to their prohibitions on imports. Hoping to get American farm support and unwilling to prolong negotiations, the president focused his efforts on Germany and that nation, fearful of trade retaliations, ended the boycott. Soon, most of the rest of the Continent followed suit. The president proved equally assertive in dealing with Great Britain on the issue of seal hunting rights in the Bering Strait islands. Last, the administration tried as had its predecessors to finance a canal across the Nicaraguan isthmus. But Congress was recalcitrant and that initiative failed.[86]

By early 1890, death seemed to strike with frightening regularity in the Harrison cabinet and its families. Blaine lost a son and a daughter; the secretary of the navy, Benjamin Tracy, lost his wife and daughter in a fire; a year later the secretary of the treasury, William Windom, died; and Harrison's wife died in 1892. By the beginning of 1893, Blaine had passed on and so had many of the nation's previous generation's political leaders: Rutherford B. Hayes, Jefferson Davis, Admiral David Dixon Porter, William Tecumseh Sherman, former vice president Hannibal Hamlin, and others.

As for Harrison, he had seriously considered not running for reelection in 1892, but the early threat of a possible Blaine candidacy fired up his competitive passions, and he entered the race. However, Blaine was weary and very ill, and it was only his wife's hatred of the president that kept the "Plumed Knight" in the race long after prudence and self-respect should have prevented it. In that summer, labor strikes were breaking out in the West and at Andrew Carnegie's steel mills in Pennsylvania, and Carnegie's ties to the GOP surely did not help the party or the president. Grover Cleveland was the Democratic nominee again. This time he won a strong victory. The Populists with General James B. Weaver on their ballot garnered as noted a million votes, and the Democrats hit hard at the rises in the tariff, carrying the solid South, New Jersey, New York, Connecticut, and even Indiana and capturing control of both houses of Congress.

In the closing months of his administration, Harrison continued his interest in foreign policy, focusing on trying to gain control of Hawaii and pushing for improvements in the harbor of the Pearl River, where he hoped to lay the groundwork for a naval station. Harrison thus accepted many of the restrictive views about what a president should do especially in dealing with Congress, but he, like Arthur and McKinley, became rather forthcoming in pressing American interests abroad in modest ways, while European states expanded their imperialist visions and their empires of ambition and exploitation.

MCKINLEY'S TRANSITION

To those students of history who view presidents in clear and concise terms and judgments, William McKinley is a particular problem. He is frequently portrayed as a weak and malleable executive, the last figure in a string of passive executives. In part, McKinley suffers by comparison with his vice president and successor, Theodore Roosevelt, and in part he has come to epitomize the presidency in the waning days of the nineteenth century. In all probability, a better assessment is that McKinley's presidency was clearly a transitional one; his administration in its management of a brief war and a longer occupation bore the imprint of the president's style and his view of America's imperialist destiny.

William McKinley was born on January 29, 1843, in Niles, Ohio. He served in the Civil War, and he rose up the ranks from private in the Ohio Volunteer Infantry to brevet major. After the war, McKinley studied law, settled in Canton, Ohio, and became associated with Rutherford B. Hayes. He served as a congressman and later as governor of Ohio and was identified with the high protectionist tariff. Friends found him to be a dignified but sensitive man whose personal life was marred by tragedy and an invalid wife. Other more critical acquaintances were to conclude that he was indecisive, uncertain, and extremely susceptible to changing public opinion. The speaker of the House, Joseph G. Cannon, once concluded that McKinley's ear was so close to the ground that it was full of grasshoppers, and another of his colleagues, Senator Thomas Platt of New York, judged that McKinley was "simply a clever gentleman, much too amiable and much too impressionable to be safely entrusted with great executive office."[87]

But entrusted he was, winning the GOP nomination in 1896 over a divided field and defeating William Jennings Bryan, the boy orator from Nebraska. McKinley and his campaign manager, Mark Hanna, ran the Republican campaign with a finesse unseen up to that time. McKinley was pictured as the advocate of prosperity and financial stability, and the GOP positioned itself for sound money and against Bryan's panacea of unlimited coinage of silver. Gold and the high tariff became the defining issues between the political parties, and workers were warned by their employers that a Bryan victory meant disaster for them. Hanna was direct and effective in raising large sums of money from the business community, portraying McKinley as the safe candidate. Indeed, Theodore Roosevelt said that Hanna had "advertised McKinley as if he were a patent medicine." McKinley undertook a front-porch campaign staying in Canton, while Bryan traveled twenty-nine thousand miles across the country giving five hundred speeches in twenty-nine states. The results showed that the conservative appeals worked; McKinley received 7,035,638 popular votes to Bryan's 6,457,945 and 271 to 176 electoral votes.[88]

As expected, the first topic on the new administration's agenda was tariff reform. The Democratic party under Cleveland had split in two over the issue, and he had been unsuccessful in resolving the dispute. Some changes in sentiment were taking place, however. The Democrats controlled Congress in 1893–94 and passed a tariff bill that raised many rates, despite their party's traditional position on free trade. McKinley meanwhile had decided to moderate his straightforward advocacy of high rates; under the influence of Secretary of State Blaine in the Harrison administration, he had come to understand the logic of trade reciprocity with foreign nations, and once he became president, he began to reconsider the whole issue.

Early in his administration he laid out his general views on other issues as well. McKinley was an early opponent of racism, although as president he showed little interest in the plight of blacks, even when the issue of lynching was brought up. His simple prescription to blacks was that they should exercise patience and self-control in facing their adversities. On the economic front, McKinley was aware of the increasing concerns being raised about the growth of trusts and corporate consolidations, but what his exact position was remained unclear. He promised support for the merit system, but was knowledgeable that patronage was the oil that made the party machinery run. He insisted that he would tolerate "no jingo nonsense" in his administration. Yet McKinley did support the building of a Nicaraguan canal, the purchase of the Danish West Indies, and U.S. control over Hawaii. He advocated the extension of trade opportunities in the Caribbean and Asia, and assumed that the benefits from such trade would work not just to the United States' advantage, but to the advantages of those people as well. Early in his term, McKinley showed a genuine concern for the Cuban nation still ruled by the Spanish, but he insisted that the United States wanted "no wars of conquest; we must avoid the temptation of territorial aggression." To spread his message on these and other issues, McKinley made himself more accessible than most of his predecessors and directly worked with the press—a novelty at that time.[89]

Discussions by the leaders of the Republican party in Congress on the tariff led them to support a bill that would increase rates on silk, change the rates on wool, substitute specific rates for ad valorem rates, and add taxes on luxury items, especially those imported from France. As deliberations continued, some American senators linked up tariff reductions for France with possible cooperation on bimetallism, which would mean a wide use of silver as a currency. Thus, high-protectionist Republicans and Western silver Republicans were involved in these trade-offs. Although McKinley played little direct part in the final bill, he did approve the compromise and signed the act. The bimetallism cause was seriously impaired, though, when the British government, faced with opposition from its colonial leaders in India to the compromise about minting silver, backed off on any agreement. Otherwise, McKinley may have proposed a sort of free silver policy after all.[90]

The administration had other more important dealings with the British, most importantly its desire to repudiate the Clayton-Bulwer Treaty, which limited American initiatives to dig a canal somewhere in Central America. The British were hoping to use that agreement to gain further concessions on the Alaskan-Canada boundary dispute and on other issues concerning fishing and hunting. Eventually, the United States simply threatened to abandon its treaty commitments altogether if the British continued to be recalcitrant, and U.S. debate shifted to whether the canal should be cut across Nicaragua or the Panama area of Colombia. Finally it was also Theodore Roosevelt who decided the matter in his own way.

The great issue that preoccupied the president's attention was not the canal or trade reciprocity, but the conflict in Cuba, and he would be forever linked with his controversial handling of the Spanish-American War and the difficult problems that resulted. The usual account is that a weak-spined president wanted to avoid war, but goaded on by the jingoist presses of William Randolph Hearst and Joseph Pulitzer, he allowed war to be forced on him and on a democracy made mad by rabid journalism. Actually, McKinley's role and the causes of the war are rather more complicated.

In Cuba in 1897, the rebels had waged a guerrilla conflict that undermined the economy and affected Spanish control. Aided by American friends, the Cubans continued their attacks, and the colonial regime sent several hundred thousand soldiers to restore order to the island. The new commander, General Valeriano Weyler y Nicolau, vigorously pursued the repression of the rebel forces, establishing concentration camps as he moved people from the countryside into fortified hamlets—a strategy similar to that employed by the United States in Vietnam in the 1960s. His efforts earned him the nickname "The Butcher," and he became a symbol of Spanish misrule.

Atrocities, real and imagined, were the stuff that many U.S. newspapers lived on and transmitted in gruesome detail to Americans at home and abroad. Publishers Hearst and Pulitzer, engaged in a fierce circulation war, outdid each other in their exposés. Democrats used the war to criticize McKinley and demanded justice for the oppressed, while some Republicans, abandoning the conservatism of many businessmen, pushed for territorial expansion. As has been seen, Cleveland opposed granting belligerency rights to the Cubans and supported Spanish rule, fearing that turmoil would lead to other European nations intervening. Even the Cleveland administration began to grow weary of Spanish inflexibility, however, and popular opposition in the United States toward the Spanish rule in Cuba increased even before McKinley's term began.[91]

To gain greater knowledge about the dispute, McKinley sent an old friend, William R. Day, to investigate the Cuban situation, and his report was clear. Cuba was "wrapped in the stillness of death and the silence of desolation" and held out little hope for an easy

or peaceful solution. The new president carried on Cleveland's balancing act and warned the Spanish government that the suppression
of the rebellion had to be carried on within humane parameters and
within a limited period of time. His assumptions were that the Spanish could not win militarily and that through diplomatic pressure,
they would end up yielding to the Cubans. At first, the Spanish
regime tried moderation, amnesty, and suspension of the relocation
policy. By the end of 1897, it appeared that U.S. diplomacy had
garnered some rewards.

A strong American pose was struck especially as European powers were becoming more assertive in Asia and Central America. But
the pacification program in Cuba produced, as one could predict,
the opposite results. It emboldened the rebels, led to rioting, and
increased Democratic party criticism that McKinley was favoring
the Spanish regime. In a show of concern and strength, the administration ordered the battleship the U.S.S. *Maine* to Havana. Meanwhile, the Spanish regime also moved toward a tougher policy on
suppressing the rebellion. Then on February 16, 1896, Secretary of
the Navy John D. Long received reports that the battleship had been
destroyed with 284 enlisted men and 2 officers killed. The sensation-
al press picked up the story and played it as the ultimate Spanish
atrocity. The cause of the explosion is still unclear to this day, although there is some evidence that it was due to internal combus-
tion and not sabotage. The president moved cautiously, and avoided
rallying the people to war. At first, he quietly explored once again
with Spain the possibility of having the United States buy Cuba and
suggested other arrangements for governing that island in turmoil.
He asked Congress for $50 million to upgrade defenses, and the
proposal sailed through the Congress without a negative vote. The
president's critics still saw his unwillingness to sound the trumpet
louder as weakness due to his closeness to wealthy Americans who
held Spanish bonds. But McKinley gave a different and more cred-
ible response, "I shall never get into a war until I am sure that God
and man approve. I have been through one war; I have seen the
dead piled up; and I do not want to see another."[92]

A board of inquiry found that the *Maine* was probably blown
up by a mine, and the Spanish government responded that it would
agree to submit the *Maine* question to arbitration. As for the president, McKinley asked for deliberateness and sent Congress a low-
keyed message, refusing to be pushed by either Democrats or
Republicans into war. But when Spain decided not to compromise

on the future of Cuba, the president lost much of his flexibility to maneuver. He appealed through the Vatican for concessions from the Spanish; on April 6, he postponed a message on the conflict in the hope of seeing some movement. Meanwhile, Spain was also delaying, trying to entice other European nations to support its position, as its government recognized that the concessions it was being asked to give would end up amounting to independence for the island.

On April 11, McKinley sent to Congress his message. Again it was not a ringing endorsement of war, but a narrative account of the situation, and a statement that expressed his personal disappointment over the lack of progress on the matter. He laid out the dangers for the United States that were inherent in the dispute and concluded "the present condition of affairs in Cuba is a constant menace to our peace, and entails upon this Government an enormous expense." The appeal declared, "In the name of humanity, in the name of civilization, in behalf of endangered American interests which give us as the right and the duty to speak and to act, the war in Cuba must stop."[93]

McKinley asked Congress to grant him the power to seek a "full and final termination of hostilities between the Government of Spain and the people of Cuba," to establish a stable government there, and to use U.S. military forces to accomplish those objectives. Congressmen on both sides of the aisle expressed again some disappointment that McKinley had not sent a stirring war message asking for a declaration of war. Democrats pushed for Cuban independence, but the Republicans in the House stood by the president, and McKinley was simply authorized to intervene to end the war, just as he had asked. In the Senate, resolutions supporting the Cuban republic and disavowing control of the island passed, but McKinley disapproved of the Senate proposal, favoring instead the House's version, and he ended up prevailing. Finally, as diplomacy failed, McKinley asked Congress on April 25 for a declaration of war. For five months, McKinley had pursued diplomacy and accommodation, hardly the strategy of a man who wanted war or went into it blindly to protect U.S. corporate interests in Cuba.

American reasons for entering the war spanned the spectrum: idealism for the spread of democracy, a revulsion toward the Spanish and their alleged atrocities, newspaper hysteria, overall social and regional tensions impacting on the United States, a desire for new markets, and a host of dynamics that merged into a tidal wave

of support. As for the Spanish, they saw one of the mainstays of
their old empire being lost at the very time other European nations
were becoming more assertive and imperialistic. And so a reluctant, but resigned McKinley prepared for three months of war, probably the most popular war the American people ever waged up to
that time.

McKinley assumed his responsibilities as a wartime commander
in chief and proved to be a master of detail and command. The
communications revolution was beginning, and the president had a
section of the White House turned into a war room, complete with
a switchboard connected to twenty telegraphic wires that kept him
in contact with the army and, to a lesser extent, the navy, and also
with the French and British cable traffic in the Caribbean. Within
twenty minutes he could reach the commanders in the field, and he
understood better than any president before him, and several after,
the conduct of armed forces under his command. The Signal Corps
had an agent in Havana who could keep the administration abreast
of activities on the island and the whereabouts of the Spanish fleet
at Santiago, and the White House also had fifteen telephone lines
to link up eight executive departments and Congress.[94]

The news coming from the Pacific was most impressive. Commodore George Dewey had easily defeated the Spanish fleet at
Manila Bay on May 1, 1898, when his armada sank seven of their
ships without the loss of any U.S. vessels. His successes not only
boded well for the war at hand, they opened up new possibilities
for the United States to become a power in Asia and the Far Pacific. As for McKinley, he had to reevaluate the United States' control of the Philippines, an extension of American power that he
probably did not foresee. But he quickly approved attempts to end
Filipino sovereignty and resolved to stand firm against anti-imperialists at home and nationalist insurgents in the islands.

McKinley also pushed Congress to annex Hawaii by joint resolution, a proposal that Democrats were most vocally against because
of the islands' multiracial population. In the House, Speaker Reed
publicly opposed the resolution, and newspapers carried the speculation that the president would simply seize Hawaii under his executive powers. Eventually, McKinley's position prevailed in Congress
once again, and the islands became part of the new American empire.

McKinley was much too sanguine about the Filipino insurgents
who had been fighting Spanish rule and who disapproved of Ameri-

can control being established over their nation. Led by Emilio Aguinaldo, the rebels at first regarded U.S. activities as disinterested and temporary, but they resorted to guerrilla warfare as their new American rulers started to settle in. As for the president, McKinley began telling visitors that while he was undecided about the fate of the Philippines, he supported "the general principle of holding on to what we get."

As the war progressed, McKinley came to realize what Lincoln had found out—how poorly prepared America was to support a fighting force, even in what proved to be a much smaller conflict than the Civil War. Opposition arose immediately in the volunteer ranks of the National Guard to serving under regular officers, and one aide of the president, George Cortelyou, observed how intense was "the struggle for place among the ambitious gentlemen who desire to serve their country in high salaried and high titled positions." In the spring of 1898, the War Department was decentralized, demoralized, underpaid, and the victim of fierce turf battles. Delays in war materials and supplies were severe and the conditions of training camps and military sites became a national disgrace. The gravest problem that affected the troops in those hot climates was not the Spanish army but widespread disease, which dangerously debilitated the American troops. Theodore Roosevelt, then in the cavalry, wrote Henry Cabot Lodge, "no words could describe to you the confusion and lack of system and the general management of affairs here."[95]

American troops prevailed in Cuba, following up on the quick successes halfway around the globe in the Philippines. The administration decided to accept an offer to negotiate a peace treaty with Spain, and the cabinet approved terms that included that nation's giving up Cuba and the neighboring island of Puerto Rico. But McKinley's advisors were divided on the question of the Philippines, postponing that issue until the peace commission made its recommendations. The Philippines' fate would be supposedly left to the outcome of the peace talks, but the president began to feel more comfortable with the new imperialist mold he was creating. On one occasion he wrote, "The true measure of duty is not what we like but what we ought to like."[96]

As the war was coming to a merciful end, the president was confronted with increasing criticism directed at his secretary of war, Russell A. Alger, over the conditions facing American fighting men. Supply, discipline, and sanitation problems were taking their toll on the battlefields and in the training camps. Some 2,500 officers and enlisted men died from typhoid alone, in contrast to the 281 who died in battle.

Once again the administration had accepted the support of the insurgents, this time in Cuba, but did not formally recognize their existence later. The war had left the economy and governmental services on the island in shambles, and it was unclear what U.S. intentions were after the conflict. On October 1, McKinley chose Lincoln's old assistant and biographer, John Hay, to be his secretary of state. Hay replaced William R. Day who was asked to serve on the peace commission and work out a treaty with Spain. McKinley also tried to add several senators to the commission, but some opposition emerged because the Senate was required to ratify any treaty that might result.

As McKinley weighed his options toward the Philippines, he received reports of Japanese and German designs on the islands— overtures that led him to accept the idea of a U.S. protectorate. Publicly he seemed vague at first, using such platitudes as "territory sometimes comes to us when we go to war in a holy cause, and whenever it does the banner of liberty will float over it and bring, I trust, blessings and benefits to all the people." The president is supposed to have told a delegation from the Methodist Episcopal Church that he had paced the floor and dropped finally to his knees for divine guidance on the issue, knowing that the Filipinos were "unfit for self-government" and having more concerns about possible foreign encroachments on the islands. He concluded that there was nothing left to do but "uplift and civilize and Christianize" the Filipinos. Unfortunately for McKinley, the Filipinos had been Roman Catholic for centuries, and either he or the Almighty who supposedly directed his responses overlooked that part of the story, if it is true at all.[97]

The treaty draft provided for the United States to acquire the Philippines, Puerto Rico and Guam, with Spain giving up Cuba and receiving a $20 million payment in return. Proudly, the president in December reported that the flag had been "planted in two hemispheres, and there it remains the symbol of liberty and law, of peace and progress." He saw in this war a new unity that triumphed over the lingering feelings of sectionalism left from the Civil War.

The president worked closely with senators to win ratification of the treaty, and the administration encouraged state legislatures to pass resolutions of support—a rare strategy in this period. The opposition in Congress was divided in objectives and tactics. As he pushed for ratification, McKinley realized that tensions were growing in the Philippines between the insurgents and the U.S. Army. To deal with these problems, the president extended military government over the territories in question, and he took the broadest view of a commander in chief's authority since Lincoln's term. By a one-vote margin of the two-thirds majority needed, the treaty passed 57 to 27.

McKinley assured his fellow citizens that the Philippines was a trust "we have not sought," but that the nation could not abandon its new responsibilities. He insisted, "No imperial designs lurk in the American mind. They are alien to American sentiment, thought and purpose. Our priceless principles undergo no change under a tropical sun. They go with the flag." The United States would redeem the Filipinos from "savage indolence and habits." It was a heady and bold prescription from a president often portrayed as vacillating and moderate in mind and deeds.[98]

By the end of 1898, the president was speaking of "benevolent assimilation" in the Philippines, and the army and the Philippine Commission were pushing legal reforms, more social services, and responsible municipal government. The president advocated the creation of an American governor general with a cabinet he would select and advised by an elected council that would include some representatives from the native population. However, opposition crystallized at home around the Anti-Imperialist League, which had a national membership of thirty thousand people, including such prominent individuals as Carl Schurz and Andrew Carnegie. The league and its allies opposed the new American expansionism, seeing it as a threat to American traditions and ideals of self-government. In the Philippines, a frustrated Aguinaldo moved from conventional warfare to guerrilla tactics as the rebels fought for self-determination against their new foreign rulers. But McKinley's position was becoming more assertive and self-confident. At Iowa Falls, he told a cheering crowd, "It is no longer a question of expansion with us. We have expanded. If there is any question at all it is a question of contraction; and who is going to contract?"

The anti-imperialists responded in 1899 that American policy was a chronicle of brutality and atrocities in the Philippines. Historian Lewis L. Gould has shown how accounts of atrocities haunted the McKinley-Theodore Roosevelt administrations, when charges were made of a vast genocide that allegedly killed millions of people, six hundred thousand on Luzon island alone. He concluded that combat death estimates ranged from fourteen thousand to fifty-seven thousand, and that the "army court-martialed far more cases than it covered up," not exactly a consoling verdict. There was evidence of torture being used, and the wholesale destruction of secular and religious property occurred all too frequently for an army claiming to be liberating the Filipinos from Spanish horrors and their "savagery."[99]

The president faced problems in Cuba as well. Congress had approved in April 1898 the Teller Amendment, which put the United States on record opposing the annexation of Cuba once the island was pacified. Concerned about possible German inroads, McKinley insisted on a stable Cuban government and on some U.S. role in the fate of the island. In expressions that again were reminiscent of Lincoln, McKinley insisted that American authority in Cuba rested on "the law of belligerent right over conquered territory." The president as commander in chief had the right to govern the island until Congress acted otherwise or until the Cubans set up a stable and firm government. Congress grew restive with such assertiveness, and there were rumors that the president wanted some sort of annexation of the island, especially after the military government was replaced by a civilian one.

As noted, the administration had pushed the British for a revision or an end to the Clayton-Bulwer Treaty of 1850, which limited the power of either nation to have exclusive control over a Central American canal. The favored U.S. route was through Nicaragua, which would link the United States to the Pacific Ocean and foster a more comprehensive version of Manifest Destiny. Recent experiences of the war there showed the increasing importance for easier passage from the Atlantic to the Pacific. After some balking, the British removed their objections to an American canal.

The administration also supported The Hague Conference on disarmament, international arbitration, and the statements on the rules of war, and the United States encouraged the establishment of a Permanent Court of Arbitration. The administration also began the initiatives toward China that became known as the "Open Door Policy." In September 1898, Secretary Hay sent to the major powers a proposal that urged each nation to respect the spheres of interest and treaty ports already established in China by other nations. Chinese tariff duties would apply inside these areas of foreign influence, and they would be permitted to collect customs duties.

Discriminatory harbor duties or railroad rates would be outlawed within those spheres, however. Hay's views did respect in some sense Chinese territorial integrity, but he was intent on assuring businessmen that the United States was watching out for their interests as that ancient nation was being divided. The British were generally supportive, while the Russians were not, and the Germans, French, Italians, and Japanese indicated that they would agree if all the others did. Hay took those tentative statements as positive responses, and informed American public opinion seemed pleased by his policy of restraint.[100]

As 1900 approached, the president prepared for a reelection campaign against Democrat William Jennings Bryan once again. On the domestic front, the president had generally avoided any real support or solicitation of black voters and moved the Republican party away from its barely residual policy of concern, which Harrison had tried to continue. He refused even to speak out against the rise in the number of black lynchings in the South and appointed few blacks to major office.

The president also showed some interest over the question of the economic power of trusts and the concentration of corporate power. As has been noted, in 1895 the Supreme Court had decided that the Sherman Anti-Trust Act required proof that a trust possess not just a monopoly of manufacturing but exert that monopoly in interstate commerce—an exacting test that would cripple the federal government's enforcement if it sought to use the regulatory provisions of the act. McKinley stayed out of the legal controversy, but he expressed some concern about the growth of trusts and seemed to be leaning toward new legislation to control those developments. In the spring of 1899, popular interest and the press focused on the trust question, and McKinley with his unerring sense of popular sentiment caught the mood once again. The president, who was facing an election and dependent on corporate support, said little publicly on the trust issue, although he did endorse the American Federation of Labor's proposal for an eight-hour day for government workers and restrictions on convict labor.

By 1900 the president and most of the GOP in Congress gave strong support to the Gold Standard Act. Typically though, McKinley approved the federal government's redeeming all its money in gold, but continuing the mix of national bank notes, paper money, and Treasury notes that could be redeemed in gold. The final bill was a compromise that reasserted the primacy of gold and pledged the

Treasury to "redeem greenbacks and other of its notes in gold alone."[101]

Facing the campaign, the Republicans needed a running mate for McKinley after Vice President Garret A. Hobart's death and chose the dynamic governor of New York and hero of the battle of San Juan Hill, Theodore Roosevelt.[102] But despite his personal popularity and the success of the war, the president had run into some opposition within his own party over the tariff policy toward Puerto Rico when he advocated lower rates due to its new status. McKinley seemed unsure and wavered, reviving criticisms once again that he was weak. His problem was compounded by controversies concerning the new government on the island of Puerto Rico. Eventually McKinley's general approach prevailed in Congress after Republican leaders insisted on party discipline and support. Judging his first term, the president pronounced that the party had brought "prosperity at home and prestige abroad," and that became his campaign theme as well.

But abroad in China, angry nationalists led the so-called Boxer Rebellion, which trapped Americans and other Western nationalists in the capital city of Peking. Joining with the European powers, McKinley sent 2,500 troops to join the China Relief Expedition to free and protect the captives, a dramatic assertion of presidential prerogatives, which some were to charge was an unconstitutional exercise of power. The multinational expedition moved in and eventually a diplomatic settlement was reached.

Having captured the Democratic nomination once again, Bryan started his campaign by denouncing McKinley's occupation policies and promising eventual independence and a protectorship for the Philippines. Soon, though, he turned his attention away from foreign affairs to the trusts and attacked the GOP's laissez faire policies. The Republicans as usual outspent, outorganized, and outpublicized the Democrats and provided McKinley with a popular margin of 7,218,491 to 6,356,734 and a margin in the electoral college of 292 to 155. The GOP controlled the Senate 55 to 31 and the House of Representatives 197 to 151. McKinley proudly hailed his victory as a triumph for all the American people, and reassured them, "Be not disturbed; there is no danger from empire; there is no fear for the Republic."[103]

The next congressional session saw the passing of a revised Hay-Pauncefote Treaty dealing with the Central American canal issue and discussions about building up the merchant marine—a natural concomitant of the United States' new role in the world. The president was granted by Congress authority to restructure the civil government of the Philippines, and McKinley delegated more powers to the American governor, William Howard Taft. With regard to Cuba, Congress approved the Platt Amendment, which would force the island to accept America's right to intervene in Cuban affairs in order to stop any foreign power from infringing on that nation's sovereignty. The United States, in turn, was granted a right to maintain naval bases on the island. The amendment was partially an expression of a genuine paternalistic concern for Cuban independence, but the United States ended up promoting and ratifying a resolution that came to symbolize imperialism and nationalist Yanqui arrogance.

As for McKinley, he pushed for the Platt wording, as he became a stronger figure in his dealings with Congress. He reiterated at one point, "Our instincts will not deteriorate by extension, and our sense of justice will not abate under tropic suns in distant seas." In his second term, he began to reconsider his position on the protective tariff and was examining a program of gradual reductions, as he emphasized even more Blaine's old notions of reciprocity. In an address in Mississippi, he concluded, "We can now supply our own markets. We have reached that point in our industrial development, and in order to secure sale for our surplus products we must open up new avenues for our surplus." The president also stepped up his scrutiny of trusts, and even Hanna warned McKinley that he might have to act against the Northern Securities Company—a cause that would help Theodore Roosevelt make his reputation as a trust buster.[104]

Enthused by his reelection and by his own growth in office, McKinley set out on a speaking engagement and on September 6, he visited the Temple of Music at the Pan-American Exposition held in Buffalo, New York. There, he was shot and seriously wounded by anarchist Leon Czolgosz. McKinley held on to life for over a week, but then died of infection and its complications.

Historians and McKinley's own contemporaries have debated whether he was a strong or a weak executive, whether he was the last Whig president, in one sense, or the first modern one. The verdict has leaned toward a negative assessment, especially when he is compared to his extraordinarily energetic and showy successor. But McKinley's hold over Congress, his knowledge of public relations, and his use of the commander in chief prerogatives were remarkably modern. In some ways, his administration with its foreign wars and national self-assertiveness may have had more profound consequences for America than Roosevelt's ebullient but short-lived crusades.

Like Eisenhower and, to a lesser extent Reagan, McKinley often led by indirection, and historians are less capable of judging such executives than men like the two Roosevelts, Wilson, and Lyndon Johnson. McKinley did have a tendency to waver occasionally, bending to the zephyrs of public opinion, but he was more in command than his colleagues realized. And there is little evidence that a reluctant McKinley was dragged into the Spanish-American War. He postponed the war, slowly closed off peace options that he regarded as inadequate, mobilized the armed forces, dictated the terms of the peace, and became the proconsul for American control over the Philippines, Cuba, and assorted islands that accrued from the war. For better or worse, it was McKinley's war and McKinley's presidency.

Conclusion

In the period of time from George Washington's oath of office at Wall Street to the reception for William McKinley at the Pan-American Exposition, the republican experiment changed enormously and so did the presidency of the republic. Founded as a reaction to royal government and prerogatives, the American states were contentious and suspicious establishments, fearful of the loss of liberty and deeply troubled by strong governments and energetic officers and magistrates. They created by design and by chance a system of overlapping powers, checks and balances, and limited grants of authority. The colonists became nationalists through the unifying experience of revolutionary rhetoric and revolutionary war. One army came before one nation. And the beleaguered general became a nationally unifying symbol—proving once again that there is indeed a role for the hero in history.

The presidency that emerged from the years of debate and dissention was a partially unformed office, a magistrate overlooking a loosely connected commonwealth. The Federalist presidents emphasized personal dignity, nonpartisanship, a zealous preoccupation with the powers of office and its prestige, a cautious hands-off relationship with Congress, and a strong control of foreign policy. Their successors, the disciples of Thomas Jefferson, followed his early lead. They made the presidency a more democratic office—not populist but democratic, an office that rested on popular appeal, which extended subtly its sway over the legislative agenda and over a more cohesive coalition of followers. Their foreign policy was more pro-French than their predecessors, but the Jeffersonians

365

believed in a foreign policy that extended the reach of their empire of liberty. It was an emphasis on imperialism, by conquest or by purchase of vast miles of territory.

The democratic impulse was greater than the presidency, indeed than the republic itself. The later Jeffersonians became followers of General Andrew Jackson, and in the process transformed the Democratic party once again and the nature of executive authority. The sons of Old Hickory were clearly beholden to the raw-boned, crude, and boisterous democracy that was growing up. They confronted Congress openly, pleaded the people's cause to the people themselves, made no apologies for using political power or creating national parties that nurtured grievances, slights, envy, and ambition. On the foreign side of the ledger, the Jacksonians seemed to wish to match their Jeffersonian brothers acre for acre in expanding the American realm. The Americans appeared insatiable in their lust for land and possessions. The empire of liberty was becoming an old-fashioned imperialist operation, except that the territories became states equal in status to the old Atlantic commonwealths. And in the process the presidency became more and more an expression of those dreams and ambitions.

Jefferson was a philosopher king; Jackson a soldier of fortune. And for every force, there is a counterforce—and a counterideology. They called themselves the Whigs—the name given to members of the opposition in Britain, who were critics of the court and the patronage of the Crown. The Whigs gave the nation a view of the presidency that was rather important, an executive of limited powers and a republic of stated and defined boundaries. The Whigs also gave the nation some major political figures: Henry Clay, Daniel Webster, and a local Illinois politician, Abraham Lincoln.

In the 1850s, minor Whigs and minor Jacksonians did battle for office and position. But all got caught up in the vortex of the fires of secessionist sentiment that led to terrible war. The limited government of the former and the exuberance of the latter were superseded by the most intense use of executive power in the nineteenth century.

He does indeed tower over the universe of his time like a colossus, this Lincoln. War creates its own necessity; the grindings of military mobilization meant executive action and energy. Americans have never seen the likes of this man or this presidency. A cautious lawyer from the prairie towns became a major international presence, a great emancipator, a determined commander in chief in a decentralized republic. He became the model of the wartime executives. And there would be other wars and other commanders in chief, all claiming to be heirs to his legacy.

The reaction to the Civil War lasted, in some ways, over a full generation. That war brought forth changes in the industrial economy and in stooped labor agriculture, in medical care and in currency systems, in the relationships of the races, and in the responsibilities of one generation to another. Sometimes the march of executive power was overshadowed by profound changes of demography, of occupational developments, and of ideas and aspirations. The Whig philosophy of limited executives seemed to reemerge in the postwar period as the nineteenth century came to a close.

That century and its demonstrations of presidential authority and restraint witnessed and stimulated the movement from colonial union to nationalism, from living in a string of far-flung states and primitive communities to a partially industrialized nation that intensely pledged its allegiance to one people, one flag, one continental commonwealth. The presidency was not just a pleasant office of magistrates applying the laws passed by others. But still it was not the nerve center of the democratic state that we know in our own times, except in exceptional periods of exceptional men.

The presidency of the Roosevelts and Wilson, Eisenhower, Truman, and Lyndon Johnson rests partially on the precedents and controversies of the nineteenth century. But that presidency is something very different in a nation that is very different. For soon the continental and the provincial, the small town people and the farm hands would be living in a republic with an international sway. And then at the midpoint of this era, it would become a superpower the likes of which can only be rivaled in Western history by imperial Rome and Victorian Britain. But that is a another story for another volume.

Thus at critical and intermittent times, the presidency both reflected and helped to direct the forces of expansion, of popular will, and of national assertiveness in the nineteenth century. It surely became a powerful republican institution, at times truly a ferocious engine of the American democracy.

Notes

These notes are meant to both acknowledge my debt to previous sources and encourage further examination. Because of the length of the total study, I have grouped together sources after each topical section. Where several sources are available, I have cited the more accessible ones which may be of interest to a broader audience.

CHAPTER 1: THE ORIGINS OF
THE AMERICAN PRESIDENCY

1. American-British colonial relations are of central concern in the work of the so-called "imperialist school" of historians, especially Charles Andrews, George R. Beer, Lawrence Gipson, and Herbert Osgood. My main source here is Beer's four volumes, especially *The Origins of the British Colonial System 1578–1600* (Gloucester, Mass: Peter Smith, reprinted 1959). See also, his *British Colonial Policy 1754–1765* (reprinted 1958) and *The Old Colonial Systems 1660–1754*, vols. 1 and 2 (reprinted 1958). A short summary of Gipson's work is *The Coming of the Revolution* (New York: Harper and Row, 1962). Another very interesting cross-oceanic examination is presented in Bernard Bailyn, *Voyages to the West* (New York: Knopf, 1986). The regional cultures in New England, Virginia, Delaware, and the backcountry are directly traced to the inhabitants of specific areas in Great Britain; see David Hackett Fischer, *Albion's Seed* (New York: Oxford University Press, 1990).
2. H. Trevor Colbourn, *The Lamp of Experience* (New York: W. W. Norton, 1965); Donald W. Hanson, *From Kingdom to Commonwealth* (Cambridge: Harvard University Press, 1970); J. H. Plumb, *The Growth of Politi-*

cal Stability in England 1675–1725 (London: Macmillan, 1967); Gordon J. Schochet, *Patriarchalism in Political Thought* (New York: Basic Books, 1975); Edward O. Smith, Jr., *Crown and Commonwealth* (Philadelphia: American Philosophical Society, 1976); Lewis Namier, *England in the Age of the American Revolution* (London: Macmillan, 1961); and Ernest H. Kantorowicz, *The King's Two Bodies* (Princeton: Princeton University Press, 1957). See also, Jack Greene, *The Quest for Power* (New York: W. W. Norton, 1963); Bernard Bailyn, *The Origins of American Politics* (New York: Vintage, 1967); John F. Burns, *Controversies between Royal Governors and Their Assemblies in the North American Colonies* (New York: Russell and Russell, 1969); Caroline Robbins, *The Eighteenth Century Commonwealthmen* (Cambridge: Harvard University Press, 1959); and Bernard Bailyn, *Ideological Origins of the American Revolution* (Cambridge: Harvard University Press, 1967).

3. John Locke, *Two Treatises on Civil Government* (New York: E. P. Dutton, 1953), pp. 199–203.

4. William Blackstone, *Commentaries on the Laws of England* (Chicago: Callahan and Co., 1899), Book 1, pp. 239–50.

5. Leonard W. Labaree, *Royal Government in America* (New York: Frederick Ungar, 1958); Evarts B. Greene, *The Provincial Governor in the English Colonies of North America* (New York: Longmans, Green, 1898); Michael G. Kammen, *Rope of Sand* (Ithaca: Cornell University Press, 1968); and Franklin B. Wickware, *British Subministers and Colonial America 1763–1783* (Princeton: Princeton University Press, 1966).

6. The various constitutions are compiled in *The Federal and State Constitutions*, ed. Francis N. Thorpe, 7 vols. (Washington, D.C.: Government Printing Office, 1909). The Massachusetts Constitution's executive article is contained in volume 3, pp. 1899–1903. See also Margaret B. MacMillan, *The War Governors in the American Revolution* (New York: Columbia University Press, 1943); Charles Thach, *The Creation of the Presidency 1775–1789* (Baltimore: Johns Hopkins University Press, 1922) and the *Works of John Adams*, ed. Charles Francis Adams, vol. 4 (Freeport, N.Y.: Books for Libraries Press, 1969).

7. Clinton Rossiter, *1787 The Grand Convention* (New York: Macmillan, 1966); Richard Hofstadter, *The American Political Tradition* (New York: Knopf, 1948), chapter 1; and John P. Roche, "The Founding Fathers: A Reform Caucus in Action," *American Political Science Review*, 60 (December 1961): 799–816.

8. The standard source is *The Records of the Federal Convention 1787*, 4 vols., ed. Max Farrand, (New Haven: Yale University Press, 1966). I have also used the one-volume edition *Notes of Delegates on the Federal Convention of 1787 Reported by James Madison*, introduction by Adrienne Koch (Athens: Ohio University Press, 1966); quotes are on pp. 45–47.

9. Important aspects of this debate are in *Notes*, pp. 60–79, 128–40.

10. *Notes*, pp. 322–25.

11. *Notes,* pp. 330–35.

12. Rossiter, *1787*, p. 222 on Washington; Franklin quote in *Notes*, p. 659.

13. Michael P. Riccards, "The Presidency and the Ratification Contro-

versy," *Presidential Studies Quarterly*, 5 (Winter 1977): 37–46; *The Federalist Papers*, introduction by Clinton Rossiter (New York: Anchor, 1961), especially important are Jay's remarks in number 64; Madison in numbers 19, 20, 38, 39, 45, 48; Hamilton in numbers 67–73. The opposition position is included in the anthology, *The Anti-Federalist Papers*, ed. Morton Borden (Lansing: Michigan State University Press, 1965), especially "Cato" (George Clinton) and "Philadelphiensis" (Benjamin Workman). See also, Elbridge Gerry, "Observations on the New Constitution and on the Federal and State Constitutions," in *Pamphlets on the Constitution of the United States*, ed. Paul Leicester Ford (Brooklyn: Historical Printing Club, 1888), p. 9.

CHAPTER 2: THE FEDERALISTS AND THE NATIONAL AGENDA

1. Background material on George Washington has grown since the Bicentennial celebration. Of special importance are the older works, Douglas Southall Freeman, *George Washington*, 7 vols. (New York: Scribner's, 1948–57); James Thomas Flexner, *George Washington*, 4 vols. (Boston: Little, Brown, 1965–72); Noemie Emery, *Washington* (New York: Putnam, 1976); Catherine L. Albanese, *Sons of the Fathers: The Civil Religions of the American Revolution* (Philadelphia: Temple University Press, 1976); Garry Wills, *Cincinnatus* (Garden City: Doubleday, 1984); Barry Schwartz, *George Washington: The Making of an American Symbol* (New York: Free Press, 1987); and Thomas A. Lewis, *For King and Country* (New York: Harper Collins, 1993).

2. Martha J. Lamb, *The Washington Inauguration* (New York and London: White and Allen, 1889); *An Account of the Inauguration of George Washington* (New York: Bankers Trust Co., 1939); Frank Monaghan, *Notes on the Inaugural Journey of George Washington* (New York: n.p., 1939); Rufus Wilmot Griswold, *The Republican Court* (New York: Appleton, 1854); and Frank Fletcher Stephens, *The Transition Period 1788–1789 in the Government of the United States* (Columbia, Mo.: E. W. Stephens, 1909).

3. Edward S. Corwin, "The President's Removal Power under the Constitution" in *Selected Essays on Constitutional Law*, Book 4, Administrative Law, ed. Douglas B. Maggs (Chicago: Foundation Press, 1938), pp. 1467–1518. See also the debate in *The Debates and Proceedings of the Congress of the United States*, compiled by Joseph Gales (Washington, D.C.: Gales and Seaton, 1834).

4. James Hart, *The American Presidency in Action, 1789* (New York: Macmillan, 1948); Leonard White, *The Federalists* (New York: Macmillan, 1956); Thach, *The Creation of the Presidency*, passim; and Carl E. Prince, *The Federalists and the Origins of the U.S. Civil Service* (New York: New York University Press: 1977).

5. Essential to a discussion of the debt situation and the banks is Forrest McDonald, *The Presidency of George Washington* (New York: W. W. Norton,

1975), pp. 50–59. Also of use are *Papers of Alexander Hamilton*, vol. 6, ed. Harold C. Syrett and Jacob E. Cooke (New York: Columbia University Press, 1961); Robert Hendrickson, *Hamilton II* (New York: Mason-Charter, 1976); and John Miller, *The Federalist Era* (New York: Harper and Row, 1960), chapters 3 and 4.

6. Richard Kohn, *The Eagle and the Sword* (New York: Free Press, 1975); Michael P. Riccards, *A Republic If You Can Keep It: The Foundation of the American Presidency, 1700–1800* (Westport, Conn.: Greenwood Press, 1987), chapter 18; George D. Hanson, *Sixty Years of Indian Affairs* (Chapel Hill: University of North Carolina Press, 1941); Jennings Wise, *The Red Man in the New World Drama* (New York: Macmillan, 1971); Reginald Horsman, *The Frontier in the Formative Years, 1783–1815* (New York: Holt, Rinehart and Winston, 1970) and his *Expansion and the American Indian Policy, 1783–1812* (Lansing: Michigan State University Press, 1967); Katherine C. Turner, *Red Man Calling on the Great White Father* (Norman: University of Oklahoma Press, 1951); John W. Caughey, *McGillivray of the Creeks* (Norman: University of Oklahoma Press, 1938); and Randolph C. Downs, *Council Fires on the Upper Ohio* (Pittsburgh: University of Pittsburgh Press, 1940). Also of interest is Anthony Wayne, *A Name in Arms: The Wayne-Knox-Pickering-McHenry Correspondence*, ed. Richard Knopf (Pittsburgh: University of Pittsburgh Press, 1960).

7. Joseph Charles, *The Origins of the American Party System* (Williamsburg: Institute of Early American History and Culture, 1956); William N. Chambers, *Political Parties in a New Nation* (New York: Oxford University Press, 1963); Jackson Turner Main, *Political Parties Before the Constitution* (New York: W.W. Norton, 1973); H. James Henderson, *Party Politics in the Continental Congress* (New York: McGraw-Hill, 1974); Bernard Fay, "Early Party Machinery in the United States," *Pennsylvania Magazine of History and Biography*, 60 (October 1936): 375–90; George D. Leutscher, *Early Political Machinery in the United States* (Philadelphia: n.p., 1903); Richard P. McCormick, *The Second Party System* (New York: W. W. Norton, 1966); and Rudolph Bell, *Party and Faction in American Politics* (Westport, Conn.: Greenwood Press, 1973).

8. Noble Cunningham, *Jeffersonian Republicans* (Chapel Hill: University of North Carolina Press, 1957); Dumas Malone, *Jefferson and the Rights of Man* (Boston: Little Brown, 1951); Samuel Flagg Bemis, *Diplomatic History of the United States* (New York: Holt, Rinehart, and Winston, 1965), chapters 5 and 6; Frederick Jackson Turner, "The Origins of Genet's Projected Attack on Louisiana and the Floridas" in his *Significance of Sections in American History* (New York: Peter Smith, 1950), pp. 52–85; Charles Marion Thomas, *American Neutrality in 1793* (New York: Columbia University Press, 1931); John J. Reardon, *Edmund Randolph* (New York: Macmillan, 1974); and Harry Ammon, "The Genet Mission and the Development of American Political Parties," *Journal of American History*, 52 (March 1966): 725–41.

9. Leland Baldwin, *Whiskey Rebellion* (Pittsburgh: University of Pittsburgh, 1938); Jacob E. Cooke, "The Whiskey Insurrection: A Reevaluation,"

Pennsylvania History, 30 (July 1963): 316–46; David O. Whitlea, "The Economic Inquiry into the Whiskey Rebellion of 1794," *Agricultural History*, 49 (July 1975): 491–504; William Miller, "The Democratic Societies and the Whiskey Insurrection," *Pennsylvania Magazine of History and Biography*, 62 (July 1938): 324–59; and William D. Barber, "'Among the Most Techy Articles of Civil Police': Federal Taxation and the Adoption of the Whiskey Excise," *William and Mary Quarterly*, 25, 3d series (January 1968): 58–84.

10. Bemis, *A Diplomatic History*, chapters 6 and 7; Alexander De Conde, *Entangling Alliances* (Durham: Duke University Press, 1958); Bradford Perkins, *The First Rapprochement* (Berkeley: University of California, 1967); A. L. Burt, *The United States, Great Britain and British North America* (New York: Russell and Russell, 1961), chapter 8; Jerald A. Combs, *The Jay Treaty* (Berkeley: University of California Press, 1970); Gerard H. Clarfield, *Timothy Pickering and American Diplomacy* (Columbia: University of Missouri Press, 1969); and Eugene Perry Link, *Democratic-Republican Societies* (New York: Columbia University Press, 1942).

11. Peter Shaw, *The Character of John Adams* (Chapel Hill: University of North Carolina Press, 1976); Joseph L. Ellis, *Passionate Sage* (New York: W. W. Norton, 1993); Page Smith, *John Adams*, 2 vols. (Garden City: Doubleday, 1962); John R. Howe, Jr., *The Changing Political Thought of John Adams* (Princeton: Princeton University Press, 1966); Ralph Adams Brown, *The Presidency of John Adams* (Lawrence: University Press of Kansas, 1978); Alexander De Conde, *The Quasi War* (New York: Scribner's, 1966); James Martin Smith, *Freedom's Fetters* (Ithaca: Cornell University Press, 1956); John Miller, *Crisis in Freedom* (Boston: Little, Brown, 1951); Eugene F. Kramer, "John Adams, Elbridge Gerry and the Origins of XYZ Affair," *Essex Institute in Historical Collection*, 94 (1958): 57–68; and William J. Murphy, Jr., "John Adams: The Politics of the Additional Army, 1798-1800," *New England Quarterly*, 52 (June 1979): 234–49.

CHAPTER 3: THE JEFFERSONIANS

1. Marshall Smelser, *The Democratic Republicans 1801–1815* (New York: Harper and Row, 1968); Forrest McDonald, *The Presidency of Thomas Jefferson* (Lawrence: University Press of Kansas, 1976), chapter 1; Rebecca Lloyd Shippen, "Inauguration of President Thomas Jefferson 1801," *Pennsylvania Magazine of History and Biography*, 25 (1901): 71–76; Margaret Bayard Smith, *The First Forty Years of Washington Society* (New York: Scribner's, 1906); Herbert Agar, "John Adams and Jefferson" in his *The People's Choice* (Boston: Houghton Mifflin, 1933), 32–71; David Brion Davis, *Was Thomas Jefferson the Authentic Enemy of Slavery* (Oxford: Clarendon Press, 1970); John Dos Passos, *The Head and Heart of Thomas Jefferson* (Garden City: Doubleday, 1954); Henry Steele Commager, *Jefferson, Nationalism and Enlightenment* (New York: G. Braziller, 1975); David Brion Davis, *The Problem of Slavery in the Age of Revolution* (Ithaca: Cornell University Press,

1975), pp. 169–84; Edward Channing, *The Jeffersonian System* (New York: Harper, 1906); J. M. Merriam, "Jefferson's Use of Executive Patronage," *American Historical Association Papers*, 2 (1887): 47; Leonard W. Levy, *Jefferson and Civil Liberties: The Darker Side* (Cambridge: Harvard University Press, 1963); Francis Luther Mott, *Jefferson and the Press* (Baton Rouge: LSU Press, 1943); and Adrienne Koch, *The Philosophy of Thomas Jefferson* (New York: Columbia University Press, 1943).

    2. There is a far-reaching literature on Jefferson and his thought. I have benefited especially from Dumas Malone's magisterial *Jefferson and His Time*, 6 vols. (Boston: Little, Brown, 1948–81); Merrill D. Peterson, *Thomas Jefferson and the New Nation* (New York: Oxford University Press, 1970); Robert M. Johnston, Jr., *Jefferson and the Presidency* (Ithaca: Cornell University Press, 1978); Claude G. Bowers, *The Young Jefferson* (Boston: Houghton Mifflin, 1943) and his *Jefferson in Power* (Boston: Houghton Mifflin, 1936); Richard F. Matthews, *The Radical Politics of Thomas Jefferson* (Lawrence: University Press of Kansas, 1984); Daniel Boorstin, *The Lost World of Thomas Jefferson* (Boston: Beacon, 1974); Fawn M. Brodie, *Thomas Jefferson* (New York: Bantam, 1974); Merrill Peterson, *The Jeffersonian Image in the American Mind* (New York: Oxford University Press, 1960); Harold L. Hillenbrand, *The Unfinished Revolution: Education and Community in the Thought of Thomas Jefferson*, 2 vols. (Stanford: Stanford University Press, 1980); Gary Wills, *Inventing America* (New York: Vintage, 1978); George Tucker, *The Life of Thomas Jefferson*, 2 vols. (Philadelphia: Carey, Lea and Blanchard, 1837); Henry Adams, *History of the United States during the First Administrations of Thomas Jefferson and James Madison*, 2 vols. (New York: Library of America, 1986); Yehoshua Arieli, *Individualism and Nationalism in American Ideology* (Cambridge: Harvard University Press, 1964), pp. 123–80; Marie Kimball, *Jefferson*, 3 vols. (New York: Coward-McCann, 1943–50); Leonard White, *The Jeffersonians* (New York: Macmillan, 1951) and *Jefferson Legacies*, ed. Peter S. Onuf (Charlottesville: University of Virginia, 1993).

    3. Richard E. Ellis, *The Jeffersonian Crisis* (New York: W.W. Norton, 1971); Jerry W. Knudson,"The Jefferson Assault on the Federalist Judiciary," *American Journal of Legal History*, 14 (1970): 55–70; C.S. Thomas, "Jefferson and the Judiciary," *Constitutional Review*, 10 (April 1926): 67–76; Charles Grove Haines, *The American Doctrine of Judicial Supremacy* (Berkeley: University of California Press, 1932), pp. 241–53; and Julian P. Boyd, "The Chasm That Separated Thomas Jefferson and John Marshall," in *Essays on the American Constitution*, ed. G. Dietz (Englewood Cliffs: Prentice Hall, 1964), pp. 3–20.

    4. Johnston, *Jefferson and the Presidency*, passim; Everett Lee Long, "Jefferson and Congress" (Ph.D. dissertation, University of Missouri, 1966); and Noble E. Cunningham, Jr., *The Process of Government under Jefferson* (Princeton: Princeton University Press, 1978); and Noble Cunningham, *The Jeffersonian Republicans in Power* (Chapel Hill: University of North Carolina, 1963). Also of special interest is Jefferson to Barnabas, Library of Congress, No. 279956, series 1; May 13, 1806–November 1806, Reel 36.

Notes

Notes 375

5. Malone, *Jefferson the President, 1801–1805* (Boston: Little, Brown, 1970), pp. 73, 81, 88; quote to du Pont on p. 91. Norman K. Risjord, *The Old Republicans* (New York: Columbia University Press, 1965); Lance Banning, *The Jeffersonian Persuasion* (Ithaca: Cornell University Press, 1970); Dumas Malone, "Presidential Leadership and National Unity: The Jefferson Example," *Journal of Southern History*, 25 (February 1969): 3–17; Carl Russell Fish, "Jefferson's Policy as to Public Office, 1801–1809," in *The Civil Service and the Patronage* (New York: Longmans, Green, 1905), pp. 29–51; Alexander B. Lacy, Jr., "Jefferson and Congress: Congressional Method and Politics, 1801–1809," (Ph.D. dissertation, University of Virginia, 1964); Dumas Malone, *Thomas Jefferson as a Political Leader* (Berkeley: University of California, 1963); Carl E. Prince, "The Passing of the Aristocrats: Jefferson's Removal of the Federalists," *Journal of American History*, 57 (December 1970): 563–75; Gaillard Hunt, "Office Seeking during Jefferson's Administration," *American Historical Review*, 3 (January 1898): 270–91; and James Sterling Young, *The Washington Community* (New York: Columbia University Press, 1967). Also of interest are David K. McCarrell, *The Formation of the Jeffersonian Party in Virginia* (Durham: Duke University Press, 1937); Harry Ammon, "The Jeffersonian Republicans in Virginia," *Virginia Magazine of History and Biography*, 71 (April 1963): 153–67; William Nisbet Chambers, *Political Parties in a New Nation* (New York: Oxford University Press, 1963), pp. 170–90; Alfred Young, "The Mechanics and the Jeffersonians: New York 1789–1801," *Labor History*, 5 (Fall 1965): 247–76; William A. Robinson, *Jeffersonian Democracy in New England* (New Haven: Yale University Press, 1916); Alfred Young, *The Jeffersonian Republicans of New York* (Chapel Hill: University of North Carolina Press, 1968); Staughton Lynd, "Beyond Beard" in *Towards a New Past*, ed. Barton J. Berstein (New York: Pantheon, 1968); Charles Beard, *Economic Origins of Jeffersonian Democracy* (New York: Macmillan, 1915); Carl F. Prince, *New Jersey's Jeffersonian Republicans* (Chapel Hill: University of North Carolina Press, 1967); Paul Goodman, *The Democratic Republicans of Massachusetts* (Cambridge: Harvard University Press, 1964); James H. Broussard, *The Southern Federalists* (Baton Rouge: Louisiana University Press, 1928); Richard Buel, *Securing the Revolution* (Ithaca: Cornell University Press, 1972); and David Hackett Fischer, *The Revolution of American Conservatism* (New York: Harper and Row, 1967).

6. Malone, *Jefferson the President, 1801–1805*, p. 987; Paul E. Norton, "Jefferson's Plan for Mothballing the Frigates," *US Naval Institute Proceedings*, 82 (July 1956): 737–41; Donald Jackson, "Jefferson, Meriwether Lewis and the Reduction of the United States," *Proceedings of the American Philosophical Society*, 124 (April 29, 1980): 91–96; Joseph G. Henrich, "The Triumph of Ideology: The Jeffersonians and the Navy, 1779–1807" (Ph.D. Dissertation, Duke University, 1971); Julia H. Macleod, "Jefferson and the Navy: A Defense," *Huntington Library Quarterly*, 8 (1945): 153–84; Mary P. Adams, "Jefferson's Military Policy with Special References to the Frontier 1805–1809" (Ph.D. dissertation, University of Virginia, 1958); and Theodore J. Crackel, *Mr. Jefferson's Army* (New York: New York University Press, 1987).

7. Malone, *Jefferson the President, 1801–1805*, p. 105; Raymond Walter, *Albert Gallatin* (New York: Macmillan, 1957); Alexander Balinsky, *Albert Gallatin* (New Brunswick: Rutgers University Press, 1958); and Joseph Doffman, "The Economic Philosophy of Thomas Jefferson," *Political Science Quarterly*, 55 (1940): 98–121.

8. Malone, *Jefferson the President, 1801–1805*, p. 112.

9. *Ibid.*, p. 131.

10. *Ibid.*, p. 176.

11. *Ibid.*, p. 225.

12. *Ibid.*, p. 235.

13. Arthur P. Whitaker, *The Mississippi Question 1795–1803* (Gloucester: Peter Smith, 1962), p. 25; Stuart Seely Sprague, "Jefferson, Kentucky and the Closing of the Port of New Orleans, 1802–1803," *Register of the Kentucky Historical Society*, 70 (October 1972): 312–17; William Appleman Williams, *The Contours of American History* (Cleveland: World Publishing Company, 1961), pp. 188–92; and Mary P. Adams, "Jefferson's Reaction to the Treaty of San Ildefonso," *Journal of Southern History*, 21 (May 1955): 173–88.

14. Whitaker, *Mississippi*, p. 180.

15. *Ibid.*, pp. 123–38.

16. C. Peter Magrath, *Yazoo: Law and Politics in the New Republic* (Providence: Brown University Press, 1966).

17. Malone, *Jefferson the President, 1801–1805*, pp. 270–79; Napoleon's quote is on p. 294.

18. *Ibid.*, p. 320.

19. George Drago, *Jefferson's Louisiana* (Cambridge: Harvard University Press, 1975); James K. Hosman, *The History of the Louisiana Purchase* (New York: Appleton, 1902); Alexander De Conde, *This Affair of Louisiana* (New York: Scribner's, 1976); Lawrence S. Kaplan, *Jefferson and France* (New Haven: Yale University Press, 1967); Arthur Burr Darling, *Our Rising Empire* (New Haven: Yale University Press, 1940); Clifford L. Egan, "United States, France and West Florida, 1803–1807," *Florida Historical Quarterly*, 47 (1969): 227–52; J. W. Bradley, "W. C. C. Claiborne and Spain: Foreign Affairs under Jefferson and Madison," *Louisiana History*, 12 (1971): 297–314 and 13 (1972): 5–26; and R. A. McLenore, "Jeffersonian Diplomacy in the Purchase of Louisiana 1803," *Louisiana Historical Quarterly*, 18 (1935): 246–53.

20. Malone, *Jefferson the President, 1801–1805*, p. 350.

21. *Ibid.*, p. 436.

22. *Ibid.*, p. 452; and Henry Adams, *John Randolph* (New York: Chelsea House, 1983), chapter 6.

23. Robert Dawidoff, *The Education of John Randolph* (New York: W. W. Norton, 1979), and Dumas Malone, *Jefferson the President, Second Term 1805–1809* (Boston: Little, Brown, 1974), p. 23.

24. Malone, *Jefferson the President, 1805–1809*, p. 56.

25. Malone, *Jefferson the President, 1805–1809*, pp. 60–63, and Bradford

Perkins, *Prologue to War* (Berkeley: University of California, 1961), pp. 3, 5, 23, 50, 92, 112.

26. Malone, *Jefferson the President, 1805–1809*, p. 93.

27. *Ibid.*, p. 110.

28. *Ibid.*, pp. 193, 208.

29. *Ibid.*, p. 218; Milton Lomask, *Aaron Burr: The Conspiracy and Years of Exile, 1805–1836* (New York: Farrar, Straus and Giroux, 1982); Dumas Malone and Gary Wills, "Executive Privilege," *New York Review of Books*, 21 (July 18, 1974): 36–40; Gary Wills, "The Strange Case of Mr. Jefferson's Subpoena," *New York Review of Books*, 21 (May 21, 1974): 15–19 and his "An UnAmerican Politician," *New York Review of Books*, 21 (May 16, 1974): 9–12; Thomas Perkins Abernethy, *The Burr Conspiracy* (New York: Oxford University Press, 1954); Nathan Schachner, *Aaron Burr* (New York: Frederick A. Stokes, 1936); Jonathan Daniels, *Ordeal of Ambition* (Garden City: Doubleday, 1970); and *Reports of the Trials of Colonel Aaron Burr*, 2 vols. (New York: Da Capo, 1969).

30. Edward Corwin, *John Marshall and the Constitution* (New Haven: Yale University Press, 1919), p. 95; and Malone, *Jefferson the President, 1805–1809*, pp. 314–20.

31. Corwin, *John Marshall*, p. 98.

32. Malone, *Jefferson the President, 1805–1809*, pp. 383–85; and Herbert Heater, "Non Importation 1806–1812," *Journal of Economic History*, I (1941): 150–78.

33. Malone, *Jefferson the President, 1805–1808*, pp. 436, 452, 473; Burton Spivak, *Jefferson's English Crisis* (Charlottesville: University Press of Virginia, 1979); Herbert Briggs, *The Doctrine of Continuous Voyage*, vol. 44 in Studies in History and Political Science (Baltimore: Johns Hopkins University Press, 1926); Douglas W. Tanner, "Jefferson, Impressment and the Rejection of the Monroe-Pinckney Treaty," *Essays in History*, 13 (1968): 7–26; Anthony Steel, "Impressment in the Monroe-Pinckney Treaty," *American Historical Review*, 57 (1952): 352–69; James F. Zimmerman, *Impressment of American Seamen* (New York: Columbia University Press, 1925); and Bradford Perkins, *Prologue to War*, passim.

34. Reginald C. Stuart, *The Half Way Pacifist* (Toronto: University of Toronto, 1978); Louis Sears, *Jefferson and the Embargo* (Durham: Duke University Press, 1927); Schuyler D. Hoslett, "Jefferson and England: The Embargo as a Measure of Coercion," *Americana*, 34 (1940): 39–54; Richard Mannix, "Gallatin, Jefferson and the Embargo of 1808," *Diplomatic History*, 3 (1979): 151–72; Nelson S. Dearmont, "Federalist Attitudes toward Government Secrecy in the Age of Jefferson," *Historian*, 37 (February 1975): 227–40; Merrill D. Peterson, "Thomas Jefferson and Commercial Policy, 1783–1793," *William and Mary Quarterly*, 22, 3d series (October 1965): 584–610; Milton B. Rich, *The Presidents and Civil Disorder* (Washington: Brookings Institute, 1941), pp. 31–37; and David Lindsay, "George Canning and Jefferson's Embargo, 1807–1809," *Tyler's Quarterly*, 1 (1952): 43–47.

35. Walter Wilson Jennings, *The American Embargo 1807–1809*, vol. 8,

University of Iowa Studies in the Social Sciences, 1921–1929 (Iowa City: University of Iowa, 1929).

36. Malone, *Jefferson the President, 1805–1809*, chapter 31, quote on p. 668.

37. The major biography of James Madison is still Irving Brant, *James Madison*, 6 vols. (Indianapolis: Bobbs Merrill, 1941–61), especially *James Madison, The President 1809–1812* and *James Madison, Commander in Chief 1812–1836*. See also his *The Fourth President* (Indianapolis: Bobbs Merrill, 1970) and *James Madison and American Nationalism* (Princeton: Van Nostrand, 1968). Other studies of interest are Ralph L. Ketchum, *James Madison* (New York: Macmillan, 1971); Robert Allen Rutland, *James Madison and the Search for Nationhood* (Washington: Library of Congress, 1981) and his *James Madison* (New York: Macmillan, 1987). Rutland's *The Presidency of James Madison* (Lawrence: University Press of Kansas, 1990) came out after the completion of this chapter. Other works are Drew McCoy, *The Last of the Fathers* (New York: Cambridge University Press, 1989); Edward M. Burns, *James Madison, Philosopher of the Constitution* (New Brunswick: Rutgers University Press, 1938); Gaillard Hunt, *The Life of James Madison* (New York: Doubleday, Page and Co. 1902); Roy J. Honeywell, "President Jefferson and His Successors," *American Historical Review*, 46 (1940): 64–75; Joseph M. Bessette and Jeffrey Tulls, *The Presidency in the Constitutional Order* (Baton Rouge: LSU Press, 1981); and Adrienne Koch, *Jefferson and Madison: The Great Collaboration* (New York: Knopf, 1950).

38. Brant, *Madison: The President*, p. 23.

39. *Ibid.*, p. 58; Adams, *History of the United States during the Administrations of Thomas Jefferson and James Madison*, passim; and Lawrence S. Kaplan, "Jefferson, the Napoleonic Wars and the Balance of Power," *William and Mary Quarterly*, 3d series, 14 (April 1957): 196–217; quote in Brant, *Madison: The President*, p. 59.

40. Brant, *Madison: The President*, p. 89. No first lady so captured the public imagination in that century as Dolley (Dolly) Madison and some of the works on her life are Virginia Moore, *The Madisons* (New York: McGraw Hill, 1979); Katherine S. Anthony, *Dolly Madison* (Garden City: Doubleday, 1949); *Memoirs and Letters of Dolly Madison* (Boston: Houghton Mifflin, 1886); and Alice Curtis Desmond, *Glamorous Dolly Madison* (New York: Dodd, 1946).

41. Brant, *Madison: The President*, p. 125.

42. *Ibid.*, p. 173.

43. *Ibid.*, p. 183; Joslin Cox, *The West Florida Controversy 1798–1813* (Baltimore: Johns Hopkins University Press, 1918); and Issac J. Cox, "Pan American Policy of Jefferson and Wilkinson," *Mississippi Valley Historical Review*, 1 (September 1914): 212–39.

44. Brant, *Madison: The President*, p. 243.

45. Bradford Perkins, *Prologue to War*, passim; Kendrie C. Babcock, *The Rise of American Nationality, 1811–1819* (New York: Harper and Row, 1969);

Notes 379

and Ernest M. Lander, Jr., *Reluctant Imperialists: Calhoun, the South Carolinians and the Mexican War* (Baton Rouge: LSU Press, 1981).

46. Brant, *Madison: The President*, pp. 363, 329, 333.

47. J. C. A. Stagg, *Mr. Madison's War* (Princeton: Princeton University Press, 1983), p. 87, and Lawrence Kaplan, "France and Madison's Decision in War, 1812," *Mississippi Valley Historical Review*, 50 (1964): 652–71.

48. Stagg, *Mr. Madison's War*, p. 110, and Norman K. Risjord, "1812: Conservatives, War Hawks, and the Nation's Honor," *William and Mary Quarterly*, 3d series, 18 (April, 1961): 196–211.

49. Stagg, *Mr. Madison's War*, p. 148; the narrative of the campaigns and the diplomacy follow closely his account. See also, William Gribbin, *The Churches Militant: The War of 1812 and American Religion* (New Haven: Yale University Press, 1973).

50. Stagg, *Mr. Madison's War*, p. 224, and George Rogers Taylor, "Agrarian Discontent in the Mississippi Valley Proceeding the War of 1812," *Journal of Political Economy*, 39 (1931): 471–505.

51. Stagg, *Mr. Madison's War*, p. 247.

52. *Ibid.*, p. 302.

53. *Ibid.*, pp. 343–58, and J. S. Martel, "A Sidelight on Federalist Strategy during the War of 1812," *American Historical Review*, 33 (1928): 553–56.

54. Theodore Dwight, *History of the Hartford Convention* (New York: DaCapo, 1970).

55. Stagg, *Mr. Madison's War*, pp. 388–413, and Abbott Smith, "Mr. Madison's War: An Unsuccessful Experiment in the Conduct of National Policy," *Political Science Quarterly*, 57 (1978): 116–36.

56. Ralph Ketchum, "James Madison: The Unimperial President," *Virginia Quarterly Review*, 54 (1978): 116–36.

57. Dwight, *History of the Hartford Convention*, passim, and Stagg, *Mr. Madison's War*, pp. 472–77.

58. Stagg, *Mr. Madison's War*, p. 499.

59. Brant, *Commander in Chief*, p. 380.

60. *Ibid.*, p. 403.

61. Theodore Clarke Smith, "War Guilt in 1812," *Massachusetts Historical Society Proceedings*, 64 (1931): 319–45.

62. Harry Ammon, *James Monroe: The Quest for National Identity* (New York: McGraw Hill, 1971), p. 362; Arthur Styron, *The Last of the Cocked Hats* (Norman: University of Oklahoma Press, 1945); Daniel Coit Gilman, *James Monroe* (Baltimore: Houghton Mifflin, 1896); William Penn Cresson, *James Monroe* (Chapel Hill: University of North Carolina Press, 1946); Edmund Berkeley and Dorothy Smith Berkeley, "The Piece Left Behind," *Virginia Magazine of History and Biography*, 75 (April 1967): 174–80; and Henry Ammon, "James Monroe and the Election of 1808 in Virginia," *William and Mary Quarterly*, 3d series, 20 (January 1963): 33–56.

63. Ammon, *James Monroe*, p. 367.

64. *Ibid.*, p. 369.

65. *Ibid.*, p. 377.

66. Carl Schurz, *Henry Clay* (Boston: Houghton Mifflin, 1887), chapter 7, and Robert V. Remini, *Henry Clay* (New York: Norton, 1991), passim.

67. Ammon, *James Monroe*, p. 392.

68. Robert V. Remini, *Andrew Jackson and the Course of American Empire* (New York: Harper and Row, 1977), chapters 22 and 23.

69. Ammon, *Monroe*, pp. 431–44.

70. *Ibid.*, pp. 449–55.

71. *Ibid.*, p. 472.

72. Frederick Merk, *The Monroe Doctrine and American Expansionism, 1842-1847* (New York: Knopf, 1966); Fred Somkin, *Unquiet Eagle* (Ithaca: Cornell University Press, 1967); Ernest R. May, *The Making of the Monroe Doctrine* (Cambridge: Harvard University Press, 1975); Bradford Perkins, *Castlereagh and Adams* (Berkeley: University of California, 1964); and Theodore A. Cook, "The Original Intention of the Monroe Doctrine," *Fortnightly Review*, 70 (1898): 357–68.

73. Ammon, *James Monroe*, pp. 497–539.

74. The cabinet in Monroe's administration is discussed in *America: The Middle Period*, ed. John B. Boles (Charlottesville: University of Virginia Press, 1973). Also of interest is Richard Ellis and Aaron Wildavsky, *Dilemmas of Presidential Leadership* (New Brunswick: Transaction Press, 1989), chapter 5.

75. George A. Lipsky, *John Quincy Adams, His Theories and Ideas* (New York: Crowell, 1950), p. 15.

76. Mary W. M. Hargreaves, *The Presidency of John Quincy Adams* (Lawrence: University Press of Kansas, 1975), p. 19; E. M. Carroll, "Politics during the Administration of John Q. Adams," *South Atlantic Quarterly*, 23 (April 1924): 23, 41–54; John Torry Morse, *John Quincy Adams* (Boston: Houghton Mifflin, 1882); *Diary of John Quincy Adams*, ed. Allan Nevins (New York: Longmans, 1928); Robert A. East, *John Quincy Adams* (New York: Bookman Associates, 1962); Jack Shephard, *Cannibals of the Mind* (New York: McGraw Hill, 1980) and his *The Adams Chronicles* (Boston: Little, Brown, 1975); and Harold J. Callanan, "The Political Economy of John Quincy Adams," (Ph.D. dissertation, Boston University, 1975).

77. Samuel Flagg Bemis, *John Quincy Adams and the Union* (New York: Knopf, 1956), p. 65. Also see his earlier *John Quincy Adams and the Foundations of American Foreign Policy* (New York: Knopf, 1949).

78. Bemis, *Adams and the Union*, p. 69.

79. Michael J. Birkner and Robert R. Thompson, "The Pre Civil War Cabinet's Role in Presidential Policy Making, with a Special Focus on the Administration of John Quincy Adams," *American Political Science Association Convention*, August 29–September 1, 1985.

80. Hargreaves, *The Presidency of John Quincy Adams*, p. 68.

81. *Ibid.*, pp. 87, 200, and L. H. Parsons, "Perpetual Harrow Upon My Feelings: John Quincy Adams and the American Indians," *New England Quarterly*, 46 (Summer 1973): 339–79.

82. Hargreaves, *The Presidency of John Quincy Adams*, p. 11.

83. *Ibid.*, chapters 4, 6, 7; *John Quincy Adams and American Continental Empire*, ed. Walter LaFeber (Chicago: Quadrangle Books, 1965); C. W. Hackett, "Development of John Quincy Adams' Policy with Respect to a Confederation and the Panama Congress, 1822–1825," *Hispanic American Historical Review*, 8 (November 1928): 496–526; E. P. Crapol, "John Quincy Adams and the Monroe Doctrine," *Pacific History Review*, 48 (August 1979): 413–18; and R. R. Stenberg, "J.Q. Adams: Imperialist and Apostate," *Southwestern Social Science Quarterly*, 16 (March 1936): 37–49.

84. Bemis, *Adams and the Union*, pp. 131–32; Marie B. Hecht, *John Quincy Adams* (New York: Macmillan, 1972), and Dan Merrill Martin, "John Quincy Adams and the Whig Ideology," (Ph.D. dissertation, Princeton University, 1968).

85. Bemis, *Adams and the Union*, pp. 133–36.

86. *Ibid.*, pp. 143–48.

CHAPTER 4: THE JACKSONIANS

1. Albert Somit, "The Political and Administrative Ideas of Andrew Jackson," (Ph.D. dissertation, University of Chicago, 1947), p. 45.

2. *Ibid.*, p. 19.

3. *Ibid.*, p. 13. The major biography of Jackson is Robert V. Remini, *Andrew Jackson*, 3 vols. (New York: Harper and Row, 1977–84). Also of use are his *The Election of Andrew Jackson* (Philadelphia: Lippincott, 1963), *The Revolutionary Age of Andrew Jackson* (New York: Avon, 1976), and *Martin Van Buren and the Making of the Democratic Party* (New York: Columbia University Press, 1962). Of interest is Ronald P. Formisano, "Towards a Reorientation of Jacksonian Politics," *Journal of American History*, 63 (June 1976): 42–65. Other biographies include Harold C. Syrett, *Andrew Jackson* (Indianapolis: Bobbs Merrill, 1953); J. W. Ward, *Andrew Jackson* (New York: Oxford University Press, 1955); William G. Summer, *Andrew Jackson as a Public Man* (Boston: Houghton Mifflin, 1882); James Parton, *Life of Andrew Jackson*, 3 vols. (Boston: Houghton Mifflin, 1859) and his *Presidency of Andrew Jackson* (New York: Harper, 1867); Marquis James, *Andrew Jackson*, 2 vols. (Indianapolis: Bobbs Merrill, 1933, 1937); and John Spencer Bassett, *Life of Andrew Jackson* (New York: Scribner's, 1916).

4. Somit, "Ideas of Andrew Jackson," p. 22, and Edwin A. Miles, "The Jacksonian Era," *Writing Southern History*, ed. Arthur S. Link and Rembert W. Patrick (Baton Rouge: LSU Press, 1966): 125–46.

5. Robert Remini, *Andrew Jackson and the Course of American Freedom* (vol. 2 of his biography), pp. 16–17.

6. *Ibid.*, p. 173.

7. *Ibid.*, p. 179, see also Remini, *The Election of Andrew Jackson*, passim.

8. Remini, *Course of American Freedom*, p. 189.

9. *Ibid.*, p. 199.

10. *Ibid.*, p. 218; Arthur M. Schlesinger, Jr., *Age of Jackson* (Boston: Little, Brown, 1945), chapters 21 and 32, and a useful later review in the *New York Review of Books*, December 7, 1989, pp. 48–52.

11. Remini, *Course of American Freedom*, pp. 233–35.

12. Claude Bowers, *The Party Battles of the Jackson Period* (Boston: Houghton Mifflin, 1922), and Richard B. Latner, *The Presidency of Andrew Jackson* (Athens: University of Georgia Press, 1979).

13. Remini, *Course of American Freedom*, pp. 241–47, and his "Martin Van Buren and the Tariff of Abominations," *American Historical Review*, 63 (July 1958): 903–17.

14. Arthur H. De Rosier, Jr., *The Removal of the Choctaw Indians* (Knoxville: University of Tennessee Press, 1970); Michael P. Rogin, *Fathers and Children: Jackson and the Subjugation of the American Indian* (New York: Knopf, 1975); F. P. Prucha, "Andrew Jackson's Indian Policy," *Journal of American History*, 56 (December 1969): 527–39; Robert Remini, *The Legacy of Andrew Jackson* (Baton Rouge: LSU Press, 1988); Ronald N. Satz, *American Indian Policy in the Jacksonian Era* (Lincoln: University of Nebraska Press, 1975); Herman J. Violan, *Thomas L. McKenney: Architect of America's Early Indian Policy* (Chicago: Swallow Press, 1974); and Joseph C. Burke, "The Cherokee Cases," *Stanford Law Review*, 21 (February 1969): 500–531.

15. Remini, *Course of American Freedom*, pp. 293–304.

16. *Ibid.*, p. 368; Schlesinger, *Age of Jackson*, chapters 7–10; Leonard D. White, *The Jacksonians* (New York: Macmillan, 1954), chapter 24; and John M. McFaul, *The Politics of Jacksonian Finance* (Ithaca: Cornell University Press, 1972).

17. Remini, *Course of American Freedom*, pp. 370–72.

18. *Ibid.*, pp. 390–92.

19. Robert Remini, *Andrew Jackson and the Course of American Democracy*, passim (vol. 3 of his biography); Chauncey S. Boucher, *Nullification Controversy in South Carolina* (New York: Russell and Russell, 1968); William W. Freehling, *Prelude to Civil War: Nullification Controversy in South Carolina, 1816–1832* (New York: Harper and Row, 1965); Frederic Bancroft, *Calhoun and the South Carolina Nullification Movement* (Baltimore: Johns Hopkins University Press, 1928); Paul Bergeron, "The Nullification Controversy Revisited," *Tennessee Historical Quarterly*, 35 (1976): 263–75.

20. Merrill Petersen, *Olive Branch and Sword* (Baton Rouge : LSU Press, 1982).

21. Remini, *Course of American Democracy*, pp. 70–75.

22. *Ibid.*, p. 83.

23. *Ibid.*, pp. 106–11.

24. *Ibid.*, p. 128.

25. *Ibid.*, p. 143; Schlesinger, *Age of Jackson*, chapters 18 and 19.

26. Rogin, *Fathers and Children*; Richard Drinnon, *Facing West* (New York: New American Library, 1980), and Remini, *Course of American Democracy*, pp. 300–312 and citations in note 14.

27. John M. Belohlavek, *"Let the Eagle Soar": The Foreign Policy of Andrew Jackson* (Lincoln: University of Nebraska Press, 1985), p. 2.

28. *Ibid.*, p. 28.

29. *Ibid.*, p. 113.

30. *Ibid.*, p. 119: Carl Schurz, *Henry Clay* (Boston: Houghton Mifflin, 1887), chapter 16; K. Jack Bauer, "The United States Navy and Texas Independence," *Military Affairs*, April 1970, pp. 44–48; E. C. Barker, *President Jackson and the Texas Revolution* (n.p., 1907), pp. 789–809; Joseph C. McElhannon, "Relations Between Imperial Mexico and the United States," *Essays in Mexican History*, ed. Thomas E. Cotnet and Carlos E. Casteneda (Austin: University of Texas Press, 1958), pp. 127–41; Richard R. Stenberg, "The Texas Schemes of Jackson and Houston, 1829–1836," *Southwestern Social Science Quarterly*, 15 (1934): 229–50; and *The Autobiography of Sam Houston*, ed. Donald Day and Harry Herbert Ullom (Norman: University of Oklahoma, 1957).

31. Remini, *Course of American Democracy*, chapters 19 and 23.

32. *Ibid.*, pp. 315–27.

33. Robert V. Remini, *Martin Van Buren and the Making of the Democratic Party* (New York: W. W. Norton, 1959). Some of his own experiences on the subject are in *The Autobiography of Martin Van Buren* (New York: Augustus M. Kelly, 1969).

34. James C. Curtis, *The Fox at Bay: Martin Van Buren and the Presidency 1837–1841* (Lexington: The University Press of Kentucky, 1970), and Edward M. Shepard, *Martin Van Buren* (New York: Chelsea House, 1983).

35. Major L. Wilson, *The Presidency of Martin Van Buren* (Lawrence: University Press of Kansas, 1984); quotes are on pages 73 and 78.

36. *Ibid.*, p. 95. The Whigs are profiled in the interesting volume by Daniel Walker Howe, *The Political Culture of American Whigs* (Chicago: University of Chicago, 1979).

37. Wilson, *Presidency of Van Buren*, pp. 99–100; quote is from the *Albany Evening Journal*, July 9, 1838.

38. John Niven, *John C. Calhoun and the Price of Union* (Baton Rouge: LSU Press, 1988), chapter 12, and Sydney Nathans, *Daniel Webster and Jacksonian Democracy* (Baltimore: Johns Hopkins University Press, 1973).

39. Wilson, *Presidency of Van Buren*, pp. 125–28, and Donald B. Cole, *Martin Van Buren and the American Political System* (Princeton: Princeton University Press, 1984), pp. 285–378.

40. Wilson, *Presidency of Van Buren*, pp. 130–31.

41. *Ibid.*, pp. 139–41.

42. *Ibid.*, p. 144; John Niven, *Martin Van Buren, The Romantic Age of American Politics* (New York: Oxford University Press, 1983), chapters 25 and 26.

43. Wilson, *Presidency of Van Buren*, pp. 196–207, and Norma Lois Peterson, *The Presidencies of William Henry Harrison and John Tyler* (Lawrence: University Press of Kansas, 1989), chapter 2.

44. Norma Lois Peterson, *The Presidencies of William Henry Harrison and John Tyler* (Lawrence: University Press of Kansas, 1989), chapter 2, and Freeman Cleavers, *Old Tippecanoe* (New York: Scribner's, 1939).

45. Oliver Perry Chitwood, *John Tyler: Champion of The Old South* (New

York: Russell and Russell, 1964), p. 207. Also of use is Robert J. Morgan, *A Whig Embattled: The Presidency under John Tyler* (Lincoln: University of Nebraska Press, 1954).

46. Peterson, *Presidencies of Harrison and Tyler*, p. 263.

47. Chitwood, *Tyler*, pp. 239–51.

48. *Ibid.*, pp. 295–98, and Merrill D. Peterson, *The Great Triumvirate* (New York: Oxford University Press, 1987).

49. Chitwood, *Tyler*, pp. 300–302, 325. To add to his problems, Tyler was president during the dispute in Rhode Island over its 1663 charter which disenfranchised large numbers of people. A rump convention, headed up by T. W. Dorr as "governor," passed a "People's Constitution." The officials, elected under the old charter, regarded this as insurrection, and Tyler supported the latter group in giving guarantees against any alleged uprising.

50. Peterson, *Presidencies of Harrison and Tyler*, pp. 318–49.

51. Robert V. Remini, *Andrew Jackson and the Course of American Democracy, 1833–1845* (New York: Harper and Row, 1984), chapter 32.

52. Peterson, *Presidencies of Harrison and Tyler*, pp. 229–30; Chitwood, *Tyler*, p. 359; Robert Seaget II, *And Tyler Too* (New York: McGraw Hill, 1963) on his second marriage.

53. Martha McBride Morrel, *Young Hickory* (New York: E. P. Dutton, 1949); Charles Sellers, *James K. Polk: Jacksonian 1795–1845* (Princeton: Princeton University Press, 1957) and his companion volume: *James K. Polk: Continentalist, 1843–1846* (Princeton: Princeton University Press, 1966); and Eugene I. McCormac, *James K. Polk* (Berkeley: University of California Press, 1922).

54. Charles A. McCoy, *Polk and the Presidency* (Austin: University of Texas, 1960), pp. 53, 70, 74. On Manifest Destiny see Albert K. Weinberg, *Manifest Destiny* (Baltimore: Johns Hopkins University Press, 1935); Frederick Merk, *Manifest Destiny and Mission in American History* (New York: Knopf, 1963) and his *The Monroe Doctrine and American Expansion* (New York: Knopf, 1966); Thomas Hietala, *Manifest Destiny* (Ithaca: Cornell University Press, 1985); Kinley J. Brauer, *Cotton versus Conscience* (Lexington: University of Kentucky, 1967); Richard R. Stenberg, "Polk and Fremont 1845–1846," *Pacific Historical Review*, 7 (September 1938), pp. 211–27 and his "Failure of Polk's Mexican War Intrigue of 1845," *Pacific Historical Review*, 4 (1935): 39–68; William C. Binkley, *The Expansionist Movement in Texas 1836–1850* (New York: DaCapo, 1970); Fred Sorekin, *Unquiet Eagle* (Ithaca: Cornell University, 1967); George L. Rives, "Mexican Diplomacy on the Eve of War with the United States," *American Historical Review*, 18 (January 1913): 275–94; Eugene C. Barker, "The Influence of Slavery in the Colonization of Texas," *Mississippi Valley Historical Review*, 9 (June 1924): 3–36; John C. McElhannon, "Relations Between Imperial Mexico and the United States, 1821–1823," in Comer and Castaneda, eds., *Essays in Mexican History*, pp. 127–43; *The Autobiography of Sam Houston*, ed. Donald Day and Harry H. Ullon (Norman: University of Oklahoma Press, 1954), chapter 16.

55. McCoy, *Polk and the Presidency*, p. 82.

56. Frederick Merk, *The Oregon Question* (Cambridge: Harvard University Press, 1967); Norman A. Graebner, *Empire on the Pacific* (New York: Ronald Press, 1955); and Thomas P. Martin, "Free Trade and the Oregon Question, 1842–1846," *Facts and Factors in Economic History*, ed. Edwin Francis Gay (Cambridge: Harvard University Press, 1932).

57. McCoy, *Polk and the Presidency*, p. 92.

58. *Ibid.*, p. 96.

59. Paul H. Bergeron, *The Presidency of James K. Polk* (Lawrence: University Press of Kansas, 1987), chapter 4; Robert W. Johannsen, *To the Halls of the Montezumas* (New York: Oxford University Press, 1985); Glenn W. Price, *Origins of the War with Mexico* (Austin: University of Texas Press, 1967); David M. Pletchan, *The Diplomacy of Annexation* (Columbia: University of Missouri Press, 1973); John H. Schroeder, *Mr. Polk's War* (Madison: University of Wisconsin Press, 1973); and John Eisenhower, *So Far from God* (New York: Random House, 1989).

60. McCoy, *Polk and the Presidency*, pp. 123, 131.

61. Bergeron, *Presidency of James K. Polk*, chapter 7.

62. McCoy, *Polk and the Presidency*, p. 155

63. *Ibid.*, p. 164.

64. *Ibid.*, p. 196; Eric Foner, "The Wilmot Proviso," *Journal of American History*, 56 (April 1969): 262–79, and Chauncey S. Boucher, "That Aggressive Slavocracy," *Mississippi Valley Historical Review*, 8 (June 1921): 113–79.

65. McCoy, *Polk and the Presidency*, p. 178.

CHAPTER 5: THE DECLINE
OF THE EXECUTIVE

1. Holman Hamilton, *Zachary Taylor: Soldier in the White House* (Indianapolis: Bobbs Merrill, 1951), p. 205; K. Jack Bauer, *Zachary Taylor* (Baton Rouge: LSU Press, 1985); and Daniel Walker Howe, *The Political Culture of the American Whigs* (Chicago: University of Chicago Press, 1980); Hamilton also deals with Taylor in his earlier volumes *Zachary Taylor: Soldier of the Republic* (Indianapolis: Bobbs Merrill, 1941) and *The Three Kentucky Presidents: Lincoln, Taylor, and Davis* (Lexington: University of Kentucky Press, 1978). In 1991, Taylor's body was examined after a claim was made that he died from arsenic poisoning; that claim was discounted by forensic experts when the examination was completed.

2. Hamilton, *Soldier in the White House*, p. 48.

3. Bauer, *Taylor*, p. 233.

4. Hamilton, *Soldier in the White House*, p. 125.

5. Joseph Nathan Kane, *Facts about the Presidents* (New York: Ace Books, 1975).

6. Hamilton, *Soldier in the White House*, p. 175.

7. *Ibid.*, p. 265.

8. *Ibid.*, p. 299.

9. Bauer, *Taylor*, p. 305, and Merrill D. Peterson, *The Great Triumvirate* (New York: Oxford University Press, 1987), pp. 450–72.

10. Robert J. Rayback, *Millard Fillmore* (Buffalo: Henry Stewart, 1959), p. 252. Other biographies are W. L. Barre, *The Life and Public Services of Millard Fillmore* (New York: Burr Franklin, 1971); Ivory Chamberlain, *Biography of Fillmore* (Buffalo: Thomas and Lathrop, 1856); William E. Griffis, *Millard Fillmore* (Ithaca: Cornell University Press, 1915); and William E. Griffis, "Millard Fillmore and His Part in the Opening of Japan," *Buffalo Historical Society Publications*, 9 (1906): 53–80. Also of interest is Charles M. Snyder, *The Lady and the President* (Lexington: University Press of Kentucky, 1975).

11. Rayback, *Fillmore*, p. 271, and Gerald M. Capers, *Stephen A. Douglas* (Boston: Little, Brown, 1959), chapter 3.

12. Rayback, *Fillmore*, p. 278.

13. *Ibid.*, p. 308.

14. Griffins, "Millard Fillmore and His Part," passim.

15. Rayback, *Fillmore*, p. 335.

16. This account is based on the only major biography of Pierce: Roy Franklin Nicholas, *Franklin Pierce: Young Hickory of the Granite Hills* (Philadelphia: University of Pennsylvania, 1931).

17. Nicholas, *Pierce*, p. 251.

18. *Ibid.*, pp. 283–84.

19. *Ibid.*, p. 300.

20. *Ibid.*, p. 433.

21. *Ibid.*, p. 454.

22. *Ibid.*, p. 533, passim.

23. Buchanan's career is covered in several older biographies, including George T. Curtis, *Life of James Buchanan* (New York: Harper and Brothers, 1883); Philip G. Auchampaugh, *James Buchanan and His Cabinet on the Eve of Secession* (Lancaster, Pa.: Lancaster Press, 1926); John B. Moore, *The Works of James Buchanan* (New York: Antiquarian Press, 1960); and the president's own *Mr. Buchanan's Administration on the Eve of the Rebellion* (New York: D. Appleton, 1866).

24. Elbert. B. Smith, *The Presidency of James Buchanan* (Lawrence: University Press of Kansas, 1975), p. 11. Although it came out after this chapter was completed, I have enjoyed Kenneth M. Stampp, *America in 1857* (New York: Oxford University Press, 1990).

25. Philip S. Klein, *President James Buchanan* (University Park: Pennsylvania State University Press, 1962), which is a fair and sympathetic presentation.

26. Smith, *Presidency*, passim, and Don E. Fehrenbacher, *The Dred Scott Case* (New York: Oxford University Press, 1978).

27. Smith, *Presidency of Buchanan*, p. 45; James A. Rawley, *Race and Politics* (Philadelphia: Lippincott, 1969); and Alice Nichols, *Bleeding Kansas* (New York: Oxford University Press, 1954).

28. Smith, *Presidency of Buchanan*, p. 55.
29. *Ibid.*, p. 59.
30. *Ibid.*, p. 65.
31. *Ibid.*, p. 86.
32. Stephen B. Oates, *To Purge this Land with Blood* (New York: Harper and Row, 1970), chapters 16–21; Osward G. Villard, *John Brown* (Garden City: Doubleday, Doran, 1929); and Jeffrey S. Rossback, *Ambivalent Conspirators* (Philadelphia: University of Pennsylvania Press, 1982).
33. Smith, *Presidency of Buchanan*, p. 151.
34. *Ibid.*, p. 157, and James M. McPherson, *Battle Cry of Freedom* (New York: Oxford University Press, 1988), p. 253.
35. *Ibid.*, p. 170.
36. David M. Potter, *The Impending Crisis, 1848–1861* (New York: Harper and Row, 1976); Roy Franklin Nichols, *The Disruption of the American Democracy* (New York: Macmillan, 1948); Michael F. Holt, *The Political Crisis of the 1850s* (New York: Norton, 1978); and Don E. Fehrenbacher, *Prelude to Greatness* (Stanford: Stanford University Press, 1962).

CHAPTER 6: THE PRESIDENCY GOES TO WAR

1. The historical literature on Lincoln is immense and I have included only the sources from which I have drawn specific judgments and information. For a good bibliographical essay on the period, see James M. McPherson, *Battle Cry of Freedom* (New York: Oxford University Press, 1988). A useful modern biography is Stephen B. Oates, *With Malice toward None* (New York: Harper and Row, 1977). The single most important source for this narrative is James G. Randall, *Lincoln the President*, 4 vols. (New York: Scribner's, 1945–55) although I do not accept the basic premise that Lincoln was simply a conservative. Also of use are Norman A. Graebner, *The Enduring Lincoln* (Urbana: University of Illinois Press, 1959); Joel H. Sibley, "Always a Whig in Politics," a paper presented at the Annual Symposium of the Abraham Lincoln Association, February 12, 1986; and M. E. Bradford, "Lincoln and the Language of Hate and Fear: A View from the South," *Continuity*, 9 (1985): 87–108.
2. This discovery of the nonliberal side of Lincoln is expressed in Richard Hofstadter, *The American Political Tradition* (New York: Knopf, 1948), chapter 5.
3. Randall, *Lincoln*, vol. 1, p. 123. For very different understandings of Lincoln and his formative years see Dwight G. Anderson, *Abraham Lincoln: The Quest for Immortality* (New York: Knopf, 1982); George B. Forgie, *Patricide in the House Divided* (New York: W. W. Norton, 1979); Charles B. Stozier, *Lincoln's Quest for Union* (New York: Basic Books, 1982); Stephen B. Oates, *Abraham Lincoln, The Man behind the Myths* (New York: Signet, 1984); Donald Riddle, *Congressman A. Lincoln* (Urbana: University of Illi-

nois Press, 1957); *The Historian's Lincoln*, ed. Gabor Boritt (Urbana: University of Illinois Press, 1988); David Donald, *Lincoln Reconsidered* (New York: Vintage, 1961), chapters 4, 7, and 10; Carl Sandburg, *Abraham Lincoln, The Prairie Years* (New York: Harcourt, Brace and Co., 1929); Don E. Fehrenbacher, *Prelude to Greatness* (Stanford: Stanford University Press, 1962); and David M. Potter, *The Impending Crisis* (New York: Harper and Row, 1971).

4. Randall, *Lincoln*, vol. 1, p. 206; Reinhard H. Luthin, *First Lincoln Campaign* (Cambridge: Harvard University Press,1944); and *Ethnic Voters in the Election of Lincoln*, ed. Frederick C. Luebke (Lincoln: University of Nebraska Press, 1971).

5. Randall, *Lincoln*, vol. 1, p. 207; David M. Potter, *Lincoln and His Party in the Secession Crisis* (New Haven: Yale University Press,1942); Harold M. Hyman, "The Narrow Escape from a 'Compromise of 1860': Secession and the Constitution," *Freedom and Reform*, ed. Harold M. Hyman and Leonard Levy (New York: Harper and Row, 1967), pp. 149–66; Eric Foner, *Free Soil, Free Labor, Free Men* (New York: Oxford University, 1970); and David Donald, *Charles Sumner and the Coming of the Civil War* (New York: Knopf, 1960).

6. Randall, *Lincoln*, vol. 1, p. 215.

7. *Ibid.*, p. 225.

8. *Ibid.*, p. 235.

9. The standard study of the Fort Sumter crisis is Richard N. Current, *Lincoln and the First Shot* (Philadelphia: Lippincott, 1963). Also useful is Potter, *Lincoln and His Party*, pp. 337–66; Potter, *The Impending Crisis*, pp. 570–83; and Kenneth Stampp, *And the War Came* (Chicago: University of Chicago Press, 1964).

10. Randall, *Lincoln*, vol. 1, p. 344.

11. *Ibid.*, p. 350.

12. Michael P. Riccards, "The Presidency in Sickness and in Health," *Presidential Studies Quarterly*, 7 (Summer 1977): 215–30.

13. David Donald, *Lincoln Reconsidered*, pp. 187–208.

14. Clinton Rossiter, *Constitutional Dictatorship* (Princeton: University Press, 1948), and Edward S. Corwin, *The President: Office and Powers 1787–1984*, 5th edition (New York: New York University Press, 1984), pp. 167, 264–67, 495–97.

15. Randall, *Lincoln*, vol. 1, pp. 228–30.

16. The best study of these legal problems and difficulties remains James G. Randall, *Constitutional Problems Under Lincoln* (Urbana: University of Illinois Press, 1951) which is supplemented in an informed way by Harold M. Hyman, *A More Perfect Union* (Boston: Houghton Mifflin, 1975); and Mark Neely, Jr., *The Fate of Liberty* (New York: Oxford University Press, 1991).

17. Randall, *Lincoln*, vol. 2, p. 7.

18. *Ibid.*, p. 28.

19. Oates, *With Malice toward None*, pp. 224, 225, 241–43.

20.   Foreign policy is considered in Norman A. Graebner, "Northern Diplomacy and European Neutrality," in *Why the North Won the War*, ed. David Donald (New York: Macmillan, 1962), pp. 55–78; and Jay Monaghan, *Diplomat in Carpet Slippers* (Indianapolis: Bobbs Merrill, 1945).

21.   For a balanced judgment see Stephen W. Sears, *George B. McClellan* (New York: Ticknor and Fields, 1988).

22.   Randall, *Lincoln*, vol. 2, p. 69.

23.   Burke Davis, *They Called Him Stonewall* (New York: The Fairfax Press, 1988).

24.   Randall, *Lincoln*, vol. 2, p. 92.

25.   T. Harry Williams, *Lincoln and the Radicals* (Madison: University of Wisconsin Press, 1960).

26.   On confiscation see J. G. Randall and David Donald, *The Civil War and Reconstruction* (Boston: D. C. Heath, 1961), pp. 372–73; Hans L. Trefousse, *The Radical Republicans* (New York: Knopf, 1969); *Lincoln and Civil War Politics*, ed. James A Rawley (New York: Holt, Reinhart and Winston, 1969); Edward Boykin, *Congress and the Civil War* (New York: McBride, 1955); Robert S. Harper, *Lincoln and the Press* (New York: McGraw Hill, 1951); J. F. C. Fuller, *Grant and Lee* (London: Eyre and Spottswoode, 1932); and Nancy S. and Dwight Anderson, *The Generals* (New York: Knopf, 1988). The president's ambivalences are discussed in Kenneth Stampp, *The Era of Reconstruction 1865–1877* (New York: Knopf, 1965), pp. 44–45.

27.   The emancipation question is also presented in James M. McPherson, *The Struggle for Equality* (Princeton: Princeton University Press, 1964); La Wanda Cox, *Lincoln and Black Freedom* (Urbana: University of Illinois Press, 1985); and James M. McPherson, *The Negro Civil War* (New York: Pantheon, 1965). The crucial issue of blacks in the Union army is presented in Joseph T. Glatthaar, *Forged in Battle* (New York: Free Press, 1990). Over 180,000 blacks served in the Union army and more than 36,000 died in the war. On Greeley, see Randall, *Lincoln*, vol. 2, p. 158.

28.   Christopher Dell, *Lincoln and the War Democrats* (Madison, N.J.: Fairleigh Dickinson University Press, 1975); Joel Silbey, *A Respectable Minority* (New York: W. W. Norton, 1977); and Frank L. Klement, *Copperheads in the Middle West* (Chicago: University of Chicago Press, 1960).

29.   William F. Zornow, *Lincoln and the Party Divided* (Westport, Conn.: Greenwood Press, 1972); William B. Hesseltine, *Lincoln and the War Governors* (New York: Knopf, 1948); Carl R. Fish, "Lincoln and the Patronage," *American Historical Review*, 8 (1924): 53–69; Harry J. Carman and Reinhart Luthin, *Lincoln and the Patronage* (Gloucester: Peter Smith, 1964); and Allan G. Bogue, *The Congressman's Civil War* (New York: Cambridge University Press, 1989).

30.   Oates, *With Malice toward None*, pp. 327–30.

31.   Randall, *Lincoln*, vol. 2, p. 241.

32.   *Ibid.*, p. 255.

33.   *Ibid.*, p. 288.

34.   Richard E. Beringer, et al., *Why the South Lost the Civil War* (Ath-

ens: University of Georgia Press, 1986); and David M. Potter, "Jefferson Davis and the Political Factors in Confederate Defeat," in *Why the North Won the Civil War*, pp. 91–112.

35.   Clement Eaton, *Jefferson Davis* (New York: Free Press, 1977), p. 127; Reinbert W. Patrick, *Jefferson Davis and His Cabinet* (Baton Rouge: LSU Press, 1944); D. S. Freeman, *The South to Posterity* (New York: Scribner's, 1939); Paul D. Escort, *After Secession: Jefferson Davis and the Failure of Confederate Nationalism* (Baton Rouge: LSU Press, 1978); and William C. Davis, *Jefferson Davis* (New York: Harper/Collins, 1991).

36.   Eaton, *Davis*, p. 139.

37.   *Ibid.*, p. 144.

38.   Eli N. Evans, *Judah P. Benjamin: The Jewish Confederate* (New York: Free Press, 1988).

39.   Emory M. Thomas, *The Confederate Nation, 1861–1865* (New York: Harper and Row, 1979).

40.   Eaton, *Davis*, chapter 22.

41.   Wilfred Buck Yearns, *The Confederate Congress* (Athens: University of Georgia, 1960).

42.   Hofstadter, *American Political Tradition*, chapter 5.

43.   Randall, *Lincoln*, vol. 3, pp. 135–36.

44.   Corwin, *The President*, pp. 166–68; Richard P. Longaker, *Presidency and Civil Liberties* (Ithaca: Cornell University Press, 1961); and Herman Belz, "Lincoln and the Constitution," *Congress and the Presidency*, 15 (Autumn 1988): 147–64.

45.   *Ibid.*, pp. 165–66; 266, 288, 356, 501–2.

46.   Randall, *Lincoln*, vol. 3, p. 218.

47.   Oates, *Abraham Lincoln*, pp. 120–21, 18–20.

48.   Randall, *Lincoln*, vol. 3, p. 208.

49.   Dell, *Lincoln and the War Democrats*, chapter 12; quote on Vallandingham in Randall, *Lincoln*, vol. 3, p. 227.

50.   Randall, *Lincoln*, vol. 3, p. 130.

51.   Oates, *With Malice toward None*, chapter 10.

52.   Randall, *Lincoln*, vol. 4, p. 248.

53.   *Ibid.*, chapters 7 and 11, and Harold M. Hyman, "Election of 1864," in *History of American Presidential Elections, 1789–1968*, ed. Arthur M. Schlesinger, Jr. and Fred Israel, vol. 2 (New York: Chelsea Publishing Company, 1985).

54.   William S. McFeeley, *Grant* (New York: W. W. Norton, 1981), chapters 12 and 13, and Randall, *Lincoln*, vol. 4, p. 150. Also of interest are the works of Bruce Catton, some of which are contained in his *Bruce Catton's Civil War* (New York: The Fairfax Press, 1984); Selby Foote, *Civil War*, 3 vols. (New York: Vintage, 1968); and also Trevor H. Dupuy, *Military Life of A. Lincoln: Commander in Chief* (New York: Franklin Watts, 1969); T. Harry Williams, *Lincoln and His Generals* (New York: Knopf, 1952); Kenneth P. Williams, *Lincoln Finds a General* (New York: Macmillan, 1950); John Shepley Tilley, *Lincoln Takes Command* (Chapel Hill: University of North

Carolina Press, 1941); and *Lincoln, the War President*, ed. Gabor S. Boritt (New York: Oxford University Press, 1992).

55. Cox, *Lincoln and Black Freedom*, passim; Eric Foner, *Reconstruction* (New York: Harper, 1988), chapters 1 and 2; William Hesseltine, *Lincoln's Plan for Reconstruction* (New York: Quadrangle, 1960); and William Harris, *Presidential Reconstruction in Mississippi* (Baton Rouge: LSU Press, 1967); and a more sympathetic Hans L. Trefousse, *Radical Republicans* (New York: Knopf, 1969).

56. Williams, *Lincoln and the Radicals*, chapters 11, 13, 14.

57. Randall, *Lincoln*, vol. 4, p. 193.

58. Hyman, *A More Perfect Union*, pp. 267–70.

59. Randall, *Lincoln*, vol. 4, p. 310; Oates, *With Malice toward None*, pp. 404–5.

CHAPTER 7: THE NATIONAL CLERK

1. Kenneth M. Stampp, *The Era of Reconstruction, 1865–1877* (New York: Vintage, 1965), p. 50.

2. *Ibid.*, p. 51, and Hans L. Trefousse, *Andrew Johnson* (New York: W. W. Norton, 1989).

3. Willard Hays, "Andrew Johnson's Reputation," *East Tennessee Historical Society Publications* 31 (1959): 1–31 and 32 (1960): 18–50; Lately Thomas, *The First President Johnson* (New York: Morrow, 1968); Robert W. Winston, *Andrew Johnson, Plebian and Patriot* (New York: Holt, 1928); Lloyd Paul Stryer, *Andrew Johnson* (New York: Macmillan, 1929); George F. Milton, *The Age of Hate: Andrew Johnson and the Radicals* (New York: Coward, McCann, 1930); David Karsner, *Andrew Johnson, The Gentle Savage* (New York: Brentano's, 1929); and Clifton Hall, *Military Governor of Tennessee* (Princeton: Princeton University Press, 1916).

4. Stampp, *Reconstruction*, pp. 83–87; and Trefousse, *Johnson*, p. 225, 236.

5. David Donald, *The Politics of Reconstruction 1863–1867* (Cambridge: Harvard University Press, 1984), chapter 1.

6. James E. Sefton, *Andrew Johnson and the Uses of Constitutional Power* (Boston: Little, Brown, 1980), p. 122; and Trefousse, *Johnson*, p. 233.

7. Sefton, *Johnson*, p. 125.

8. *Ibid.*, p. 138. Expressions such as these have led to the simple conclusion that Johnson was just another provincial racist politician, see LaWanda Cox and John H. Cox, *Politics, Principle and Prejudice, 1865–1866* (New York: Atheneum, 1963).

9. Foner, *Reconstruction*, chapters 5 and 6.

10. Sefton, *Johnson*, p. 158.

11. *Ibid.*, p. 165.

12. *Ibid.*, p. 174; Edmund G. Ross, *History of the Impeachment of Andrew Johnson* (New York: B. Franklin, 1965); Michael Les Benedict, *Impeach-*

ment and the Trial of Andrew Johnson (New York: W. W. Norton, 1973); and Eric L. McKitrick, *Andrew Johnson and Reconstruction* (Chicago: University of Chicago Press, 1960). On Grant and the army, see Charles Fairman, *Reconstruction and Reunion 1864–68*, part one (New York: Macmillan, 1971), chapter 10. The major cases were *Ex parte Milligan*, the *Test Oath* cases, *Ex parte McCardle*, and *Georgia v. Grant, Meade, and others.*

13. Sefton, *Johnson*, p. 181, and on Ross, see Trefousse, *Johnson*, p. 324 and p. 317 on Roman parties.

14. Ulysses S. Grant III, *Ulysses S. Grant: Warrior and Statesman* (New York: William Morrow, 1969); Louis A. Coolidge, *Ulysses S. Grant* (Boston: Houghton Mifflin, 1917); and General Horace Porter, *Campaigning with Grant* (New York: The Century Co., 1897).

15. Martin E. Mantell, *Johnson, Grant and the Politics of Reconstruction* (New York: Columbia University Press, 1973).

16. Eric Foner, *Reconstruction, 1863–1877* (New York: Harper and Row, 1988), and Richard N. Current, *Those Terrible Carpetbaggers* (New York: Oxford University Press, 1989).

17. Coolidge, *Ulysses S. Grant*, p. 283.

18. Allan Nevins, *Hamilton Fish*, 2 vols. (New York: Frederick Ungar Publishing Company, 1936).

19. William S. Mc Feely, *Grant* (New York: W. W. Norton, 1981), pp. 319–29.

20. Coolidge, *Grant*, p. 355, and Sidney Ratner, "Was the Supreme Court Packed by President Grant?" *Political Science Quarterly*, 50 (September 1935): 343–58.

21. Coolidge, *Grant*, pp. 375–78.

22. *Ibid.*, p. 398, and Laurie Tatum, *Our Red Brothers and the Peace Policy of President Ulysses S. Grant* (Lincoln: University Nebraska, 1970).

23. Coolidge, *Grant*, p. 416.

24. McFeely, *Grant*, chapter 23.

25. *Ibid.*, chapter 24, and Nevins, *Fish*, p. 763.

26. Nevins, *Fish*, pp. 787–88.

27. *Ibid.*, p. 807, and Robert C. Prickett, "The Malfeasance of William Worth Belknap, Secretary of War, October 13, 1869 to March 2, 1876," *North Dakota History*, 17 (January 1950): 5–51.

28. Nevins, *Fish* is the best account of these scandals.

29. C. Van Woodward, *Reunion and Reaction* (Garden City: Doubleday, 1956), pp. 14–18.

30. Harry Barnard, *Rutherford B. Hayes and His America* (Indianapolis: Bobbs Merrill, 1954), p. 402.

31. Van Woodward, *Reunion*, p. 23.

32. Kenneth E. Davidson, *The Presidency of Rutherford B. Hayes* (Westport, Conn.: Greenwood Press, 1972), p. 138.

33. *Ibid.*, p. 139.

34. *Ibid.*, p. 141.

35. Charles R. Williams, *The Life of Rutherford B. Hayes* (Boston: Houghton Mifflin, 1914), vol 2, p. 28.

36. Davidson, *Presidency of Hayes*, p. 153.
37. *Ibid.*, p. 165.
38. *Ibid.*, pp. 175–76 and Williams, *Life*, p. 113.
39. Davidson, *Presidency of Hayes*, p. 188.
40. Barnard, *Rutherford B. Hayes*, pp. 442–44.
41. Davidson, *Presidency of Hayes*, p. 217.
42. Justus D. Doenecke, *The Presidencies of James A. Garfield and Chester A. Arthur* (Lawrence: University Press of Kansas, 1981), p. 22; Allan Peskin, *Garfield* (Kent, Ohio: Kent State University Press, 1978); Robert G. Caldwell, *James A. Garfield, Party Chieftain* (New York: Dodd, Mead, 1931); John M. Taylor, *Garfield of Ohio* (New York: W. W. Norton, 1970). See also Harry J. Brown, *The Garfield Orbit* (New York: Harper and Row, 1978) and Hendrik Booraem V, *The Road to Respectability: James A. Garfield and His World, 1844–1852* (Lewisburg, Pa: Bucknell University Press, 1988)
43. Doenecke, *Garfield and Arthur*, p. 38. Also of interest are Allan Peskin, "President Garfield and the Southern Question: The Making of a Policy That Never Was," *Southern Quarterly*, 16 (1978): 375–86; Vincent P. DeSantis, *Republicans Face the Southern Question* (Baltimore: Johns Hopkins University Press, 1959); and Stanley P. Hitshorn, *Farewell to the Bloody Shirt* (Bloomington: Indiana University Press, 1962).
44. *Ibid.*, p. 42.
45. The best biography of Arthur is Thomas C. Reeves, *Gentleman Boss: The Life of Chester Alan Arthur* (New York: Knopf, 1975).
46. Doenecke, *Garfield and Arthur*, p. 76.
47. *Ibid.*, p. 56.
48. *Ibid.*, pp. 74, 167; David Saville Muzzey, *James G. Blaine* (New York: Dodd, Mead 1935), and A. C. Wilgus, "James G. Blaine and the Pan American Movement," *Hispanic American Historical Review*, 5 (November 1922): 667–708.
49. David M. Pletcher, *The Awkward Years: American Foreign Relations Under Garfield and Arthur* (Columbia: University of Missouri Press, 1962); Alice Felt Tyler, *The Foreign Policy of James G. Blaine* (Minneapolis: University of Minnesota Press, 1927); and James B. Locky, "James Gillespie Blaine," in *The American Secretaries of State and Their Diplomacy*, ed. Samuel Flagg Bemis, vol. 7 (New York: Knopf, 1928), pp. 261–97.
50. Doenecke, *Garfield and Arthur*, pp. 134–35; and Pletcher, *Awkward Years*, passim.
51. Doenecke, *Garfield and Arthur*, p. 141.
52. Ari Hoogenboom, *Outlawing the Spoils* (Urbana: University of Illinois Press, 1961).
53. Allan Nevins, *Grover Cleveland: A Study in Courage* (New York: Dodd, Mead and Co., 1932), p. 4.
54. Horace Samuel Merrill, *Bourbon Leader: Grover Cleveland and the Democratic Party* (Boston: Little, Brown, 1957), p. 17.
55. *Ibid.*, pp. 58–67.
56. Henry Jones Ford, *The Cleveland Era* (New Haven: Yale University Press, 1920).

394   Notes

57. Arthur Wallace Dunn, *From Harrison to Harding* (New York: Putnam, 1922), and Merritt, *Bourbon Leader*, p. 202.

58. J. Rogers Hollingsworth, *Whirligig of Politics: Democracy of Cleveland and Bryan* (Chicago: University of Chicago Press, 1963).

59. Nevins, *Cleveland*, p. 226.

60. *Ibid.*, pp. 235–38.

61. *Ibid.*, p. 251.

62. *Ibid.*, pp. 270–82.

63. *Ibid.*, pp. 332–33.

64. Besides Nevins's splendid biography to which this chapter is obviously indebted, some of the other studies are Robert McElroy, *Grover Cleveland, the Man and the Statesman* (New York: Harper, 1923); Richard E. Welch, *The Presidencies of Grover Cleveland* (Lawrence: University Press of Kansas, 1988); and Denis T. Lynch, *Grover Cleveland: A Man Four Square* (New York: Liveright, 1932).

65. Nevins, *Cleveland*, p. 349, see also Marcus Cunliffe, *The Presidency* (Boston: Houghton Mifflin, 1987), chapter 6.

66. Nevins, *Cleveland*, p. 377.

67. Robert F. Wessen, "Election of 1888," *History of American Presidential Elections, 1789–1968*, vol. 2; and Nevins, *Cleveland*, p. 439.

68. Nevins, *Cleveland*, p. 445 and passim.

69. *Ibid.*, p. 467.

70. Hollingsmith, *The Whirligig of Politics*, p. 1.

71. H. Wayne Morgan, *From Hayes to McKinley* (Syracuse: Syracuse University Press, 1969), chapters 10–12, and Nevins, *Cleveland*, pp. 519–40.

72. Thomas Bailey, *A Diplomatic History of the American People* (Englewoods Cliffs, N.J.: Prentice Hall, 1980), pp. 418–35; some background is provided in Donald Marquand Dozer, "The Opposition to Hawaiian Reciprocity, 1876–88," *Pacific Historical Review*, 14 (1945): 157–83; and Nevins, *Cleveland*, pp. 560–87.

73. John B. Hicks, *The Populist Revolt* (Minneapolis: University of Minnesota Press, 1931). For a study of the depression see W. Jelt Lanch, *The Causes of the Panic of 1893* (Boston: Houghton Mifflin, 1907); Charles Hoffman, "The Depression of the Nineties," *Journal of Economic History*, 16 (June 1956): 137–64; Samuel Rezneck, "Unemployment, Unrest and Relief in the United States during the Depression of 1893–1897," *Journal of Political Economy*, 61 (August 1953): 324–45; and Joel H. Silbey, *The American Political Nation* (Stanford: Stanford University, 1991), pp. 235–38. For a rather interesting defense of Cleveland's reactions to the depression, see Walter LaFeber, "The Background of Cleveland's Venezuelan Policy: A Reinterpretation," *American Historical Review*, 66 (July 1961): 947–67, which argues that Cleveland favored bad monetary measures, high tariffs, and overprotectionism and that he saw the solution as increased foreign trade, a repeal of the Sherman Silver Purchase Act, and more competitive U.S. industries.

74. Merrill, *Bourbon Leader*, p. 31.

75. Edward S. Corwin, *The President*, 5th ed. (New York: New York University Press, 1984), pp. 155–56.

76. Charles W. Calhoun, *Gilded Age Cato: The Life of Walter Q. Gresham* (Lexington: The University Press of Kentucky, 1988); George Young, "Intervention Under the Monroe Doctrine: The Olny Corollary," *Political Science Quarterly*, 57 (June 1942): 247–80; George Lincoln Burr, "The Search for the Venezuela-Guiana Boundary," *American Historical Review*, 4 (April 1899): 470–77; Paul A. Varg, "The Myth of the China Market, 1890–1914," *American Historical Review*, 73 (February 1968): 742–58; Nevins, *Cleveland*, p. 635.

77. The election figures are in Nevins, *Cleveland*, p. 651, and the discussions of the following treasury bond issues are on pp. 652–88; Tillman is quoted on p. 675.

78. Nevins, *Cleveland*, p. 704, and Louis W. Koenig, *Bryan* (New York: Putnam, 1971), chapters 13 and 14.

79. Homer E. Socolofsky and Allan B. Spetter, *The Presidency of Benjamin Harrison* (Lawrence: University Press of Kansas, 1987), p. 16.

80. *Ibid.*, p. 40. The major biographical treatment of Harrison has been done by Harry J. Sievers in his three-volume work, *Benjamin Harrison, Hoosier Warrior 1833–1865* (Chicago: Henry Regnery, 1952); *Benjamin Harrison, Hoosier Statesman* (New York: University Publishers, 1959); and *Benjamin Harrison, Hoosier President* (Indianapolis: Bobbs Merrill, 1968).

81. Socolofsky and Spetter, *Presidency of Harrison*, p. 51.

82. *Ibid.*, p. 55.

83. Arthur Wallace Dunn, *From Harrison to Harding*, vol. 2 (New York: Putnam, 1922), chapters 1–4, and Fred Wellborn, "The Influence of the Silver Republican Senators 1889–1891," *Mississippi Valley Historical Review*, 14 (December 1928): 462–80.

84. John K. Mahon, "Benjamin Franklin Tracy: Secretary of the Navy, 1889–1893," *New York Historical Society Quarterly*, 44 (April 1960): 179–201; and Benjamin F. Cooling, *Benjamin Franklin Tracy* (Hamden, Conn.: Archon, 1973).

85. Socolofsky and Spetter, *Presidency*, pp. 89–115.

86. David S. Muzzey, *James G. Blaine* (New York: Dodd, Mead and Co, 1934); Tyler, *The Foreign Policy of James G. Blaine*, passim; and Michael J. Devine, *John W. Foster* (Athens: Ohio University Press, 1981).

87. Useful studies of McKinley's rise are Charles S. Olcott, *Life of McKinley*, 2 vols. (Boston: Houghton Mifflin, 1916); Margaret Leech, *In the Days of McKinley* (New York: Harper, 1959); Howard W. Morgan, *William McKinley and His America* (Syracuse: Syracuse University Press, 1963); and Lewis L. Gould, *The Presidency of McKinley* (Lawrence: Regents Press of Kansas, 1980).

88. Louis W. Koenig, *Bryan* (New York: Putnam, 1971), chapters 14 and 15, and Michael E. McGerr, *The Decline of Popular Parties: The American North, 1865–1928* (New York: Oxford University Press, 1986), pp. 144–45.

89. Gould, *The Presidency of McKinley*, pp. 34–35.

90. *Ibid.*, pp. 25–47.
91. W. A. Swanberg, *Citizen Hearst* (New York: Collier Books, 1961), book 3. Pulitzer at first opposed U.S. involvement but came around to supporting the war because it meant circulation increases for his newspaper, p. 137. See Charles H. Brown, *The Correspondents' War* (New York: Scribner's, 1967).
92. Gould, *The Presidency of McKinley*, pp. 71–78.
93. *Ibid.*, pp. 85–88.
94. The treatment of McKinley and his role as commander in chief is from Gould, *The Presidency of McKinley*, pp. 96–101.
95. *Ibid.*, p. 107; and Leech, *In the Days of McKinley*, chapters 7–11.
96. Gould, *The Presidency of McKinley*, p. 121.
97. *Ibid.*, pp. 131–41; Dunn, *From Harrison to Harding*, vol. 1, pp. 278–96; Louis A. Perez, Jr., "Supervision of a Protectorate: The United States and the Cuban Army, 1898–1908," *Hispanic American Historical Review*, 52 (May 1972): 250–71; and David F. Healy, *The United States in Cuba 1898–1902* (Madison: University of Wisconsin Press, 1963).
98. Gould, *The Presidency of McKinley*, pp. 143–45.
99. *Ibid.*, pp. 185, 189; Ernest May, *Imperial Democracy* (New York: Harcourt, Brace and World, 1961); Walter LaFeber, *The New Empire* (Ithaca: Cornell University Press, 1963); Robert L. Beismer, *Twelve Against Empire* (New York: McGraw Hill, 1968); and E. Berkeley Tompkins, *Anti-Imperialism in the United States* (Philadelphia: University of Pennsylvania Press, 1970).
100. Thomas J. McCormick, *China Market* (Chicago: Quadrangle Books, 1967); Marilyn B. Young, *Rhetoric of Empire* (Cambridge: Harvard University Press, 1968); and Kenton J. Clymer, *John Hay: The Gentleman as Diplomat* (Ann Arbor: University of Michigan Press, 1975).
101. Gould, *The Presidency of McKinley*, pp. 161–71.
102. Edmund Morris, *The Rise of Theodore Roosevelt* (New York: Coward, McCann and Geoghegan, 1979), p. 610.
103. Gould, *The Presidency of McKinley*, p. 231.
104. *Ibid.*, pp. 240, 248, 249, 252.

Index